MW01199631

LIBRARY OF HEBREW BIBLE/
OLD TESTAMENT STUDIES

545

Formerly Journal for the Study of the Old Testament Supplement Series

THE SENSES OF SCRIPTURE

Sensory Perception in the Hebrew Bible

Yael Avrahami

B L O O M S B U R Y

NEW YORK · LONDON · NEW DELHI · SYDNEY

Bloomsbury T&T Clark
An imprint of Bloomsbury Publishing Inc

1385 Broadway	50 Bedford Square
New York	London
NY 10018	WC1B 3DP
USA	UK

www.bloomsbury.com

Bloomsbury is a registered trade mark of Bloomsbury Publishing Plc

First published 2012
Paperback edition first published 2014

Library of Congress Cataloging-in-Publication Data
A catalog record for this book is available from the Library of Congress

ISBN: HB: 978-0-567-53092-9
PB: 978-0-567-46091-2

Typeset by Jones Ltd, London

CONTENTS

PREFACE

Said the Eye one day, "I see beyond these valleys a mountain veiled with
blue mist. Is it not beautiful?"
The Ear listened, and after listening intently awhile, said, "But where is
any mountain? I do not hear it."
Then the Hand spoke and said, "I am trying in vain to feel it or touch it,
and I can find no mountain."
And the Nose said, "There is no mountain, I cannot smell it."
Then the Eye turned the other way, and they all began to talk together
about the Eye's strange delusion. And they said, "Something must be the
matter with the Eye."

—Gibran Khalil[1]

When I embarked on my journey into sensory perception in the Hebrew
Bible I felt like the eye in Khalil Gibran's parable. If you do not choose
the synchronic or diachronic way—they said—how would you know
where to go? Indeed, the journey was long and as can be read in the first
chapter, I went gleaning in other fields, but hopefully was not harmed.
As the project went on, first submitted as a Doctoral Dissertation at the
University of Haifa (2008) and now in a revised version presented before
you, I was lucky enough to meet many people who trusted in my way,
and at times even saw things eye to eye with me. It is my pleasure to
thank my advisor, Meir Malul, who gave me full trust and freedom
throughout my Ph.D. studies. During my years at the University of Haifa,
I received a stipend from the Graduate Studies Authority. Great debt is
also due to Paul Stoller of Westchester University, who patiently and
pleasantly discussed matters of sensory anthropology and phenomenological anthropology with me. I was fortunate to study with Paul at
Temple University in 2005 thanks to the Fulbright Grant for Doctoral
Dissertation Students.

Many other scholars have shared their insights, advice, and many
times their manuscripts with me. Special thanks go to Michael Carasik,
Talia Sutzkover and Dominika Kurek-Chomycz, who shared their
dissertations with me before their publication, to Shalom Paul who

1.   "The Eye," in *The Madman* (repr.; Whitefish: Kessinger Publishing, 2004), 33.

solved any problem I could think about, to Shani Tzoref who trusted me during my years at the University of Sydney, and to Moshe Lavee, whose friendship can support the most desperate of academics. Ed Greenstein, Frank Polak and Alan Cooper read the Hebrew dissertation and gave valuable and friendly advice which, no doubt, improved this study greatly. Any failure to implement their advice or to include their recommended references is my own responsibility.

Whenever I faced a writer's block, I was lucky to be supported by wonderful people who shared not only their sympathy but also their escape routes—Hilit Surowitz, Sue Beecher, Joanne Clarke, Laurence Toltz, and Sally Tadmor. Finally, endless thanks go to my colleague and friend, Mark Leuchter, who convinced me that my work deserves an audience, and helped me find the right stage for it. The process of transferring the dissertation into a book was supported by the Committee for Higher Jewish Education, Emanuel Synagogue Woollahra, and the Council of Christians and Jews in Australia. Recently, there seems to be an emergent interest in sensory perception, the Hebrew Bible and its receptive cultures. I was happy to meet two enthusiastic scholars to share the passion of sensory perception with me. Deborah Green, Greg Schmidt Goering and I started a new consultation at the SBL Annual meeting dedicated to sensory perception, and I finally feel surrounded with eyes, rather than noses and ears.

A few changes were made to the structure of my original dissertation during the process of turning my work into a book. The chapter dedicated to the olfactory sense was mostly left aside—a recognition that some major aspects of it were separately discussed either by Deborah Green or by Dominika Kurek-Chomycz in their respective dissertations. Moreover, this chapter was the only chapter to go beyond the questions of the sensorium and into the investigation of a particular sense. I have chosen to present a more coherent and focused discussion presently and hope that it would serve as a starting point for new and intriguing investigations. At times, matters were discussed more lengthily because of their peculiarity to most biblical scholars; other times, obvious notions were commented upon briefly.

Finally, a note must be said on biblical citations in this study. For methodological reasons, the book was written in a descriptive manner, including many biblical citations. The reader should feel immersed in biblical sensory vocabulary and its context, and such an aim is achieved, in my view, by citing the verses rather than merely writing about them. As a result, many of the cited verses are not discussed at length, especially when the relevant information is self-evident. To provide the most free-flowing reading experience, all citations were given in English. The

NRSV was chosen as the default translation (unmarked), and whenever a different translation was found to be more accurate it was indicated. The vocabulary referred to in the discussion was added in Hebrew in parentheses. However, "what was originally expressed in Hebrew does not have exactly the same sense when translated into another language. Not only this book, but even the Law itself, the Prophecies, and the rest of the books differ not a little when read in the original" (Sirach, Prologue).

ABBREVIATIONS

AB	The Anchor Bible
ABD	*Anchor Bible Dictionary*. Edited by D. N. Freedman. 6 vols. New York, 1992
ANESSup	Ancient Near Eastern Studies, Supplement
ANET	*Ancient Near Eastern Texts Relating to the Old Testament*. Edited by J. B. Pritchard. 3d ed. Princeton, 1969
AOAT	Alter Orient und Altes Testament
BAR	*Biblical Archaeology Review*
BASOR	*Bulletin of the Schools of Oriental Research*
BDB	Brown, F., S. R. Driver, and C. A. Briggs. *A Hebrew and English Lexicon of the Old Testament*. Oxford, 1907
BH	Biblical Hebrew
BHK	*Biblia Hebraica*. Edited by R. Kittel. Stuttgart, 1905–1906, 1925^2, 1937^3, 1951^4, 1973^{16}
BHS	*Biblia Hebraica Stuttgartensia*. Edited by K. Elliger and W. Rudolph. Stuttgart, 1983
BZAW	Beihefte zur Zeitschrift für die alttestamentliche Wissenschaft
CAD	*The Assyrian Dictionary of the Oriental Institute of the University of Chicago*. Chicago, 1956–
CahRB	Cahiers de la Revue biblique
CBQ	*Catholic Biblical Quarterly*
CDLB	*Cuneiform Digital Library Bulletin*
CRRAI	Proceedings of the Recontre Assyriologique Internationale (Compte rendu de la Recontre Assyriologique Internationale)
EH	*Encyclopedia Hebraica*. Edited by J. Klausner, B. Netanyahu, Y. Leibowitz, N. Rotenstreich, Y. Gutman, and J. Prawer. Jerusalem, 1948–89
EncJud	*Encyclopaedia Judaica*. 16 vols. Jerusalem, 1972
ER	*The Encyclopedia of Religion*. Edited by M. Eliade. 16 vols. New York, 1987
FRLANT	Forschungen zur Religion und Literatur des Alten und Neuen Testaments

Gesenius	*Gesenius' Hebrew Grammar*. Edited by E. Kautzsch. Translated by A. E. Cowley. 2d. ed. Oxford, 1910
HALOT	Koehler, L., W. Baumgartner, and J. J. Stamm, *The Hebrew and Aramaic Lexicon of the Old Testament*. Translated and edited under the supervision of M. E. J. Richardson. 4 vols. Leiden, 1994–99
HAR	*Hebrew Annual Review*
HB	Hebrew Bible
HCOT	Historical Commentary on the Old Testament
HTR	*Harvard Theological Review*
ICC	International Critical Commentary
IEJ	*Israel Exploration Journal*
IESS	*International Encyclopedia of the Social Sciences*. Edited by D. L. Sills. New York, 1968–
JANES	*Journal of the Ancient Near Eastern Society*
JBL	*Journal of Biblical Literature*
JCS	*Journal of Cuneiform Studies*
JHS	*Journal of Hebrew Scriptures*
JNES	*Journal of Near Eastern Studies*
JNSL	*Journal of Northwest Semitic Languages*
JPS	The New Jewish Publication Society Translation
JSOT	*Journal for the Study of the Old Testament*
JTS	*Journal of Theological Studies*
LHBOTS	Library of Hebrew Bible/Old Testament Studies
MG	*Mikraot Gedolot Haketer*. Edited by M. Cohen. Ramat Gan, 2000–2007
MKCS	M. Malul, *Knowledge, Control and Sex: Studies in Biblical Thought, Culture and Worldview*. Tel Aviv-Jaffa, 2002
NEB	*The New English Bible*. Oxford and Cambridge, 1970
NETS	*A New English Translation of the Septuagint and the Other Greek Translations Traditionally Included under That Title*. Edited by A. Pietersma and B. G. Wright. New York 2007
NICOT	New International Commentary on the Old Testament
NIV	New International Version
NRSV	New Revised Standard Version (Anglicized Version)
OBO	Orbis Biblicus et Orientalis
Or	*Orientalia*
OTL	Old Testament Library
OTS	Old Testament Studies
PAAJR	*Proceedings of the American Academy of Jewish Research*
RB	*Revue Biblique*
SBLSP	*Society of Biblical Literature Seminar Papers*

SJOT	*Scandinavian Journal of the Old Testament*
SVTP	Studia in Veteris Testamenti pseudepigraphica
TDOT	*Theological Dictionary of the Old Testament*. Edited by G. J. Botterweck and H. Ringgren. Translated by J. T. Willis, G. W. Bromiley, and D. E. Green. 8 vols. Grand Rapids, 1974–
TLOT	*Theological Lexicon of the Old Testament*. Edited by E. Jenni, with assistance from C. Westermann. Translated by M. E. Biddle. 3 vols. Peabody, Mass., 1997
UF	*Ugarit-Forschungen*
VT	*Vetus Testamentum*
VTSup	Vetus Testamentum Supplements
WCJS	*Proceedings of the World Congress for Jewish Studies*
ZA	*Zeitschrift für Assyriologie und Vorderasiatische Archaeology*
ZAH	*Zeitschrift für Althebräisch*
ZAR	*Zeitschrift für Altorientalische und Biblische Rechtsgeschichte*
ZAW	*Zeitschrift für die Alttestamentliche Wissenschaft*

LIST OF TABLES

Introduction:
Common Sense

What would Western epistemology look like had Plato lived in ancient Israel rather than ancient Greece? What if philosophical, reflective writing had been a widespread literary genre in eighth-century B.C.E. Jerusalem? In a way, this book attempts to provide an answer. In this book, I attempt to reveal the category "sensorium" as it is embedded in the Hebrew Bible—the number of senses included in the category, its definition, and its function in biblical thought and practice. In order to achieve this goal, I explore Biblical Hebrew throughout the Hebrew Bible in search of associative patterns, contextual patterns, and bits of implicit and unintentional information that reveal cultural categories. Loaded with recent anthropological evidence that a strong correlation exists between the ways senses are talked about and the way they are used in various cultures, I aim to provide at the end of this book a definition for a biblical sensory category.

The senses are mentioned countless times in the Hebrew Bible, in all genres, periods, and schools. Sensory vocabulary serves to describe concrete encounters with reality, as well as a diverse range of derived meaning, at times common to some or all modalities, at times unique to one. And while it is clear that the Hebrew Bible has a different take on what the senses are than the common, Platonic model known to us, it is also clear that it has some interest in it.[1] The subtitle of this book, *Sensory Perception in the Hebrew Bible*, reflects, therefore, the avenue of this study. I am interested in sensory perception and the perception of the senses, as it is described, implicitly and explicitly, in the Hebrew Bible. The choice to discuss the sensorium, rather than a particular sense, was conscious. I hope to provide a preliminary study and to fill the gap

---

1. Cf. S. A. Geller, "Textual Juxtaposition and Comparative Study," in *Approaches to Teaching the Hebrew Bible as Literature in Translation* (ed. B. N. Olsen and Y. S. Feldman; New York: Modern Language Association of America, 1989), 72-79 (76–77).

in biblical epistemological scholarship. I do hope that many of the matters tackled in this book will be revisited and expanded in the future by other scholars as well as myself.

Before addressing the subject, I will present previous anthropological studies of the senses, studies which provide the background to my choice of subject and methodology. I will also summarize the current state of scholarship about the senses in biblical studies. Lastly, I will present my theoretical choices and methodologies. The first chapter, hence, should lead the reader from my intellectual background through to my methodological choices. The second chapter will try to reveal the components of the biblical sensory category. Linguistic associative patterns between different modalities will be examined, and seven senses will be presented as culturally associated: sight, hearing, kinaesthesia, speech, taste, touch, and smell. The complex web of association between these modalities will lead to the suggestion of a septasensory model.

The third chapter will aim to provide a definition to the sensory category. I will explore the contextual patterns in which sensory vocabulary is used. In general, sensory vocabulary appears in literal contexts of embodied experience as well as multiple derived contexts. I will demonstrate that in the Hebrew Bible, the senses are embodied experiences, whereby each sense is semantically associated with a particular organ that operates it. The senses represent ability and sovereignty, as expressed in the use of sensory imagery to describe learning and thought, help and harm, actual judgment and moral judgment. The senses are used as metaphors for life, and as an indicator of ability and sovereignty. The fourth chapter will further develop the definition of the sensorium by exploring the theological concept of divine creation of the senses and its implications. Reviewing this religious notion will further clarify the definition of sensory experience as a mark of sovereignty and the status of people with sensory disabilities.

The fifth and final chapter will focus on the sense of sight and aim at solving the dispute regarding the centrality of sight vs. hearing in biblical thought. I will start by referring to this dispute, and to the implications of the study of sight on the understanding of the entire biblical sensorium. I will than explore in detail major contexts in which sight vocabulary is used: sight as metaphor for evidence and the way it is rhetorically and theologically employed; sight as metaphor for thought and inquiry; sight as metaphor for life and its place in the dichotomies life/death, light/darkness; sight as empathy; and sight as subjective opinion—all closely linked to the perception that sight is the most intimate and immediate sensory experience. In addition to these contexts, I will present evidence that sight is the main sense through which the supernatural in perceived in the narrative, and that sight is a central key to understanding various biblical narratives. I will conclude that sight was the prototype for the sensorium in the Hebrew Bible, that the supremacy of sight is expressed at all levels of the biblical text, despite the fact that it is a different kind of sight to the one ruling the Platonic pentasensory model. All in all, this book aims to reveal the biblical common sense of sensory perception, and I do hope that it will make sense to my audience too.

Chapter 1

MAKING SENSE OF THE SENSORIUM

Embarking on a journey to reveal embedded cultural notions in an ancient text is not a straightforward task. My own preparation for this journey included delving into various oceans far from what my teachers perceived as classic training for a biblical scholar. In this chapter, I intend to present the tools which I found most useful in the task of bringing together lively theories of cultural anthropology and a dead culture. This chapter, therefore, aims at presenting previous scholarship, the theoretical background, and the chosen methodologies of the current book. The discussion will start with the general field of cultural perception of the senses, and will end with particular tools for the investigation of the biblical sensory perceptions—in other words, we will move from theory to practice. Finally, this chapter situates this book in the broader intellectual field of the humanities and explains both the methodology and style chosen for discussing the biblical material.

The Sensorium and Cultural-Anthropological Perspective

The sensorium and sensory perception has long been the focus of psychology, especially neuro-psychology and of the philosophy of consciousness, known as epistemology.[1] Both fields regard the senses as tools for discerning the world. Both share a basic assumption regarding the universal use of the senses. Scholars in both fields attempt to reach a more complete description of the way people learn about their world through sensory, as well as other kinds of perception. Contrarily, the cultural study of the senses, or sensory anthropology, takes a different view, namely, a non-universalistic one. Instead of focusing exclusively on how the senses are used as tools for learning about the world, sensory

---

1. See M. Merleau-Ponty, *Phenomenology of Perception* (trans. C. Smith; repr. 1958, London: Routledge, 2004), 8–10, where a discussion of the difficulties of such a study are detailed.

anthropology looks at different uses of the senses in the lifeworld,[2] which include emotions, communication, and expressions of social and cultural relationships. Sensory anthropology explores the ways members of different cultures experience the world via the senses. Furthermore, sensory anthropology recognizes that the modern, Western perception of the senses is infused with distinct anthropological biases, such as the mind–body dichotomy, the centrality of sight, and the textual lens through which cultural topics are examined. In essence, sensory anthropology explores the sensory map of a given culture.

Despite the challenge inherent in defining the concept of "culture," there is consensus that culture is a human phenomenon, an ensemble of features that distinguishes a specific human group from another. Hence, culture is a human construction that is not genetically predetermined and is not uniform across different groups.[3] Cultural anthropology, therefore, studies the human, the variable, the relative—rather than the universal. The study of the senses has been revolutionized in the past twenty years through cultural anthropology, and is now studied in cultural context, rather than as part of a philosophical or biological debate. After casting off the shackles of accepted Western cultural perspectives, sensory anthropologists now reject the ethnocentric perspective, sprouting from the Greek–Western philosophical tradition.[4]

The first philosopher to distinguish between the senses and the mind was Parmenides (early fifth century B.C.E.), though it was Plato (423–347 B.C.E.) who popularized this distinction.[5] Plato's disciple Aristotle (384–322 B.C.E.) went further, and established a hierarchy of senses, from the figurative to the concrete: sight–hearing–smell–taste–touch. Western philosophers remained loyal to this hierarchy until Hegel, more

2. The term, originally *Lebenswelt*, was coined by Edmond Husserl, and is widely used in contemporary phenomenological anthropology. See n. 181, and A. Schutz, "Phenomenology and the Social Sciences," in *Phenomenology and Sociology* (ed. T. Luckmann; Harmondsworth: Penguin, 1978), 119–42 (121).

3. P. L. Berger, *The Sacred Canopy: Elements of a Sociological Theory of Religion* (New York: Anchor, 1990), 5–10.

4. It is claimed that the distinction between the senses and the mind and the strict hierarchy of the senses in Western philosophy are so widely accepted, that they seem like a natural, universal epistemology. Cultural anthropology attempts to avoid ethnocentrism and distance itself from its own cultural perceptions in order to appreciate and understand other cultures.

5. In his "Allegory of the Cave," Plato compares the reality that is perceived by the senses to shadows on a cave's wall. These shadows are only a twisted and partial representation of the true reality outside. The senses are, in this allegory, a cave that restricts the mind from reaching the true forms.

than two millennia later. Over the centuries, there were many changes in the way sensory experience was evaluated, yet their distinctiveness from the mind and their hierarchy remained unchallenged.[6] This state of phenomenology led to Alfred Whitehead's declaration that Western epistemological tradition is nothing more than a series of footnotes to Plato.[7] This understanding of the senses endured in the two major Western faiths, Christianity and Judaism.[8]

The *supremacy* of sight may be ascribed to Aristotle, and the negation of the senses as a tool for learning about the world may be ascribed to Descartes (1641), but the *exclusivity* of sight from a philosophical perspective is ascribed to Kant (1790). Yet Kant is merely a loyal representative of his time. Many scholars agree with Michel Foucault that the eighteenth century was the tipping point when sight became the superior sense in popular Western culture.[9] In addition, this shift in the evaluation of the sense of sight also found expression in modern (observance) science, in evolutionary theories, and later in Freud's psychological theories. These changes in philosophy, culture, and science were accompanied by semantic shifts in sensory vocabulary of various European languages.[10] For example, the phrase "seeing is believing"

6.   A. Synnott, "Puzzling Over the Senses: From Plato to Marx," in *The Varieties of Sensory Experience: A Sourcebook in the Anthropology of the Senses* (ed. D. Howes; Toronto: University of Toronto Press, 1991), 61–76 (62–64).

7.   See A. N. Whitehead, *Process and Reality* (New York: Macmillan, 1929), 39, cited by P. Stoller, *The Taste of Ethnographic Things* (Philadelphia: University of Pennsylvania Press, 1989), 48.

8.   With regard to Christianity, see Synnott, "Puzzling Over the Senses," 65–69. With regard to Judaism, see M. D. M. Leventhal, "The Torah and the Senses (A)" (Hebrew), *Zohar* 6 (2001): 87–102, and "The Torah and the Senses (B)" (Hebrew), *Zohar* 7 (2001): 83–100. Leventhal reviews scholars of various streams and periods to find agreement concerning the supremacy of sight, and to a certain extent of hearing as abstract. Some scholars rank the olfactory sense among the supreme/ abstract senses. Interestingly, the halachic status of the sense of taste was unstable, and went down when Maimonides restricted its usage for halachic decisions ("The Torah and the Senses [A]," 96). It is quite probable that such a change was influenced by Maimonides' acquaintance with Platonic ideas.

9.   M. Foucault, *The Birth of the Clinic: An Archaeology of Medical Perception* (trans. A. M. Sheridan Smith; New York: Tavistock, 1973), 54–63, 107–23. Foucault describes the change in sensory experience (the way the senses are used) as well as the way this change is represented in language (vocabulary and semantics).

10.   See the previous note, as well as Stoller, *Taste of Ethnographic Things*, 7–8; Synnott, "Puzzling Over the Senses," 70; C. Classen, "Foundations for the Anthropology of the Senses," *International Social Science Journal* 153 (1997): 401–12 (402).

clearly expresses the superiority of sight. Interestingly, the original phrase was: "Seeing is believing, but touching is the truth." Such changes hint at the fact that the cultural and semantic map of the senses evolves from era to era and from place to place.[11]

Modern scientific evidence seemed to have supported the classic philosophical hierarchy, with the scientific revolution emphasizing sight above the other senses. This is partially due to the fact that scientific development in recent centuries has focused primarily on observation, whether distant (via telescope) or near (via microscope). The centrality of science in Western ideology and perception reinforces a belief in and a preference for the sense of sight from early childhood. Moral justifications are also proposed to support the hierarchy of the senses. Some researchers champion the superiority of the figurative, loftier and heavenly senses, as opposed to the inferior, beast-like direct or process senses. This hierarchy is also supported by evolutionary arguments, including the irrefutable biological superiority of sight among primates, including humans.[12] Some scholars also used the relative height of the sense organs in the human body as a visual-physical justification for this hierarchy of the senses. This argument is of a circular nature, being based on visual evidence and the assumption that the thing which is higher is necessarily better. More recently, based on the conceptual revolution prompted by the theory of relativity and quantum theories, the status of the senses has been further undermined in science and in popular Western culture, relative to the status of the mind in philosophy.[13]

Early cultural researchers adopted a rigid approach to the traditional hierarchy of the senses. In the early nineteenth century, Laurence Oken created a hierarchy of the races according to their prominent senses: the European eye man, the Asian ear man, the American nose man, the Australian tongue man, and the African skin man. This hierarchical explanation was based on an evolutionary assumption that the development of lower senses among "undeveloped" cultures came at the expense of their intellectual development.[14] Moreover, the ethnocentric bias of

11. D. Howes, "Sensorial Anthropology," in Howes, ed., *The Varieties of Sensory Experience*, 167–92 (169); A. Dundes, "Seeing is Believing," in *Interpreting Folklore* (Bloomington: Indiana University Press, 1990), 86–92.

12. D. Ackerman, *A Natural History of the Senses* (New York: Random House, 1990), 30.

13. T. Yanai, *Following the Thoughts: On the Universe, Nature, and Man* (Ramat-Gan: Poetica, 1994 [Hebrew]), 50–51.

14. Classen, "Anthropology of the Senses," 405; D. Howes, *Sensual Relations: Engaging the Senses in Culture and Social Theory* (Ann Arbor: University of Michigan Press, 2004), 5.

Western researchers was the reason for choosing the sense of sight as the main research tool. Examples include ethnographies filled with descriptions of visual details, but lacking other sensory data; photographs of body decorations that conceal other aspects, such as fragrance; or presentation of jewellery, without reference to the sounds made when worn. This bias was also evident in ethnographic museums, where musical instruments, attire, and decorations were on display "for viewing only," at the expense of their other qualities, such as sound, fragrance, and texture.[15] The exception to this rule was the anthropologist Franz Boas. In 1883, as part of the debate on the Eskimos' colour spectrum, he proposed exploring cultural differences in the use of the senses.[16] His students, Margaret Mead and Rhoda Metraux, pioneered the exploration of sensory differences as a manifestation of customs and values, rather than as something based on evolutionary development (1953).[17] This change of approach was so dramatic that these researchers and their disciples became known as "sensualists." It would take many years before their view—that we can only understand cultures by examining all their senses—entered the mainstream of anthropological study.[18]

The most significant change in sensory research occurred in the field of communication. Meloy and Wober first introduced the concept of sensotypes and their analytical abilities, and made the connection between sensotypes and communication media in various cultures.[19] The communication scholar Marshall McLuhan and his student Walter Ong postulated a direct correlation between sense and its functions, such as smell–memory and sight–analytical thinking. During the 1960s, McLuhan and Ong explored the Western cultural bias towards sight, and showed how the emphasis on and technological development of different senses in different cultures led to the pre-eminence of that sense over others. In

15. S. Feld, "Sound as a Symbolic System: The Kaluli Drum," in Howes, ed., *The Varieties of Sensory Experience*, 79–99 (80). A change to the normal rules can be observed in "touch-me" museums, which are largely designed for children, though the old "do not touch" rule normally still applies in the main exhibition.

16. K. L. Guerts, *Culture and the Senses: Bodily Ways of Knowing in an African Community* (Berkeley: University of California Press, 2002), 11. One of his students, Edward Sapir, continued the investigation of the link between verbal and cultural categories, and demonstrated the impossibility of creating a hierarchy of languages based on their complexity; see H. Goldberg, O. Ziv, and E. Basker, *Anthropology: Man, Society, Culture* (Tel Aviv: Cherikover, 1978 [Hebrew]), 165. Edward Sapir will be mentioned later in the context of the Sapir–Whorf Hypothesis.

17. Margaret Mead and Rhoda Métraux belong to the American branch of cultural anthropology, whose founding father is Franz Boas.

18. Howes, *Sensual Relations*, 10–15.

19. M. Wober, "Sensotypes," *Journal of Social Psychology* 70 (1966): 181–89.

other words, various cultures invest technologically in their preferred sense, and in that way enhance it further. In Western culture, this phenomenon found expression in the invention of the printing press and scientific instruments such as the telescope and microscope, which added significantly to previous pre-eminence of the sense of sight. As a consequence, entire cultures were created based on reading and writing. The expansion of the sense of sight created a distance from the observed object and led to the development of abstract thought. These changes found expression in the fields of art (such as the "invention" of perspective drawing), philosophy (describing the world as observed), and science (modern scientific thought). Irreversible human changes took place among people who could read and write. Cognitive distancing led to the development of a bias towards the creation of systematic but imaginative worlds and the development of schizophrenic tendencies.[20]

Importantly, McLuhan and Ong divided the human world into literate and oral cultures, with core differences between them. Literate cultures, claimed Ong, favour the sense of sight and differentiate sight from the other senses. Oral cultures, on the other hand, favour the sense of hearing, experiencing the world harmoniously, and communicating through a mix of all the senses. Literate cultures and oral cultures also differ in other ways: static vs. dynamic; modern vs. conservative; and seeing the world as a view vs. experiencing the world as an event.[21] Similarly to Wober's theory of sensotypes, McLuhan and Ong explain cultural differences through assumed biological differences between hearing and sight. Hearing is synaesthetic, contemporary, and can activate feelings. Sight is indirect, controlled, analytic, and distancing.[22] Soon enough, the contrast oral–literal, and its pair aural–visual, found a match in the dichotomy between modern thought (and culture) and primitive thought (and culture).[23] Followers of McLuhan and Ong, such as Bernard Hibbits, focus on the gap between modern literate cultures and simple cultures, or as Hibbits calls them, "performative cultures."[24]

20. W. J. Ong, "World as View and World as Event," *American Anthropologist* 71 (1969): 634–47 (643). This theory explains how a philosophical preference born in ancient Greece became a popular perception in the Western world.

21. Ibid., 637–44.

22. Howes, "Sensorial Anthropology," 171.

23. As an example, see C. R. Hallpike, *The Foundations of Primitive Thought* (Oxford: Clarendon, 1979). Hallpike finds similar characteristics to those found by Ong, the main difference between the two being the emphasis that Hallpike puts on the distinctions between static-abstract thinking and dynamic-concrete thinking.

24. B. J. Hibbits, "'Coming to Our Senses': Communication and Legal Expression in Performance Cultures," *Emory Law Journal* 41 (1992): 874–960 (941–43).

The dichotomy proposed by Ong and his followers attracted much criticism, particularly because of its strict and rigid categorization.[25] Despite the fact that contemporary scholars prefer to discuss each culture in its own right, based on the principle of cultural relativism, and on a recognition of the impossibility of dividing all the world's cultures into just two categories, the contribution of this theory should not be dismissed. McLuhan and Ong made a highly significant contribution to the cultural research of the senses by highlighting awareness of Western scholars' bias in favour of sight, and suggesting the possible existence of alternative sensory systems. The more that senses were perceived as a critical tool for learning about the world; and the more the core differences between the sensory categories of different cultures were acknowledged; the more obvious it became that scholars raised in the Western philosophical tradition were prisoners of their own sensorium.[26] This can be summarized by the following quotation from Dundes:

> Ruth Benedict used to explain why so many social theorists failed to notice custom or culture: "We do not see the lens through which we look." A conscious recognition of our visual bias may help make the lens visible. We must never forget the possible relativity of our own sensory perception categories.
>
> Inventories of the same or similar sense categories found in other cultures may help. Clifford Geertz reports, for example, that the Javanese have five senses (seeing, hearing, *talking*, smelling, and feeling), which do not coincide exactly with our five. The delineation of such differences may teach us just how culture-bound or culture-specific our own observations of nature might be. We tend to delude ourselves into thinking we are studying the nature of nature, foolishly forgetting that we cannot observe raw or pure nature. We can perceive nature only through the mediation of culture, with its panoply of culturally relative cognitive categories.
>
> Much of the study of "natural history" often turns out to be "cultural history" in disguise. Theories and ideas about the natural world are invariably couched in terms of a specific human language and are based upon data obtained from human observations. With human observation expressed in human language, one simply cannot avoid cultural bias. Searching for culture-free descriptions of nature may be a worthwhile goal, and perhaps man will one day succeed in achieving it. In the meantime, we must be wary of mistaking relatives for absolutes, of mistaking

---

25. Howes, "Sensorial Anthropology," 173, and *Sensual Relations*, xix; Classen, "Anthropology of the Senses," 403. See also Daniel Chandlers' review and criticism of the "Great Divide" theories in "Biases of the Ear and Eye: 'Great Divide' Theories, Phonocentrism, Graphocentrism and Logocentrism," cited 10 July 2000. Online: http://www.aber.ac.uk/media/Documents/litoral/litoral.html.

26. Stoller, *Taste of Ethnographic Things*, 57; M. Herzfeld, "Anthropology: A Practice of Theory," *International Social Science Journal* 153 (1997): 301–18 (313).

culture for nature. Cross-cultural comparisons of sense categories may not only reveal critical differences in the specific senses, but also whether or not the apparent priority of vision over the other senses is a human universal. For the moment, we can do little more than wait and *see*.[27]

As evolutionary and universal theories were gradually replaced by relativistic anthropological theories, it was increasingly recognized that the senses must be understood in their cultural context, and that the world is perceived differently by different cultures.[28] Michael Herzfeld sums up the way in which the exposure of differences in sensory experience influenced anthropologists: "Because visual idioms of representation have become quite literally the common sense of the modern, industrial world, they have also become relatively invisible—a revealing metaphor in itself."[29]

First coined by Roy Porter in 1986, the term "sensory anthropology" only gained popularity after Paul Stoller's *The Taste of Ethnographic Things* (1989) was published.[30] Stoller reviews the history of modern thought and the emergence of the superiority of sight. He describes how ethnographers preferred to describe visual facts in their field work. Stoller further claims that the beliefs and the preferences of visual culture led ethnographers to the creation of a systematic reflective documentation that established order and found examples behind reality. Ethnographic studies, asserts Stoller, are conducted by Western scholars with a Western epistemology that seeks a uniform reality behind a world of diverse phenomena.[31] Therefore, the study of the senses must be accompanied by a change in scholarly approach and by an abandonment of the scientific-visual approach. Cultural study of the senses must rely on existential philosophy—the sole modern Western philosophy that denies the traditional divide between the mind and the senses.[32] This divide is reflected in the Christian body–spirit dichotomy, which over time was translated into a reason–emotional dichotomy,[33] and lately to literate–oral dichotomy. Moreover, according to the Western body–spirit dichotomy, the senses belong to the realm of the physical–emotional, and not to the

27. Dundes, "Seeing is Believing," 92 (original emphasis).
28. Classen, "Anthropology of the Senses," 401. More on cultural relativism and the senses will follow in the next chapter.
29. Herzfeld, "Anthropology: A Practice of Theory," 314.
30. Classen, "Anthropology of the Senses," 406.
31. As Stoller notes (*Taste of Ethnographic Things*, 48–54) these scholarly preferences are themselves based on Platonic modes of thought.
32. Ibid., 25.
33. Synnott, "Puzzling Over the Senses," 74.

realm of the rational. Any attempt to understand sensory perception in different cultures must therefore abandon this set of dichotomies.

The body–mind dichotomy, which places the senses on the biological–universal edge of the spectrum, caused a neglecting of the sensorium in studies that nevertheless recognized the cultural relativism of other fields (e.g. family structure, the meaning of symbols etc.). The debate over the universality of embodied experiences became more strident after Pierre Bourdieu introduced the term *habitus*, and after the *practice* theory gained popularity in the 1980s. The terms *habitus* and practice describe culture as something experienced physically, something constantly implemented by individuals. Cultural conventions and social behaviours are not arterial, independently existing abstractions, but daily actions that are internalized, enacted, and embodied.[34] Phenomenological anthropology—influenced by the mentioned development—shifts the focus of the debate. In comparison to previous anthropological discourse, phenomenological anthropology examines the embodied experience of learning and knowledge, and thus of course the use of senses.[35] A good example is body decoration, regarded by classic anthropologists as a symbol of figurative ideas expressed visually on the body. Phenomenological anthropology examines the physical-personal experience during the creation of body decoration. It also examines the rituals and learning experience during which the decoration is created, and without which it is meaningless:[36] "Cultural phenomenology focuses on how embodied experience, thought, feeling and psychological orientations all interrelate. Embodiment and orientation are central themes within phenomenological anthropology."[37]

The inherent criticism in this approach to traditional cultural anthropology, and its refusal to take account of personal experiences such as emotions and sensation, is clear from the following critiques:

34. S. B. Ortner, "Theory in Anthropology Since the Sixties," *Comparative Studies in Society and History* 26, no. 1 (1984): 126–66 (146); D. Howes, "To Summon all the Senses," in Howes, ed., *The Varieties of Sensory Experience*, 3–21 (3).

35. See T. J. Csordas, "Somatic Modes of Attention," *Cultural Anthropology* 8, no. 2 (1993): 135–56.

36. M. Jackson, "Phenomenology, Radical Empiricism, and Anthropological Critique," in *Things as They Are: New Directions in Phenomenological Anthropology* (ed. M. Jackson; Bloomington: Indiana University Press, 1996), 1–45 (33). For the phenomenological discussion of carnal existence, see M. Merleau-Ponty, *Signs* (trans. R. C. McCleary; Northwestern University Studies in Phenomenology and Existential Philosophy; Chicago: Northwestern University Press, 1964), 155.

37. Guerts, *Culture and the Senses*, 15.

> Tied to tropes of interiority and granted ultimate facility by being located in the natural body, emotions stubbornly retain their place, even in all but the most recent anthropological discussions, as the aspect of human experience least subject to control, least constructed or learned (hence most universal), least public, and hence least amenable to socio-cultural analysis.[38]

> Until very recently, cultural anthropologists have never dealt very well with the affective dimensions of culture. We have reveled in "structures" and "systems" of all kinds, from the Radcliffe–Brownian to the Levi-Straussian; and we have used all manner of power-laden idealist concepts as "ideology," "hegemony," and the like. Yet the realm of the emotions, which are indisputably connected to values, has been banished to a small corner of psychological anthropology and has not received comparable attention.[39]

In the early 1990s, as part of a growing interest in the cultural experience or the experience of culture, anthropologists rejected this neglect of the cultural elements of feelings. In the context of this book, this criticism touched on the investigation of the senses in their cultural context. Both the study of feelings and the study of the senses explore the interface between the study of culture, society, and experience. They originate in different research histories, yet both received theoretical support within phenomenological anthropology. From the '90s, phenomenological thinking has held sway in the academic agenda. The uniqueness of phenomenological anthropology lies in its focus on the human-experiential aspect of society and culture.[40]

An important aspect of this new approach is the examination of somatic social construction. The term "social construction" refers to the socio-cultural creation of pseudo-biological perceptions and sensations. One of the first fields which dealt with social constructions was the field of gender studies. Unlike sex, which is a biological fact, gender is a socio-cultural reality, created through the process of social construction. Similarly, anthropologists of the senses deal with social construction of sensory experience. In other words, sensory experience is not dictated solely by biological features, but rather also by cultural preferences.[41]

---

38. L. Abu Lughod and C. A. Lutz, "Introduction: Emotion, Discourse and the Politics of Everyday Life," in *Languages and the Politics of Emotion* (ed. C. A. Lutz and L. Abu-Lughad; Cambridge: Cambridge University Press, 1990), 1–23 (1).

39. J. K. Chance, "The Anthropology of Honor and Shame: Culture, Values and Practice," *Semeia* 68 (1994): 139–51 (139).

40. I will discuss in greater detail the influence of phenomenological anthropology below (pp. 53–55).

41. For an ancient Near Eastern example, see P. Abrahami, "Masculine and Feminine Personal Determinatives before Women's Names at Nuzi: A Gender

This is why any cultural study of the sensorium should abandon the traditional distinction between the senses and the mind—particularly when the culture under study makes no such distinction itself. It is equally wrong to assume that use of the senses has a solely epistemological or solely physical significance. The scholar must remember that such categories are alien to the culture under study.

In fact, and despite the above discussion, the pentasensory model is far from a consensus in our own culture. Physiologists, for example, define the term "sense" very broadly: sense is any action based on a receptor (a sense cell), including the senses of temperature, pain, and acceleration.[42] A philosophically modified count itemizes nine senses, and defines them as an ability to absorb content that reaches *consciousness*.[43] As mentioned before, the pentasensory category with which we are all familiar has its origin with Plato, whose definition has helped shaped both the Western and the Jewish worlds. The difference between counting five senses or fifteen[44] is arbitrary, since some senses can be combined or divided according to different methods of categorization, while others might not be categorized as senses at all. The difference, therefore, lies in the way we define and categorize the senses. The category "sensorium" in a given culture would include all items that agree with its definition. Empiricists use the classic philosophical definition "human actions through which we actively receive knowledge of the world." Hence, if A is B, it belongs to C. In other words, if sight is "a human action…" it belongs to the category "sensorium," but if vibration is not "a human action…," it does not belong to the category. As the definition comes from the epistemological terms of reference, a certain group of senses would be included in the category. Physiologists, however, define senses as "human actions that are based on receptors," and get a different list of modalities included in their sensorium.

An epistemological exploration of the senses must acknowledge that every school of consciousness will produce a different definition of sensory actions. Not only can different senses be included in the same category, but the definitions of the category differ, depending on where

---

Indicator of Social or Economic Independence?," *CDLB* 1 (2011). Online: http://cdli.ucla.edu/pubs/cdlb/2011/cdlb2011_001.html. Cited 10 October 2011.

42. T. Atzmon, "How Many Senses Do We Really Have?" Online: http://www.ynet.co.il/articles/0,7340,L-2975031,00.html. Cited 12 September 2004.

43. Y. Steiner, C. Ormian, and Y. Leibovitch, "Senses" (Hebrew), *EH* 17 (1983): 213–23 (221–22).

44. Sight, hearing, touch, heat, coldness, pressure, pain, olfaction, static, balance, movement, weight, vibration, and intuition.

we are, what time period we live in, and what culture we belong to. The gap between biological and cultural definitions explains why different cultures define the senses differently.[45] This gap also accounts for the partial uniformity found across cultures. The field of language can set another example. According to Chomsky, different cultures choose certain practices out of available universal biological/neurological structures.[46] While discussing the super-structure is a "closed theory," enabling only the demonstration of more examples, the discussion of the cultural-specific practices is contextual, distinctive in its nature. In fact, when it comes to the senses, even physiologists and psychologists have a problem with definition, and often use culturally biased categories.[47]

With this theoretical background, one must mention, finally, the Concordia Sensoria Research Team (CONSERT), including Constance Classen, David Howes, and Anthony Synnott, who embarked on a cultural study of the senses in the 1990s. Their assumptions can be summarized thus:[48]

1. The hierarchy of the senses depends on the cultural tradition, which varies from culture to culture.
2. The senses encode ethical values that are learned as part of the socialization process, in real practices during childhood. The sensory hierarchy is experienced as natural, and forms the basis for physical experience.
3. Sensory preferences are expressed in language, in expressions, in symbols, and in proverbs.
4. Different sensory hierarchies can exist in different parts of the same culture, based on religious, political, or gender factors.

The Concordia researchers define the purpose of sensory anthropology as a description of different synchronous sensoria, together with a description of diachronic changes in the value of a particular sense.[49]

---

45. Like any anthropological investigation, we balance on the rope between the biological and the cultural, the universal and the relative, and so forth (see pp. 32–36). See R. Benedict, *Patterns of Culture* (Introduction by F. Boaz; Preface by M. Mead; New York: New American Library, 1960). In the second chapter, Benedict describes the rainbow of possible phenomena, out of which each culture "chooses" certain colours or parts.

46. N. Chomsky, *Language and Problems of Knowledge: The Mangua Lectures* (Current Studies in Linguistics 16; Cambridge: MIT, 1988), 133–41.

47. Merleau-Ponty, *Phenomenology*, 11.

48. Guerts, *Culture and the Senses*, 17–18; Howes, "To Summon all the Senses," 3, and "Sensorial Anthropology," 178; Classen, "Anthropology of the Senses," 401–3.

49. Classen, "Anthropology of the Senses," 409–10.

Moreover, their research does not centre solely round a description of the senses, semantic categorization, and expressions that describe the senses, or the use of the senses. Rather, it attempts to synthesize between the study of sensation and the study of the use of sensation.[50] The Concordia team points to the correlation between the senses and the social and cultural definitions as proof that anthropology should focus both on conceptual-sensory aspects of the senses and on their everyday aspects.[51] The importance of this duality lies in the correlation between verbal-descriptive cultural expression and experiential-practical cultural expression, which impacts on and highlights the difficulty of studying the senses in the Hebrew Bible. Are we studying what people thought about the senses, or are we studying the practical way in which people used the senses?[52] According to the Concordia school, there is a close correlation between what we think and how we think. Concordia scholars repeatedly highlight Western culture's verbal preference for sight metaphors, alongside its practical preference for the use of sight.[53] The purpose of the cultural study of the senses is to reveal the uniqueness and correlation of sensory meanings and sensory behaviours that are exclusive to a particular culture.[54]

This approach overlaps with phenomenological anthropology only partially. For example, Paul Stoller, who calls for "sensuous scholarship," represents the American heritage of cultural-anthropology, dealing with meaning. Like Michael Jackson and Robert Desjarlais, Stoller investigates the bodily experience of "being in the world," hence the study of the senses in embedded harmonically within the study of culture. In contrast, the British heritage (including Canada) is generally focused on cultural and social structures. Consequently the Concordia school of anthropology of the senses is implicitly based on functional-structural anthropology, and studies the senses per se. The current study is interested in gaining the good of both.

50.   Howes, "Sensorial Anthropology," 175.

51.   Howes, *Sensual Relations*, 56. A similar idea appeared already in M. Mead, "The Study of Culture at a Distance," in *The Study of Culture at a Distance* (ed. M. Mead and R. Métraux; Chicago: University of Chicago Press, 1953), 3–53 (16). Mead claims that there is no room for distinction between the study of how the senses are used and how they are socially constructed.

52.   M. Carasik, *Theologies of the Mind in Biblical Israel* (New York: Lang, 2006), 1–2.

53.   So Dundes, Hibbits, Classen, Howes, and others.

54.   Classen, "Anthropology of the Senses," 401.

In sum, the past two decades have seen a distinct change of direction in the cultural study of the senses, mainly in North America. The shift was rooted in social-scientific criticism of textual-visual symbolism, and a move to "discourse" vocabulary. Gradually, anthropologists of the senses attempted to avoid the verbal metaphor of culture as well.[55] The cultural study of the senses has now become an integral part of the study of embodied experience. In the early days of anthropology, culture was defined as "that complex whole which includes knowledge, belief, art, morals, law, custom, and any other capabilities and habits acquired by man as a member of society."[56] Today, many anthropologists would define culture as a way in which a particular group experiences the world.[57]

The Sensorium in Biblical Scholarship

In a presidential address to the Society of Biblical Literature, in 1982, Lou Silberman urged us to "listen to the text." Silberman was not interested in recovering the sound of Biblical Hebrew, or in the study of sensory preference. His primary interest lay in the linguistic-cultural totality of the text, and therefore his call is highly relevant to the present study.[58] When discussing the sensorium in biblical scholarship, a difficulty is raised; namely, the matter was not a focus of interest for biblical scholars. Existing scholarship is largely limited to lexical discussion, sporadic verses, or tangible areas. For example, some studies of body parts shed partial light on sensory organs, yet mostly refrain from discussion of the sensorium.[59] Studies of non-verbal communication too are tangential to the study of the senses. Meir Malul's 1988 study of mostly non-verbal legal symbolic gestures indicates a highly dominant sensory motif in the biblical legal system, and a clear indication of a performance society.[60] Meir Gruber, in his study of non-verbal communication in the Bible, also addresses actions that convey non-verbal

---

55. Howes, "To Summon All the Senses," 7.

56. E. B. Tylor, *Primitive Culture: Researches into the Development of Mythology, Philosophy, Religion, Language, Art, and Custom* (2 vols.; London: Murray, 1920 [1871]), 1:1. This is the Classic definition by Edward Burnett Tylor, one of the founding fathers of modern anthropology. For further discussion, see Goldberg, Ziv, and Basker, *Anthropology*, 158.

57. Howes, "To Summon All the Senses," 8.

58. L. H. Silberman, "Listening to the Text," *JBL* 102 (1983): 3–26 (17–20).

59. E.g. P. Dhorme, *L'emploi métaphorique des noms de parties du corps en hébreu et en akkadien* (Paris: Gabalda, 1923).

60. M. Malul, *Studies in Mesopotamian Legal Symbolism* (AOAT 221; Kevelaer: Butzon & Bercker, 1988), 155–57.

communication that is independent of the sense of hearing.[61] These studies conclude that the senses featured in the biblical text were experienced, and served biblical culture in an interpersonal communication capacity, as well as for legal and public order purposes. Like all the other senses, sight served these same purposes concretely and performatively, without any figurative or reflective meanings.[62]

Another seemingly related direction is the call for aural understanding of the text. Given the view that the source of the text was oral/aural, an interest in the sound of the text is based on the assumption that visual treatment of the text fails to reflect its original qualities. An aural reading attempts to reproduce the imagined sounds, rhythm, and non-verbal knowledge of the original text.[63] The obvious problem with "hearing" the Hebrew Bible is that the sound of the original text is not known. And since hearing the Hebrew Bible has nothing to do with the use of the senses or perception of the senses in biblical times, this area will remain outside the scope of this book. Another sensory issue which raised scholarly discussion and is not central to the present survey is the question of hearing and sight in prophetic experience. There is broad consensus that prophecy has evolved from a concrete prophetic description of what is seen, to a more figurative prophetic description of what is heard.[64]

While a call for attentive reading is heard every now and then in biblical scholarship, only rarely do we hear demand for greater focus on the entire sensorium. In the following pages, I will, therefore, focus on studies specifically related to sensory experience, perception, and imagination in ancient Israel. These are generally divided to two strands—the study of scents and smell, and studies of perception or mind in ancient Israel.

---

61. M. I. Gruber, *Aspects of Non-Verbal Communication in the Ancient Near East* (Studia Pohl. Dissertationes scientificae de rebus Orientis antiqui 12/1–2; Rome: Pontifical Biblical Institute, 1980), 8.

62. M. Malul, *Knowledge, Control and Sex: Studies in Biblical Thought, Culture and Worldview* (Tel Aviv-Jaffa: Archaeological Center, 2002), 31.

63. One example for this call is F. Bark, "Listen Your Way In with Your Mouth: A Reading of Leviticus," *Judaism* 48, no. 2 (1999): 198–209.

64. See, among others, L. H. Brockington, "Audition in the Old Testament," *JTS* 49 (1948): 1–8; Y. A. Zeligman, "The Problem of Prophecy in Israel, Its Origin and Its Character" (Hebrew), *Eretz Israel* 3 (1954): 123–32; Z. Weisman, "Patterns and Structures in the Visions of Amos" (Hebrew), *Beit Mikra* 14, no. 4 (1970): 40–57. Such an approach sees hearing as more abstract than seeing and demonstrates the instability of sensory hierarchy. A review of lexicons and introductions demonstrates that the sensory experience in biblical prophecy is no longer a leading theme in the field.

Biblical Scents, Biblical Smell

Saul Levin stated in 1979 that many obscure biblical verses could have been better understood had we given greater focus to the sensory experiences embedded in the text.[65] Levin highlighted the sensory deficit in modern research, a theme taken up thirty years later in Malul's *Knowledge, Control and Sex* (hereafter *MKCS*). Specifically, Levin points to the preference for Abel's offering, which is based on a preference for the smell of the meat as opposed the scent of the plant. Levin's suggestion raises questions about the sensory aspects of sacrifice. Even if there were good reasons for preferring the meat, such as rarity and symbolism, we cannot easily dismiss Levin's arguments. The smell that arose from the meat offering is ten times more pungent (though whether it was also more pleasant, we cannot say) than the smell of the semolina cake. This interesting remark remained unnoticed by scholars who investigated sacrificial rites, and who, all-in-all, remained loyal to the concept of gradual abstraction in Israelite religion. In short, sacrifice was first understood as food for the gods (mostly in popular religion, and only hinted at in the Hebrew Bible), later it was understood as scent for the gods (mostly in pre-exilic literature, and represented by the phrase ריח ניחוח), and finally as an offering lacking any sensory aspect (mostly in Ezekiel, represented by abstention).[66] This appealing model must be taken cautiously for its evolutionary assumptions, a matter to be discussed later. The question of the role of smell, alongside taste and touch, was dealt with in John Durham's unpublished dissertation, the conclusions of which never received scholarly attention.[67]

Interestingly, the olfactory sense received relatively broad attention, mainly in the last decade. Ian Ritchie, a Concordia school scholar, rejected the Platonic sensory model with regard to the sense of smell in

65. S. Levin, "The More Savory Offering: A Key to the Problem of Gen. 4:3–5," *JBL* 98 (1979): 85.

66. L. Köhler, *Old Testament Theology* (trans. A. S. Todd; Philadelphia: Westminster, 1957), 186; A. Hurvitz, *A Linguistic Study of the Relationship Between the Priestly Source and the Book of Ezekiel: A New Approach to an Old Problem* (CahRB 20; Paris: Gabalda, 1982), 53–58. For evaluation of the matter, see D. Kurek-Chomycz, "Making Scents of Revelation: The Significance of Cultic Scents in Ancient Judaism as the Backdrop of Saint Paul's Olfactory Metaphor in 2 Cor 2:14–17" (Ph.D. diss., Katholieke Universiteit Leuven, 2008), 24–27.

67. J. I. Durham, "The Senses Touch, Taste, and Smell in Old Testament Religion" (Ph.D. diss., University of Oxford, 1963). A copy of the dissertation was unavailable to me, though was partially accessed via Kurek-Chomycz, "Making Scents of Revelation."

the Hebrew Bible.[68] Ritchie claims that scholars and translators alike ignored the significance of judgment in Isa 11:13[69] because they rejected the regular semantic domain of the sense of smell and the world of senses of ancient Israel. Despite its importance, the main drawback of Ritchie's arguments is a lack of theoretical basis for his comparison between ancient Israel and contemporary Africa. While he speaks of cultural relativism in one place,[70] he mentions "the sensory world of ancient Israel and Africa" in another.[71] Ritchie's reading is supported by Meir Malul, who discusses the legal status of the olfactory sense.[72] Both claim that the verse reflects the actual usage of smell for judgment here and (according to Malul) in Gen 27 (Jacob's Imposture).[73]

The olfactory sense received some lexical attention too. In two articles, Pieter de Boer claimed that a conceptual gap between the researcher and the biblical narrator leads to a lack of understanding of the text. In his analysis of the meaning of the verb "to smell" (ריח) and the phrase "pleasing odour" (ריח ניחוח), he claimed that the basic meaning of both is the dispersal of scent, and not smelling.[74] According to de Boer, the latter expression refers to the scent that God disperses as proof of having accepted the offering.[75] Furthermore, de Boer demands that we abandon our assumption that sight and hearing are more abstract than the sense of

---

68. With regard to Isa 11:13, see I. D. Ritchie, "The Nose Knows: Bodily Knowing in Isaiah 11.3," *JSOT* 87 (2000): 59–73 (68).

69. "He shall sense (lit. 'smell,' והריחו) the truth by his reverence for the Lord: He shall not judge by what his eyes behold, nor decide by what his ears perceive" (JPS).

70. Ritchie, "The Nose Knows," 65.

71. Ibid., 70. It seems that Ritchie internalized his informants' perception, and senses a direct link between African customs and biblical manners. This is a theoretical trip, even if Ritchie's conclusion concerning Isa 11:3 is correct.

72. M. Malul, "Fabrication of Evidence in the Bible: Jacob's Imposture and Joseph's Blood-Stained Coat" (Hebrew), *Diné Israel* 22 (2003): 203–20 (217), cf. *MKCS*, 162–65.

73. It seems that, as far as Isa 11:3 is concerned, the verses discuss a future king with extraordinary abilities, rather than actual legal practice. The matter is discussed in my dissertation, "The Sensorium and Its Operation in Biblical Epistemology with Particular Attention to the Senses of Sight and Smell" (Ph.D. diss., The University of Haifa, 2008 [Hebrew]), 181–82, as well as in Kurek-Chomycz, "Making Scents of Revelation," 10–12.

74. P. A. H. de Boer, "Job 39:25—ומרחוק יריח מלחמה," in *Words and Meanings* (Festschrift David Winton Thomas; ed. P. R. Ackroyd and B. Lindars; Cambridge: Cambridge University Press, 1968), 29–38.

75. P. A. H. de Boer, "An Aspect of Sacrifice. II. God's Fragrance," in *Studies in the Religion of Ancient Israel* (VTSup 23; Leiden: Brill, 1972), 27–47. Detailed objection to de Boer's thesis is found in my dissertation, "The Sensorium," 161–62.

smell, as the differentiation between types of senses led researchers—especially theologians —to ignore the evidence of the role of taste and smell in ceremonial ritual.[76]

The use of aromatic spices in the Song of Songs has received some attention too,[77] notably their ability to create and enhance sexual attraction.[78] Patrick Hunt gave special attention to the role of smell metaphors in the Song of Songs. He analyses the poetic use of images from the world of sensation (sight, hearing, touch, smell, and taste), noting that they help to create the rich character of the poetry. The images, Hunt notes, serve as mnemonic devices. These images are designed to awaken familiar memories and experiences among the audience.[79] According to Hunt, the Song of Songs exemplifies the centrality of the sense of sight because every image also incorporates a visual element.[80] As Hunt uses the Platonic hierarchy of the five senses to support his poetic analysis, he does not enter the debate about whether this categorization originates in the biblical text or not.[81]

The growing interest in the sense of smell in biblical and cognate literature finds expression in two dissertations and a monograph, all dealing with biblical perception and metaphors of scents, and their transformation in later literature. Deborah Green discusses scent metaphors in three domains—priesthood, sexuality, and gardens—and explores the ways in which these metaphors are transformed in rabbinic literature.[82] Dominika Kurek-Chomycz discusses cultic scents in the Hebrew Bible, and the light they shed on understanding the olfactory metaphor of Paul in the New Testament (2 Cor 2:14–17).[83] Lastly, Susan Ashbrook Harvey discusses olfactory imagination in early Christianity, and the way that

76. De Boer, "An Aspect of Sacrifice," 41–42.

77. A. Brenner, "Aromatics and Perfumes in the Song of Songs," *JSOT* 25 (1983): 75–81.

78. S. Bachar, "Perfume in the Song of Songs: An Erotic Motif and Sign of Social Class," *Shnaton* 15 (2005): 39–51.

79. P. N. Hunt, "Sensory Images in Song of Songs 1:12–2:16," in *"Dort Ziehen Schiffe dahin...": Collected Communications to the XIVth Congress of the International Organization for the Study of the Old Testament* (ed. M. Augustin and K.-D. Schunck; Frankfurt am Main: Lang, 1996), 69–78 (70).

80. Ibid., 73.

81. Ibid., 76.

82. D. A. Green, "Soothing Odors: The Transformation of Scents in Ancient Israelite and Ancient Jewish Literature" (Ph.D. diss., University of Chicago, 2003). A much revised version is found in *The Aroma of Righteousness: Scent and Seduction in Rabbinic Life and Literature* (University Park: Penn State University Press, 2011).

83. Kurek-Chomycz, "Making Scents of Revelation."

"Christianity participated in the ancient uses of and attitudes towards smell…"[84] Her work on Christian olfactory imagination is focused more on the influence of Greco-Roman culture than the Hebrew one.

These last three studies are all examples of the emerging interest in sensory imagination in ancient times, and in the Hebrew Bible, yet their interest in the olfactory sense brings to light the absence of such discussion of other senses, apart from sporadic references.[85] Investigation of sensory experience, perception, and metaphor is still largely restricted to specific words or exceptional verses.

In Search of the Biblical Mind

Several studies on the character of biblical thought also discuss the use of the senses, or the way the senses were perceived. It is notable that various scholars who discuss the matter contrast biblical thought to modern thought, and refer to the "mind" as the subject of their research. The mode of thinking in early Israel is described as "Eastern mind,"[86] "Hebrew mind,"[87] "biblical mind,"[88] as well as "Semitic mind"[89] and "primitive."[90] The utilization of the term "mind" is borrowed, clearly, from the traditional Western body–mind dichotomy. Moreover, all these terms are implicitly associated with the "savage mind." This term was coined by the anthropologist Lucien Levi-Bruhl in 1926, who introduces a primitive vs. modern thought dichotomy. It is necessary to mention that Levi-Bruhl's theory has not withstood the test of time, either in terms of the history of anthropological theory or in terms of ethnographic reality. In a book titled *The Savage Mind*, anthropologist Claude Lévi-Strauss demonstrated that there is no real distinction between mythic and

84. S. Ashbrook Harvey, *Scenting Salvation: Ancient Christianity and the Olfactory Imagination* (Berkeley: University of California Press, 2006), 3.

85. For example, the taste metaphor in Ps 34:9 (L. A. Schökel, "Contemplar y Gustar," *Estudios Biblicos* 57 [1999]: 11–21). Reference to specific exegetical attempts will be made throughout the book.

86. E. Ullendorff, "Thought Categories in the Hebrew Bible," in *Studies in Rationalism, Judaism and Universalism* (Festschrift L. Roth; ed. R. Lowe; London: Routledge & Kegan Paul, 1966), 273–88 (278).

87. S. Sandmel, "The Ancient Mind and Ours," in *Understanding the Sacred Text: Essays in Honor of Morton S. Enslin on the Hebrew Bible and Christian Beginnings* (Festschrift M. S. Enslin; ed. J. Reumann; Valley Forge: Judson, 1972), 29–44 (38).

88. D. Bakan, "Infanticide and Sacrifice in the Biblical Mind," *Midway* 8 (1967): 37–47.

89. J. Pedersen, *Israel: Its Life and Culture* (2 vols.; London: Cumberlege, 1954). "Semitic mind" is used throughout the book.

90. *MKCS*, 126, and throughout.

scientific thinking, as all systems of classification and categorization are scientific systems. In his book, therefore, Lévi-Strauss goes against any claim for essential gaps between modes of thinking of plain and complex cultures.[91]

Studies of biblical thought conducted by scholars such as Samuel Sandmel, Edward Ullendorff, and Thorleif Boman contributed to the perpetuation of the discarded savage–modern dichotomy, and further relate it to other traditional distinctions between Western and Eastern thought, Hebrew and Greek thought, and finally between us (the scholars) and them (the Israelites).[92] For example, Boman maintains a sharp contrast between the Hebrew, dynamic thought found in the Hebrew Bible, and Greek, static thought.[93] Despite the fact that his book was systematically challenged by James Barr,[94] and that Louis Feldman accused Boman of basing his research on a stigmatic contrast between the Hebrew and Greek mind, the dichotomy survived in biblical scholarship.[95] Michael Carasik ascribes this to the huge influence of psychologist Julian Jaynes' 1976 work, *The Origin of Consciousness in the Breakdown of the Bicameral Mind.*[96] Christopher Hallpike's 1979 book,

91. C. Lévi-Strauss, *The Savage Mind* (trans. D. Weightman; Chicago: University of Chicago Press, 1966).

92. Seeing the Bible (or the Israelites) as the "other" is a rooted practice which has Christian theological origins on the one hand (J. Barr, *The Semantics of Biblical Language* [London: Oxford University Press, 1961], 1–7), as well as Western-intellectual ones (namely Orientalism).

93. T. Boman, *Hebrew Thought Compared with Greek* (trans. J. L. Moreau; New York: Norton, 1970).

94. M. Tsevat, "An Aspect of Biblical Thought: Deductive Explanation" (Hebrew), *Shnaton* 3 (1978): 53–58 (53). See also the original criticism in Barr, *Semantics*, 8–20, 21–45.

95. L. H. Feldman, "Hebraism and Hellenism Reconsidered," *Judaism* 43, no. 2 (1994): 115–26 (121). Interestingly, alongside the essentialist dichotomy between Hebrew and Greek modes of thinking found in some scholarly works, other scholars (mainly from the social-scientific approach) attribute both Hebrew and Greek cultures to a larger pan-Mediterranean culture. For recent detailed review of the comparison between Hebrew and Greek thought in biblical studies, see A. C. Hagedorn, *Between Moses and Plato: Individual and Society in Deuteronomy and Ancient Greek Law* (FRLANT 204; Göttingen: Vandenhoeck & Ruprecht, 2004), 14–37.

96. Carasik, *Theologies of the Mind*, 5. In his book, Jaynes describes a neurological change in the human brain which resulted in changes of thought patterns. Such changes are reflected in Mesopotamia, Biblical Israel, and Ancient Greece. See J. Jaynes, *The Origin of Consciousness in the Breakdown of the Bicameral Mind* (Boston: Houghton Mifflin, 1976). Despite its isolation within evolution theory, Jaynes's theory was happily adopted by influential scholars of religion, such as

The Foundations of Primitive Thought, may have also contributed to the survival of this dichotomy, by differentiating between action and reflection.[97] Notably, the inclusion of ancient Israel in the comprehensive discussion of axial-age civilizations did not cause great difference in scholarly popular perception.[98]

Despite slight differences among these studies, and despite core differences in their initial point of reference,[99] they reach similar conclusions. Table 1 shows how biblical thought contrasts with Western-modern-Greek thought in biblical scholarship:[100]

Table 1. *Biblical Thought vs. Western Thought*

Biblical Thought	*Western Thought*
Elastic	Inflexible
Intuitive	Conscious
Active	Reactive
Creative	Disciplined
Concrete	Abstract
Sensory	Mind
Dynamic	Static
Synthetic	Analytic

Robert N. Bellah and others (see Carasik, *Theologies of the Mind*, 7). This approach differs from that of biblical scholars such as Sandmel or Malul, who find that thought patterns change culturally, not neurologically.

97. Hallpike, *Foundations of Primitive Thought*, 32ff. The influence of Hallpike on *MKCS* must be noticed. For a short criticism of Hallpike, see E. L. Greenstein, "Some Developments in the Study of Language and Some Implications for Interpreting Ancient Texts and Cultures," in *Semitic Linguistics: The State of the Art at the Turn of the Twenty-First Century* (ed. S. Izre'el; Israel Oriental Studies 20; Winona Lake: Eisenbrauns, 2002), 441–79 (455 n. 22).

98. See the articles by Uffenheimer, Weinfeld, Machinist, and Tadmor in S. N. Eisenstadt, ed., *Origins and Diversity of Axial Age Civilizations* (SUNY Series in Near Eastern Studies; New York: State University of New York Press, 1986).

99. Despite the similarity of their conclusions, Pedersen and Boman differ dramatically in their starting points; Boman assumes that the structure of language can indicate the content of cultural patterns. Pedersen, on the other hand, assumes the existence of primitive psychology, and embarks on a journey to find its verbal expression in the Hebrew Bible. See also Barr, *Semantics*, 22, 42.

100. Mainly Sandmel, "Ancient Mind," 44; Boman, *Hebrew Thought*, 19; *MKCS*, 6, 128, and elsewhere; Tsevat, "Aspect of Biblical Thought," 53, and elsewhere.

These contrasts resemble the differentiation made by Hibbits and Ong between literate and oral societies (or performance cultures), between the experienced, real world and the written, imagined world. In terms of this book, the most significant contrast in the table is the emphasis on sensory perception in performance societies.

A recent study on biblical thought is Meir Malul's *Knowledge, Control and Sex*, which devotes a substantial section to a discussion of the senses. Published in 2002, this book focuses on a description of the semantic overlaying of knowledge (and sensation) concepts, sexuality, and control in the Hebrew Bible and in the ancient Near East. Malul dedicates much of his discussion to the senses for two reasons: first, the senses are a central tool for perception, an epistemic system in all senses;[101] additionally, sensory verbs are frequently used to describe learning and thought processes in the Hebrew Bible and the ancient Near East.[102] Malul itemizes the different senses mentioned in the Hebrew Bible, including sight, hearing, speech, smell, taste, touch, mobility, and the sexual sense. He argues that biblical thought has an entirely concrete and even physical character, and that it was driven by the sense of touch that lies at the core of all the senses in biblical culture.[103] In his book, Malul contrasts shared knowledge and concrete learning that typifies oral societies with individual knowledge and abstract learning, which typifies the modern world. Malul moves from a general discussion of the dichotomy of types of thought towards a specific discussion about the character of biblical thought. The importance of the book is its pioneering stress that the sensory categorization found in the Hebrew Bible has no equivalent in the categorization identified by Western scholars. For example, kinaesthesia is a category that biblical research has hitherto ignored as a sensory category.[104]

The drawback of the book, it seems to me, is the maintenance of the dichotomy between biblical and Western-modern thought.[105] It is important to note the shift apparent in *MKCS* from the Hebrew–Greek contrast, to the primitive–modern contrast. While this shift might seem reasonable, it actually involves a risky leap of logic. The Hebrew vs. Greek thought debate relates specifically to the mutual impact of these two

101. Malul, "Fabrication of Evidence," 215.
102. *MKCS*, 100.
103. Ibid., 128.
104. I want to thank Professor Étan Levine for pointing out the matter in the early stages of my research.
105. For background on the Hebrew–Greek dichotomy, see Feldman, "Hebraism and Hellenism"; Barr, *Semantics*, 8–20; Hagedorn, *Between Moses and Plato*, 14–17.

cultures. Their relationship, and especially the legacy that each culture left behind, has left an imprint on Western thought, Christian and Jewish alike.[106] The primitive vs. modern thought debate, however, is part of an attempt to make universal and essential dual distinction between all cultures in the world. The confusion between these two contrasts—the particular and the universal—leads consequently to a universal explanation based on a particular case. Such a leap is a classic example of how ethnocentricity works in practice.

As mentioned above, another problem of the studies mentioned is their frequent use of the terms "Hebrew/primitive/biblical mind." The term "mind" is a product of Western philosophy that evokes an essential distinction between body and mind, and between mental and physical perception. Such a distinction is alien to the biblical worldview. In fact, it seems that Israelite culture made no distinction between sensory and physical perception, as will be demonstrated in this book. If indeed no distinction exists between mind and emotion in biblical culture, it is not enough to explore the senses as a thinking tool or as an epistemic system. They must be seen as a tool for emotive experience, or involvement in the world. A similar example is evident in the work of Terence Collins, who shows the psychosomatic element of emotion in the Hebrew Bible. He argues that the Hebrew Bible does not differentiate between physical and emotional sensations, and that we need to revisit descriptions of pain and weeping in the biblical text.[107] Exploring the senses as an emotional tool might lead to new and surprising conclusions. One example is Menachem Zvi Kaddari's discussion of sensory terms such as "he saw" and "he heard" to describe empathy[108] or the sense of amazement.[109]

Researchers clearly need to liberate themselves not just from the Western bias that prioritizes the sense of sight, or from the pentasensory paradigm, but also from the consensus that every discussion of the senses is a discussion about thought or epistemology. Moreover, as Michael Carasik notes, while the term "thought" in studies of Western culture translates into the *content of thought*, it actually means the *process of thought* when this same term is used to describe biblical culture. In terms

---

106.   For the phenomenon in Christianity, see Barr, *Semantics*, 19, as well as n. 92.

107.   T. Collins, "The Physiology of Tears in the Old Testament," *CBQ* 33 (1971): 19–38, 185–97 (18).

108.   M. Z. Kaddari, "What is the Difference Between '*raʾah b-*' and '*raʾah et*' in Biblical Hebrew?" (Hebrew), *Mehkarim be-Lashon* 5–6 (1982): 67–78 (75).

109.   M. Z. Kaddari, "*Ma raʾita ki...* (Gen 20, 10)," in Augustin and Schunck, eds., *Dort Ziehen Schiffe dahin...*, 79–84 (82).

of what members of biblical culture thought about thought, Carasik concluded that biblical culture emphasized memory more than originality, and authoritative (divine) knowledge more than original (human) knowledge.[110] If we are to accept the anthropological studies of the senses discussed above, we should not find a sharp distinction between these two interpretations of the word "thought."[111]

Another major question arises in the discussion of biblical thought: When did the essential shift from "first level" to "second level" thinking occur in ancient Israel? Some scholars claim that "second level" (linear, figurative) thought only appears in Ecclesiastes, if at all.[112] Others see a core difference between communal and individual thought in the very earliest times, as reflected in first temple prophecy.[113] This debate reveals the contradiction inherent in the dichotomy presented in some of the studies mentioned above. On the one hand, there is a stress on the creative aspect of biblical thought, especially as expressed in internal commentaries, in glosses, in editorial processes, and in the expressions of the dynamic character of biblical thought, as displayed in the lack of textual consistency.[114] On the other hand, biblical thought is described as unscientific and unreflective,[115] a claim that perpetuates the historic argument regarding the existence of a communal personality in the Hebrew Bible.[116] How can a culture be creative, yet not reflective, when the creativity of human thought (in the form of interpretation of divine massage) within the Hebrew Bible is, in fact, the most prominent feature of the Hebrew Bible.[117]

Notable in this context are studies of Greek-influenced interpretation of biblical verses which mention the senses, and relate to variant different thought and perception processes. Annewies van der Hoek shows

110. Carasik, *Theologies of the Mind*, 11–12.

111. See n. 52, above.

112. P. Machinist, "Fate, *miqreh*, and Reason: Some Reflections on Qohelet and Biblical Thought," in *Solving Riddles and Untying Knots: Biblical, Epigraphic, and Semitic Studies* (Festschrift J. C. Greenfield; ed. Z. Zevit, S. Gitin, and M. Sokoloff; Winona Lake: Eisenbrauns, 1995), 159–75 (174); N. Shupak, "Learning Methods in Ancient Israel," *VT* 53 (2003): 416–26 (421).

113. H. Gunkel, *The Legends of Genesis: The Biblical Saga and History* (trans. W. H. Carruth; Introduction by W. F. Albright; New York: Schocken, 1964), 132.

114. Sandmel, "Ancient Mind," 37–38. For terms of creative thinking in biblical Hebrew, see Carasik, *Theologies of the Mind*, 176.

115. *MKCS*, 32–38, and elsewhere.

116. See pp. 48–50, below.

117. B. M. Levinson, *Legal Revision and Religious Renewal in Ancient Israel* (New York: Cambridge University Press, 2008).

how Philo's commentary on the story of the creation of Adam and Eve is influenced by Platonic ideas. Philo finds a dichotomy between logic and senses as ascribed to Adam and Eve respectively in the creation story.[118] Another study is Charles Fritsch's review of the Greek translations of the verb "to see" (ראה) and how they reflect changes in perception from the concrete to the abstract. Fritsch suggests that two factors influenced the translation. One is the Greek language itself, which translates every term associated with sight as abstract thought. The second factor is Jewish theology at the end of the Second Temple period, which proscribes the ability to see God or any other personification of God.[119] Notwithstanding the sharp distinction in earlier studies between biblical thought and other modes of thought, an inherent ontological contradiction cannot be found. It seems that we must allow a recognition of more complex cultural variations than that.[120] The form of thought presented in the Hebrew Bible is indeed associative rather than logical, yet every form of human thought is associative.[121] Any categorization is based on associations, as is any symbolism, including the use of language. All forms of thought are based simultaneously on the capacity for abstraction, and on the capacity for association.[122]

This review of "biblical thought" scholarship is essential to this book from a methodological perspective, as well as through its reference to sensory hierarchy. The recurring methodological discrepancies inherent in these studies are apparent whenever the perception of senses in the Hebrew Bible is discussed. A prime example is the argument about the sensory hierarchy. Boman states that it is futile to talk of a worldview among the Israelites, since they themselves did not regard the sense of sight as the primary method of describing the world:[123] "In the entire

118.   A. Van der Hoek, "Endowed with Reason or Glued to the Senses: Philo's Thoughts on Adam and Eve," in *The Creation of Man and Woman: Interpretations of the Biblical Narratives in Jewish and Christian Traditions* (ed. G. P. Luttikhuizen; Leiden: Brill, 2000), 63–75 (72).

119.   C. T. Fritsch, "A Study of the Greek Translation of the Hebrew Verbs 'to See', with Deity as Subject or Object," *Eretz Israel* 16 (1982): 51*–56*. The few existing studies of this kind demonstrate the difficulty of using any literature of Greek influence when attempting to solve the riddle of a difficult verse.

120.   Feldman, "Hebraism and Hellenism," 124. See pp. 65–69, below.

121.   W. J. Soll, "Babylonian and Biblical Acrostics," *Biblica* 69 (1988): 305–23.

122.   Merleau-Ponty, *Signs*, 39–42.

123.   Despite the lack of reference, it is clear that Boman uses Ong's distinction between worldview and world as event. The link between the two is clear through Ong's citation of Boman in referring to biblical culture as an oral culture; see W. J. Ong, "The Shifting Sensorium," in Howes, ed., *The Varieties of Sensory Experience*, 25–30 (25–26).

Old Testament, we do not find a single description of an objective 'photographic' appearance. The Israelites give us their impression of the thing that is perceived."[124] The claim that hearing is the dominant sense in the Hebrew Bible is repeated by other researchers who make an ontological distinction between a hearing Judaism and a seeing Hellenism. Based on the injunction against any physical representation of God, these researchers claim that the biblical God is a hearing God.[125] Furthermore, the extensive employment of hearing metaphors in the semantic fields of study and thought in Biblical Hebrew seems to support such bias.[126] Interestingly, Carasik reached the exact opposite conclusion. He claims that real learning in the Hebrew Bible is expressed solely through sight metaphors, while hearing expresses obedience and memorizing. Carasik also uses evolutionary arguments to claim that the superiority of the sense of sight is a human biological given that is not unique to biblical culture.[127] Carasik presents a spectrum of worldviews on senses in the Hebrew Bible. He claims that while Proverbs generally gives prominence to the ear as the most important learning organ, the culture of Deuteronomy presents sight as the dominant sense because of its personal and direct character.[128] Both these examples have a significant religious import.[129] They also demonstrate that the evaluation of sight and hearing in biblical thought cannot be solved by simple chronological means.

Carasik adds that in the biblical context, the means for learning about the world were the eye, the ears, and the heart (mind). Smell, taste, and touch played a much more minor role:

---

124. Boman, *Hebrew Thought*, 74, cf. pp. 204–8.

125. Y. Meshorer, "Two Extraordinary 'YHD' Coins," *Eretz Israel* 25 (1996): 434–37 (435).

126. For example, N. Shupak, *Where Can Wisdom Be Found? The Sage's Language in the Bible and in Ancient Egyptian Literature* (OBO 130; Fribourg: University Press Freiburg, 1993).

127. Carasik, *Theologies of the Mind*, 219.

128. Contra the unsound view of H. Avalos, as expressed in "Introducing Sensory Criticism in Biblical Studies: Audiocentricity and Visiocentricity," in *This Abled Body: Rethinking Disabilities in Biblical Studies* (ed. H. Avalos, S. Melcher, and J. Schipper; Semeia Studies 55; Atlanta: Society of Biblical Literature, 2007), 47–60.

129. M. Carasik, "To See a Sound: A Deuteronomic Rereading of Exodus 20:15," *Prooftexts* 19, no. 2 (1999): 257–65 (mainly 259). For inner-cultural variation of sensory perception, see R. Desjarlais, *Sensory Biographies: Lives and Deaths Among Nepal's Yolmo Buddhists* (Berkeley: University of California Press, 2003).

Seeing was by far the most important sense, according to all biblical understandings of the mind. As we pointed out, this is not in any case a trait particular to some human cultures and not others, but a biological one that is characteristic not merely for all humans, but of all primates. We argued from the text of the Bible, too, that (with the extremely rare exception of taste) sight was the only sense used in biblical Hebrew as a metaphor for thinking.[130]

The argument that sight is the dominant sense has led many researchers to conclude that the ancient custom of "evil eye" originated in the region of the ancient Near East, including the Hebrew Bible. But Thomsen has pointed out that the phrase "evil words" was much more common in the ancient Near East than "evil eyes."[131] His study points to the exceptional view of Hans Wolff, who looks for the human capacity which defines "man" in biblical thought: "This will no doubt be enough to show that with the human organ of speech we are coming particularly near to man's specific being. The capacity of language provides the essential condition for the humanity of man."[132] This matter will be discussed in detail later, in Chapter 5.

Malul takes a different view in *MKCS*: it is not the hierarchy of senses that determines their value in the Hebrew Bible, but the way in which they are used—always concrete, never figurative.[133] Yet, in another place, Malul contends that taste and smell are the most important senses. He states that the story in Gen 37:31–36 "reflects a perception whereby smell is the strongest sense in creating a clear mental image for man and in making up his mind" (my translation).[134] The contradictory conclusions presented above underline the need to revisit the question of sensory hierarchy portrayed in the Hebrew Bible, if indeed such hierarchy existed.

To sum up, research into the study of the senses in the Hebrew Bible has been sporadic at best, with an almost total lack of interest in the perception of the sensorium as such. Studies of biblical epistemology in the broader sense tend to neglect the scholarly bias caused by the

130.   Carasik, *Theologies of the Mind*, 219.
131.   M. L. Thomsen, "The Evil Eye in Mesopotamia," *JNES* 51 (1992): 19–32 (28). For a different view, see J. N. Ford, " 'Ninety-Nine by the Evil Eye and One from Natural Causes': KTU^2 1.96 in Its Near Eastern Context," *UF* 30 (1998): 201–78. Ford parallels the concept of evil eye, as found in a text from Ugarit, to belief in the evil eye in the ancient and contemporary Near East.
132.   H. W. Wolff, *Anthropology of the Old Testament* (trans. M. Kohl; London: SCM, 1974), 78.
133.   *MKCS*, 253.
134.   Malul, "Fabrication of Evidence," 216.

centrality of the sight in Western thought. In addition, they ignore the possibility of cultural relativism of the use of the senses. *MKCS* stands out as the only clear and comprehensive examination of different modalities and their use from a cultural perspective. Awareness of cultural relativism compels the scholar to acknowledge cultural difference between him/herself and the subject of the study, without artificially negating the two.[135] Many studies display a strong tendency towards defining the Hebrew Bible as the "other," or as a mirror image of Western culture and contemporary sensibilities.

In his book *Orientalism*, Edward Said showed that Western thought is visual and textual, and its source of knowledge is visualism and textualism.[136] That perception leads to the imagining of the Orient as the complete "other," a phenomenon which came to be known as Orientalism. Biblical scholarship, especially when it comes to the investigation of perception, shows strong orientalistic tendencies itself. At the opening of the third millennium, scholars are still thinking of the Levant as an all-embracing cultural phenomenon that has not changed in place or time for the past few thousand years. Orientalism in biblical scholarship perceives the Bible as the "other," oral–aural culture.[137]

Theoretical Considerations

The state of the study of the senses within cultural anthropology leads to some theoretical considerations for the scholar interested in the Hebrew sensorium. In the following pages I will present the basic stands, borrowed from anthropology, and more particularly phenomenological anthropology. Generally, the adopted notions are related to the view that sensory experience and thought about the senses are culturally specific, and that in the study of cultural phenomena the scholar must prefer the "native" data and vocabulary over external theories. These two notions will be discussed below through the presentation of cultural relativism, the theory–practice debate, and the emic–etic distinction. Given that I use

135. C. Geertz, *The Interpretation of Cultures: Selected Essays* (New York: Basic, 1973), 15–16. Geertz emphasizes the need for scholarly awareness to the limitation of cross-cultural understanding. Scholars must "translate" their findings and insights to make them comprehensible for readers of their own culture.

136. E. W. Said, *Orientalism* (trans. A. Zilber; Tel-Aviv: Am-Oved, 2000 [Hebrew]), 94ff; Ritchie, "The Nose Knows," 73.

137. Discussion of this phenomena is not yet widespread. Related discussion can be found in I. Davidson Kalmar and D. Penslar, "Orientalism and the Jews: An Introduction", in *Orientalism and the Jews* (ed. I. Davidson Kalmar and D. Penslar; Waltham: Brandeis University Press, 2005), xiii–xl.

textual data for cultural investigation, this study's assumptions about language and culture will also follow. The theoretical considerations will then lead to the methodological choices of this book.

Cultural Relativism

"Interpretation would be impossible if expressions of life were completely strange. It would be unnecessary if nothing strange were in them. It lies, therefore, between these two extremes."[138] Proof of the existence of cultural universalism, says Ullendorf, lies in the ability to translate any sentence or phrase from one language to another (and thus from one culture to another), so that the sentence will be accurately understood once it is translated. The fact that it is impossible precisely to translate individual words is proof of the existence of cultural relativism.[139] Ullendorf and Dilthey represent the two extremes to which cultural anthropology has been pulled over the past 150 years.[140] In the dawn of cultural anthropology, the young science was influenced by evolutionary and other late nineteenth-century and early twentieth-century theories that highlighted what was similar (universal) among different human cultures. Later, the cumulative evidence from ethnographic studies and their comparative analysis led to an emphasis on what is different and unique in each culture and society. These extremes were also reflected in the "nature or nurture" debate (i.e. to what extent is the development and behaviour of individuals influenced by either their genes or their culture?).

The basic assumption of the school of cultural relativism is that any cultural phenomenon—symbol, social institution, custom—can only be fully understood within the context of that culture. Any comparison between a cultural phenomenon and similar phenomena among other cultures may sharpen—but cannot explain—our understanding of the particular phenomenon. A distinction should be made between human physiological-universal and cultural traits, with prominence given to the latter. As our research review shows, there is an assumption that culture is something human, variable and relative:

---

138. Wilhelm Dilthey, in J. Z. Smith, *Imagining Religion: From Babylon to Jonestown* (Chicago Studies in History of Judaism; Chicago: University of Chicago Press, 1988), xii.

139. Ullendorff, "Thought Categories," 275.

140. Note that "anthropology" originally (in the seventeenth century) denoted the "study of man," and that its reference to cultural aspects of human life is a later development. Nowadays a distinction between archaeological/biological anthropology and social/cultural/linguistic anthropology is maintained. See Goldberg, Ziv, and Basker, *Anthropology*, 18–20.

A mischievous definition—but a useful one—for social and cultural anthropology is "the study of common sense." Yet common sense is, anthropologically speaking, seriously misnamed: it is neither common to all cultures, nor is any version of it particularly sensible from the perspective of anyone outside its particular cultural context... Common sense— the everyday understanding of how the world works—turns out to be extraordinarily diverse, maddeningly inconsistent, and highly resistant to scepticism of any kind. It is embedded in both sensory experience and practical politics—powerful realities that constrain and shape access to knowledge.[141]

Obviously, access to any foreign culture is based on a level of understanding that would be impossible unless humans shared a basic nature. In fact, it seems that the very existence of the cultural space produced by differing human conceptions is a characteristic common to all humankind, while the content of this creation varies considerably from culture to culture.[142] In this context, even factors previously regarded as biological, such as the definition of male and female gender, are now seen as a by-product of institutional, social, and cultural organizations.[143] This is not to deny human's biological unity, but it does show that biological data cannot explain every social action.[144]

The solution of the universal-particular conflict is usually presented in terms of a uniform biological basis—for example, the ability to create language. Cultural choices made by different groups created different languages with different sounds, symbols, and categorizations. Eating could also be described as a biological need, something natural and universal. But what we eat is determined by cultural boundaries that restrict choice. The way we eat is determined by societal conventions that are an extension of the "natural" choices of how to eat.[145] The study of the use of senses must be similar to the study of language or food. While all humans can see, hear, smell, and taste, not every culture uses or describes these abilities in the same way. Senses such as balance or speech could be included in the same categories as hearing and sight. Taste and touch are often regarded as a single, identical sense. The senses of taste and

141. Herzfeld, "Anthropology: A Practice of Theory," 301.
142. Schutz, "Phenomenology and the Social Sciences," 128; Berger, *The Sacred Canopy*, 6.
143. See pp. 13–14, above.
144. M. Z. Rosaldo, "The Use and Abuse of Anthropology: Reflection on Feminism and Cross-Cultural Understanding," *Signs* 5, no. 3 (1980): 389–417 (415 n. 58). Rosaldo's words regarding gender definitions are true for any pseudo-biological experience, including sensory experience.
145. Smith, *Imagining Religion*, 40.

smell are often regarded as a single sense. There are cultures that identify five senses, and there are those that identify only two: visual senses and non-visual ones.[146] Consider the following examples, which demonstrate cultural differences in the use and description of the senses:

1. Western convention equates thinking man with seeing man. But we find in the Malay culture of Southern Malaysia a clear preference for speech as the dominant way of defining human activity. Humans are defined in contradistinction to orang-utan primates, which in the Malay language is *orang* (man) *hutan* (forest), hence "men of the forest" that do not have the power of speech.

2. For the Sedang Moi tribe in Indochina, the ear is the seat of logic. Even people who do not or cannot speak, like some of the shamans, are regarded as having reached the pinnacle of human achievement.[147]

3. Among Anlo-speaking peoples in Southern Togo, a loss of hearing is regarded as the most severe defect. The centrality of hearing is expressed in language (hearing as the central metaphor), as well as in the high social and ethical value placed on the sense of balance, itself a function of the functioning ear.[148]

4. Among the members of the Hausa tribe in Niger, people are described according to their taste: men are sharp, women are sweet, and children are salty.[149] Members of Niger's Songhay tribe base their images of control and magic on food images. Much of the study and mastery of magic includes eating rituals.[150]

These examples demonstrate that the division of the senses into five categories is by no means shared by all cultures.

How do we explain these cultural differences in the use and imagination of the sensorium? One theory is that the cultural preferences absorbed by children during their education via linguistic categories, and via specific sensory-skills enhancement, influence how the senses are used for the rest of their lives. Some of the physiologically potential

146.   Classen, "Anthropology of the Senses," 401.

147.   G. Devereux, "Ethnopsychological Aspects of the Terms 'Deaf' and 'Dumb'," in Howes, ed., *The Varieties of Sensory Experience*, 43–46.

148.   Guerts, *Culture and the Senses*, 5.

149.   I. D. Ritchie, "Fusion of the Faculties: A Study of the Language of the Senses in Hausaland," in Howes, ed., *The Varieties of Sensory Experience*, 192–202 (200).

150.   P. Stoller, *Sensuous Scholarship* (Philadelphia: University of Pennsylvania Press, 1997), 7–9.

senses will be developed, others will be discarded. Furthermore, the way the various senses are used will differ. We often find that in certain professions, one sense becomes more developed than others. Wine tasters, for example, have an unusually well-developed sense of smell and taste. Musicians have an unusually well-developed sense of listening. Foucault showed that until the eighteenth century, physicians needed a well-developed sense of smell, since this was their main means of diagnosing disease.[151] People who lack an essential sense often successfully enhance the use of their other senses, such as a blind person who develops his sense of hearing and touch. The same process happens in all cultures.

A more extreme example of how senses can be culturally enhanced is children raised without human education—so-called wolf children. Rare documentation of feral children and their sensory abilities displays various sensory adjustments: some kids experienced physical pain when they tried to use senses they had never used before. When they saw bright or strong colours for the first time, they felt physical pain. They could not distinguish between a photograph and the real three-dimensional world around them. Others could hear the faintest sound of a nut cracking open (= food), yet could not hear a gun being fired right next to their ears. Yet other children could not physically distinguish hot from cold.[152] Apparently, just as feral children were unable to learn a language intuitively, they were unable to learn to use their senses in a way that was appropriate to a particular culture. Their senses developed in a way that ensured their acclimatization to the conditions in which they were raised. There is documentary evidence that after these children were discovered, the substantial efforts made to change their "sensory habits" and to acclimatize them to their adoptive society only rarely succeeded.[153]

In part at least, sensory experience is a skill. And since every skill is culturally dependent, different cultures create different profiles of the sensory system. Even when someone has an idiosyncratic sensory profile, this must be understood in the context of the senses in his culture.[154] The cultural influences on the use of the senses prove that it is dangerous to assume a direct biological connection between a sense and its inner phenomenological component—for example, the correlation between sight and linearity, between smell and memory, and between touch and

151.   Stoller, *Taste of Ethnographic Things*, 8; Howes, "Sensorial Anthropology," 180.

152.   C. Classen, "The Sensory Orders of 'Wild Children'," in Howes, ed., *The Varieties of Sensory Experience*, 47–60 (51–52).

153.   Ibid., 57.

154.   Howes, "Sensorial Anthropology," 168; Desjarlais, *Sensory Biographies*, 4.

engagement with the world. Even if these connections exist, such as the proven multiple connections between the smell and memory centres in the brain, we cannot take their cultural expression for granted. A culture can assign a function to a certain sense that is different from its biological function.[155] Cultural sensory preferences influence both the semantic field of the senses in language, and the actual use of the senses. Children learn language as a thinking tool, and they learn how to use their senses as techniques for engaging with the world. The senses shape the way children understand their world.[156] Any discussion of thinking about the senses, therefore, cannot be separated from a discussion of the senses themselves, and as far as the theory on cultural relativity of the senses is concerned, a strong link between language and cultural practice exists.[157]

Finally, the relativistic approach rejects dichotomous theories of cultures. As such, dichotomy does not reflect existing cultural diversity.[158] Similarly, repeated comparisons with Western culture (which is usually the scholar's own culture) are not desirable, as they perpetuate this dichotomy by defining the culture under study as alien, inaccessible, and impenetrable.[159] The study must examine each homogenous culture in its own right, with its power struggles and differences. It must make comparisons with the scholar's own culture only for clarification purposes, whether as a contrast or as a typological similarity.

The present work follows this approach, and focuses on the Hebrew Bible. Examples from contemporary or ancient Near Eastern cultures will be made for clarification purposes only. Despite the historical and geographical proximity between ancient Israel and the ancient Near East, and the proximity of perceptions found between the Hebrew Bible and some texts in Ugaritic, Akkadian, Aramaic, and Moabite, this material is complex and deserves thorough study in its own right. An in-depth discussion of sensory perception in each separate language and culture would have to be conducted before grand comparison.

---

155.   Howes, *Sensual Relations*, 53. One example is the connection between the olfactory sense and the remembrance centre of the brain. Despite the fact that this is a physiological connection, training or neglecting the connection will influence the use of the olfactory sense. So, in some cultures, the olfactory sense will neither be perceived as evoking memories, nor evoke memories in true experience.

156.   Howes, "Sensorial Anthropology," 183.

157.   What feature of language is represented here will be discussed below, in the meanwhile it is crucial to state that the semantic and contextual elements are the parts meant here, and not the structural-grammatical one.

158.   One might say that it reflects a Western mode of thought, or even a human mode of thought *à la* Levi-Strauss, but not reality.

159.   Herzfeld, "Anthropology: A Practice of Theory," 308.

Data and Theory, Who Comes First?

"There is nothing in the mind that has not previously been in the senses," says the famous maxim of empiricism.[160] To paraphrase, when it comes to cultural investigation, there should be nothing in the theory that has not previously been in the data. Any discussion of theory and practice highlights the gap between the scholar's theory and the reality he/she is actually researching. There is also a gap in every culture between the description of the social principles and actual life, between ideology and practice.[161] The link between these two conflicts is that anthropologies in the past tended to base their conclusions on the ideology presented by informants from the culture under study, and to create an abstract explanation far removed from the customs and implementation of the cultural codes. In what follows, I will first discuss the gap between the scholarly theory and reality, and then its relevance to the current book.

Is it possible to describe a cultural research without reduction and creation of an essentially external construction? Admittedly, order is an essential part of culture, namely, an explanation of the world, the categorization of the world, the creation of behavioural norms. Yet in some ways, theoretical descriptions can themselves create the illusion of order in culture. Cultural systems, unlike philosophical systems, are varied and filled with conflicts and power struggles.[162] Anthropology, which has long described different cultures as sets of rules and regulations, often created a false impression of a static human reality that can be described scientifically and objectively, and that can reveal the set of rules that guides the individuals in that culture. Not only does such an approach separate culture from reality as a separate objective entity, but it also creates its own mystification as a factor that is external to humanity: "Objective knowledge bestows a semblance of order on one's world, but at a price. The price is what Whitehead called 'the fallacy of misplaced concreteness.' In becoming tokens of the real, concepts easily become mistaken for the real, and are manipulated magically as if they give

---

160.   For the origin of the maxim see P. F. Cranefield, "On the Origin of the Phrase NIHIL EST IN INTELLECTU QUOD NON PRIUS FUERIT IN SENSU," *Journal of the History of Medicine* (1970): 77–80.

161.   See the anthropological distinctions between norm, belief, and occurrence, in *MKCS*, 71–74.

162.   H. Eilberg-Schwarz, "The Problem of the Body for the People of the Book," in *Women in the Hebrew Bible* (ed. A. Bach; New York: Routledge, 1999), 53–73 (53); B. E. F. Beck, "The Metaphor as Mediator Between Semantic and Analogic Modes of Thought," *Current Anthropology* 19, no. 1 (1978): 83–97; Mead, "Study of Culture," 10; and, with regards to the Hebrew Bible, Machinist, "Fate, *miqreh*, and Reason," 165.

control over life."[163] This fallacy grows further when anthropological theories are applied, and even forced on biblical data, a matter to be discussed later.

This is not a mere philosophical argument. It is linked to research methods that reflect the conflict of theory and practice within the culture itself. One of the problems that anthropologists repeatedly face is the gap between the social-cultural principles they learn from informants, and the actions they observe and are involved in.[164] Edmund Leach uses a famous example from the Trobriand Islands, where researchers were told of the custom whereby a man marries the daughter of his father's sister. Yet demographic research revealed only a single example of such a marriage during the course of an entire year's research.[165] Another example is the gap between the official principle and the practice of family honour among Bedouin tribes. While hundreds of women violate the behavioural codes of family honour every single day, only very few Bedouin women are murdered in the name of family honour each year.[166] This last fact is interesting, as the theory about "family honour" in Mediterranean societies is often used in biblical studies, despite its dependence on questionable data. Despite the holism of society, language, and culture, they contain a wide and diverse range of opinions and actions. What happens in reality is not always the same as what should happen.

At first glance, the Hebrew Bible appears to be closer to the declarative-official aspect of the culture in which it developed, yet it also contains details that demonstrate actual reality.[167] Such details can be revealed through research tools such as "innocent speech" and linguistic categories, which reveal cultural principles even when using language to describe an ideal situation.[168] This complexity is expressed through commandments that were never observed, through an agenda-driven description of history, and through repeated descriptions of the same event (such as the creation story and other historical events). It is extremely difficult to distinguish between theory and practice in a culture

---

163. Jackson, "Phenomenology and Anthropological Critique," 5. See the criticism of previous biblical scholars in Barr, *Semantics*, 22.

164. This matter is linked to the crisis of representation in anthropology. See Stoller, *Taste of Ethnographic Things*, 125.

165. E. R. Leach, "The Comparative Method in Anthropology," *IESS* I (1968): 339–45.

166. J. Ginat, *Blood Disputes Among Bedouin and Rural Arabs in Israel: Revenge, Mediation, Outcast and Family Honor* (Pittsburgh: University of Pittsburgh Press in cooperation with Jerusalem Institute for Israel Studies, 1987), 204.

167. Chance, "Anthropology of Honor and Shame," 145.

168. Further details in the next section.

that is not accessible to us, yet such difficulty arises in the study of living cultures as well. As mentioned before, the gap between the source theory (in this case: anthropology) and its use as a descriptor of the culture reflected in the biblical text should be noted. There is a risk that a set of rules derived from another culture will be used to try and understand biblical culture, and that ethnographic details (i.e. the conclusions of a specific ethnographic study) will be used, instead of using theory and core assumptions as the basis for research.[169]

My core assumption is that a system described as a generalization of the culture being studied supplies the scholar with a conceptual framework for discussing the culture, but cannot predict social activity.[170] Cultural structures, hence, are similar to linguistic structures. The grammatical rules of a language are based on the actual use of the language, yet do not exist "above" or "in front of" it. Although we can use these grammatical rules to speak the language with varying degrees of proficiency, we cannot use them to predict linguistic performance.[171]

Furthermore, the rules induced in human-cultural science are different from rules induced in the natural sciences, which extend beyond description to prediction. Semantic and cultural structures exist, but they are not rigid. They have no existence apart from their implementation. The attempt by scholars of human phenomena to imitate the natural sciences, to find regularity and consistency, produces the gap between theory and practice. The typologies discovered by the researcher often become independent entities.[172] And so, from the 1970s onwards, voices calling for a revolution in the "human" sciences started to be raised. Clifford Geertz called for a discussion of meaning: "Believing, with Max Weber, that man is an animal suspended in webs of significance he himself spun, I take culture to be those webs, and the analysis of it to be therefore not an experimental science in search of law but an interpretive one in search of meaning."[173] Geertz further defines the difference between description and explanation to be used in the newly suggested "interpretive science":

169. See also the discussion of the emic approach below. Using facts in place of theory is quite common in the contemporary social-scientific approach to biblical studies, which uses the pan-Mediterranean theory.

170. Geertz, *Interpretation of Cultures*, 26.

171. J. J. Gumperz, "Sociolinguistics and Communication in Small Groups," in *Sociolinguistics: Selected Readings* (ed. J. B. Pride and J. Holmes; Harmondsworth: Penguin, 1972), 203–24 (215); Schutz, "Phenomenology and the Social Sciences," 131.

172. Schutz, "Phenomenology and the Social Sciences," 140.

173. Geertz, *Interpretation of Cultures*, 5.

Such a view of how theory functions in an interpretative science suggests that the distinction relative in any case, that appears in the experimental or observational sciences between "description" and "explanation" appears here as one, even more relative, between "inscription" ("thick description") and "specification" ("diagnosis")—between setting down the meaning particular social actions have for the actors whose actions they are, and stating, as explicitly as we can manage, what the knowledge thus attained demonstrates about the society in which it is found and, beyond that, about social life as such.[174]

Other voices took it a step forward and called for a discussion on practice, where culture is living and transmitted, and total rejection of the search for regularity itself.[175] If the goal of cultural research is not to create a systematic set of rules, because of the gap created between itself and reality, a further definition of the research subject is required.

First, we must acknowledge the gap between knowledge by which we live, and the knowledge through which we explain life. This gap between action and doctrine, practice and theory, experience and idea is inherent to daily reality. In fact, what drives action is not a particular rationale but the common sense that drives the lifeworld.[176] We must acknowledge that the human, orderly picture of the world is a fabrication, one whose truth only lies in its contextual application. In other words, we use "fictions," but should be ready to change them when necessary. These fictions are neither myths nor truths trying to preserve themselves.[177] The study of culture from an interpretive point of view is, therefore, the study of awareness to the world, of a cultural way to experience happenings in the lifeworld and to idealize them. Such awareness to the world is normally unconscious and varies from culture to culture.[178]

To expand, the study of a cultural common sense focuses on the shared cultural background, the immediate (concrete and figurative) environment that leads someone to feel at home in his culture.[179] It is a shift of discussion from what the text (or culture) says, to what it talks about.[180] In phenomenological anthropology, this is known as lifeworld, an expression that has its origin in the German word *Lebenswelt* coined

---

174. Ibid., 27, and cf. the citation of Silberman regarding biblical studies below.

175. Ortner, "Theory in Anthropology," 144. See also pp. 11–12, above.

176. Jackson, "Phenomenology and Anthropological Critique," 2–4.

177. Silberman, "Listening to the Text," 5.

178. Schutz, "Phenomenology and the Social Sciences," 124.

179. See Herzfeld, "Anthropology: A Practice of Theory," 103.

180. Paul Ricouer, in P. Rabinow and M. W. Sullivan, "The Interpretive Turn: Emergence of an Approach," in *Interpretive Social Science* (ed. P. Rabinow and M. W. Sullivan; Berkeley: University of California Press, 1979), 1–24 (12).

by Edmond Husserl.[181] The term is used to describe the fact that we do not study an abstract transcendental body of knowledge, but the totality of existing factors—abstract ideas, but also customs, semantic categories, symbols, and so forth. The term lifeworld tries to avoid the cultural bias of a related term, *Weltanschauung*, a comprehensive view of the world and human life. *Weltanschauung* incorporates a bias towards the sense of sight and towards the existence of a figurative system that controls action.[182] The difference between the two terms is one of theoretical context, more than contextual usage. Using the term lifeworld directs the study towards the investigation of what there is,[183] of the context of a cultural common sense. When it comes to the Hebrew Bible, we are searching for its cultural-context, the biblical sense.

A short note is due on the difference between the term lifeworld, and the basic term of biblical scholarship, *Sitz im Leben*, "setting in life," which describes the concrete background against which a specific text was created. Lifeworld is a broader reality in which texts were indeed created, but such reality cannot prove how they were created. Lifeworld is more similar to the discussion of cultural milieu, the environment that includes customs and ideas in which these texts were created.[184] The common sense behind biblical compositions could have been common to members of Israelite culture, but was by no means consistent, often circular and contextual. Such cultural logic exists in every culture, not just in "simple" cultures. My aim is to discover this cultural context while avoiding the construction of an artificial theoretical system. To achieve this aim, I follow Silberman's suggestion for biblical scholars, as well as Stoller's suggestion for anthropologists:

> The rules are quite simple: suspend explanations; describe. Ihde wrote: "Phenomenology calls for the suspension of 'theories' which attempt to go behind or under experience, for a suspension of 'constructs' which are elaborated to account for such a phenomenon."[185]

181.   Schutz, "Phenomenology and the Social Sciences," 121–24, 133–34; Jackson, "Phenomenology and Anthropological Critique," 13–14. One must note, however, that Edmund Husserl was in search of a united *Lebenswelt* before diverse phenomena, while his followers talk about diverse *Lebenswelt*.

182.   See *MKCS*, 3. Malul summarizes Wilhelm Dilthey's term as an image of the real world which is the basis for judgments and evaluations that create a coherent system of purposes, ideals, and operative principles. The operative principles connect the *Weltanschauung* to the *praxis*.

183.   Merleau-Ponty, *Phenomenology*, 7.

184.   In such a way, Gunkel's term is extended to three domains: reference, situation, and context. See D. A. Knight, "The Understanding of 'Sitz im Leben' in Form Criticism," *SBLSP* 1 (1974): 105–25.

185.   Silberman, "Listening to the Text," 11.

> Despite its self-evident status, ethnography, rather than cultural material-
> ism, structuralism, or any other "ism," has been and will be our core con-
> tribution.[186]

The choice of description over theory, patterns over rules, and the
previously mentioned cultural-particular over universal, led to the choice
of the emic over the etic approach.[187] The etic approach is an objective
approach that uses external, scientific criteria and concepts in an effort
to understand the phenomenon being studied. The emic approach is a
subjective approach which looks from within, and uses local criteria. The
emic approach is critical for the study of culture, since it is interested in
holistically examining the local world of knowledge. Some describe the
emic approach as a search for the native's point of view. This point of
view is, in a way, similar to the cultural common sense presented earlier:
"Understanding the form and pressure of, to use the dangerous word one
more time, native's inner lives is more like grasping a proverb, catching
an allusion, seeing a joke, or, as I have suggested, reading a poem—than
it is like achieving communion."[188]

On Language and Culture

When it comes to language, using an emic approach implies interest in
the performance of language, which reveals the associative world of
members of that culture. In order to do that, the terms and phrases of that
language are to be used, rather than external ones. As Geertz puts it,
we prefer to use "experience near" rather than "experience distant"
terms.[189] Moreover, from a linguistic point of view, the etic approach is a
domain-centred approach where researchers assume that there is a
particular idea or experience, which they then proceed to codify within
the language or culture under study. The emic approach is a structure-
centred approach that examines given structures within that culture and
the existing terms in the language, in order to find the concepts that exist
in that culture.[190] Having said that, the gap between the field of notions
and the field of terms neutralizes any attempt simply to choose one of the

---

186. Stoller, *Taste of Ethnographic Things*, 130. Cf. Geertz, *Interpretation of
Cultures*, 9–10; Herzfeld, "Anthropology: a Practice of Theory," 313.

187. Mead, "Study of Culture," 12–15.

188. C. Geertz, "From the Native's Point of View," in Rabinow and Sullivan,
eds., *Interpretive Social Science*, 225–42 (241). Thorough discussion of the emic and
the etic in biblical studies is found in upcoming publications by Dan Wu, which we
discussed in August 2011. Most important is his emphasis on the dialectic character
of both approaches.

189. Ibid., 226–27.

190. Guerts, *Culture and the Senses*, 38–39.

two approaches.[191] Sapir-Warf's view that language dictates our perception of reality, so that only terms that exist in a language also exist in our ability to conceptualize, seems too extreme.[192] The link between language and reality is a dialectic link, where language dictates reality but is also formed by reality.[193] There are also non-linguistic components that incorporate categories and understanding of reality. Language is thus just one medium—indeed, the main medium—of meaning. It is a highly accessible medium for our study of the Hebrew Bible.

These two possibilities are also found in sensory research. Researchers such as Howes, Dundes, Hibbits, and others focus on a description of words and expressions that demonstrate the centrality of one particular sense. Other researchers also describe the performative prominence of different categories, including the use of the senses. Relating this to the senses in the Hebrew Bible, we can state that the sense of sight is linguistically elaborated, while the sense of smell is performatively elaborated.[194] This is akin to synaesthesia in the Hebrew Bible, and its linguistic or experiential basis. While not every image that involves senses is needed to reflect an experience of synaesthesia, it is possible to have a mixed experience that is not thus described. The linguistic category should not be seen as sole proof of thought categories in a culture. Some terms are unclear but are swallowed into the language, in narrative and in practice.

Transferring the emic approach to biblical studies must go through language, which is the major native data available for ancient Israel. While ethnographic research is influenced and strengthened by the researcher's unmediated experience, biblical material precludes any such experience. The main source is the biblical text itself, with all the challenges this poses, including language that is unclear, laconic, and tendentious.[195] While revealing unconscious cultural categories through

191. Kaddari, "What is the Difference?," 67. See also C. Lévi-Strauss, *Structural Anthropology* (trans. C. Jacobson and B. Grundfest Schöpf; New York: Basic, 1963), 38.

192. Carasik, *Theologies of the Mind*, 3.

193. Ullendorff, "Thought Categories," 286–87; Ong, "Shifting Sensorium," 26. See also Berger's discussion of the dialectic link between culture and reality. Culture is simultaneity created by and creates reality (*The Sacred Canopy*, 7–12).

194. According to previous studies. Chapter 5 of this book demonstrates the linguistic elaboration of sight. The centrality of scents in cultic ritual can point to cultural elaboration. For the distinction between linguistic and performative elaboration, see Csordas, "Somatic Modes," 137; Guerts, *Culture and the Senses*, 5.

195. See *MKCS*, 29. For the attempts to use anthropological methods in the study of distance cultures (in time/space), see Mead and Métraux, eds., *The Study of Culture at a Distance*.

semantic research is relevant to ethnography,[196] it is crucial for biblical studies. Language often unconsciously reflects common cultural categories and contexts, as opposed to conscious textual content such as stories, poems, and legal material. Later, we will explore the research tools based on these assumptions. The examination of language as an indicator of the culture resembles the approach that sees culture as a living and performing entity, and not as an abstract set of rules.

Language has many aspects that deserve study: structure, history, phonetics. But all these look at language or a group of languages from a theoretical perspective known as *langue*. A discussion of the *langue* teaches us that every language has its own structure, history, and sounds. But any study of language is based on the generalized use of the language in practice, in other words: how it is spoken, the *parole*.[197] Our examination of biblical language will focus on the performance of the language, on its *parole*. Studying the way a language is used can teach us about the thought processes, the categories, and the associations shared by all those who speak the language. As we saw earlier, we can understand the performance of a language but we cannot predict it.[198] Language is not just a means of expression. It is a cultural tool for understanding and constructing the world, indistinguishable from experiencing the world:[199]

> Humankind has a variety of media and means of communication at its disposal, each with the ability to transfer messages, with a unique focus and stress on this or that segment of the human sensorium. Language is one very important medium of communication which has commanded human thought to the point of actually conditioning, rather than just articulating it. *All this is true for traditional "pre-literate" cultures as it is for contemporary Western cultures...* In short, language has become a medium of reflection rather than a reflection of action.[200]

196.   See B. Good, "The Heart of What's the Matter: The Semantics of Illness in Iran," *Culture, Medicine and Psychiatry* 1 (1977): 25–58.

197.   The original distinction between *langue* and *parole* is found in F. de Saussure, *Course in General Linguistics* (trans. R. Harris; London: Duckworth, 1982), 13–15.

198.   M. J. Buss, "The Idea of Sitz im Leben—History and Critique," *ZAW* 90 (1978): 157–70 (168). While using de Saussure's classic definition, I do not find that *parole* is a repetition and/or realization of a set of rules and norms (see Ortner, "Theory in Anthropology," 180). I adopt the phenomenological approach, in which *parole* precedes *langue* and not vice versa (see Jackson, "Phenomenology and Anthropological Critique," 35). See also Greenstein, "Some Developments," 444–45.

199.   See n. 194.

200.   *MKCS*, 36 (my emphasis).

In other words, although some experiences are not verbally expressed, many experiences receive their significance through linguistic expression.[201]

The performance of language has its origin in, and shapes, the life-world. Our discussion on the performative aspect of language allows us to acknowledge the diversity of reality.[202] We do not investigate a utopian linguistic structure, but cultural preferences, power struggles, and basic values that are reflected in the practical performance of the language. The use of language demands prior cultural knowledge, as does behaviour in society. The linguistic preferences are demonstrated in vocabulary, metaphors, and associative patterns. Together, they form an associative and synchronous whole of semantic networks that express feelings, experiences, thoughts, and events.[203] Naturally, the medium of language cannot reflect every single reality. Not everything of significance has a lingual expression, and not everything absent from the language is also absent from the way members of that culture view the world. But even if we accept the limitations of language, we need a command of the language under study, so that we can spot irony, illusion, and abstraction that exist in the spoken language.[204]

Language reflects culture, but understanding language requires knowledge that is usually acquired naturally and gradually through informal study, the knowledge that allows us to understand metaphors, humour, or criticism.[205] Searching for the symbolic basis of the culture, as opposed to searching for its operating principles, could help us understand and not just recognize the cultural codes.[206] We need to understand the associative space of the language, because words have no intrinsic meaning on their own. Words can only be understood relative to the cultural system and context in which they are spoken. This leads Merleau-Ponty to present the paradox created by the character and essence of language: it is impossible to learn a language without knowing it. He claims that the solution to this paradox lies in the use of speech, just as Zeno's tortoise paradox was solved by using movement. Once more, this leads to the

---

201.   Merleau-Ponty, *Signs*, 42. Yet, searching for pre-verbal experience is, at times, the aim of phenomenological investigation.

202.   Schutz, "Phenomenology and the Social Sciences," 134; Abu Lughod and Lutz, *Emotion, Discourse and Politics*, 9.

203.   Good, "The Heart of What's the Matter," 26.

204.   Herzfeld, "Anthropology: A Practice of Theory," 305–6. See also Merleau-Ponty, *Signs*, 44–46.

205.   Gumperz, "Sociolinguistics and Communication," 220.

206.   Geertz, *Interpretation of Cultures*, 9.

inescapable conclusion that language only exists in its performance, as *parole*.[207]

I propose a more practical definition of the paradox: social linguistics distinguishes between linguistic competence, the ability to learn a foreign language and to speak it according to the rules of grammar, and communicative competence, the ability to choose from a linguistic repertoire that includes the appropriate vocabulary for the appropriate situation. This ability can only be acquired by practicing the language, by speaking the language in different contexts in the social and cultural space.[208] This ability is actually part of the shared cultural pre-learning that empowers any behaviour within a defined human society. This knowledge belongs to humanity's store of cognitive blueprints, the knowledge blueprints that create expectations of what is happening in the world. By learning these blueprints, and by learning the historical context of cultural knowledge, the researcher gains access to the cultural worlds view under study.[209] The creation of knowledge blueprints is influenced mainly by the environment, and since culture is a dominant part of the environment, we inevitably return to the correlation between language and culture.

For an example of this correlation, let us revisit Boman and Barr, who both assume a link between language and culture, but reach almost opposite conclusions. Boman links the *grammatical* structure of language to the *type* of thought of those that speak it. Barr links the *semantic* structure of language to the *content* of the thought of those who speak it.[210] Neither scholar bases his findings on the content of the biblical text, but on the language itself. Similarly, while we cannot accept the text as direct documentation of reality, we can approach the language as direct documentation of reality. Language is a kind of cultural matrix within which humankind operates. This is in harmony with the approach whereby, morphologically speaking, actions in themselves are meaningless, and only become significant as part of context, commentary, or symbolism.[211] Despite its literary character, Biblical Hebrew is not a language in a vacuum, and while syntactical and grammatical features can be detached from daily language and context, semantics and associative

---

207. Merleau-Ponty, *Signs*, 39.

208. Gumperz, "Sociolinguistics and Communication," 205.

209. G. B. Palmer, *Toward a Theory of Cultural Linguistics* (Austin: University of Texas Press, 1996), 4.

210. Boman, *Hebrew Thought*, 27–42; Barr, *Semantics*, 21–45.

211. Rosaldo, "Use and Abuse of Anthropology," 400; Geertz, *Interpretation of Cultures*, 18.

patterns rarely can. In the context of Biblical Hebrew, the phenomenon of word pairs in poetry provides a fine example: "The lists of pairs that scholars have collected are not part of a poetic or even literary tradition. They are much more: they are a window into what psycholinguistics would call the language behaviour, and ultimately the whole conceptual world, of speakers of Biblical Hebrew and Ugaritic."[212]

I agree with Berlin that studying a language through existing texts reveals the cultural world of the "authors" and of the "audience" who shared common values and concepts,[213] but does not necessarily reveal the writing process. In the biblical context, we must assume some cultural unity between the authors of the text and their target audience. Even if we accept that people in biblical times belonged to a predominantly oral society, we cannot assume an unbridgeable cultural gap between the literate and illiterate members of the same society. This is also true for texts that a priori were written down and which have no oral source.[214]

Lastly, the correlation between language and culture is expressed in their holism: "An analogy between language and cultural structure means that just as language is an integrated, coherent structure, it is also a social structure whose different components…touch one another and cross one another in a multitude of different and complex ways. From every anchor point, the viewer can discern the structure in a holistic and dynamic way".[215] Holism is a key concept in cultural research, and important for the link between various experience horizons in a given culture. Discussion of one leads us to—and complements—a discussion of the other. When we examine a language or culture, we find both structure and consistency, as well as holism. Words, like actions, have no meaning without context and correlation.[216] Yet, although a linguistic or cultural system is holistic, it is by no means uniform. As we saw in our discussion of cultural relativism, holistic research relates to any culture as a totality, and refrains from inter-cultural comparisons on particular details. It

---

212.   A. Berlin, "Parallel Word Pairs: A Linguistic Explanation," *UF* 15 (1983): 7–16 (repr. in *The Dynamics of Biblical Parallelism* [Bloomington: Indiana University Press, 1985], 64–72); see also M. O'Connor, *Hebrew Verse Structure* (Winona Lake: Eisenbrauns, 1980), 96–100. See the further discussion below, pp. 55–60.

213.   For the unity between author/editor and the audience, see Boman, *Hebrew Thought*, 22.

214.   Soll, "Acrostics," 321. See also Greenstein, "Some Developments," Part 5.

215.   M. Malul, "A Holistic-Integrative Investigation of Biblical Culture: A Case Study: The Motif of Spying and Conquering a Territory in the Bible" (Hebrew), *Shnaton* 14 (2004): 141–57 (143, my translation).

216.   Merleau-Ponty, *Signs*, 42.

refrains from atomization.[217] The existence of continuity and correlation in the lifeworld among fields such as religion, science, and justice does not prove that the lifeworld is balanced and harmonious. At the same time, models found in language—metaphors, images, and shared contexts—show conscious and unconscious understandings that guide the type of thought of the participants of a particular culture, and are an authentic representation of that culture.[218]

Sensory Experience and the Individual

My focus on the senses comes from a cultural-relativistic perspective. I seek the experience of reality rather than an abstract theoretical construct. I am dealing with the realm of sensation, which together with feelings and thought belongs to the subjective formation. Another basic premise that underlies this study is the existence of the experiencing subject in all cultures. This core assumption is rooted in the theoretical tendencies I presented so far, and deserves its due attention. This is despite the fact that it does not influence significantly my methodology, mainly due to the laconic nature of the text under study. It requires clarification for yet another reason, as it stands in stark contrast to the assumption of many biblical scholars: biblical modes of thinking were not systematic, abstract, or reflective. They were modes of participation in the world.[219] These modes of thought are described within dichotomous theories, as discussed before, and are often linked to this level or another of communal personality. The idea of communal personality within the Hebrew Bible is almost as old as biblical studies.[220] See, for example, the words of Hermann Gunkel (1901): "This is in accord with the conditions of antiquity, in which the individual was much less sharply distinguished from the mass of the people than in modern times."[221] Such a concept was presented by major anthropologists, such as Emile Durkheim (1912): "Since all conscious minds are drawn along

---

217. See also S. Talmon, "The 'Comparative Method' in Biblical Interpretation—Principles and Problems," in *Congress Volume: Göttingen 1977* (ed. J. A. Emerton; VTSup 29; Leiden: Brill, 1978), 320–56 (mainly 328–29).

218. *MKCS*, 41–42.

219. See *MKCS*, 9 (following Hallpike).

220. The expression "corporate personality," just like "primitive thinking," was coined by Levy-Bruhl (see pp. 22–24, above). This term is based, therefore on basic assumptions which are no longer accepted by contemporary anthropologist (i.e. the developmental-dichotomist assumption). Such rejection of a theory must be followed by a re-examination of its verbal expressions.

221. Gunkel, *The Legends of Genesis*, 43.

in the same current, the individual type almost overlaps with the general type. While everything is uniform, everything is simple."[222]

In terms of the Hebrew Bible, Rogerson has already suggested that we should only talk of "communal responsibility," in family groups, but not of real communal personality,[223] and Kaminsky has provided us with a reassessment of "communal responsibility in terms of its meaning and function in the Hebrew Bible: the terms and their meanings in the Hebrew Bible."[224] In anthropology, allegedly ethnographic proofs of the existence of cultures without emotional experience or sense of individuality, such as the Balinese culture, have been refuted long ago.[225] Similarly, we no longer accept statements that simple societies do not create abstract knowledge systems. In fact, these knowledge systems seem to have influenced the very development of anthropology. A good example is the theoretical discussion of kinship and the graphic display of this discussion. The informant who drew the "ideal" kinship system for the well-known scholar Evans-Prichard used shapes to symbolize the social relationships in his culture. These shapes became abstract neutral symbols, through which completely different cultures are still described to this day.[226] Another example is the dreamtime paintings of different aboriginal groups in Australia. These paintings are a figurative representation of highly concrete myths, and they demonstrate a highly developed level of abstraction in a culture that is materially very simple.

In other words, it is impossible to deny the existence of the individual or the subject in the Hebrew Bible or in any human society: "Every

222. E. Durkheim, *The Elementary Forms of Religious Life* (trans. C. Cosman; abridg. with Introduction and notes M. S. Cladis; Oxford: Oxford University Press, 2001), 7.

223. J. W. Rogerson, "The Hebrew Conception of Corporate Personality: A Re-examination," *JTS* 21 (1970): 1–16.

224. J. S. Kaminsky, *Corporate Responsibility in the Hebrew Bible* (JSOTSup 196; Sheffield: Sheffield Academic, 1995).

225. See U. Wikan, *Managing Turbulent Hearts: A Balinese Formula for Living* (Chicago: University of Chicago Press, 1990); N. Scheper-Hughes, *Death Without Weeping: The Violence of Everyday Life in Brazil* (Berkeley: University of California Press, 1992).

226. See Herzfeld, "Anthropology: A Practice of Theory," 307, for further examples. The first scholar to emphasize inner-cultural interpretation as a scholarly tool was Victor Turner, who demonstrated an informant's ability to abstract and interpret his own cultural symbols. See V. Turner, "Muchona the Hornet, Interpreter of Religion," in *In the Company of Man* (ed. J. Casagrande; New York: Harper Bros, 1959), 333–56 (repr. as Chapter 4 in V. Turner, *The Forest of Symbols: Aspects of Ndembu Ritual* [Ithaca: Cornell University Press, 1967]). Cf. Mead, "Study of Culture," 11.

argument for the death of the subject is authored by a human subject. By dismissing the subject, Bourdieu and Foucault would deprive us of the very site where life is lived, meanings are made, will is exercised, reflections take place, consciousness finds expression, determinations take effect, and habits are formed or broken."[227] Note that Jackson (as myself) does not only talk about the act of the individual, but about the subject, the aware and reacting individual.[228]

The subject is defined by two main criteria: reflection and awareness. I contend that the very use of language requires reflective skill. As for awareness, let us examine Martin Buber's statement regarding the existence of self. Buber differentiates between the attitude to the world of primitive and advanced societies, along similar lines to those we have already examined: thought [= distance] vs. experience [involvement].[229] Buber also claims that primitive man uses the I–Thou relation which is based on mutuality and reciprocity, while the I–It relationship is one of separateness and detachment. Buber claims that the I–Thou duality, which is at the basis of all human language, contains within it a distinction between the self and the other.[230] Therefore, even if we find different levels of awareness in different cultures, the ability to speak requires at least an awareness of a degree of separation between the individual and other—a kind of unaware awareness. In addition, use of language demands a symbolism skill and a categorization skill, both of which are forms of abstraction in representing the world, from concrete to figurative representation.

Nonetheless, not all awareness or reaction to the environment translates into analytical thought, in that it does not extend beyond the existence of the lifeworld: "Analytic thought interrupts the perceptual transition from one moment to another, and then seeks in the mind the guarantee of a unity which is already there when we perceive. Analytic thought also interrupts the unity of culture and then tries to reconstitute it from outside."[231] Unlike analytical thought, reflective thought starts in physical life itself and not through abstract external strength. Just as we

227.   Jackson, "Phenomenology and Anthropological Critique," 22.

228.   For further discussion, see T. Asad, *Genealogies of Religion: Discipline and Reasons of Power in Christianity and Islam* (Baltimore: The Johns Hopkins University Press, 1993), 16; Ortner, "Theory in Anthropology," 150; Merleau-Ponty, *Signs*, 153.

229.   M. Buber, *The Dialogue on Man and Being* (trans. [Chapters 1–3] T. Wislovsky; Philosophical Writings 1; Jerusalem: Bialik Institute, 1959 [Hebrew]), 14–18.

230.   Ibid., 18–19.

231.   Merleau-Ponty, *Signs*, 69.

do not need to know how our muscles work in order to walk, and we do not need to know our cultural categories in order to use them, so a lack of awareness of reflection or the individual does not negate their existence.[232] In fact, any creation—including folk or oral creation—demonstrates the existence of the subject, its reaction to the world and the way it interprets the world. The phenomenological approach that anchors this study contends that humans experience their world in a unique manner, namely, subjectively. This means that when there is an I–Thou connection, as Buber and others define it, or any other form of interpersonal communication, a discourse exists between two subjective perspectives. Culture, too, exists in the space between different (individual) subjects. Human-cultural existence is impossible without the existence of the subject, and the subject cannot gain access to the cultural space without awareness.[233]

The dichotomy objectivity vs. subjectivity itself belongs to a phenomenology alien to the Hebrew Bible. The contrasts that accompany this dichotomy, awareness and reflection vs. lack of awareness and activism, are therefore irrelevant to our discussion. The awareness that I ascribe to the subjects in this study is not of the "I think that...," but of the "I can" awareness. Awareness is a trans-body phenomenon, not something separate from the body and controlling it.[234] Any discussion of the subject, hence, focuses on embodiment, which is the basic given of subjective and social existence. The body is where self and culture are embodied, and hence an experiencing subject must be assumed for the study of sensory experience.[235] Like the study of emotions, sensory research is inseparable from phenomenological research of culture, to which the existence of the subject is essential.[236]

In summary, it is impossible to speak of the lack of a subject in biblical society or indeed in any society. Objective (scientific) thought is acquired with great effort in some cultures. Subjective thought is natural, and is found in every culture in the world. Objective thought covers the essential truth while recognizing the relativism of human perception. Subjective thought is not aware of the relativism of human perception, but exists inside it. Subjective thought is not aware of the gap between relative and absolute truth because of its inherent truthfulness, yet nevertheless exists inside this relativism. To some degree, every culture uses

232. Ibid., 66–68.
233. Schutz, "Phenomenology and the Social Sciences," 125.
234. Jackson, "Phenomenology and Anthropological Critique," 31–32.
235. Csordas, "Somatic Modes," 136.
236. Stoller, *Taste of Ethnographic Things*, 29.

both thought methods in parallel. So, in every culture there is routine action that maintains the existing cultural customs, alongside reflective action which changes them.[237] To translate the last words for biblical scholars, it is enough to say that any exegesis is created in the meeting point of preserving a sacred scripture, while reflecting upon it for the purpose of adjustment.

If we go back to the theory–practice debate, when a set of values or rules is examined in the context of a given culture, asking how the culture dictates the behaviour of the individual (a question that is asked from a static perspective) is the wrong question. Instead, the researcher should try and explore how these rules are constantly maintained, created, and changed.[238]

In the context of the Hebrew Bible, the very possibility of the subject being revealed in the text could lead us to a different understanding of communal personality or communal responsibility. I will show in later chapters that expressions associated with sight, a metaphor for learning through personal experience and involvement,[239] hint at awareness of the existence of personal opinions.[240] Moreover, the very existence of a justice system in the Hebrew Bible and in biblical culture demonstrates awareness of the demand for clarification and examination of different opinions (a recognition of subjectivity). Amusingly, the uniform thread of the text, to which the figurative and reflective thought level of the biblical text is normally attributed, tries to create uniformity of reality and to communicate a conformity that negates the individual.[241] At the same time, reading between the lines reveals that there are truly various opinions as to the role of the subject in the Hebrew Bible, or at least varying opinions and experiences of biblical figures as they are depicted in the Hebrew Bible.

237.   A discussion of choice is beyond the scope of the present enquiry. Cf. Ortner, "Theory in Anthropology," 150.

238.   Ibid., 146.

239.   Carasik, *Theologies of the Mind*, 219. According to such theory, seeing is embodied, while hearing is abstract.

240.   For example, בעיני, which represents an evaluation or an opinion (Z. Livnat, "*Beʿeiney* + Noun Phrase in Biblical Hebrew: Semantic-Syntactic Investigation," *WCJS 11* 4, no. 1 [1994] 9–14, repr. in *Beit Mikra* 164 [2000] [Hebrew]); the expression טוב בעיני, which expresses agreement and voluntary approval (M. Malul, "Law in the Narratives: A Study of the Expressions הִכִּירוֹ and וַיִּיטַב בְּעֵינֵיהֶם in 2 Sam 3:36," *JNSL* 17 [1991]: 23–36), and לפני, which expresses the "thinking/acting" element (E. Rubinstein, "*lipnēy* + NP: From Place Indication to Indication of the 'Thinker' and the 'Cause': A Study into Biblical Hebrew," *Leshonenu* 40 [1986]: 57–66 [Hebrew]).

241.   See n. 31, above.

The Hebrew Bible as Cultural Evidence

Finally, we must address the assumption that the concepts and ideas reflected in the biblical text can be discussed holistically. This raises the criticism that the linguistic approach to the text as a single entity could lead to a static understanding of the culture represented in the Hebrew Bible. Such criticism is based on the claim that the biblical text includes linguistic and conceptual components from different periods, different locations, and different social groups. I acknowledge the difference and diversity of the biblical text, yet maintain that there are different ways of explaining this diversity. Besides diachronic explanations, we should be open to possibility of contemporaneous different views and aspects. In any case, consistency and order are the hallmark of philosophy, but do not characterize a cultural product that was never designed to be an objective or systematic written description of the world.

Having said that, some earlier studies demonstrate the possibility of finding uniformity or inner truth of some matters in the biblical text that is above the conflicts, particularly in the semantic and conceptual realm. This is not the dominant theme in biblical research, which prefers an atomistic discussion of small units of text.[242] Biblical scholarship generally focuses on the text—how it was shaped, where it originated, and how was it transmitted. Most schools of biblical research are characterized by focus on the text. They all share a wish to find the source. The source that they are searching for is sometimes the original text (*Ur*-text) and sometimes the original context (*Sitz im Leben*). This search is the inheritance of the nineteenth-century evolutionary tradition. At that time, it was assumed that finding the origin meant understanding the essence, and that finding the origin proved the historical facts and authentic character of the text being studied.[243] In this study, I strengthen Meir Malul's suggestion that we abandon a text-oriented approach in favour of a human-oriented approach. In this way, the text becomes a means of revealing the lifeworld that created it.

I do not look at the text for an authentic description of historical events, even if some of the text does offer precisely that. I look at the text as something created in a particular culture, something containing authentic cultural facts.[244] Don Seeman describes this type of historicity

---

242. J. F. A. Sawyer, *Semantics in Biblical Research: New Methods of Defining Hebrew Words for Salvation* (London: SCM, 1972), 12; Barr, *Semantics*, 9.

243. Merleau-Ponty, *Signs*, 147; Sawyer, *Semantics*, 7.

244. *MKCS*, 91. See also Williams, for revealing authentic experience in ancient Greek literature, even when there is no way of revealing the historicity of that experience (B. Williams, *Shame and Necessity* [Berkeley: Berkeley University Press, 1993], 48).

as "cultural poetics," the cultural, a priori, common sense of a culture.[245] To borrow the words of Malul,

> The historian looks for the specific events, places, personae, and the like in the sources, and tries to reconstruct a diachronic history with reference to unfolding events and occurrences that are tied to points of time and place. The anthropologist, on the other hand, is not interested in specific events and people; rather, the concern lies in revealing typologies, in exemplifying patterns of behaviour, social formations, customs, and institutions.[246]

Malul proposes that we adopt neither the synchronic approach favoured by literary biblical researchers, nor the diachronic approach favoured by researchers of text development. Instead, we should adopt a typological approach that finds patterns and principles reflected in the biblical text itself.[247] This approach looks for cultural formations, or as we defined it earlier, pre-learned culture, consisting of ideas or customs. Searching for typologies does not ignore differences in the text, but assumes that these formations are a collective representation of the culture.[248] If the reality represented in the text contains essential conflict, it will hover over the data, but will not preclude finding a common denominator that frames our cultural and inter-cultural understanding.[249] We talk of "Western culture" or "the Western perspective," even though there are different cultures, different regions, and different eras in it. There is no shortage of general cultural and conceptual formations for the researcher. It is eminently possible to reach important conclusions about the culture reflected in the Hebrew Bible, even though the text covers different times, different views, and different customs. The researcher must remain sensitive to the likelihood that there will also be exceptional findings. These only confirm the expected existence of divergent views.

To conclude this chapter, presenting and discussing the theoretical considerations has more than a theoretical significance. It is essential for an understanding of the methodological considerations that will follow. The presented debates also indicate my chosen research approach. I have discussed a number of issues on which any researcher interested in cultural notions and the Hebrew Bible must make a stand: universalism vs. cultural relativism; atomism vs. holism; theory vs. practice; structure

---

245. D. Seeman, "'Where Is Sarah Your Wife?' Cultural Poetics of Gender and Nationhood in the Hebrew Bible," *HTR* 91, no. 2 (1998): 103–25, and "The Watcher at the Window: Cultural Poetics of a Biblical Motif," *Prooftexts* 24, no. 1 (2004): 1–50; see also Good, "The Heart," and for biblical studies, Knight, "Sitz im Leben."

246. *MKCS*, 16. Cf. Mead, "Study of Culture," 15–18.

247. *MKCS*, 75–89, and elsewhere.

248. Ibid., 73.

249. Jackson, "Phenomenology and Anthropological Critique," 20.

vs. usage; etic vs. emic approach. Clearly, not every human phenomenon belongs to either of these extremes, but in this study, I have generally chosen the second alternative. These complement each other: relativism, holism, practice, usage, and emic approach. These assumptions are expressed in phenomenological anthropology, which is built on the foundations of existential philosophy. It is just as difficult to characterize phenomenological anthropology as a theoretical approach as it is to so characterize the philosophy that begat it,[250] because it does not create general and closed theories. Nevertheless, its influence on this study is considerable, both in terms of the basic assumptions, the influence on the structure and writing of this study, especially the preference for description over theory, and—importantly—the very positing of the research questions. Phenomenological approaches to cultural research opened up discussion on areas that remained outside cultural research, including a discussion on the senses, emotions, and experience. In the anthropological trinity, human experience–society–culture, British anthropologists tried to codify society, while American anthropologists tried to codify culture. It was the phenomenologists who focused their attention on codifying human experience.

Methodological Considerations

Having presented my cultural assumptions, I now present the tools that help reveal this "cultural given," this shared milieu enjoyed by those who spoke the language, and which is denied to the modern reader. To understand any category, one must answer two questions: (1) What is included in the category? And, (2) What is the definition of the category? When it comes to the sensorium, we will attempt to reveal the list of senses included in the biblical category, and to provide a definition of it. For that aim, two types of information are used—associative and contextual—and although they overlap at times, they will be presented separately, for the convenience of the discussion.

Associative Patterns
In a cultural context, a word is never just a word: words evoke other words, idioms, images, feelings, memories. Some associations are universal, others cultural, and some idiosyncratic. Cultural linguistic associations can be studied through a certain text, as the repetition of association within the text reflects these associative patterns. Within the

---

250. H. J. Blackham, "An Introduction to Existentialist Thinking," in *Reality, Man and Existence: Essential Works of Existentialism* (ed. H. J. Blackham; New York: Bantam, 1965), 1–15.

Hebrew Bible, we can use paradigmatic and syntagmatic associative relations, as well as word pairs (mainly in parallelism) and clusters, typical of biblical poetry. A link between two terms, which repeats in one or more of these axes, implies that both terms belong to one semantic field. In simpler words, I would say that the associative patterns reveal for us that certain terms are "similar" in a certain way, and therefore belong to the same category.

I shall start with the prominent feature of Hebrew poetry—word pairs. Reoccurring word pairs demonstrate the speaker's immediate association.[251] For example, the pair eye–heart (עין||לב) appears about 40 times in the Hebrew Bible, usually within parallelism.[252] For example: "The precepts of the Lord are right, rejoicing the heart (לב); the commandment of the Lord is clear, enlightening the eyes (עינים)" (Ps 19:9). The eye and the heart are hence imagined as the seat of the emotion of joy, and its opposite, sadness: "Because of this our hearts (לבנו) are sick, because of these things our eyes (עינינו) have grown dim" (Lam 5:17). The quoted verses demonstrate how a parallel word pair links both terms to the same semantic space—in this case, the emotional space. However, from other parallels we learn that the eye and the heart can also belong to the knowledge space: "What do you know that we do not know? What do you understand that is not clear to us?... Why does your heart (לבך) carry you away, and why do your eyes (עיניך) flash" (Job 15:9, 12). Even when the eye and the heart are in conflict, the conflict originates from an understanding that these two organs are similar: "For not as man sees [does the Lord see]; man sees only what is visible (לעינים), but the Lord sees into the heart (ללבב)" (1 Sam 16:7, JPS). Whether we regard this as contrasting skills (using the eye or the heart as a thought organ), or whether the contrast describes a different focus (focusing on the outward and not the inward), the eye and the heart are organs that can be compared. They belong to the same cultural category.

Similarly, we find links between terms that appear together in clusters in the same context. One example is another eye–heart pairing, this time with the addition of the ear: "But to this day the Lord has not given you a mind (לב) to understand, or eyes (עינים) to see, or ears (אזנים) to hear" (Deut 29:3). Although there is no actual parallelism, there is an obvious parallel between the use of all three organs to denote understanding and learning. This type of cluster teaches us about how terms are clustered

---

251.   Word pairs are based on various associative patterns, see Berlin, "Parallel Word Pairs"; O'Connor, *Hebrew Verse Structure*, 96–100.

252.   W. G. Watson, "The Unnoticed Word Pair 'eye(s)' // 'heart'," *ZAW* 101 (1989): 398–408.

into categories, and teaches us about the categories themselves. We also learn that sight, hearing, and knowledge, which are performed via the eye, the ear, and the heart, belong to a category of actions that serve thought. Another example is the passage spoken by Barzillai the Gileadite: "I am now eighty years old. Can I tell the difference between good and bad? Can your servant taste what he eats and drinks? Can I still listen to the singing of men and women? Why then should your servant continue to be a burden to my lord the king?" (2 Sam 19:36). In his words, Barzillai compares his knowledge ability with his ability to taste and to hear. We again see a correlation between knowing, eating, and hearing in a single category. In this verse, the link between the actions is negative—these are the actions that the eighty-year-old Barzillai claims he can no longer perform fully.

Generally, associative patterns found in word pairs and clusters belong to types of patterns, long recognized in semantic theory, namely the paradigmatic and the syntagmatic links. A paradigmatic connection is created between elements that in certain contexts could replace each other. These elements could be synonyms, antonyms, or words belonging to the same category—but they differ in degree (good/excellent) or accuracy (king/David).[253] The paradigmatic connection between different terms demonstrates that they belong to a shared category and to a single semantic space. So, for example, God's response to the people is expressed alternatively as opening his eyes, hearing, and speaking. There is a clear correlation between these three actions.

A syntagmatic connection between elements creates a bigger unit of meaning; for example, word pairs, phrases, or expressions.[254] When such a unit is broken down, it retains its associative connection. For example, when Rachel hides the household idols from her father she asks him not to "be angry." Literally, she asks him not to be angry in his eyes (אל יחר בעיני אדני, Gen 31:35; cf. 45:5). This enigmatic expression is understood through the syntagmatic link between חרה and אף (nose), in the common phrase, meaning to be angry.[255] Yet in Rachel's words, we do not only complete intuitively the missing word "nose" (אף), but also unconsciously replace it with the existing word "eyes." As the eyes are here (within the phrase "in the eyes of...") the seat of reason or opinion, Rachel's words soften the message of the original phrase (denoting bursting anger). For our purpose, it creates an associative link between the eye and the nose.

---

253. Berlin, "Parallel Word Pairs," 10–12.
254. Ibid., 12–15; *MKCS*, 85–86.
255. Gen 45:5; Exod 32:22; Deut 6:15; Judg 6:39 and elsewhere.

Another example for the use of the syntagmatic links for the identification of associative patterns is found in phrases that denote a beginning of action, through the verb "to lift" (נשא):[256] the frequently appearing phrase "and he lifted his eyes and saw"[257] denotes a sudden seeing, or a new action. The phrase "he lifted his voice" expresses the beginning of an oral expression,[258] and the phrase "to lift the legs and go" marks the beginning of a new event, rather than actual walking: "Jacob resumed his journey (וישא רגליו) and came to the land of the Easterners" (JPS, Gen 29:1).[259] Despite the fact that the common phrase "to lift the eyes and see" might serve discourse function, rather than hold its semantic content, the repetition of the phrase created a syntagmatic link between the form נשא (*wayyiqtol*), the eyes, and seeing. And so, when a similar phrase is found, where the legs or the voice are mentioned, an immediate associative link is made between seeing and walking, seeing and speech.

Another tool which helps in the mapping of associative patterns is the investigation of metaphors, and in our case, more particularly, synaesthesia.[260] Metaphors are, generally, an implied comparison between two unlike things, and serve both to help us understand the world and to shape our experience of the world.[261] Lyric literature introduces us to intensively symbolic language that shapes practices. Moreover, metaphors are not limited to analogies, but also serve as a brokering tool between the

---

256.   Greenstein, "Some Developements," 445–46.

257.   Gen 22:13; Num 24:2; Josh 5:13; Judg 19:17 and elsewhere.

258.   E.g. Gen 29:11.

259.   See the use of הלך *wayyiqtol* as mark of narrative development, rather than narrative event (e.g. Gen 35:22; Exod 2:1). For further details, see Greenstein, "Developments in the Study of Language," 445–46.

260.   I will not supply a full discussion of the growing publications on metaphors in the Hebrew Bible, but will provide the essential information relevant for the present book. A comprehensive review of the matter, excluding some recent developments, is found in A. L. Weiss, *Figurative Language in Biblical Prose Narrative: Metaphor in the Book of Samuel* (VTSup 107; Leiden: Brill, 2006).

261.   H. Eilberg-Schwarz, *The Savage in Judaism* (Bloomington: Indiana University Press, 1990), 117. Some scholars choose to distinguish between metaphor and simile; see, for example, N. Wasserman, "'Sweeter than Honey and Wine...' Semantic Domains and Old Babylonian Imagery," in *Landscapes: Territories, Frontiers and Horizons in the Ancient Near East* (ed. L. Milano et al.; CRRAI 44/III; Padua: Sargon, 2000), 191–96 (117). We must note, however, that at times what seems like a metaphor to us might be conceived as reality to the intended reader (see Jackson, "Phenomenology and Anthropological Critique," 9; M. Malul "The Ceremonial and Juridical Background of Some Expressions in Biblical Hebrew," in *Studies in Bible and Exegesis* [Festschrift M. Garsiel; ed. S. Vargon et al.; Ramat Gan: Bar-Ilan University Press, 2009 (Hebrew)], 299–302.

concrete world and its abstract understanding.[262] An analysis of meta-phors yields cultural perceptions, or cultural mapping—the way in which a given culture extends its own categories.[263] Whether we regard meta-phors as merely a literary convention or frozen expressions with no experiential basis at the time they were written, these literary conven-tions and expressions were created a priori in some culture. There is always a cultural logic behind metaphors, even if at a certain point that logic becomes lost.[264] For example, an accumulation of metaphorical formations that blend the field of sight and the field of eating, such as "the sweetness of light" (מתוק האור), enhance the associative pattern sight–taste found in other formations too.

The last example points to a universal linguistic phenomenon unique to sensory metaphors, known as synaesthesia—presenting one sensory experience through images from another sensory field. Normally, two types of synaesthesia are discerned: experiential synaesthesia—per-ceiving with a different sense than the sense aroused; and linguistic syn-aesthesia—describing something experienced with one sense through words from the semantic field of another sense. Scholars discuss whether linguistic synaesthesia is based on regular metaphorical logic (the transfer of meaning from one field to another), or whether there exists a pre-linguistic experiential cooperation between the senses that forms the basis of these metaphors (i.e. all linguistic synaesthesia is experiential at some point). For our purpose, the main issue is that synaesthesia enhances the associative links between different sensory terms.[265]

262. Beck, "The Metaphor as Mediator," 84–85.

263. George Lakoff and Mark Johnson, *Metaphors We Live By* (Chicago: University of Chicago Press, 1980). For a discussion related to biblical studies, see Z. Kotzé, "A Cognitive Linguistic Methodology for the Study of Metaphor in the Hebrew Bible," *JNSL* 31, no. 1 (2005): 107–17.

264. Cf. Collins, "Physiology of Tears," 20.

265. *MKCS*, 131–32; B. Kedar-Kopfstein, "Synästhesien im biblischen Althebräisch in Übersetzung und Auslegung," *ZAH* 1, no. 1 (1988): 47–60; 1, no. 2 (1988): 147–58 (87); R. Tsur, "Literary Synaesthesia: A Cognitive Approach," *Hebrew Linguistics* 29–30 (1990): 75–86. When dealing with this matter, Marks states: "Despite the many concurrences among modalities, analogies among the senses cannot completely overcome their ontological isolation. Even in unity, the senses show diversity. A sound, a light, an odor may all be phenomenally bright—perhaps it can be meaningful to say equally bright—but they remain nevertheless a sound, a light and an odor. The pen that I see is the same pen that I hold, but even though the pen is unitary the sight and the touch are not the same. Similarity across the senses must necessarily be one step removed from similarity within a sense, for there is, by definition, no continuity between modalities" (L. E. Marks, *The Unity of the Senses: Interrelations among the Modalities* [New York: Academic, 1978], 88).

Examples of linguistic synaesthesia will be presented throughout the present work, and the question of an authentic experience behind these metaphors is sometimes a central exegetical matter.[266] The classic example is the revelation in Sinai: "When all the people witnessed (lit. saw, ראים) the thunder and lightning, the sound of the trumpet, and the mountain smoking, they were afraid and trembled and stood at a distance" (Exod 20:18). Whether the verse attempts to describe a synaesthetic experience, or merely uses the root "to see" in its broader sense "to experience," "to perceive," is nearly impossible to determine.[267]

Other examples can be given: "Then the Lord said to Moses, 'Stretch out your hand toward heaven so that there may be darkness over the land of Egypt, a darkness that can be felt'" (Exod 10:21). The description of darkness as something that can be touched (וימש חשך) is a linguistic synaesthesia, one which at first sight blends the fields of sight and the tactile faculty. However, it also evokes the descriptions of blind people, groping (touching) darkness as they walk,[268] and therefore is based on true (non-synaesthetic) experience. Parallels between the root "to touch" (משש) and other words from the semantic field of sight (e.g. Ps 115:5–7) strengthen the first, associative connection. We see that associative links between terms repeat in various forms (word pairs, parallels, metaphors, paradigmatic replacement etc.). The repetition of associative links between two modalities creates an associative pattern, such as sight–touch, or sight–hearing. Such associative patterns imply that the two fields belong to one category.

Contextual Patterns

Determining the content of the biblical sensorium is only the first step towards the definition of that category. Revealing such definition is based on the reappearing context of sensory vocabulary, which creates a contextual pattern. For example, sight appears often in the context of learning and investigation, and at the same time serves commonly as an idiom and/or metaphor for learning and investigation. Similarly, walking is often mentioned in the context of learning and investigation, and at the same time serves commonly as an idiom and/or metaphor for learning

---

266. For a review of linguistic synaesthesia and its reception, see Kedar-Kopfstein, "Synästhesien."

267. See Ibn-Ezra on Exod 20:14 ("the five senses link in one place," MG Exodus, 66, my translation). For contemporary explanations, see Carasik, "To See a Sound"; S. A. Geller, "Fiery Wisdom: Logos and Lexis in Deuteronomy 4," *Prooftexts* 14, no. 2 (1994): 103–39.

268. Deut 28:19. Cf. Job 5:14; 12:25.

and investigation. The repetition of context of both modalities (already established to have an associative pattern that links them) implies that part of the definition of the sensorium would be "a vehicle of learning and investigation."

Some of the associative forms presented before can further help in the discerning of the definition of the sensorium. For example, synaesthetic expressions demonstrate contextual link, and not only associative link, between modalities. Both sight and the olfactory sense appear in context of moral judgment. Adjectives from each field are used to express moral judgment, such as beautiful/fragrant (= good) and ill-looking/foul (= bad).[269] The similarity of context is expressed in the following synaesthetic expression: "They said to them, 'May Lord look upon you and judge you, for you have made us stink in the sight of Pharaoh and his courtiers; you have put a sword in their hand to kill us'" (Exod 5:21, my translation).[270] The expression "to make so and so stink in the sight of" (הבאשתם את־ריחנו בעיני) is clearly synaesthetic, despite the effort of modern translations to avoid it.[271] Yet the link between sight and odour here must be sought after in corresponding contexts of moral judgment, and not in a synaesthetic metaphor. Bad smell is a moral attribute, and the eyes are a common locus for moral judgment. The appearance of sight and smell in this same context not only helps us to better understand Exod 5:21, but also to understand the sensorial category. A repetitive similarity of contexts for various modalities indicates that such context is part of the definition of the sensory category.

The paradigmatic principle which I presented before as an aid in revealing associative patterns can be applied to reveal a correlation between the different contexts in which the terms appear.[272] Using different terms, loss of sight is portrayed in the Hebrew Bible in the context of old age, i.e.: "When Isaac was old and his eyes were dim so that he could not see (ותכהין עיניו מראות)…" (Gen 27:1). This loss of sight is regarded as irreversible: "Remember that my life is a breath; my eye will never again see good (= well)" (Job 7:7). In other contexts, blindness can also be a form of a curse, both physically and metaphorically: "you shall

269. For further discussion, see pp. 167–72.
270. Compare the discussed words of Rachel, as a demonstration of the syntagmatic principle (p. 57) above.
271. For example, "you have brought us into bad odour *with* Pharaoh"; "You have made us stink in the *nostrils* of Pharaoh" (the NEB translation seems to be based on Rashi).
272. See *MKCS*, 81–84, for paradigmatic patterns and their link to cultural categories.

grope about (ממשש) at noon as blind people grope (ימשש) in darkness, but you shall be unable to find your way; and you shall be continually abused and robbed, without anyone to help" (Deut 28:29). In a similar threat, the prophet Zachariah draws a telling parallel between blindness and madness: "In that day, says the Lord, I will strike every horse with panic (תמהון), and its rider with madness (שגעון). But on the house of Judah I will keep a watchful eye (אפקח את עיני), when I strike every horse of the peoples with blindness (עורון)" (Zech 12:4). A third context of blindness is as antonym for wisdom: "The wise have eyes in their head, but fools walk in darkness..." (Qoh 2:14). The appearance of blindness in the context of the elderly, punishment, and foolishness creates an associative link between old age and punishment, old age and foolishness.[273]

Common Knowledge—Common Sense
The context of perception of a sense or the sensorium can also be sought after in common knowledge, expressed in proverbs and through innocent speech. Proverbs are generally considered as "common knowledge" in the culture that produced them. Although we often find contradictory proverbs, they still teach us something about the declarative level of certain categories.[274] For example, when Qohelet declares "Better is the sight of the eyes than the wandering of desire; this also is vanity and a chasing after wind" (Qoh 6:9), he criticizes an existing proverb. Yet the very fact that the proverb gets mentioned tells us something about an existing preference for personal investigation (seeing) over passive acceptance of knowledge, or of logic over desire.[275] In any case, it strengthens the link between sight and investigation found elsewhere, and poses the eye and desire (נפש) at a comparable level. Qohelet may be

---

273.   One term can belong to a few categories, for example, when we look at old age through the lens of blindness, we can discern the liminality of old people. In such a way, the discussion of old age is separated from the discussion of "the elderly" (as an institution). An associative examination of the elderly (זקנים) would yield mostly positive contexts, while an associative examination of old age would yield a different result. Understanding old age through its paradigmatic context would shed light on Moses' description: "Moses was one hundred and twenty years old at his death; his eyes were not dimmed and his strength had not faded away" (Deut 34:7, my translation). Despite his old age, Moses is not "old."

274.   A. Tylor, "The Wisdom of the Many and the Wit of One," in *The Wisdom of Many: Essays on the Proverb* (ed. W. Mieder and A. Dundes; New York: Garland, 1981), 3–9; Ritchie, "Fusion of the Faculties," 195.

275.   See JPS: "Is the feasting of the eyes more important than the pursuit of desire?"

attacking the proverb he quotes, but he nevertheless presents us with a common thought process.

The proverb just cited leads us to the important principle of innocent speech, which has its origin in Talmudic tradition.[276] According to this principle, even tendentious texts reveal authentic knowledge, since they must use normative language and normative knowledge. The evidence based on this principle can either be positive or negative. An example of the positive is the polemical claim made by the scriptural author: "The wondrous feats that you saw with your own eyes, those prodigious signs and marvels…" (Deut 29:2, JPS). This claim demonstrates the narrator's belief in the centrality of testimony based on sight, even though this is not the purpose of the verse. Also inferred here is the claim that the people actually saw God being revealed, which is contrary to other traditions that deny the visual-concrete characteristic of the revelation.[277] We also find unintentional evidence through negative evidence. One example is the frequently repeated phrase about idols lacking senses: "There you will serve other gods made by human hands, objects of wood and stone that neither see, nor hear, nor eat, nor smell" (Deut 4:28).[278] The polemic description of idols as having no powers demonstrates, even unwittingly, a perception of the Israelite God who does see, hear, eat, and smell. This unconscious disclosure indicates that the use of the senses is not perceived as anthropomorphism, but as a sign of his power and his authority.[279]

A word must be said regarding the micro-level of context, that is, the basic semantic load of a studied term. The semantic context consists of both diachronic (etymological and historical) elements and synchronic (contextual) elements. For example, Malul finds that for etymological reasons the word "good" (טוב) has a semantic component of eating and being satisfied. Can we accept that in common associative terms, the Hebrew Bible presents us with such an associative pattern? Was that a natural association for the "native speaker" of Biblical Hebrew?

In seeking to understand a particular term, I place utmost emphasis on synchronic semantic investigation methods:[280] the range of meanings and

---

276. "Innocent speech," המשיח לפי תומו in Hebrew, is a talmudic term, denoting information revealed unintentionally. See *MKCS*, 75.

277. See Carasik, "To See a Sound," 259.

278. Cf. Pss 115:5–7; 135:16–17.

279. De Boer, "An Aspect of Sacrifice," 37.

280. See Sawyer, *Semantics*, 113–16. Another discussion of these principles (albeit focused on lexicography rather than cultural concepts) is C. Cohen, "The 'Held Method' for Comparative Semitic Philology," *JANES* 19 (1998): 9–23 (10–14).

contexts for a particular word as it is used is my main database, rather than the "precise original denotation of each term…its narrowest meaning before its connotative value broadens its usage into synonymous ambiguity with other terms conceptually related by etymologically and semantically distant."[281] Although the "original" meaning might teach us something about the term's semantic space, it does not explain the understanding of the term in an actual usage. In order to understand any word, we need to focus on the meanings and contexts within which the word appears.

Moreover, I prefer to explain the biblical language on its own, without recourse to comparisons to other languages, since etymological parallels are often not semantic parallels: "Etymological equivalents which are not also semantic equivalents do not help us arrive at a better contextual understanding of the word in question. Therefore, while they are surely important for the study of general linguistic and phonological structure of the language concerned, they are irrelevant philologically."[282] As stated earlier, the discovery of semantic fields, and an analysis of the contexts in which the words appear, provide us with the inner logic of the language in a way that a diachronic description cannot do. Nonetheless, an existing semantic shift or contextual shift in the meaning of a term *within* the Hebrew Bible will be dealt with if applicable.

So far, I have described the main tools used in understanding the senses and their usage in biblical times, as portrayed in the biblical text. I distinguished between associative patterns mainly explaining the content of the sensory category, and contextual patterns, mainly teaching us about the definition of the sensory category. Both forms of patterns are good models for revealing unconscious cultural perceptions. An associative or contextual pattern can explain the boarder category—sensorium— but also a particular semantic field within it. A demonstration of such investigation is given in Chapter 5, where a focus on the sense of sight and its related associative patterns and contexts is expanded.

Associative models help us define the content and character of the term "sense" as reflected in the biblical text. I use the term "associative models" because I wish to avoid describing a rigid set of rules based on the core assumptions itemized earlier. My analysis of the sensory categories and the associative models linked to the senses will create a holistic description of our understanding and usage of the senses as reflected in the biblical text, with all its inherent complexity and diversity.

---

281.   C. H. Brichto, *The Problem of "Curse" in the Hebrew Bible* (JBL Monograph Series 13; Philadelphia: Society of Biblical Literature and Exegesis, 1963), 14.
282.   Cohen, "Held Method," 15 n. 40.

Chapter 2

NUMBER OUR SENSES

On the face of it, the five senses that we are familiar with are identical to the senses described in the Hebrew Bible, as is hinted by the story of the stolen blessing (Gen 27:1–30).[1] At the same time, the data presented in the previous chapter concerning cultural relativism of sensory perception demand that we take a further look at the pentasensory count, when it comes to the Hebrew Bible. The earliest hypothetically Hebrew text to mention the five senses is the Wisdom of Jesus the Son of Sirach:[2]

> The Lord created a human being out of earth,
>   and he returned him into it again.
> He gave them days in number and a fixed time,
>   And he gave them authority over the things upon it.
> He clothed them in a strength like himself,
>   And in his image he made them.
> He placed the fear of him[3] upon all flesh,
>   Even to have dominion over beasts and birds.
> [*They received use of the five faculties of the Lord,*]
>   [*But, apportioning a sixth, he gave them the gift of mind,*]
> [*and the seventh, reason, the interpreter of his faculties.*]
> Deliberation and tongue and eyes,
>   Ears and heart for thinking he gave them.
> With knowledge of understanding he filled them,
>   And good things and bad he showed to them. (Sir 17:1–7, NETS)[4]

In his reworking of some major biblical creation themes, Sirach seems to provide a simple answer to the question of how many senses are included in the biblical sensorium. Ben Sira tries to describe and count the different senses that God gave humankind, and even uses the general term "five faculties."[5] A closer look into this paragraph reveals its

---

1. A. Bar-Am, "The Story of the Five Senses" (Hebrew), *De'ot* 5 (1999): 76–87.
2. No Hebrew version of these verses has yet been found.
3. "Of human being" (remark within NETS).
4. Italics in NETS.
5. "Actions" is probably a more accurate translation of *energèma(tōn)*. The translation provided demonstrates how the English term "five faculties" is associatively

complexity. What are these five faculties? Are they inclination, tongue, eyes, ears, and heart, as indicated in v. 6? Ben Sira clearly echoes the biblical perception that the senses are a divine creation,[6] and unquestionably hints at various biblical verses.[7] Despite this affinity with the Hebrew Bible, Sirach demonstrates here a descriptive attitude to the senses, unknown in earlier Hebrew literature. What is more, a closer look at v. 5 reveals its deviation from the parallelistic structure of the chapter. In fact, v. 5 is missing from most manuscripts, and is considered a later, Christian insertion (hence the use of parentheses above).[8]

Notably, the foreign nature of a categorical term for the senses in Sirach moves it even further from the Hebrew Bible, and enhances the lack of such terminology in our focus text. Moreover, Biblical Hebrew has no term to describe the sensory category, and the Hebrew abstract noun "sense" (חוש) makes its first appearance within the phrase "the sense of sight" in a Midrash collection of the twentieth century.[9] Within the Hebrew Bible, we find only one occurrence of the root: "for apart from him who can eat or who can have enjoyment (יחוש)?" (Qoh 2:25).[10] In short, we do not find in the Hebrew Bible any verbal category that parallels the modern terms "sense" or "sensorium." The terms "sense," "sensory," "sensorium," and so forth, as used in this book, are therefore "experience distant," and the reader should attempt to detach them from

embedded in the translator's mind. The same translation is given in the NRSV. I wish to thank Professor Frank Polak for pointing out the inaccuracy of the common translation.

6. See Chapter 4.

7. For biblical references, see E. S. Hartom, *Ben-Sira: Partially Translated and Interpreted* (Tel Aviv: Yavneh, 1963 [Hebrew]), 63–64.

8. M. Z. Segal, *The Complete Ben-Sira* (Jerusalem: Bialik Institute, 1953 [Hebrew]), 105. For Greek/stoic influence on such verses, see also H. W. Hollander and M. de Jonge, *The Testament of the Twelve Patriarchs: A Commentary* (SVTP 8; Leiden: Brill, 1985), 822.

9. The expression חוש הראיה ("sense of sight") first appears in the words of Rabbi Yochanan ben-Zakkai, first attested in J. D. Eisenstein, *Ozar Midrashim* (2 vols.; New York: Eisenstein, 1915 [Hebrew]), 214. Cf. E. Ben-Yehuda, *The Dictionary of Hebrew Language, Old and New* (Jerusalem: Ben-Yehuda, 1948–59), 1476 n. 2. The root II חוש mainly maintains the meanings "unease," "pain," "to feel" in Middle Hebrew, and does not get the Modern abstract meaning "sense" until much later (see *The Historical Dictionary of the Hebrew Language*; online: http://hebrew-treasures.huji.ac.il/).

10. Some scholars derive also חושי (Job 20:2) and חושה (Ps 141:1) from the same root (see *MKCS*, 137 n. 43). The common translation for the root is "pleasure" or "sensation" (see BDB, 301; T. Kruger, *Qohelet: A Commentary* [Hermeneia; Philadelphia: Fortress, 2004], 59).

their meaning in contemporary epistemology.[11] Can we therefore deduce that this category never existed in the culture reflected in the Hebrew Bible? As stated before, we cannot assume that a category similar to the modern sensory category operated—intentionally or unintentionally—in the culture depicted in the Hebrew Bible.[12] This chapter forms the first step towards the examination of whether such a category operated on a non-verbal, associative level.

The absence of a generalized term such as "sense" also makes it difficult to identify which experiences or human actions were perceived as belonging to this category. A way out of this dead-end must be to start from actions that are indisputably and universally described as sensory, such as sight and hearing. Such a starting point serves as a temporary working assumption from which an associative pattern between these senses and other human actions and experiences is examined. Such inquiry should lead to the "senses" hinted at in the Hebrew Bible. Even before that, my exploration begins with three passages that appear to offer sensory itemization:

A. Their idols are silver and gold, the work of human hands.
   They have mouths, but do not speak; eyes, but do not see.
   They have ears, but do not hear; noses, but do not smell.
   They have hands, but do not feel; feet, but do not walk;
   they make no sound in their throats. (Ps 115:4–7)

B. The idols of the nations are silver and gold, the work of human hands.
   They have mouths, but they do not speak; they have eyes, but they do not see;
   They have ears, but they do not hear, and there is no breath in their mouths. (Ps 135:15–17)

C. There you will serve other gods made by human hands, objects of wood and stone that neither see, nor hear, nor eat, nor smell. (Deut 4:28)

---

11. It would have been preferable to use the native term and to avoid the inevitable associative context of the scholar's language. See, for example, Guerts, who consistently uses the Anlo term *seselelame* and not the English term "sense" (*Culture and the Senses*, 40).

12. Kaddari assumes that it is possible find the verbal term for universal concepts in a given language ("What is the Difference?"). Some scholars even assume that universal concepts can be found with no matching verbal term; see, for example, A. Shapira, "On 'Dignity' in the Bible" (Hebrew), *Beth Mikra* 44, no. 2 (1999): 128–45 (131); L. Huber-Bechtel, "The Biblical Experience of Shame/Shaming: The Social Experience of Shame/Shaming in Biblical Israel in Relation to Its Use as Religious Metaphor" (Ph.D. diss., Drew University, 1983). See also pp. 42–46, above.

These three passages are fundamental sources for any discussion of the senses in the Hebrew Bible.[13] Not only do they provide us with similar lists, but they are all connected to the same theme—idolatry. All three passages describe human actions that cannot be performed by idols, and all three passages explain this lack of ability on the fact that the idols are created by humans.[14] Yet despite the similarity among these three passages, each of them presents a slightly different list of actions that idols cannot perform, as Table 2 shows:

Table 2. *Comparison of Biblical Passages that Mention*
the Senselessness of Idols

	Ps 115:4–7	*Ps 135:14–17*	*Deut 4:28*
Sight	+	+	+
Hearing	+	+	+
Speech	+ (×2)[15]	+	
Eating			+
Breathing		+[16]	
Smell	+		+
Touch	+		
Walking	+		

Already at this point, these three passages direct us to explore beyond the horizons of the pentasensory model. In these passages, sight, hearing, smell, taste, touch, speech, breathing, and walking are listed alongside

13. De Boer, "An Aspect of Sacrifice." We must note the thematic similarity in Dan 5:23: "…You have praised the gods of silver and gold, of bronze, iron, wood, and stone, which do not see or hear or know; but the God in whose power is your very breath, and to whom belong all your ways, you have not honoured."

14. On the creation of the senses as part of the sensory category, see Chapter 4.

15. Dahood (following Friedman) distinguished "talking" (ידברו) from "making emotion-related sounds" (יהגו בגרונם, M. Dahood, *Psalms III* [AB 17a; Garden City: Doubleday, 1970]). Understanding expressions of tears and crying elsewhere supports such an explanation (Collins, "Physiology of Tears"). Others interpret both acts as speech (Wolff, *Anthropology of the Old Testament*, 78).

16. That is, if we understand "there is no רוח in their mouth" to stand for "lifeless," "breathless" (C. A. Briggs and E. G. Briggs, *Critical and Exegetical Commentary on the Book of Psalms* [ICC 16; Edinburgh: T. & T. Clark, 1969], 480). For the expression אין יש, see Dahood, *Psalms III*, 262. Cf. 1 Sam 11:9. It seems that this translation fits the syntax of the verse, where the word "indeed" (אף) denotes a summary of previous statements. The problem with such translation is that elsewhere breath (רוח) as a marker of life is linked to the nose, and not to the mouth (see pp. 124–25), while breath (רוח) in the mouth denotes speech (e.g. Ps 33:6). In any case, if breathing is the meaning of רוח בפיהם it would be a summary motto and could not be counted as a sense in this list.

each other. While speech and walking, which are not considered as senses in Western epistemology, are mentioned here,[17] eating (with its hint of the sense of taste) and touch, which are included in the Western sensorium, receive only partial mention in these passages. Table 2, therefore, provides us with the list of modalities, or list of semantic fields worth examining for the establishment of the sensory category of the Hebrew Bible.

The comparison of these passages demonstrates agreement on the correlation between sight and hearing, two senses whose frequent appearances in the biblical text have already been discussed.[18] A quick concordance check of the words and verbs associated with actions in all three passages shows that sight and hearing also appear most frequently in the text as nouns, verbs, and even within personal names. The statistical centrality of sight and hearing in the biblical text makes them a natural starting point for our discussion. Below, the strength of the link between sight and hearing will be discussed first, following by a discussion of each sense mentioned in Table 2. The discussion will use the associative models introduced earlier, in order to ascertain whether they can be included in one category.[19]

Sight and Hearing

The correlation between sight and hearing in the Hebrew Bible is self-evident. There are frequent parallels between sight–hearing and eye–ear in the context of knowledge, learning, and understanding.[20] When Job tries to prove to his friends that his knowledge is not inferior to theirs, he asserts: Look, my eye has seen all this, my ear has heard and understood

17. That is despite the fact that idioms of movement still exist in contemporary Hebrew (ירד לסוף דעתו) and English ("understand"); see *MKCS*, 140 n. 61; J. L. Palache, *Semantic Notes on the Hebrew Lexicon* (trans. N. J. Z. Werblowsky; Leiden: Brill, 1959), 54. Similarly, the equilibrium sense is used as a metaphor for emotional stability and general mood in English, but is not elaborated in discourse or practice. Some African communities do elaborate equilibrium sense in both domains; see Guerts, *Culture and the Senses*, 5; Wober, "Sensotypes."

18. Watson, "Unnoticed Word Pair."

19. Note that the current discussion will not revolve around the philology of sensory vocabulary in detail (for such discussion, see *MKCS*). The aim of the current discussion is to present the associative patterns that link the various senses.

20. Kedar-Kopfstein, "Synästhesien," 50–54. H.-J. Kraus, "Hören und Sehen in der althebräischen Tradition," in *Biblische-theologische Aufsätze* (Neukirchen–Vluyn: Butzon & Bercker 1972), 84–101 (repr. from *Studium Generale* 19 [1966]: 115–23).

it" (Job 13:1).[21] The parallel verbs "to see" (ראה) and "to hear" (שמע) and the words "eye" (עין) and "ear" (אזן) are not merely used as word pairs or literary devices. The frequent use of these combinations as word pairs points to an even broader associative context of the two actions.[22] The strongest support for the associative pattern sight–hearing lies in parallels of less common sight and hearing vocabulary, in the context of understanding or thought. In a different part of Job's dispute with his friends, Elihu challenges Job's ability to understand: "Hear (האזינה) this, O Job; stop (עמד) and consider (התבונן) the wondrous works of God" (Job 37:14). The challenge is enhanced by the following two verses, both opening with the rhetorical question, "do you know?" (התדע). The seemingly abstract meaning of "consider" is, in fact, a concrete meaning, "to watch."[23] It is in complete harmony with the notion that understanding and acknowledgment of creation come from watching the created universe.

Another parallel is found between "to hear" and "to gaze": "He who planted the ear, does he not hear (ישמע)? He who formed the eye, does he not see (יביט)?" (Ps 94:9).[24] The eye and the ear, sight and hearing, are examples of God's creative power and understanding. God's response to humans through hearing and sight is expressed in yet another parallel: "Surely God does not hear an empty cry, nor does the Almighty regard it (ישורנה)" (Job 35:13). The verb שור, too, has the concrete meaning "to watch," commonly translated in a more abstract way.[25]

The parallel between sight and hearing in these examples is not limited to common roots or word pairs, but is expanded to other parallels (i.e. בין||אזן, שמע||נבט, and שמע||שור), and thus demonstrates an associative semantic link between sight and hearing. Finally, just as sight and hearing are concretely and metaphorically linked, so too are blindness and deafness. A good example is Lev 19:14: "You shall not revile the deaf or put a stumbling block before the blind; you shall fear your God: I

21. See also Deut 29:3; 2 Kgs 19:16; Isa 6:10; 32:3; Jer 5:21; Ezek 40:4; 44:5; Job 9:11; Qoh 1:8 and many more

22. Berlin, "Parallel Word Pairs," 8; W. G. E. Watson, *Classical Hebrew Poetry: A Guide to Its Techniques* (JSOTSup 26; Sheffield: Sheffield Academic, 1984; repr., New York: T&T Clark International, 2008), 130–43.

23. The root בין is linked semantically to the field of sight, particularly in Hithpael. In a few cases the Hithpael form of בין means "to see," or parallels another sight verb (1 Kgs 3:21; Isa 14:16; 52:15; Jer 2:10; Ps 37:10; Job 31:1). The root עמד in this verse belongs to the field of kinaesthesia, which will be discussed below, pp. 75–86.

24. Cf. Isa 42:18; 51:1–2.

25. See Chapter 3, n. 92.

am the Lord."[26] Again, because being deaf and being blind are presented as similar, the associative link between sight and hearing is strengthened.

The paradigmatic principle offers us another hint for this link. The phrase "to open" (פקח) + "eye" appears 18 times in the Hebrew Bible. Sometimes this phrase is concrete, describing a restoring of sight, "to open (לפקח) the eyes that are blind…" (Isa 42:7).[27] In other instances, the phrase is used metaphorically to describe understanding, or more accurately sudden understanding, as in the story of eating from the tree of knowledge: "Then the eyes of both were opened (ותפקחנה), and they knew that they were naked…" (Gen 3:7). At times, opening the eyes enables a person to see or recognize something that was hidden before. For example, when Hagar sees the water we are told, "Then God opened (ויפקח) her eyes and she saw a well of water. She went, and filled the skin with water, and gave the boy a drink" (Gen 21:19).[28] The phrase "to open the eyes" repeats, in another metaphoric sense, that of divine help. See, for example, Isaiah's plea to God on the people's behalf: "Incline (הטה) your ear, O Lord, and hear; open (פקח) your eyes, O Lord, and see…" (2 Kgs 19:16).[29]

While this phrase is quite common, it does not have a distinct meaning, and is used in a range of meanings, normally attributed to sight in general: seeing, understanding, divine help, and more. The paradigmatic correlation between the root "open" and sight is so strong that the adjective "seeing" (פקח), derived from the root "to open" (פקח), serves as the antonym of "blind" (Exod 4:11; 23:8). Only once does this root describe an action not related to the eyes: "He sees many things, but does not observe them; his ears are open (פקוח), but he does not hear" (Isa 42:20). In this case, hearing, parallel to sight, is linked to a verb that almost exclusively appears in the context of sight.[30] While the image of opening the eyes is anchored in physical reality (despite having different derivations), the metaphor of opening the ears is borrowed from the world of sight.

We have seen before that opening the eyes is an idiom for divine help and guard. Such description is also found in the root פתח, similarly meaning "to open." See its use in Solomon's prayer: "Now, O my God,

---

26. Cf. Exod 4:11; Isa 42:18–20; 43:8.

27. In addition to 18 occurrences of עין + פקח, I count פוקח עורים (Ps 146:8).

28. Cf. 2 Kgs 6:17, 20.

29. Cf. Isa 37:17; cf. Dan 9:18.

30. See also T. Sutskover, "The Semantic Field of 'Seeing' in the Book of Genesis and the Coherence of the Text" (Ph.D. diss., Tel-Aviv University, 2006 [Hebrew]), 2, 35–37.

let your eyes be open (פתוחות) and your ears attentive (קשבות) to prayer from this place" (2 Chr 6:40).[31] Metaphorical opening and closing of the eye and the ear, which symbolize the ability to see and hear, appears frequently in the prophecies of Isaiah in the context of repairing disabilities: "Then the eyes of the blind shall be opened (תפקחנה), and the ears of the deaf unstopped (תפתחנה)" (Isa 35:5). Note that both verbs in the verse mean "to be open" and the similarity between opening of ear and eye is demonstrated.[32] In this last verse, the meaning of "open ear" is concrete—hearing. In other instances, Isaiah uses the metaphoric meaning "to understand" by using similar vocabulary: "You have never heard (שמעת), you have never known (ידעת), from of old your ear has not been opened (לא־פתחה)..." (Isa 48:8). Thirdly, Isaiah uses the image of the open ear to describe obedience: "The Lord God has opened (פתח) my ear, and I was not rebellious, I did not turn backward" (Isa 50:5). Like the original image, "open eye," the image "open ear" is not specific and can bear the range of meanings normally attributed to hearing, such as help and obedience.

The parallel between sight and hearing in descriptions of divine help or an appeal for help is not limited to the image of opening/closing the eyes/ears. Sight and hearing are used separately as metaphors for divine help, as we see in the expressions "called out unto the Lord" and "he saw their suffering." At times, these expressions appear in proximity to one another, as in the description of the suffering of the Israelites in Egypt: "We cried to the Lord, the God of our ancestors; the Lord heard (וישמע) our voice and saw (וירא) our affliction, our toil, and our oppression" (Deut 26:7). A more idiomatic example is found in the Psalms: "The eyes of the Lord are on the righteous, his ears [attentive] to their cry" (Ps 34:16, JPS).[33] Still in the realm of help metaphors, we find a further connection between sight and hearing, based on the paradigmatic principle. The root עלם Hiphil ("to hide," "to conceal") appears to denote lack of attention when used with the eyes as its object, probably closer to

---

31. Cf. the similar idea, with different phrasing, in 1 Kgs 52: "that your eyes may be open (פתחות) night and day toward this house, the place of which you said, 'My name shall be there,' that you may heed (lit. 'hear,' לשמוע) the prayer that your servant prays toward this place." The combination of sight with the verb פתח ("to open"), in parallel to the listening ear, repeats elsewhere (1 Kgs 8:29, 52; 2 Chr 6:20; 7:15; Neh 1:6).

32. Note the common metaphor of the open ear, and the opening of the ears in Akkadian. See Malul, "Piercing a Slave's Ear," 135–58 (mostly n. 64).

33. Square brackets show that this word is implied from the Hebrew, while only the preposition is found in the Hebrew. See also Pss 94:9, 12; 106:44.

the meaning "to shut [the eyes]":[34] "When you stretch out your hands, I will hide (אַעְלִים) my eyes from you; even though you make many prayers, I will not listen (שמע); your hands are full of blood" (Isa 1:15).[35] This verse returns to the image of listening and watching as help. In a similar verse, the root עלם commonly used with the eyes, is describing the ear: "You heard my plea, 'Do not close (אַל־תַּעְלֵם) your ear to my cry for help, but give me relief!'" (Lam 3:56). We find again, that the paradigmatic link between עלם and "eye" leads to an associative link between "eye" and "ear" when the latter is found as the object of עלם.

Further evidence for the semantics of sight and hearing comes from biblical names. Names, especially those with a theophoric element, often serve as a window on the worldview of a given culture.[36] Sight and hearing reappear as expressions of divine help in quite a few names. The name Shemaiah(u), "Yahweh has listened," for example, appears more than 40 times, and relates to 25 different biblical characters.[37] Six people are called Elishama, "God heard,"[38] and six called Ishmael, "El heard," or, "may El hear."[39] There are also names that combine sight with a theophoric element, such as Hazael ("El has looked") king of Aram (1 Kgs 19:15 and further) and Pekahiah ("Yahweh has opened [the eyes]") king of Israel (2 Kgs 15:22–26).[40] The frequent use of sight and hearing words combined with a theophoric element in names supports

---

34. *HALOT* 2:83–84. See also S. E. Balentine, *The Hidden God: The Hiding of the Face of God in the Old Testament* (Oxford: Oxford University Press, 1983), 7–14.

35. Cf. Lev 20:4; 1 Sam 12:3; Ezek 22:26; Job 42:3; Prov 28:27 and others.

36. For discussion of the hypothesis, see J. H. Tigay, *You Shall Have No Other Gods: Israelite Religion in the Light of Hebrew Inscriptions* (Atlanta: Scholars Press, 1986), 5–9.

37. The man of God (1 Kgs 12:22; 1 Chr 11:2), the false prophet (Jer 29:24, 31), the father of prophet Uriah (Jer 26:20) and many others. Translation of the name taken from *HALOT* 4:1578.

38. The chieftain of Ephraim (Num 1:10), Elishama the scribe (Jer 36:20), Elishama the priest (2 Chr 17:8) and others. Translation of the name taken from *HALOT* 1:57.

39. The son of Hagar (Gen 16:11), the murderer of Gedaliah (2 Kgs 25:25), Ishmael the chief (2 Chr 23:1) and others, translation of name taken from *HALOT* 2:447. Many other names include a component of the root שמע: Simeon, Shimei, Shema, Shimea, Eshtemoa, Mishma and Shimeath. See Meshorer, "Two 'YHD' Coins," 435.

40. The names Pekahiah and Pekah could refer to opening of the womb (*HALOT* 3:959). Other names using the root ראה are Reaiah, Reuben. Names using the root חזה are Hazaiah, Hezion, and Hozai (2 Chr 33:19, could mean "seer" and may not be a PN).

the perception of providential care through sight and hearing metaphors, mentioned above.[41] The frequent appearance of names containing references to sight and hearing is parallel to the frequent appearance of other roots and nouns that describe sight and hearing as opposed to other senses. Sight and hearing emerge as a metaphor for divine help, both when they appear on their own and when they are correlated. In the latter case, the parallel is not limited to seeing–hearing or eye–ear pairs, but also appears in the broadest context of the two actions.[42]

In summary, the associative pattern sight–hearing recurs at different levels of the biblical text. Conceptually, the roots of seeing and hearing recur as dominant word pairs.[43] Poetically, the see–hear (ראה‖שמע) and eye–ear (עין‖אזן) word pairs appear together frequently in different parallel constructs. These two word pairs are not used statically, but semantically/associatively and expand to other related terms. The contexts in which these senses are mentioned are overlapping too. Both sight and hearing are used as a metaphor for learning, acknowledgment, attention, and divine aid. Finally, note the many examples of synaesthetic sight–hearing images, particularly striking in the descriptions of prophetic experience, which are sometimes described as a vocal and sometimes as a visual experience.[44]

The frequent mentions of sight and hearing, especially in texts that describe the thought process, led Michael Carasik to conclude that the eyes and ears were the vehicles that deliver knowledge from the world to the mind, while smell, taste, and touch played a much more minor role.[45] I will reserve judgment on this for now, since I have not yet established that these are indeed the five senses of the culture represented in the Hebrew Bible. It is clear to me, though, that the statistical richness of expressions and images from the world of sight and hearing make them culturally conspicuous, and a good starting point for the discussion. Later in the book I shall offer my own explanation for this richness.

---

41. This multitude of theophoric names that include an element of sight or hearing stand out next to the paucity of names with other sensory elements. The other sense attested is the tactile sense, which represents divine support, such as in the names Ahaziah, Yehoahaz, Hezekiah, and Amaziah. Similarly, there are names which represent a firm posture (related to kinaesthesia), such as Jeconiah and Jehoiakim.

42. For the senses as idioms for aid, see pp. 130–41.

43. A. Frisch, "*rʾh* and *šmʿ* as a Pair of Leading Words" (Hebrew), *WCJS* 12, no. 1 (1997): 89–98.

44. For more on prophetic experience, see pp. 266–69; more on the connection between sight and hearing, see Chapter 5.

45. Carasik, *Theologies of the Mind*, 219.

Kinaesthesia

Walking, which appears in Ps 115:7 in parallel with sight, hearing, touch, smell, and speech, raises the possibility of a conceptual link between walking and sensory actions. In the following pages, I will provide additional examples for such a link—images, parallels, and metaphors that indicate the relevance of walking to the biblical sensory category. Apart from this verse, we find an associative pattern between walking and three main actions—hearing, sight, and speech—which appear in various contexts as detailed below.[46]

The walking–hearing associative link is particularly strong in Deuteronomy, Jeremiah, and the wisdom literature.[47] The commandment to obey God is expressed in parallel by the verbs "to hear" (שמע), "to keep" (שמר), and "to walk" (הלך).[48] In Deuteronomy we find: "Today you have obtained the Lord's agreement: to be your God; and for you to walk (וללכת) in his ways, to keep (ולשמור) his statutes, his commandments, and his ordinances, and to obey (ולשמע) him" (Deut 26:17). Note that "to obey" God is literally "to listen to his voice." Descriptions of obedience to God expressed through the metaphor of listening and walking are also used by the prophet Jeremiah: "But this command I gave them, 'Obey (שמעו) my voice, and I will be your God, and you shall be my people; and walk (והלכתם) only in the way that I command you, so that it may be well with you.' Yet they did not obey (שמעו) or incline their ear, but, in the stubbornness of their evil will, they walked (וילכו) in their own counsels, and looked backward rather than forward" (Jer 7:23–24).[49] At times, the parallel hearing–walking in the context of obedience/disobedience is further stressed by a parallel with the verb "to do." Jeremiah's reproof of the nation's action in the land provides a fine example: "...and they came and took possession of it. But they did not listen (שמעו) to you or follow (הלכו) your teaching; they did (עשו) nothing of what you

46. See also *MKCS*, 140ff.
47. For verbal and ideological similarities between the Deuteronomistic School, the book of Jeremiah, and wisdom literature, see M. Weinfeld, *Deuteronomy and the Deuteronomic School* (Oxford: Oxford University Press, 1972), 244–81.
48. See also Chapter 4 in Carasik, *Theologies of the Mind*, 139–76.
49. Cf. Jer 9:12; 11:6–8, 10–11; 13:10–11; 16:12; 26:3–5. In all these verses Jeremiah uses the metaphor "listening is obeying" alongside the metaphor "walking is obeying." In some cases, we find the term "to walk in the stubbornness/stiffness(?)" (שרירות) of the heart, belonging to the same semantic field. The associative pattern eye–ear–heart is quite common, and likewise the heart is described as hearing (*HALOT* 4:1572).

commanded them to do (לעשות). Therefore you have caused all this misfortune to befall them" (Jer 32:23, JPS). This verse demonstrates a poetic blend between walking and hearing in two ways: the path not taken is a verbal path of teaching (תורתך). The verbal character of the teaching is strengthened by its parallels in the verse: command (צויתה) and voice (קול). This vocal aspect is further enhanced by the verb "to cause" (II קרא), which serves as a pun with the common verb "to call" (I קרא). In other words, God causes, but also announces the punishment for, Judah's disobedience.

This parallel description of walking a vocal path and of listening repeats elsewhere: "So I gave them over to their stubborn hearts, to follow (והלכו) their own counsels (מועצותיהם). O that my people would listen (שמע) to me, that Israel would walk (יהלכו) in my ways!" (Ps 81:13–14). Similar parallels are found in Proverbs, with the nuanced context of obedience, that of education and learning.[50] The wise man advises the sons: "And now, my child, listen (שמעו) to me, and do not depart (תסורו) from the words of my mouth" (Prov 5:7), and elsewhere: "And now, my children, listen (שמעו) to me: happy are those who keep (ישמרו) my ways" (Prov 8:32). Even without a parallel to the verb "to walk," there is a clear parallel between listening to a voice, obeying, and walking in these examples. Hearing is therefore parallel not only to walking but to kinaesthesia in general. An associative correlation is created between the two actions, based on a range of metaphors and images, and not merely on literary conventions regarding the use of word pairs.

The hearing–walking correlation is also apparent when the paradigmatic principle is applied to the use of the word "plan," "advice" (עצה). The noun is clearly an oral–aural performance, as is clear from the expressions "hear the plan that the LORD…and the purposes" (שמעו עצת ה'...ומחשבותיו, Jer 50:45); "Listen to advice and accept instruction" (שמע עצה וקבל מוסר, Prov 19:20); and "you have done this and have not listened to my advice" (ולא שמעת לעצתי, 2 Chr 25:16).[51]

At the same time, the advice is parallel to the way, or the path: "Fools think their own way is right, but the wise listen to advice" (שמע לעצה, Prov 12:15). The phrase "to walk in the advice" encapsulates the above parallels and serves to reinforce the associative pattern walking–hearing: "Happy are those who do not follow (הלך) the advice of the wicked, or take the path (עמד) that sinners tread, or sit (ישב) in the seat of scoffers"

50. In Proverbs, there is a strong parallel between study and obedience to teacher, parent, and God.

51. Also the parallel שמע||עוץ: Exod 18:19; Jer 38:15. The verbal element of advice (עצה) links walking to speech, which will be dealt with shortly.

(Ps 1:1).[52] This verse also shows that walking itself is parallels to other kinaesthetic experiences: walking, standing, and sitting all represent here behaviour, involvement, and presence.[53]

Walking, and more broadly kinaesthesia, is not only an image for hearing, but is often compared with the sense of sight. Walking in the path of the commandments is not just hearing, but also walking in the light, an image from the world of sight: "Your word is a lamp to my feet and a light to my path" (Ps 119:105). Note that the synaesthetic expression "to walk in the light" could be based on real practices of walking in the dark, but could also be an idiom which presumes the metaphor (words [instructions] are light). Such synaesthetic metaphor is found in biblical wisdom literature and is further developed in apocryphal sapiential work.[54] If we follow the latter explanation, a triangular synaesthetic association is created: sight–hearing–walking. If we reject this assumption, we still have an image of walking in the light that could be metaphoric too. Another verse from Psalms will clarify this notion: "For you have delivered my soul from death, and my feet from falling, so that I may walk (להתהלך) before God in the light of life" (Ps 56:14). Walking in the ways of God is walking in the light, and walking in the light is life.

A more common example of the walking–sight associative pattern appears in the context of investigation. In contrast to learning through obedience, walking and sight are perceived as a new discovery, based on a personal experience, not walking along an existing path.[55] This idea is reflected in the expressions "walk and see" (לך וראה) and "go and see" (צא וראה): "Come and see (לכו וראו) what God has done: he is awesome in his deeds among mortals" (Ps 66:5).[56] When the psalmist calls for witnesses, he asks them to experience things personally, through approaching and watching. Walking and sight are therefore associated through their quality—personal acquiring of knowledge.

52. See also 2 Chr 22:5.

53. Another parallel between kinaesthesia and hearing is found in Ps 141:1: "A psalm of David. I call you, O Lord, hasten to me (חושה); give ear (האזינה) to my cry when I call you" (JPS). This translation derives חושה from I חוש, "to hasten." *HALOT*, however, derives the word from II חוש, "to take note" (1:288), which is similar to the meaning of the root in Modern Hebrew. See *MKCS*, 137 n. 43.

54. See G. S. Goering, "Sapiential Synesthesia: The Conceptual Blending of Light and Word in Ben Sira's Wisdom Instruction," unpublished.

55. This is closely linked to the biblical understanding of the epistemic process: knowledge comes from personal experience (= sight), which is then transmitted and taught (= hearing/speech). See Carasik, *Theologies of the Mind*, 261, and the further elaboration given below, pp. 248–51.

56. Cf. 1 Sam 23:22; 2 Kgs 6:13; 7:14; cf. Amos 7:5; Isa 66:24; Lam 2:16; Song 3:11.

Such overlapping between sight and walking is especially prevalent in descriptions of acquiring knowledge by theft—in other words, spying.[57] At first, this looks like a natural description. In order to spy, you have to go (walk) to the enemy's location and observe. But in terms of semantic networks, there is no such thing as a purely natural description. Other actions surely took place, such as listening in or investigation, but the biblical narrator did not "choose" to describe the act of espionage using these actions. When Saul tries to find David, he commands his people: "Go (לכו) and make sure once more; find out exactly (ודעו וראו) where he is, and who has seen him there; for I am told that he is very cunning" (1 Sam 23:22). Note that here too, the verbs "to walk" (הלך) and "to see" (ראה) are clustered with "to know" (ידע). In some cases, standing (when it does not describe the halting of an action) can itself actually symbolize participation, as in learning and knowledge. We find an example of this in a parallel to hearing and sight: "For who has stood (עמד) in the council of the Lord so as to see (וירא) and to hear (וישמע) his word? Who has given heed (הקשיב) to his word so as to proclaim (וישמע) it?" (Jer 23:18). The physical presence required for witnessing (sight and hearing) is therefore described by approaching. Sight and movement are the fundamentals for knowing a hidden fact. The last example is taken from God's reply to Job. In a set of rhetorical questions, mostly asking whether Job has performed divine deeds, two sets of questions ask about Job's knowledge:

> Have you entered (הבאת) into the springs of the sea,
> or walked (התהלכת) in the recesses of the deep?
> Have the gates of death been revealed (נגלו) to you,
>   or have you seen (ראית) the gates of deep darkness?
> Have you comprehended (התבוננת) the expanse of the earth?
> Declare, if you know (הידעת) all this?
> ...
> Have you entered (הבאת) the storehouses of the snow,
> or have you seen (תראה) the storehouses of the hail? (Job 38:16–18, 22)

In these questions we find again the parallelism sight–walking/coming–knowing. This association has further nuances: walking over the land, or setting foot on the land, marks both examining it, but also controlling it, something strongly expressed in the denominative root "to spy" (רגל, lit. to set foot), to which I shall refer later. Similarly, sight marks authority, as well as spying, and is used both in a concrete and in an abstract way to

---

57. *HALOT* 1:1158, and further in Malul, "Holistic-Integrative Investigation," 147–52; *MKCS*, 114–44.

express these notions.[58] For example, when Joseph accuses his brothers of spying, he describes them as spies (מרגלים). The word appears seven times in the chapter and only twice is it explained: "He said to them, 'You are spies (מרגלים); you have come (באתם) to see (לראות) the nakedness of the land!'" (Gen 42:9, cf. v. 12). It is coming and looking that marks their act; it is a way that demonstrates the associative link between sight–kinaesthesia.

A further correlation between kinaesthesia and sight is expressed in the context of the organs that perform these actions—the foot and the eye. These organs appear in parallel in different contexts. Among the curses in Deut 28 we find the threat of unease and misery during exile:[59] "Among those nations you shall find no ease, no resting place for the sole of your foot (כף־רגלך). There the Lord will give you a trembling heart (לב), failing eyes (עינים), and a languishing spirit" (נפש, Deut 28:65). This verse demonstrates how emotional response is closely linked to physical sensation. It also demonstrates how an abstract experience is described by means of concrete experience: the stumbling feet, the failing eyes, the short breath (נפש), and the trembling heart are all psychosomatic expressions, but also metaphors for the helplessness of the exilic condition. This metaphor of helplessness is not unique to Deuteronomy and parallels the eyes, the feet, and the נפש (spirit/breath) elsewhere: "You have delivered me (נפשי) from death, my eyes (עיני) from tears, my feet (רגלי) from stumbling" (Ps 116:8, JPS). In this parallelism, the eyes and feet are both parallel to the synecdoche נפש. As difficulties of sight and movement are compared in these last two examples, the associative link sight–movement is further supported.

The eyes and the feet parallel in yet another description of seemingly physical difficulty: "As for those peoples that warred against Jerusalem, the Lord will smite them with this plague: their flesh shall rot away while they stand on their feet (רגליו); their eyes (עיניו) shall rot away in their sockets; and their tongues (לשונו) shall rot away in their mouths" (Zech 14:12, JPS).[60] This description of a plague compares various organs without distinguishing between the internal and the external effect of the disease or danger. As the punishment to the nations seems to be a

---

58. Daube in Malul, "Holistic-Integrative Investigation," 148–50, and Malul in the same study. Also compare to other sensory idioms of control, discussed on pp. 142–45, below, and elsewhere.

59. For such an interpretation, see G. von Rad, *Deuteronomy: A Commentary* (trans. D. Barton; OTL; London: SCM, 1966), 176.

60. In this citation the parallel with the tongue, representing speech, is highlighted; see also pp. 120–24.

physical one, it stresses their inability to act. A similar correlation between sensory body parts is found in descriptions of the weakness of the body, which can be at times understood as fear:[61] "Therefore my loins (מתני) are seized with trembling; I am gripped by pangs like a woman in travail, too anguished to hear, too frightened to see" (Isa 21:3, JPS).[62] This description compares tremors (i.e. a kinetic experience) to sight and hearing. Similarly, when the psalmist wishes anguish on his enemies, he says: "Let their eyes be darkened so that they cannot see, and make their loins (מתניהם) tremble continually" (Ps 69:24).[63] We learn from these verses that different organs, including those responsible for the different senses, represent a whole. At a cognitive level, the sight–walking correlation is thus juxtaposed with a physical correlation of human actions, and offers a hint about the performative character of the biblical epistemology.

    Sight, hearing, and walking are also linked by the paradigmatic principle in the use of the verb "to lift" (נשא), which often appears together with "eyes" as the subject. The meanings of this phrase are manifold. First, it can highlight a sudden sight: "And he lift up his eyes and looked (וישא עיניו וירא), and, lo, three men stood by him" (Gen 18:2, KJV).[64] In other occurrences, this phrase indicates expectation and trust: "To you I lift up my eyes (נשאתי את עיני), O you who are enthroned in the heavens! As the eyes of servants look to (עיני...אל) the hand of their master, as the eyes of a maid to (עיני...אל) the hand of her mistress, so our eyes look (עינינו אל) to the Lord our God, until he has mercy upon us" (Ps 123:1–2).[65] Lastly, it can express personal investigation: "Lift (שאו) up your eyes (עיניכם) on high and see: Who created these?" (Isa 40:26). In total, the phrase וירא[66] + עין + נשא occurs 34 times, and the phrase עין + נשא

61. See pp. 163–67.

62. For more on the idiom of warrior as birthing woman, see T. Philip, "Woman in Travail as a Simile to Men in Distress in the Hebrew Bible," in *Sex and Gender in the Ancient Near East* (ed. S. Parpola and R. M. Whiting; CRRAI 47/II; Helsinki: Neo-Assyrian Text Corpus Project, 2002), 499–505.

63. Collins discusses internal and external expressions of crying ("Physiology of Tears," 196).

64. The phrase is quite common and is a literary formula. See F. H. Polak, "Linguistic and Stylistic Aspects of Epic Formulae in Ancient Semitic Poetry and Biblical Narrative," in *Biblical Hebrew in Its Northwest Semitic Setting* (ed. S. E. Fassberg and A. Hurvitz; Winona Lake: Eisenbrauns, 2006), 285–304.

65. Note that the same expression is used to describe idolatry, since lifting the eyes to (= trusting) the idols is forbidden (e.g. Ezek 18:6, 12, 15; 23:27; 33:25).

66. The root "to see" (ראה) in this phrase always appears with *waw*, either *wayyiqtol*, *weqatal*, or *waw* + imperative.

15 more; a strong paradigmatic link is created. In one particular instance, a similar phrase, נשא + רגליו + וילך, appears: "Then Jacob went on his journey, and came to the land of the people of the east" (Gen 29:1). In this last phrase, we find an expression of similar concrete meaning (lifting in order to start an action), similar semantic content (the beginning of an action), and possibly a similar discourse function (the beginning of an episode).[67] The fact that the phrase, with its multiple possible functions, appears only once with the foot and walking associates it immediately with the more common phrase for sight.

Interestingly, the verb "to lift" (נשא) appears quite frequently (17 times) in a similar structure with the word "voice" (קול), and a complement verb. Thus, the physical imagery of lifting becomes audio imagery. In most cases, the phrase describes weeping: "And Esau lifted up his voice and wept (וישא קולו ויבך)" (Gen 27:38).[68] It is possible, therefore, that an associative link sight–speaking is in the background of the associative usage of the expression to denote movement. Notably, the root "to lift" is itself a movement, and appears frequently as the action of the hand, and as a discourse marker of a beginning. Hence, any abstract use of the root in the field of sight or speech is a synaesthetic use.[69]

So far, I have looked at how walking and mobility are parallel to sight, hearing, and to some extant speech.[70] Interestingly, the association between movement, in the broader sense, and sight is expressed also in the synaesthetic description of blindness as unmoving eyes, assuming sight to be a type of movement. Eli's old age is thus described: "Now Eli was ninety-eight years old and his eyes were set (עיניו קמה), so that he could not see (לראות)" (1 Sam 4:15). Ahijah's blindness is similarly described: "Now Ahijah could not see (לראות), for his eyes were dim (קמו עיניו) because of his age" (1 Kgs 14:4).

These last two examples indicate that a correlation among the senses is evident not just when compared with sensory actions, but also with sensory organs, and even with the consequences of the non-functioning of the sensory system. An examination of the different disabilities that appear in the Hebrew Bible will reveal how their description contributes to an understanding of the correlation between kinaesthesia and the

---

67. Mostly, the root הלך (*wayyiqtol*) marks the beginning of an episode on its own, such as in Gen 25:22; Exod 2:1. See Greenstein, "Developments in the Study of Language," 446.

68. As well as Gen 21:16; 29:11; Judg 2:4; 21:2; 1 Sam 11:4; 24:17; 2 Sam 3:32; 13:36; Job 2:12; Ruth 1:9, 14. As for crying sounds, see Collins, "Physiology of Tears," 25.

69. See below for speech and the senses, pp. 84–93.

70. I shall return to the associative link movement–sound below.

senses. There are several examples of a parallel between walking, sight, and speech. The frequent co-mention of the blind and the lame gives the impression of a common association. Some scholars even see the use of blind (עור) and lame (פסח) as indicating any defect, from the head to the foot.[71] It is clear from several sources that a lame person is one who cannot walk or whose legs are damaged, for example, Mephiboshet, who is "crippled in his feet" (נכה רגלים, 2 Sam 9:3), is also "lame (פסח) in both his feet" (v. 13).[72] The lame person appears together with the blind person in ritual contexts, where people with disabilities may not offer certain sacrifices,[73] and in the description of David's conquest of Jerusalem (2 Sam 5:8).[74] A further context in which the blind and the lame are mentioned alongside each other is the description of marginalized people. Job describes the righteousness of his path as helping the blind and the lame (Job 29:15), and Jeremiah counts the blind and the lame together with the pregnant woman and the young mother who will return to Zion (Jer 31:7).[75] In these instances the associative link sight–movement is enhanced by the associative link inability of sight–inability of movement.

71. S. M. Olyan, "'Anyone Blind or Lame Shall Not Enter the House': On the Interpretation of Second Samuel 5:8b," *CBQ* 60 (1998): 218–27 (225, 226 n. 12). The word "foot" (רגל) is normally used as a merism together with "head" (קדקד, Deut 28:35; 2 Sam 14:25; Job 2:7; ראש, Lev 13:12; Isa 1:6), though it is possible to find a merism of foot and eye, where the eye represents the face or the head. The main difference between a merism of body parts and a merism of deficiencies is that the second merism refers to the ability, and not only to the shape of an organ/whole body. From such merisms we learn that the ability of the legs is semantically equivalent to the ability of the eyes.

72. See 2 Sam 19:27; Job 29:15. The term נכה רגלים means that his feet were beaten (BDB, 646), while the term פסח שתי רגליו is a functional description. For thorough discussion of Mephibosheth, his disability, and his function in the David narrative, see J. Schipper, *Disability Studies and the Hebrew Bible: Figuring Mephibosheth in the David Story* (LHBOTS 441; New York: T&T Clark International, 2006), mainly 29–60, 108–23.

73. Deut 15:21, and referred to by Mal 1:8. See also, pp. 208–22.

74. There is much debate as to the identity of the blind and the lame in this verse. See pp. 208–22, below, and Olyan, "Anyone Blind or Lame"; S. Vargon, "The Blind and the Lame," *VT* 66 (1996): 498–514.

75. The pregnant and birthing woman are not liminal figures, but they are in a liminal state, due to the associative link between birth and death in biblical society; see the discussion in T. Philip, "Descriptions of the Birthing Women in the Bible and in the Ancient Near East: The Birthing Women and the Prophet Who Do Not See and Hear" (Hebrew), in *Shai le-Sara Japhet: Studies in the Bible, Its Exegesis and Its Language* (Festschrift S. Japhet; ed. M. Bar-Asher et al.; Jerusalem: Bialik Institute, 2007), 415–26.

Infirmity of the leg is not compared only to infirmity of sight. It also appears in parallel to the infirmity of speech: "Then the lame (פסח) shall leap (ידלג) like a deer, and the tongue of the speechless sing for joy (ותרן לשון אלם). For waters shall break forth in the wilderness, and streams in the desert" (Isa 35:6). The wondrous nature of the coming day finds expression in the correlating change of fate for the lame and the dumb. A similar parallel is found elsewhere: "As legs hang limp on a cripple (פסח), so is a proverb in the mouth of dullards" (Prov 26:7).

The associative link speech–movement demonstrated in the above verses is not restricted to parallel inabilities. The root "to spy" (רגל), mentioned before, is used at least twice to describe slanderous speech. See the complaint of Mephibosheth about his servant's deeds: "He [Ziba] has slandered (וירגל) your servant to my lord the king" (2 Sam 19:28).[76] The denominative verb, normally describing spying by walking, is here referring to verbal accusations carried out by Ziba. A similar usage of the verb is found in the description of the righteous, "who do not slander (רגל) with their tongue, and do no evil to their friends, nor take up a reproach against their neighbours" (Ps 15:3). The walking/movement–speech associative link is also apparent in the root רכל. In addition to the possible etymological link to the root רגל,[77] this root by itself includes nuances of meanings related both to movement and slanderous speech. The meaning of the verb, "to trade," and the noun, "trader" (רוכל), both refer to moving from one place to the other. The noun "slander" (רכיל), which in five occurrences in the Hebrew Bible appears as a complement to the verb "to walk" (הלך), describes "to walk about talking,"[78] to speak an evil rumour, or to gossip. Thus for example: "Beware of your neighbours, and put no trust in any of your kin; for all your kin are supplanters, and every neighbour goes around like a slanderer (רכיל יהלך). They all deceive their neighbours, and no one speaks the truth; they have taught their tongues to speak lies; they commit iniquity and are too weary to repent" (Jer 9:3–4 [4–5]).

In ancient times, there was a clear physical connection between the transmission of information and the people who did the transmitting: traders and other passers-by. But the semantic shift of the root to actual speech, performed kinaesthetically (with "to walk"), is enhanced when the word "slander" (רכיל) parallels the word "secret" (סוד), clearly a term

76. Vargon, "The Blind and the Lame," 508.
77. BDB, 940; E. Lipiński, "רכל *rkl*; רֹכֵל *rōkēl*; רָכִיל *rākîl*; רְכֻלָּה *rekullâ*; מַרְכֹּלֶת *markōlet*," *TDOT* 14:498–99 (198).
78. *HALOT* 4:1236–37. See Lev 19:16; Jer 6:28; 9:3; Prov 11:13; 20:19; and another occurrence of אנשי רכיל (Ezek 22:9).

from the verbal realm: "A gossip goes (הולך רכיל) about telling secrets (סוד), but one who is trustworthy in spirit keeps a confidence" (Prov 11:13; cf. 20:19). The word secret, which comes from the semantic field of speech,[79] strengthens the associative correlation between kinaesthesia and speech as reflected in the root רכל. Lastly, the dual kinaesthetic–sound image encapsulated in this root reappears in another Biblical Hebrew root, namely, דום/דמם, which incorporates two separate meanings—stopping and silence: "And the sun stood still (וידם), and the moon stopped (עמד), until the nation took vengeance on their enemies…" (Josh 10:13); "But when I was silent and still (נאלמתי דומיה), not even saying (החשיתי) anything good, my anguish increased" (Ps 39:3, JPS). The etymological matter was discussed at length by Baruch Levine,[80] yet for my purpose it demonstrates an associative link—stillness–silence—which enhances the associative link kinaesthesia–speech.

To sum up, I have demonstrated that walking and, more generally, movement, is associatively linked to hearing, sight, and speech/sound. These associative patterns are established on parallels, word pairs, dual meanings (etymology), paradigmatic principles, and synaesthetic descriptions. In the following pages I will look at the correlation between speech and the other senses.

Speech

"All things are wearisome; more than one can express (לדבר); the eye is not satisfied with seeing (לראות), or the ear filled with hearing (משמע)" (Qoh 1:8). This verse is part of Qohelet's description of intellectual despair. The inability to talk about, see, and hear the perceived matters is a strong bodily idiom. Michael Carasik explains this associative parallel through two metaphors: speech is thought, and sight is thought. Speech in the Hebrew Bible is a verbal thought, namely, speech is not only a representation of information extracted from the mind, but the actual process of thought.[81] See, for example, the thoughts of Esau: "Now Esau hated Jacob because of the blessing with which his father had blessed him, and Esau said to himself (ויאמר…בלבו), 'The days of mourning for my father are approaching; then I will kill my brother Jacob'" (Gen 27:41). When Esau speaks within his mind (לב), he is in fact planning,

---

79. For example: "But is they have stood (עמדו) in my council, then they would have proclaimed my words…" (Jer 23:22; cf. Job 15:8).

80. See B. A. Levine, "Silence, Sound, and the Phenomenology of Mourning in Biblical Israel," *JANES* 22 (1993): 89–106.

81. Carasik, *Theologies of the Mind*, 94–103.

thinking. David's thought processes are described in a similar manner: "David said in his heart (ויאמר...אל־לבו), 'I shall now perish one day by the hand of Saul; there is nothing better for me than to escape to the land of the Philistines; then Saul will despair of seeking me any longer within the borders of Israel, and I shall escape out of his hand'" (1 Sam 27:1).[82] In these two examples, the complete phrase "to speak" + "to/in" + "mind" (אמר ב/אל לבו) is describing thought and planning. Yet the usage of speech as an image or metaphor for thought is found also in the usage of other, completely verbal, terms: "The tongue (לשון) of the wise produces much knowledge (דעת), but the mouth (פי) of dullards pours out folly (אולת)" (Prov 15:2, JPS). In this instance, the content of speech reflects knowledge, and is even identified with the content of the information. A similar image exists in parallel to thinking/planning: "You are plotting (תחשב) destruction. Your tongue (לשונך) is like a sharp razor, you worker of treachery" (Ps 52:4). Coming back to the words of Qohelet—"All things are wearisome; more than one can express (לדבר); the eye is not satisfied with seeing (לראות), or the ear filled with hearing" (משמע, Qoh 1:8)—since the whole opening chapter of the book expresses Qohelet's despair from his personal investigation, and the practicality of knowledge, this verse exemplifies that despair, of reality which is more than possible to comprehend—speak, see, or hear. A few verses later, this parallel, between speech and sight as means of thought, is demonstrated again: "I said to myself (דברתי...עם לבי), 'I (אני) have acquired great wisdom, surpassing all who were over Jerusalem before me; and my mind (לבי) has had great experience (lit. "saw," ראה) of wisdom and knowledge'" (v. 16). The king's personal investigation, his sight,[83] is processed through his "internal speech."

The nuanced parallel between speech and hearing is found in images for learning: "The Lord God gave me a skilled tongue (לשון למודים), to know how to sustain[84] to the weary with words (דבר). Morning by morning, He rouses, He rouses my ear to listen skilfully (לשמע כלמודים)" (Isa 50:4, JPS [with slight modification]).[85] The skill of speech and that of hearing are both necessities for learning. Interestingly, the similarity is

---

82. Carasik (ibid.) discerns that speech within the heart is not only non-vocal, but rather an expression of planning, as is clear from the above examples. This expression repeats in Gen 17:17; Deut 7:17; 8:17; 9:4; 1 Sam 27:1; 1 Kgs 12:26; Isa 14:13; 47:8, 10; 49:21; Jer 13:22; Hos 7:2; Obad 3; Zeph 1:12; 2:15; Qoh 2:15.

83. Note that the book of Qohelet has a marked tendency for using the root ראה, as well as other sight expressions, in sharp contrast to Proverbs.

84. The meaning of the Hebrew is uncertain, with the *hapax* לעות having no immediate meaning. As such, interpretive suggestions are multiple.

85. For more on speech as thought/understanding, see pp. 159–60.

both practical (learning through recitation and listening), and semantic, as various roots in Biblical Hebrew can express both the production of sound, and its perception.

One example is the common root שמע, for which the common meaning in the Qal is "to hear." In the Hiphil we find the causative meaning, "to cause to hear"—yet quite often the meaning in context involves the production of sound: "He shall not cry (יצעק), nor lift up (ישא),[86] nor cause his voice to be heard (ישמיע...קולו) in the street" (Isa 42:2, KJV); "Who declared it (הגיד) from the beginning, so that we might know, and beforehand, so that we might say, 'He is right'? There was no one who declared it (מגיד), none who proclaimed (משמיע), none who heard (שמע) your words" (Isa 41:26).[87] These last two examples demonstrate the fluidity of meaning in the root שמע, but also the associative link hearing–speech. Moreover, about half of all the occurrences of the verb שמע (Hiphil) have a complement subject that describes a sound, such as "voice" (קול),[88] "word" (דבר),[89] "shout" (זעקה, Jer 48:4; תרועה, Jer 49:2), and more. Clearly, an essential condition for activating hearing is the existence of a voice—which in our context means creating the voice. Naturally, other derived words demonstrate this semantic shift hearing–speech. One example is the noun "byword/report" (שמועה), as found in the words of Ezekiel—"Was not your sister Sodom a byword in your mouth (שמועה בפיך) in the day of your pride?" (Ezek 16:56). Note how the mention of the mouth prevents the misunderstanding of the byword as a passive, heard matter. In some instances, the oral–aural act of pronouncing parallels sight: "But this is why I have let you live: to show you (הראותך) my power, and to make my name resound (ספר שמי) through all the earth" (Exod 9:16).

Another form of the verb שמע includes synaesthetic elements. In both Piel and Pual, שמע can denote summoning to battle. For example, in the Piel: "Saul summoned (וישמע) all the people to war, to go down to Keilah, to besiege David and his men" (1 Sam 23:8);[90] and in the Hiphil: "Summon (השמיעו) archers against Babylon, all who bend the bow. Encamp all around her; let no one escape. Repay her according to her

---

86. The root נשא appears here alongside speech, and should be read in light of the phrases עין + נשא and נשא + קול, which were mentioned earlier.

87. And many more. See *HALOT* 4:1574, where שמע in Hiphil is translated as "cause to hear," "announce," "make oneself heard/known."

88. Deut 4:36; Judg 18:25; Josh 6:10; Isa 30:30; 42:2; 58:4; Ezek 27:30; Pss 26:7; 66:8; Song 2:14; Neh 8:15; 1 Chr 15:16; 2 Chr 5:13.

89. Deut 4:10; 1 Sam 9:27; Jer 18:2.

90. Cf. 1 Sam 15:4.

deeds; just as she has done, do to her—for she has arrogantly defied the
Lord, the Holy One of Israel" (Jer 50:29).[91] The summons to gather
warriors highlights the link between voice, hearing, and kinaesthesia
that we saw earlier in the use of the roots רגל and רכל. A report, which
is both an oral and aural experience, is carried by, and experienced, as
mobility.[92] As summons to fight is answered with hearing, and as hearing is a basic metaphor for obedience, we have further merging of the
above meanings in another noun derived from שמע—"subjugated"/
"bodyguard" (משמעת).[93] The response to calling out is hearing and coming, and the associative link between hearing–speech–kinaesthesia is
enhanced.

Another example of the blending of speech and hearing is the root
חרש, in this case the context being an inability to hear or to make sounds.
From the infrequent appearance of this root, it is clear that the noun
"deaf" (חֵרֵשׁ) signifies inability to hear: "You shall not revile the deaf
(תקלל חרש) or put a stumbling block before the blind; you shall fear your
God: I am the Lord" (Lev 19:14). It is clear that this term describes only
the inability to hear, as those with speech disability are called "mute"
(אלם). The distinction between the two appears elsewhere: "But I am like
the deaf (חרש), I do not hear; like the mute (אלם), who cannot speak" (Ps
38:14). Despite the fact that the deaf has disfunctioning ears,[94] the verbal
form of חרש almost always portrays an inability to speak, or silence. For
example: "They said to him, 'Keep quiet (החרש)! Put your hand over
your mouth, and come with us'…" (Judg 18:19); "But they were silent
(ויחרישו) and answered him not a word, for the king's command was,
'Do not answer him.' But they remained silent and said nothing" (Isa
36:21).[95] The predicted meaning of the root—to cause unhearing—is
actually to be silent. This verb can also describe God's silence, which
serves as a metaphor for his lack of help, similarly to a lack of hearing or
a lack of sight. The psalmist begs God: "O God, do not keep silent
(דֳמִי);[96] be not quiet (תחרש), O God, be not still (תשקט)" (Ps 83:1, NIV).[97]

---

91. Cf. 1 Kgs 15:22; Jer 51:27.

92. See also the phrase "arriving report" (שמועה באה), 2 Sam 13:30; 2 Kgs 2:28;
Ezek 21:12.

93. 1 Sam 22:14; 2 Sam 23:23; Isa 11:14; 1 Chr 11:25.

94. See Isa 43:8: "Bring forth the people who are blind, yet have eyes, who are
deaf, yet have ears!"

95. There are three meanings to II חרש in Hiphil: "to be silent, to create silence,
to be deaf or act as a deaf" (BDB, 361).

96. The noun used here is דֳמִי, meaning "rest" or "silence"; cf. Isa 62:6.

97. Cf. Pss 35:22; 39:1; 50:3; Job 31:35.

Clustering the root חרש with two other silence words demonstrates its meaning.

Furthermore, the two other silence words mentioned—coming from the roots II דמה and שקט—have a strong associative link to kinaesthesia, and the verse in context finds parallels between both acts (note v. 2). Finally, in only one instance do we find the verbal form of חרש used specifically to denote lack of hearing, which further blurs the already fuzzy semantic boundary between hearing and speech: "The nations shall see and be ashamed of all their might; they shall lay their hands on their mouths; their ears shall be deaf (תחרשנה)" (Mic 7:16). The peculiarity of this occurrence of the root is strengthened on comparison with Judg 18:19, cited above, where laying the hands on the mouth and חרש have the same meaning.[98] The semantic proximity between the two actions reaches its peak in the following verses: "Pay heed (הקשב), Job, listen (שמע) to me; be silent (החרש), and I will speak (אדבר). If you have anything to say, answer me; speak, for I desire to justify you. If not, listen (שמע) to me; be silent (החרש), and I will teach you wisdom" (Job 33:31–33). Although NRSV translates חרש twice as "be silent," note that, mainly in v. 31, it could be either a synonymous parallel to "to listen" (שמע), or an antonymous one to "to speak" (דבר). Is it impossible simultaneously to listen and speak? Could there be two experiences in the same action? Is speech really separate from hearing?[99]

The semantic proximity between hearing and speech is not restricted to the use of identical roots, but extends to images of speech and hearing actions, such as silence and deafness in similar symbolic contexts. Hearing and speech signify responsiveness and help. Their absence describes a lack of ability. However, as I demonstrated above, when it comes to learning, speech and hearing serve different purposes and metaphors.

Further associations are found through examination of the root ענה. The most basic meaning of the root is assumed to be that of opening,[100] yet its common meaning in Biblical Hebrew is "to start speaking" or "to answer" a question. This meaning of the root is highly significant, because in more than one third (about 120) of the occurrences, it appears in conjunction with the verb "to say" (אמר). Examples include: "and they shall declare" (וענו ואמרו, Deut 21:7): "All the people answered" (ויען כל־העם ויאמרו, 1 Kgs 18:24); "Isaac answered (ויען), saying (ויאמר) to

98. Cf. Job 21:5 where laying the hands on the mouth parallels silence.
99. Ong and McLuhan treat hearing-speech as one faculty. Such definition exists in various cultures; see Howes, "Sensorial Anthropology," 171–72.
100. E. Levine, "Biblical Women's Marital Rights," *PAAJR* 63 (1997): 87–135 (103).

Esau..." (Gen 27:37).[101] The root ענה does not just describe speech or the beginning of speech, but also signifies responding to a request. This meaning is close to what we identified earlier: speech, hearing, and sight are metaphors for help.[102] That meaning was displayed in the root חרש as an idiom for God's silence as unhelpful. The root ענה also denotes responding to a request, either as human or divine aid. Such meaning is found in the prose, in Jacob's words: "then come, let us go up to Bethel, that I may make an altar there to the God who answered (הענה) me in the day of my distress and has been with me wherever I have gone" (Gen 35:3).

The same meaning is found in biblical poetry: "Answer me (ענני) when I call, O God of my right! You gave me room when I was in distress. Be gracious to me (חנני), and hear (שמע) my prayer" (Ps 4:1).[103] In this last verse we see a parallel between answering and hearing, while in other verses this parallel appears in the context of knowledge: "Before they call I will answer (אענה), while they are yet speaking I will hear" (אשמע, Isa 65:24)—God knows even before his senses absorb the information.[104] The differences of meanings between knowledge, response, and help in this verse are hazy. In the human context, we again find verbal response/ speech and hearing to mean response, this time as a kind of obedience to God. God's supreme ability to hear and answer (= know, help) is enhanced when his words from v. 12 are taking into consideration:[105] "I will destine you to the sword, and all of you shall bow down to the slaughter; because, when I called, you did not answer, when I spoke, you did not listen, but you did what was evil in my sight, and chose what I

---

101.   And many others. A similar phrase is ענה דבר (1 Kgs 21; 2 Kgs 18:36; Isa 36:21), with ענה and דבר as parallel or clustered verbs (Josh 22:21; 1 Kgs 12:7; Jer 23:23; Job 40:5 and elsewhere).

102.   For detailed analysis, see pp. 130–41.

103.   See also Pss 17:6; 27:7; 55:20; 143:1.

104.   J. N. Oswalt, *The Book of Isaiah: Chapters 40–66* (NICOT; Grand Rapids: Eerdmans, 1997), 661.

105.   This contrast is similar to the contrast between hearing as obedience with human subject, and aid with divine subject. It is possible that this gap in meaning is not as sharp as it seems at first sight. Both hearing and speech are used as a metaphor for response; the type of response depends on the location in a particular relationship, in this case a covenant relationship. The strong party responds to the weak party and by doing so aids it. The weak party responds, and therefore obeys the strong party. See also pp. 130–41, below. For a basic discussion of covenant as fundamental metaphor in biblical culture, see G. E. Mendenhall and G. A. Herion, "Covenant," *ABD* 1:1179–202 (1180–81 more specifically for the matter of hierarchy).

did not delight in" (Isa 65:12).[106] The main stanza of interest for the present purpose is "I called, you did not answer, when I spoke, you did not listen" (קראתי ולא עניתם דברתי ולא שמעתם). Besides being a mirror image of v. 24 (יקראו ואני אענה...מדברים ואני אשמע), we find here again the associative link between speech and hearing, not only in the formal level of parallelism, but also in idiomatic meaning, be it knowledge, divine aid, or obedience.[107]

We therefore find both a linguistic and a semantic parallel between the verb "to respond" and the verb "to hear" in different contexts. This parallel reinforces the semantic link between speech, hearing, and kinaesthesia.[108] Speech and hearing have common roots, and speech is linked to hearing in a number of semantic realms: cognitive, obedience, divine help. Speech and hearing are even found in proximity to sight, as indicated in the lists describing the lack of senses of idols (Pss 115:4–7; 135:15–17). Such parallelism is found elsewhere. When Moses refuses to lead the Israelites, God claims: "Who gives speech (lit. 'mouth,' פה) to mortals? Who makes them mute (אלם) or deaf (חרש), seeing (פקח) or blind (עור)? Is it not I, the Lord?" (Exod 4:11). This verse poses two contrasts: the human mouth (speech) vs. the dumb and the deaf; and the seeing (someone with the ability to see) vs. blindness.[109] Here are two senses where God controls human ability: the sense of sight and the sense of hearing–speech.[110]

Speech and sight appear in parallel several times in the Hebrew Bible, as do the organs that represent these actions: the eye and the tongue/mouth/lips. We see an example in images of unethical behaviour in Proverbs.[111] There are seven abominations to Yahweh:

106.   See also Jer 7:13, 27; 35:17.

107.   As written above, learning and obedience are one in the wisdom tradition.

108.   The blurring of semantic boundary between the meaning "to hear" and the meaning "to talk" in the root ענה is demonstrated in its frequent translation to the first meaning in the LXX. See R. Kessler, "Der antwortende Gott," *Wort und Dienst* 21 (1991): 43–57.

109.   Further in the book of Exodus, we find again the contrast between עור and פקח: "...for bribes blind (יְעַוֵּר) the clear-sighted (פִּקְחִים)..." (23:8). Generally, the root פקח is used in the Hebrew Bible to describe seeing (open eyes) and, metaphorically, hearing (BDB, 824).

110.   For more on the creation of speech, see pp. 193–96. Relating cognitive weakness to deaf/mute people is not unique to the Hebrew Bible (for English, see Devereux, "Ethnopsychological Aspects"). Note the similar semantic shift in the Akkadian substantive *sukkuku*, meaning both deaf and stupid (see *CAD* 15, 68; *MKCS*, 146).

111.   For more on sensory perception as a metaphor for moral behaviour, see pp. 167–75.

> Haughty *eyes*, a lying *tongue*,
> and *hands* that shed innocent blood,
> a *heart* that devises wicked plans,
> > *feet* that hurry to run to evil,
> a lying witness who testifies falsely,
> > and one who sows discord in a family. (Prov 6:17–19)

The eyes, tongue, hands, heart (mind), and feet are compared as the sources of evil doing, and as they are also clustered with human action as a whole, they are all a synecdoche. Furthermore, speech, sight, touch, and kinaesthesia are all expressions of negative and harmful actions.[112] This indicates an associative correlation among the organs, and among the actions of those organs. We find a similar parallel in Prov 4:24–27:

> Put away from you crooked *speech*,
> and put devious *talk* far from you.
> Let your *eyes* look directly forward,
> and your *gaze*[113] be straight before you.
> Keep straight the path of your *feet*,
> > and all your ways will be sure.
> Do not swerve to the right or to the left;
> > turn your *foot* away from evil.[114]

We find again that sight, speech, and walking are associated, as all serve as a metaphor for appropriate behaviour. The associative link between speech and kinaesthesia presented previously is enhanced in this triangular parallel.

The syntagmatic principle provides a further link between speech and sight. We know that the eye and the heart serve as a word pair in the Hebrew Bible, and appear both as synonymous and antonymous in parallelism.[115] Most famous is the words directed at Samuel: "For not as man sees [does the Lord see]; man sees only what is visible (לעינים), but the Lord sees into the heart (ללבב)" (1 Sam 16:7, JPS).[116] Interestingly, the contrast between the heart/mind as an inward expression/perception and sensory organs as outward ones repeats in the contrast between the heart and the tongue: speech with the heart/mind is internal (thought), and vocal speech is external. Consider this contrast between the tongue and the heart: "The plans of the mind (לב) belong to mortals, but the

---

112. Note the absence of hearing and the olfactory sense, which normally express passive action when related to a human subject.
113. Literally "eyelids" (עפעפיך).
114. Cf. Prov 6:12; 10:10.
115. Watson, "Unnoticed Word Pair."
116. See p. 56, above.

answer of the tongue (לשון) is from the Lord" (Prov 16:1).[117] In the culture reflected in the Hebrew Bible, the heart functions as the organ of thought, and as such it is related to the senses in a complex way. The sense organs and the mind can reflect each other, but also can contradict each other.

A broader example of the parallel between speech and sight in the context of understanding can be found in Isaiah's prophecy: "Then the eyes of those who have sight (עיני ראים) will not be closed, and the ears of those who have hearing will listen (אזני שמעים תקשבנה). The minds (לבב) of the rash will have good judgment, and the tongues (לשון) of stammerers will speak readily and distinctly" (Isa 32:3–4).[118] The cited prophecy demonstrates the parallelism eye–ear–heart–tongue and the associative link between them. It also distinguishes between sight and hearing as passive and speech and thought as active, and enhances the distinction between speech and hearing.

Lastly, we also find a similarity between speech and sight in portrayals of presence or an intimate meeting. When God wants to highlight Moses' uniqueness, he describes his intimate relationship with him: "With him I speak mouth to mouth, plainly (במראה) and not in riddles, and he beholds (יביט) the likeness of the Lord. How then did you not shrink from speaking against My servant Moses!" (Num 12:8). Not only are speaking and seeing both a marker for intimate relationship, they also follow the

---

117.   See also Prov 16:9, with reference to movement: "The human mind (לב) plans the way, but the Lord directs the steps." See also the similar meaning in "The human mind may devise many plans, but it is the purpose (עצה) of the Lord that will be established" (Prov 16:21). Cf. Isa 29:13. Other examples for the parallel לב‖לשון are Pss 39:4; 45:2; Prov 7:20.

118.   The verbal form תשעינה is difficult, yet it is agreed that it means "lack of sight," as a parallel to תקשבנה further on in the verse. Similar occurrences of the same root appear in Isa 6:10: "Fatten the mind (לב) of this nation, and its ears make heavy, and its eyes seal/turn away (השע)—lest it will see with its eyes, and with its ears it will hear, and his mind (לב) will realize, turn back and be healed" (my translation). The forms תשענה, תשעינה, השע can derive from שעה, "to turn" (movement). If this is the case, שעה can denote turning towards something (Gen 14:5; Isa 31:1 and more), and figuratively to look to attend (BDB, 1043–44; *HALOT* 4:1610; J. R. Lundbom, "שָׁעָה *šāʿâ*," *TDOT* 15:349–51 [349]), or turning away from something (Isa 32:3; 6:10). Another possibility is to derive the forms תשענה and השע from שעע, "to cover, blur." Such derivation requires a change in vocalization from תִּשְׁעֶינָה to תְּשֻׁעֶינָה, meaning "to cover, to shut" (so KJV, JPS, and NRSV). Some find the phrase to "speak plainly" (צחות, Isa 32:4) to be a synaesthetic metaphor, linking speech to sight (Kedar-Kopfstein, "Synästhesien," 52). Although it is possible to ascribe צח to the semantic field of sight, it could also mean something true, or healthy (S. Talmon, צח *ṣaḥ*; צָחִיח *ṣāḥîaḥ*; צְחִיחָה *ṣeḥîḥâ*," *TDOT* 12:321–24).

same syntax—"mouth to mouth," "eye to eye"—and are both syntactically (and associatively) linked to "face to face." One example is the prophecy to Zedekiah: "And you yourself shall not escape from his hand, but shall surely be captured and handed over to him; you shall see the king of Babylon eye to eye and speak with him face to face; and you shall go to Babylon" (Jer 34:3).[119] Both these examples highlight the intimacy of meeting through the metaphor of mutual sight and speech, a parallel that reinforces the associative link between speech and the other senses.

In sum, we recognize a strong proximity between speech and hearing, both linguistically and in similar contexts. However, it has been shown that speech and hearing cannot be considered one and the same. We have also seen that the parallel between speech and sight is a recurring theme in the Hebrew Bible, and that speech and kinaesthesia are associatively linked through shared terminology[120] and parallelism. In the following paragraphs, I will further present the associative link between speech and taste, yet the data presented so far are sufficient to include speech in the biblical sensorium.

Taste

I started the discussion of the sensorium with the sensory disabilities of the idols: "There you will serve other gods made by human hands, objects of wood and stone that neither see, nor hear, nor eat, nor smell" (Deut 4:28). In this verse, the verb "to eat" (אכל) is parallel to the verbs for sight, hearing, and smell. It is noteworthy that neither a sharp semantic distinction exists between the common verb "to eat" (אכל) and the rare verb "to taste" (טעם), nor the tasting process and eating, as is evident from the following parallelism: "For the ear tastes words as the palate tastes (יטעם) food" (Job 34:3).[121] In this parallel between hearing and tasting, neither involves passive absorption. We are looking at what enters the body. This parallel between the sense of taste and the other senses appears in other biblical verses. Look at the following verses from the prophet Ezekiel:

> But you, mortal, hear (שמע) what I say to you; do not be rebellious like that rebellious house; open your mouth and eat (ואכל) what I give you... He said to me, O mortal, eat (אכול) what is offered to you; eat (אכול) this scroll, and go, speak (אכול ולך דבר) to the house of Israel. So I opened my

---

119. Here again בוא indicates physical presence.
120. Levine, "Silence, Sound," 91.
121. Cf. Job 12:11.

mouth, and he gave me the scroll to eat (וַיַּאֲכִלֵנִי). He said to me, Mortal, eat (הַאֲכֵל) this scroll that I give you and fill your stomach with it. Then I ate it (וָאֹכְלָה); and in my mouth it was as sweet as honey. (Ezek 2:8; 3:1–3)

This passage presents us with a mix of senses.[122] The prophet's appeal is verbal, through the verb "to hear," signifying a request for obedience and understanding, as is clear from the contrast with "rebellious house" in the same verse. Hearing in v. 8 is parallel to eating the scroll. Later, the prophet sees the scroll and even reads it (v. 10), but the main imagery in this part of the prophecy is clearly of eating and processing information by literally placing it in the body—the verb "to eat" (אכל) repeats six times in 2:8–3:3. From here on, eating the scroll becomes important in order to pass its content on, to speak it out (דבר, four times), so it can be heard.[123]

The semantic proximity between eating and speech is expressed through a physical link. The mouth is the representative organ of both actions. Moreover, there is a semantic, synaesthetic correlation between the two, in particular the metaphoric use of adjectives from the field of taste to describe the content of speech. Positive or correct things are portrayed as sweet: "Pleasant words are like a honeycomb, sweetness to the soul and health to the body" (Prov 16:24); or simply in the combination "sweet speech": the wise of heart is called perceptive, and pleasant (lit. sweet מֶתֶק) speech increases persuasiveness (Prov 16:21).[124] In contrast, negative or wrong things are portrayed as bitter. The evildoers are those who "whet their tongues like swords, who aim bitter words like arrows" (Ps 64:4)[125] The adjective "bitter" also describes

---

122.   For a short discussion of the matter, see below.

123.   See also Jer 15:16: "Your words were found, and I ate them, and your words became to me a joy and the delight of my heart; for I am called by your name, O Lord, God of hosts." For the semantic tie between speech and eating in Mesopotamia and a short note about Ezek 2:8–3:3, see Wasserman, "Sweeter than Honey." Interestingly, these verses are referred to in a Jewish rite of passage, one which marked the entry of young boys into school, and their transfer from infanthood into childhood. In the ceremony, the boys received either tablets with honey letters to lick, or letter-shaped honey cakes. The letters meant for reading (sight) were symbolically internalized through eating (H. E. Goldberg, *Jewish Passages: Cycles of Jewish Life* [Berkeley: University of California Press, 2003], 83–87).

124.   See the Mishnaic Hebrew term דברי טעם, and the etymological Akkadian equivalent *ṭēmu*, "decree, report, order" (speech), as well as understanding and planning. Another meaning of the noun in Akkadian is "characteristic," similar to Hebrew טעם. The meaning "taste" is not found. For discussion and examples, see *CAD* 19, 85–97.

125.   For more on the tongue as a sword, see pp. 144–59.

crying out, thus denoting a negative emotion rather than a slanderous action per se: "When Mordecai learned all that had been done, Mordecai tore his clothes and put on sackcloth and ashes, and went through the city, wailing with a loud and bitter (גדולה ומרה) cry" (Est 4:1)[126] This image, which adds a flavour dimension to vocal acts, and also gives an evaluation of the content of speech, is based indirectly on the image of eating as gaining knowledge. The different and contrary tastes (bitter vs. sweet) signify a concrete assessment of food, and an abstract assessment of anything else in reality (such as speech, human behaviour, and more).

In addition to bitter and sweet images, we also find speech portrayed by the adjective "tasteless" (תפל), which also originates from the semantic field of the taste: "Your prophets have seen (חזו) for you false and deceptive (ותפל)[127] visions; they have not exposed your iniquity to restore your fortunes, but have seen oracles for you that are false and misleading" (Lam 2:14). This verse highlights the synaesthetic link between the sense of taste and two other senses. The link with speech is clear, because "tasteless" describes the content of the prophecy, which was transmitted verbally. But it also connects to the root "to see" (חזה), which has its origin in the field of sight.[128] We find a similar combination in Jeremiah's prophecy, this time in association with the word "saw": "And I have seen folly (ראיתי תפלה) in the prophets of Samaria; they prophesied in Baal, and caused my people Israel to err" (Jer 23:13, KJV). Here too, the noun "tasteless" refers both to what the prophet sees or finds, and to the prophecy (speech) of the prophets of Samaria. In both cases, something which is tasteless is also unworthy or false.[129] As we saw in the use of sweet and bitter imagery, the imagery of something tasteless is also based on a perception that the sense of taste is a critical sense with which we learn about and analyse the world. This perception, as well as the associative link speech–taste, appear again in Proverbs, where wise words are portrayed as the fruit of the mouth, as food: "From the fruit of their mouth a man enjoys eating; but [from] the throat of the treacherous—wrongdoing" (Prov 13:2 [my translation]); "From the fruit

---

126. Cf. Gen 27:34; Zeph 1:14; Sir 29:25.

127. The interpretation of תפל is doubtful. While most translators, ancient and modern, understand it in the same manner I do, there are suggestions to read it as II תפל, meaning "whitewash."

128. See Kedar-Kopfstein, "Synästhesien," 53.

129. It is unclear to me why some translations of תפלה are so biased as to read "repulsive" (JPS), "disgusting" (NRSV). Accusing false prophets of uselessness is quite common, therefore the translations of תפל in Lam 2:14 ("folly" [JPS] and "deceptive" [NRSV]) seem more accurate.

of the mouth one is filled with good things and manual labour has its reward" (Prov 12:14).[130] Here too we find that eating and speech are blurred, as speech is the produce, the fruit, which is then consumed.

The verb "to be satisfied" (שבע), which also belongs to the semantic field of eating, is also used to describe sight, particularly in images of wishes and wish fulfilment. As the eyes want something, that wish can be fulfilled, just like the throat is fulfilled with food. In Proverbs, for example, human wishes (lit. "the eyes") are never satisfied: "Sheol and Abaddon are never satisfied (תשבענה), and human eyes are never satisfied (תשבענה)" (Prov 27:20).[131] While the first stanza shows a clear eating idiom—Sheol as a being that eats the dead—the second stanza uses a more abstract idiom of satisfying desire. It seems that the נפש, which holds hunger and desire, and its physical location (the throat) between the inwards on the one hand, and the eyes and mouth on the other hand, creates an image of a hungry and satisfied eye. Eating as satisfying the soul appears in several contexts, such as in prophecy: "Why do we fast (צמנו), but you do not see? Why humble ourselves (ענינו נפשנו), but you do not notice? Look, you serve your own interest on your fast-day, and oppress all your workers. Look, you fast only to quarrel and to fight and to strike with a wicked fist. Such fasting as you do (תצומו) today will not make your voice heard (להשמיע קולכם) on high" (Isa 58:3–4). Fasting is parallel in v. 3 to "afflicting the נפש," and both are meant to be seen and heard by God. The lack of eating is hence linked to making a voice heard. It is also striking in this verse that fasting affects the נפש, which is the seat of hunger.[132]

The affect of eating (or lack of) on the throat (נפש) resembles the affect of sight and hearing on the mind, and at times the נפש and soul/heart. The sensory organs are external organs through which concrete and abstract experiences enter the spirit/mind. The sensory organs can

---

130.   The phrase פרי פה appears again in Prov 18:20. The metaphor embedded in the phrase is that speech is a product of the mouth. The source domain "fertility, produce," represented here by the fruit (פרי, cf. the phrase "fruit of the land"), is brought in to the target domain "speech," represented here metonymically by the mouth (פה). Associatively, one must compare the phrase to "fruit of the hand" (פרי ידים, Prov 31:31) and "fruit of the womb" (פרי בטן, Gen 30:2; Deut 7:13; 28:4, 11, 18; 30:9; Isa 13:18; Mic 6:7; Pss 127:3; 132:11). For fruit as metaphor in biblical literature, see Eilberg-Schwarz, *The Savage in Judaism*, 149–54. For the associative link between the senses and sexuality, see *MKCS*, 313, as well as pp. 110–11, below.

131.   Cf. Qoh 4:8, and the parallel שבע‖ראה in Isa 53:11.

132.   Cf. Ps 35:13; see also Jer 50:19; Pss 63:6; 123:4; Prov 6:3; 13:23; 27:7 and more.

also express the content of the spirit/mind.[133] Eating satisfies the hungry soul: "The righteous have enough to satisfy their appetite (לשבע נפשו), but the belly of the wicked is empty" (Prov 13:25). Notably, the ambiguity of נפש makes it hard to decide whether in this verse it means "throat," and hence eating and being full is filling the stomach up to the throat, or whether נפש means "spirit" and the verse talks about spiritual hunger. It seems that both the physical and the spiritual/emotional effects are meant when this image is used. This is the case also when hunger and thirst are describes as empty נפש, and serve as an idiom for the feeling of unfulfilled yearning: "Just as when a hungry person dreams of eating and wakes up still hungry (וריקה נפשו), or a thirsty person dreams of drinking and wakes up faint, still thirsty (ונפשו שוקקה), so shall the multitude of all the nations be that fight against Mt. Zion" (Isa 29:8).[134] The image of hunger and satisfaction is found again when the eye is described as the locus of wanting. The image is semantically broadened when the satisfied eye becomes a description of complete experience and understanding: "All things are wearisome; more than one can express; the eye is not satisfied with seeing (לא־תשבע עין לראות), or the ear filled with hearing (תמלא אזן משמע)" (Qoh 1:8).[135]

The inability of Job to perceive is described through a complexity of images. Being full (שבע, מלא) is an image of eating, used to describe the ear and the eye which aspire to be full of understanding. We see a similar use of hunger and satisfaction imagery with stronger emphasis on hearing. While linking prosperity (food) to faith/obedience (hearing), and creating a strong allegory between eating/drinking and following God, Isaiah makes the following statement: "Why do you spend your money for that which is not bread, and your labour for that which does not satisfy (שבעה)? Listen carefully (שמעו שמוע) to me, and eat what is good

133.   Cf. Collins, "Physiology of Tears," 23–24; A. R. Johnson, *The Vitality of the Individual in the Thought of Ancient Israel* (2d ed.; Cardiff: University of Wales Press, 1964), 48; Pedersen, *Israel: Its Life and Culture*, 174–76.

134.   The difficulty of translating נפש is apparent in this verse: KJV translated "soul," while recent translations have chosen to treat it as "oneself." Establishing the meaning of the word in each and every case is far beyond the scope of the present study. I do, however, prefer to find as many meanings in the word as is possible and fitting to the context. In this case, the choice of hunger image and the emphasis on the נפש hint that the idiom here serves as a metaphor as well.

135.   The metaphor of eyes as location of will/desire is found in the phrase עין + שאל, which merges the domain of speech and sight: "Whatever my eyes desired (lit. "ask," שאלו) I did not keep from them; I kept my heart from no pleasure, for my heart found pleasure in all my toil, and this was my reward for all my toil" (Qoh 2:10).

(אכלו טוב), and delight yourselves (נפשכם) in rich food" (Isa 55:2). The prophet uses the metaphor "hearing is obedience," the consequences of which are described as eating and success. However, the pleasure of the נפש in this verse does not only refer to physical satisfaction. As we find in other sources, the נפש can also want experiential satisfaction that is described in sight or hearing terms: "As a deer longs for flowing streams, so my soul longs (נפשי תערג) for you, O God. My soul thirsts (צמאה נפשי) for God, for the living God. When shall I come and behold (אבוא ואראה) the face of God?" (Ps 42:2–3). Explicit comparison between physical and spiritual hunger/thirst and satisfaction is found in another prophecy: "The time is surely coming, says the Lord God, when I will send a famine (רעב) on the land; not a famine (רעב) of bread, or a thirst (צמא) for water, but of hearing (לשמע) the words of the Lord" (Amos 8:11). The last examples use eating imagery to describe a religious experience that borrows imagery from sight and hearing. This helps us better understand the synaesthetic combination in Ps 34: "O taste and see (טעמו וראו) that the Lord is good; happy are those who take refuge in him" (Ps 34:9).[136] While tasting here can be understood as inquiry or investigation ("taste and see" is similar to "go and see"), it could also express being satisfied through faith, as the following verses clarify: "O fear the Lord, you his holy ones, for those who fear him have no want (מחסור). The young lions suffer want and hunger (רשו ורעבו), but those who seek the LORD lack (יחסרו) no good thing" (vv. 10–11).

The associative link between taste and sight (and hearing) based on hunger and satisfaction imagery also appears in stories where eating leads to sight or to a kind of understanding and ability. In the Genesis Garden of Eden narrative, the serpent claims: "For God knows that when you eat (אכלכם) of it your eyes will be opened (ונפקחו עיניכם), and you will be like God, knowing (ידע) good and evil" (Gen 3:5). And indeed, that is the case:

> So when the woman saw that the tree was good for food (טוב...למאכל), and that it was a delight to the eyes (תאוה...לעינים), and that the tree was to be desired to make one wise (להשכיל), she took of its fruit and ate (ותאכל); and she also gave some to her husband, who was with her, and he ate (ויאכל). Then the eyes of both were opened (ותפקחנה עיני), and they knew (וידעו) that they were naked; and they sewed fig leaves together and made loincloths for themselves. (Gen 3:6–7)

---

136. For discussion, see Schökel, "Contemplar y Gustar."

In this episode, eating, sight, and knowledge are described as inter-twined. This is stressed by the inclusion of the three aspects in the words of the serpent (v. 5), in the description of the tree (v. 6), and in Adam and Eve's experience (v. 7). The image of Ezekiel eating the scroll seems more reasonable in light of this narrative.

Eating that leads to sight is not restricted to mythical times, or to prophecy. Jonathan's sudden power in the battle of Michmash is described similarly:

> But Jonathan had not heard his father charge the troops with the oath; so he extended the staff that was in his hand, and dipped the tip of it in the honeycomb, and put his hand to his mouth; and his eyes brightened (ותארנה).[137] Then one of the soldiers said, "Your father strictly charged (השבע השביע) the troops with an oath, saying, 'Cursed be anyone who eats food this day.' And so the troops are faint (ויעף)." Then Jonathan said, "My father has troubled the land; see (ראו) how my eyes have brightened (ארו עיני) because I tasted (טעמתי) a little of this honey." (1 Sam 14:27–29)

In this short paragraph, we find that Jonathan's power is his lightened eyes, in contrast to the faint people (יעף). That is because he has eaten and they have not. The irony is further stressed by the graphic and auditory similarity between the root "to place an oath" (שבע) and "to be full" (שבע). Finally, the reader is led to the conclusion that Jonathan is right, and, to use Qohelet's words: "Light is sweet, and it is pleasant for the eyes to see the sun" (ומתוק האור וטוב לעינים לראות את־השמש, Qoh 11:7).[138]

A further parallel between eating and other senses is evident in descriptions of gluttony as a metaphor for negative behaviour. For example, gluttony is contrasted to hearing (i.e. obedience): "They shall say to the elders of his town, 'This son of ours is stubborn and rebellious; he will not obey us (lit. listen, שמע בקלנו). He is a glutton and a drunkard (זולל וסבא)'" (Deut 21:20). Lack of obedience, is, therefore excessive eating, as well as lack of hearing.[139] These metaphors recur many times in biblical literature.[140] It seems to contrast eating and hearing, but the gluttony metaphor must be understood in the context of other images from the sensory category that describe evil behaviour, such as not

---

137. Such is the *qere*. The *ketib*, וַתֵּרְאָנָה (missing *yod*), means "my eyes have seen."

138. See also Goering, "Sapiential Synesthesia."

139. On excessive eating, see N. MacDonald, *Not Bread Alone: The Uses of Food in the Old Testament* (Oxford: Oxford University Press, 2008), 86–98.

140. Prov 23:20–21 and others.

walking straight or lack of attention.[141] A similar parallel is found with
sight: "Besides, all their days they eat in darkness (בחשך יאכל), in much
vexation and sickness and resentment" (Qoh 5:16).[142]

In all these instances, we see inappropriate use of the senses as a
metaphor for a negative way of life. This imagery is derived from, and is
contrasted with, the imagery of appropriate use of the senses as a sign of
life, just as we saw with eating and its parallel to sight: "…whenever a
man does eat and drink (אכל ושתה) and get enjoyment (lit. 'see good,'
וראה טוב) out of all his wealth, it is a gift of God" (Qoh 3:13, JPS).[143]
From these verses it is clear that eating, like sight-hearing, and kinaesthesia, is clearly a metaphor for a way of life. As the saying goes,
"Parents eat (יאכלו) sour grapes and their children's teeth are blunted"
(Jer 31:29, JPS; cf. Ezek 18:2).

The imagery of eating as a way of life parallel to hearing and sight is
correlated to the image of taste as substance and inner logic that appears
parallel to smell, with a similar meaning: "Moab has been at ease from
his youth, settled like wine on its dregs; he has not been emptied from
vessel to vessel, nor has he gone into exile; therefore his flavour (טעמו)
has remained and his aroma (וריחו) is unspoiled" (Jer 48:11). The prophet
uses colourful images to compare the qualities of wine with the qualities
of Moab. Interestingly, the use of concrete imagery from the field of
taste is quite rare, and appears only three more times in the Hebrew
Bible.[144] The meaning of the noun "taste" (טעם) is usually a derived
meaning that appears in descriptions of people, and especially the sense
of judgment and human awareness. The description of David in the court
of Achish serves as a good example: "So he concealed his good sense
(טעמו) from them; he feigned madness for their benefit. He scratched
marks on the doors of the gate and let his saliva run down his beard"
(1 Sam 21:13 [14], JPS).[145] This verse, like the verse that compares
Moab's character to the taste and aroma of wine, must be interpreted in
the context of the general meaning of taste as a sense of judgment and
logic: "Does not the ear test words as the palate tastes food?" (Job
12:11). Discernment is achieved through tasting and hearing, and therefore Job wonders: "Is wisdom with the aged, and understanding in length
of days?" (v. 12). How can the elders who lose some of their sensory
abilities have wisdom? The answer comes in v. 20: "[God] deprives of

141.   For more, see pp. 160–62, 177–79.
142.   Similarly Qoh 2:24; 8:15.
143.   See below, pp. 178–82, 149–54.
144.   Exod 16:31; Num 11:8; Job 6:6.
145.   Cf. Ps 34:1.

speech (שפה) those who are trusted, and takes away the discernment (טעם) of the elders." Job describes the sense of taste and hearing as tools for understanding the world, since both are part of the normal workings of the world. God the creator has the power to give sensory ability, but also to take it away. Taste in this verse can be interpreted as a tool for understanding and judgment, but also as a sense that distinguishes food.

The description of the loss of the sense of taste in old age is found with this dual meaning also in the words of Barzillai to David: "How many years are left to me that I should go up with your majesty to Jerusalem? I am now eighty years old. Can I tell the difference (האדע) between good and bad (בין־טוב לרע)? Can your servant taste (יטעם) what he eats and drinks? Can I still listen (אשמע) to the singing of men and women? Why then should your servant continue to be a burden to my lord the king?" (2 Sam 19:35–36). Barzillai claims that his old age has blunted his sense of judgment, as the parallel between eating and understanding what is good and what is evil fits the mental context of eating. Yet the second part of Barzillai's complaint is clearly about his lack of ability to enjoy the extra privileges offered in the king's palace.[146] Some translations read all his words as a description of enjoyment; note, for example, NRSV, where האדע בין־טוב לרע is translated "can I discern what is pleasant and what is not?" (v. 35). Such translation, however, ignores the semantic load of the phrase טוב ורע which elsewhere in the Hebrew Bible has either moral or intellectual load. This verse demonstrates the associative link between taste and hearing, as well as further clarifies the metaphor "tasting is discernment."

Before summarizing the data about the sense of taste/eating and the sensorium, I should mention the strong associative link eating–sexuality. As the following two examples show, these two are strongly correlated. The finest example is found in the Joseph narrative:

> So he left all that he had in Joseph's charge; and, with him there, he had no concern for anything but the food that he ate (ולא ידע עמו מאומה כי אם־הלחם אשר־הוא אוכל). Now Joseph was handsome and good-looking... "My master has no concern about anything in the house, and he has put everything that he has in my hand. He is not greater in this house than I am, nor has he kept back anything from me except yourself (ולא־חשך ממני מאומה כי אם־אותך), because you are his wife..." (Gen 39:6, 8–9)

In the description of Joseph by the narrator, and by himself, only one difference is evident—the thing over which Potiphar did not give Joseph control. In v. 6, it is his food, while in v. 9 it is his wife. The parallelism

---

146. Yet see the following discussion in Chapter 4, n. 82.

created between food and sexuality was clear to interpreters long ago.[147] Such an associative link is the common sense that yields the following riddle, and its answer:

> Three things are too wonderful for me;
> four I do not understand:
> the way of an eagle in the sky,
> the way of a snake on a rock,
> the way of a ship on the high seas,
> and the way of a man with a girl.
> This is the way of an adulteress: she eats (אכלה), and wipes her mouth,
> and says, "I have done no wrong." (Prov 30:18–20)

Whether we see v. 20 as the original explanation to the riddle, or whether we find the proximity of it to vv. 18–19 as an associative, or even interpretive, move, the euphemism, used for the sexual act here, is eating. This use of clean language is part of a broader semantic overlapping between eating and sexuality. Appropriate or inappropriate behaviour can be described by similes of eating and sexuality: "They shall eat (יאכלו), but not be satisfied (ישבעו); they shall play the whore (הזנו), but not multiply (יפרצו); because they have forsaken the Lord to devote themselves to whoredom" (Hos 4:10). Eating and having sexual intercourse are similar since they lead to a desired consequence when done appropriately. Here we note another similarity between the two actions, related also to the tactile sense, namely, the large number of prohibitions that appear in the Hebrew Bible regarding eating, sexuality, and touch (impurity and purity).[148] This contrasts to the only commandment that prohibits smell (Exod 30:38). It seems that this group (eating, sexuality, touch) creates a conceptual category that does not directly parallel the sensory category.[149]

A further parallel between eating and a portrayal of the senses is the assumed root of "to sense" (חוש) itself: "There is nothing worthwhile for a man but to eat and drink and afford himself enjoyment (והראה את־נפשו טוב) with his means. And even that, I noted, comes from God. For who eats (יאכל) and who enjoys (יחוש) but myself?" (Qoh 2:24–25, JPS). The meaning of the rare root חוש is subject to much debate. Some interpret the word as meaning anxiety, while others interpret it as enjoyment.[150] The occurrence of the root in Job 20:2 suggests a meaning

---

147. See, for example, Rahshi for these verses in *MG*.

148. Most notably, but not restricted to, Priestly literature.

149. More will be said on this matter in the conclusion to the present chapter (111–13).

150. Kruger, *Qohelet*, 59.

of feeling, similar to the Modern Hebrew meaning of the word.[151] Although the root חוש appears twice alongside eating, its ambiguity makes it hard to draw conclusions.

In summary, only a relatively small number of parallels or word pairs are common to taste and the other senses. Moreover, most examples presented above were synaesthetic examples, where eating (more than taste) serves as simile or metaphor for other senses or in a metaphor that other senses also provide. Hence the evidence for the associative link with the sensorium is less direct and the associative impression is weak compared to the data presented in previous sections. Nevertheless, there is a semantic correlation between sight, kinaesthesia, smell, and speech, particularly when using synaesthetic imagery. In most of these images, adjectives from the world of eating and taste are used to portray other sensory actions. The discussion of the definition of the sensorium in Chapter 3, will address this question again.

Olfactory

One problem with presenting the sense of smell in our discussion is the small number of biblical verses that mention smell, scents, or any other words linked to olfaction. There is also a paucity of occurrences of these words and expressions linked to the other senses. But the sense of smell does appear explicitly in the two verses we mentioned earlier, ones in which smell is listed to the other senses. In Ps 115:4–7, smell is parallel to speech, sight, hearing, touch, and walking. In Deut 4:28, smell is parallel to sight, hearing, and eating. The sense of smell also appears in connection with other senses in the story of the stolen blessing. Isaac smells Jacob's clothes and blesses him: "So he came near and kissed him; and he smelled the smell (וירח את-ריח) of his garments, and blessed him, and said, 'Ah (ראה), the smell (ריח) of my son is like the smell (ריח) of a field that the Lord has blessed'" (Gen 27:27). From this story it is evident that the use of the sense of smell complemented and paralleled hearing, taste, and touch.[152] This verse also presents us with a linguistic synaesthesia that links smell and sight in the expression "See, the smell of my son."[153] This imagery demonstrates the centrality of the sight motif and its absence in the story. The use of the different senses—including

151. Cf. Job 20:2–3, where the word חושי is translated "agitation" (NRSV), "feelings" (JPS), "haste" (KJV). See *MKCS*, 137 n. 43. See also nn. 10, 53.

152. See Malul, "Fabrication of Evidence," 215; cf. Bar-Am, "The Story of the Five Senses," 77–78.

153. See further Kedar-Kopfstein, "Synästhesien," 55.

the sense of smell—in this story, effectively replaces the use of the sense of sight.

Another synaesthetic expression that links smell and sight is found in the Exodus narrative. After Pharaoh increase the burden on the Israelite, they say to Moses and Aaron: "…The Lord look upon you and judge! You have brought us into bad odour (הבאשתם את־ריחנו) with Pharaoh (בעיני פרעה) and his officials (ובעיני עבדיו), and have put a sword in their hand to kill us" (Exod 5:21). In this phrase, Israel's image is described as a bad odour, coming through the eyes, rather than the nostrils of Pharaoh and his officials. The phrase blends together the idiom "in so and so's sight" (בעיני), which is a metaphoric idiom—"sight is subjective opinion" with the metaphor "stench is immoral behaviour."[154] The second metaphor assumes someone is there to smell (= judge) the moral behaviour, and therefore, when that someone sees the behaviour, sight and smelling are associatively linked.

Similarly, bad odour is perceived by hearing in the account of Absalom's rebellion: "Ahithophel said to Absalom, 'Go in to your father's concubines, the ones he has left to look after the house; and all Israel will hear (ושמע) that you have made yourself odious (נבאשת) to your father, and the hands of all who are with you will be strengthened'" (2 Sam 16:21). Here too, the verse should not be interpreted literally as making a stench, but as the status of the relationship between Absalom and his father, David, which is publicized via rumour.[155] Interestingly, the unique use of באש Niphal serves as a complex evaluation of Ahithophel's advice, and Absalom's deeds. In the three appearances of this form of the root (here, and 1 Sam 13:4; 2 Sam 10:6), it describes becoming odious to the other party, meaning to be rejected by it. Yet the choice of root, which links it to odour, is crucial, as other roots such as מאס could be used instead. Using באש puts a question mark on whether the act leading to it was appropriate or not. For our purpose, either the immoral behaviour, or the impossible status of the relationship, are perceived in this example as being heard, and the associative link between smell and hearing is created. In these two verses, the actions of sight and hearing are described as investigative and discerning actions achieved by smell.

Another example of sight and hearing linked with discernment, and also connected to smell, gives a more structured parallelism of the three:

154.   For the phrase "in the eyes of" (בעיני), see Livnat, "*Be'einey*," as well as 158–62, below.

155.   For the synaesthetic metaphor in both cases, see Kedar-Kopfstein, "Synästhesien," 54.

He shall sense (lit. "smell," והריחו) the truth by his reverence for the Lord:
He shall not judge by what his eyes behold (מראה עיניו),
Nor decide by what his ears (משמע אזניו) perceive. (Isa 11:3, JPS)

This much-debated verse has suffered emendation attempts alongside abstract translation.[156] Yet examination of its structure shows a simple parallelism, whereby smelling through reverence of the Lord parallels seeing through the eyes and hearing through the ears. Smelling, sight, and hearing all mark judgment. However, judgment through smell is reserved to a future leader, in a utopian time, when "The wolf shall dwell with the lamb, the leopard lie down with the kid; the calf, the beast of prey, and the fatling together, with a little boy to herd them" (v. 6).[157]

Another correlation between smell and sight is found via the syntagmatic principle. In the Hebrew Bible, the root חרה, commonly translated "to burn," yet probably meaning "to cringe," "to shut,"[158] is closely linked to the nose (אף). In 53 out of 82 occurrences, חרה (Qal) has as its subject "nose" (אף); the only occurrence of חרה Hiphil (Job 19:11) has the same subject. The phrase describes both divine, and human anger: "The Lord was angry (ויחר־אף) with his people and he abhorred His inheritance" (Ps 106:40, JPS); "Saul flew into a rage (ויחר־אף) against Jonathan. 'You son of a perverse, rebellious woman!'..." (1 Sam 20:30).[159] Such repetition creates a syntagmatic link between the two words. The syntagmatic link enables one of the words to carry the meaning of the whole phrase: "...So Cain was very angry (ויחר), and his countenance fell" (Gen 4:5).[160] In two cases, however, we find the verb חרה is coupled with the eyes, rather than the nose: "...Let not my lord

156. For the case of emendation, see J. Unterman, "The (Non)Sense of Smell in Isaiah 11:3," *Hebrew Studies* 33 (1992): 17–23 (18–20). A rejection of the view is found in Ritchie, "The Nose Knows," 66–70. A fuller discussion of the verse is found in my dissertation, "The Sensorium," 181–82. A similar discussion is found in Kurek-Chomycz, "Making Scents of Revelation," 10–12.

157. Cf. early Jewish interpretation as found in Sanhedrin 93, p. 2.

158. Arnold Ehrlich (*Miqra Kifshuto*) *apud* and further supported by Greenstein, "Developments in the Study of Language," 456. For more on the matter, see pp. 149–50.

159. Similarly, the derived nouns חרון and חרי are closely linked to the nose. Thirty-three out of 41 occurrences of the substantive חרון are part of the phrase חרון אף, and all occurrences of חרי are part of the phrase חרי אף (Exod 11:8; Deut 29:23; 1 Sam 20:34; Isa 7:4; Lam 2:3; 2 Chr 25:10). The meaning of חרון and חרי is normally described as "heat" or "blaze," yet should be translated "anger." See the above note for references.

160. But see M. I. Gruber, "Was Cain Angry or Depressed? Background of a Biblical Murder," *BAR* 6, no. 6 (1980): 35–36.

be angry (יחר בעיני אדני) that I cannot rise before you, for the way of women is upon me..." (Gen 31:35); "And now do not be distressed, or angry according to your own judgment[161] (יחר בעיניכם), because you sold me here; for God sent me before you to preserve life" (Gen 45:5). In both verses the addressee is asked not to be angry (יחר), with an uncommon complement "his eyes." In the first verse it stresses Laban's judgment, in the second, the brothers'. In both cases, an association to "nose" (אף) is suggested, and an associative link between smell and sight is created.

Finally, we find that the olfactory sense is not linguistically elaborated in Biblical Hebrew, and therefore its associative links with the sensorium is hard to establish. There is, however, sufficient information to point to at least two associative patterns: smell–taste, and smell–sight. Less obvious links are to hearing, and to the sensorium as a whole (Deut 4:28; Ps 115:4–7). As with the sense of taste, only the discussion of the definition of the sensorium will assist us in determining its place within the category.

Touch

Just as there is a hazy semantic boundary between taste and eating in biblical language, so the semantic boundary between feeling and touch is also hazy. Moreover, just as there are more references to eating than to tasting in the Hebrew Bible, so there are more references to touching than to the tactile experience. The verb "to feel" (tactically, מוש/משש) is mostly used alongside other modalities. Is Ps 115:4–7, the tactile sense parallels speech, sight, hearing, smelling, and walking. Apart from these verses, the typical context of the root is sensing when sight cannot be used. The first occurrence of this root in found in the stolen blessing passage. Isaac, whose eyes no longer function, feels Jacob in order to identify him (Gen 27:12, 21). Laban, who is searching for the idols that are hidden and cannot be seen, feels the tent (Gen 31:34, 37). Samson too uses his hands instead of his eyes in order to be supported by the pillars of the temple (Judg 15:26). In non-prose contexts, the מוש/משש is associated with faulty sight, and symbolizes the action of the blind person groping around in the dark: "You shall grope (ממשש) about at noon as blind people grope (ימשש העור) in darkness, but you shall be unable to find your way; and you shall be continually abused and robbed, without

---

161. My translation—the one provided by NRSV (and others), "angry with yourself," fails to comprehend the contrast between the brothers' subjective view and God's plan.

anyone to help" (Deut 28:29).[162] Apparently feeling becomes a token for the blind and for walking in the dark, which are signs of folly: "They meet with darkness in the daytime, and grope (ימששו) at noonday as in the night" (Job 5:14; cf. 12:25). The ultimate similarity between the blind man sensing, or sensing in darkness, and darkness itself, is the synaesthetic description of the plague of darkness: "…Stretch out your hand toward heaven so that there may be darkness over the land of Egypt, a darkness that can be felt" (וימש חשך, Exod 10:21). The plague is a total darkness, so dark that it cannot be experienced through sight, only through feeling. The parallelism and interchangeability of feeling and sight here strengthen the perception that they are similar actions, and belong to the same category.

In Ps 115:7, feeling is the act of the hand: "They have hands, but do not feel (ימישון)…"[163] The hand as the tactile organ is mentioned elsewhere in parallel to other sensory organs. For example: "Those who walk (הלך) righteously and speak (דבר) what is right, who reject gain from extortion and keep their hands (נער כפיו)[164] from accepting bribes, who stop their ears (אטם אזניו משמע) against plots of murder and shut their eyes (עצם עיניו מראות) against contemplating evil" (NIV, Isa 33:15). Some of the expressions in the verse can be understood as symbolic legal actions. But for our purposes, the fact that these actions appear in juxtaposition, even if they were not actually implemented together, demonstrates that they are semantically linked. This verse contains images of walking and speech (which have positive connotations), and touch, hearing, and sight (which have negative connotations). As we have seen, these images originate in a perception of the senses as an indicator of a way of life, and as a sign of the action's ethical value. The righteous are judged by their all-encompassing somatic behaviour.[165] Similar comparison between the hands and the eyes is found in the legal context: "…Our hands (ידינו) did not shed this blood, nor did our eyes see (ועינינו לא ראו) it done" (Deut 21:7, JPS). These words express non-involvement in the crime, non-involvement in touching, and non-involvement (no knowledge) in seeing. The hands and the eyes are paralleled, but also carry similar semantic load.

162. Note the associative pattern blindness–darkness–inability demonstrated in this verse.
163. For the somatic aspect of the senses, see pp. 114–30.
164. For the legal background of the phrase, see *MKCS*, 215–37.
165. Cf. Prov 6:16–19, discussed in this chapter, pp. 90–91.

Another parallel between the hand and a sensory organ, this time the ear, is found in the context of divine aid:[166] "No, the Lord's arm (יד) is not too short to save, or his ear (אזנו) too dull to hear" (Isa 59:1, JPS). In this parallelism, the hand and the ear are compared, and consequently the action of the hand (touch) and the action of the ear (hearing) are associated. Elsewhere the touch of God and his sight mark his power: "[Yahweh] who looks (המביט) on the earth and it trembles, who touches (יגע) the mountains and they smoke" (Ps 104:32). There is no evidence in this verse that God's tactile abilities are more concrete than his sight abilities. Both are images of his power. This example adds to the previously discussed verses that show that despite the relatively few examples, touch and sight are associated in the Hebrew Bible.

A final link to be explored is the strong semantic correlation between the tactile sense and the kinaesthetic sense, expressed in a use of joint roots, similar to hearing and speech. The main meaning of the common root נגע is "to touch."[167] Interestingly, one of the most common meanings derived from this root is arriving in a physical space or time space.[168] This recurs in different *binyanim*, and has a distinct kinaesthetic character: "If they say to us, 'Wait (דמו) until we come (הגיענו) to you,' then we will stand still (עמדנו) in our place, and we will not go up (נעלה) to them" (1 Sam 14:9). In this verse, the root נגע (Hiphil) parallels "going up," a clear kinaesthetic verb. The root is also contrasted to the roots דמם ("to stand still"/"to be silent") and עמד, "to stand," both of which come from the world of mobility. This meaning of kinaesthesia is also found in the Qal and parallels other verbs. One example is the verb "to be lifted" (נשא): "We tried to heal Babylon, but she could not be healed. Forsake her, and let each of us go to our own country; for her judgment has reached up (נגע) to heaven and has been lifted up (נשא) even to the skies" (Jer 51:9). While the movement in the root נגע here is clearly derived from physical touch, it does parallel a kinaesthetic verse, and clarifies the associative link between the two. Finally, נגע Hiphil receives temporal meanings: "The time has come (בא), the day draws near (הגיע)…" (Ezek 7:12).[169]

---

166. See further pp. 130–41, below.

167. L. Schwienhorst, "נָגַע *nāgaʿ*; נֶגַע *negaʿ*," *TDOT* 9:203–9 (204–5).

168. Further details are found in ibid., 207.

169. We see this same phenomenon with the verb "to harm," פגע, which has a tactile sense. The same root can denote "to arrive," and therefore to mix the tactile and the kinaesthetic.

Lastly, the root נגע, "to touch," and its parallel בוא, "to come," can both have sexual meaning: "So is he who sleeps (lit. comes, הַבָּא) with his neighbour's wife; no one who touches (הַנֹּגֵעַ) her will go unpunished" (Prov 6:29). The seaming parallel between touch and kinaesthesia in this verse is the euphemistic description of sexual intercourse. At the same, time it demonstrates the associative link tactile = kinaesthesia. This is similar to the euphemistic use of eating we described before.[170]

To sum up, touch is associatively related to sight, hearing, and kinaesthesia in a very clear way. It also shares some similarities with the sense of taste: both serve as a euphemism for sexual intercourse; both are regulated by biblical law.

Towards a Septasensory Model

> The underlying premise of this epistemology is fundamental: one can separate thought from feeling and action… Slowly, I uncovered an important rule: one cannot separate thought from feeling and action; they are inextricably linked… This fundamental rule in epistemological humility taught me that in Songhay, one can taste kinship, smell witches, and hear the ancestors.[171]

Stoller's comments about the perception of the senses among the Songhay reflect the way we should approach the question of the components of the sensory category in the Hebrew Bible. We must put aside our stereotypes based on the pentasensory model and subject the biblical text to a more objective examination. The expectation that the Hebrew Bible will reveal five senses corresponding to the Western-modern perception is "to elevate one's blindness or dumbness to a universal rule of perception," to use Barthes's expression.[172] This chapter has shown how difficult it is to determine how many senses there are in the Hebrew Bible. So far we have identified seven senses that are correlated semantically and associatively in a number of different ways: sight, hearing, kinaesthesia, speech, taste/eating, smell, and the sense of touch. There exists a powerful associative link between hearing and speech, one which may even have been perceived as two elements of a single sense. Another difficulty that has emerged in our discussion is that, linguistically, some

---

170. For further discussion, see *MKCS*, Chapter 5.
171. Stoller, *Taste of Ethnographic Things*, 7–8.
172. R. Barthes, *Mythologies* (trans. A. Lavers; London: J. Cape, 1972), 35. Interestingly, in a chapter titled "Blind and Dumb Criticism" Barth talks about speech as a means of perception. It seems that even within Western culture there are variations in sensory perception (see n. 17, above).

senses are far more prevalent than others. And while a semantic correlation does exist among these seven senses, some have a very strong associative correlation, while others have a more tenuous link. We have seen several examples of a strong semantic correlation between some of the senses and sexuality. Could the sex organs have been perceived as sensory organs? Could sexuality have been perceived as a sense?

Meir Malul regards sexuality as a sense in its own right. The male and female sex organs are sensory organs, similar to other senses and organs:

> The sex organs may be regarded as part and parcel of the human epistemic sensorial apparatus, besides such "classic" senses as sight, hearing, taste and smell, the sex organs coming closer to the tactile sense in their operation in the process of carnal knowledge. The sexual activity would then be perceived as an epistemic activity as much as the activities of looking, hearing and touching.[173]

Malul sees a strong associative correlation between sexuality and some of the senses, a correlation indicated by the use of the same tools that demonstrate the link between senses in this chapter. Linguistically and semantically, sexuality is parallel to eating and touching. Like sensory experience, the sexual act is described in terms of knowledge and learning.[174] A semantic parallel exists between the male sex organ and sensory organs such as the ear and the heart (mind). For example, all three can be described as "uncircumcised" (ערל).[175] We also see terms from the mentioned senses as euphemisms for the sexual act and sexuality, for example, "to see" (ראה), "to eat" (אכל), "to touch" (נגע), "to come" (בוא).[176] This raises the question: Is sexuality the eighth sense in the biblical categorization of the sensorium?

Before attempting to answer this question, let us examine a common linguistic phenomenon, the euphemism.[177] Fundamentally, a euphemism replaces words deemed unsuitable in one semantic field with words from another semantic field. One of the most prevalent uses of euphemism in the Hebrew Bible is in sexual imagery.[178] We often find the sex act or sex organs portrayed in words that usually mean something else: the verb שכב

---

173. *MKCS*, 313.

174. See the following chapter.

175. Malul, "Piercing a Slave's Ear," 149–51.

176. Cf. Malul, "Holistic-Integrative Investigation."

177. For a survey of euphemism in the Hebrew Bible, see S. M. Paul, "Euphemism and Dysphemism," *EncJud* 6:959–61.

178. See S. M. Paul, "The Shared Legacy of Sexual Metaphors and Euphemisms in Mesopotamian and Biblical Literature," in Parpola and Whiting, eds., *Sex and Gender in the Ancient Near East*, 489–98.

could mean "to lie down"; the verb ענה could mean "to open"; the verb צחק could mean "to laugh"; and the verb אחז could mean "to hold." All these can mean (in the Qal or the Piel) "to have sex," or "to fondle."[179] Different organs are used to portray sex organs: "thigh," "knees," and "bosom" describe the male sex organ, while "mouth" describes the female.[180] The use of euphemism is particularly and irrefutably prevalent when using sensory terms to describe sex. Indeed, the interpretation of the associative correlation created by this phenomenon may help us determine whether sex belongs in the biblical sensory category.

Sexual imagery in the Hebrew Bible can be interpreted either through euphemisms or through synaesthesia. If we use euphemisms to explain sexual imagery, a category gap is created between the sexual indicator which cannot be openly described, and the specific sensory indicator. This conclusion is supported by the fact that we do not find a specific vocabulary for sex acts, unlike the vocabulary used to describe the other senses. We also find no overt linguistic parallel between the main words used to describe sex organs—ערוה, מבושים, and the main sensory organs. However, if we interpret sexual imagery through synaesthesia, the frequent association between sexuality and sensuality supports the notion that they both belong to a single category. Does our perception of sexual imagery as euphemism rather than synaesthesia reflect a stereotype that makes it difficult for us to regard sexuality as a sense? There would appear to be no irrefutable answer to the question of sexuality as the eighth sense. I do, however, tend to see, for the mentioned reason, sexuality as shared definition of the sensory category, like knowledge, help, moral judgment etc., rather than an item within it.

The question of whether sexuality belongs to the biblical sensory category parallels the difficulty in determining how many senses there are in the Hebrew Bible. While the multitude of associations among the different senses indicates the intentional or unintentional existence of a sensory category in the Hebrew Bible, it is still difficult to determine exactly which senses belong to this category. We can talk about sensation with all the body, which also includes the sexual experience. As in

---

179. All in the context of sexuality: "to lie down" (שכב, Gen 34:7; Lev 15:33; Num 5:19; Isa 13:16 and many more); "to come, arrive" (בוא, Gen 29:21; Deut 22:13; 2 Sam 3:7; Ezek 23:44 and elsewhere); "to open" (ענה Piel, Gen 34:2; Deut 22:24; 2 Sam 13:32 and more); "to enjoy" (צחק Piel, Gen 21:9; 26:8; 39:17; Exod 32:6); "to grasp" (תפש, Gen 29:12; Deut 22:28).

180. In this respect, see "the thigh" (ירך, Gen 24:9; 46:26; Judg 8:30); "knees" (ברך, Gen 50:23; Job 3:12); "the bosom" (חיק, Gen 16:5; Deut 13:7; 2 Sam 12:8; Mic 7:5 and others); "the mouth" (פה, Prov 30:20).

every culture, the culture reflected in the Hebrew Bible gives verbal expression to only some of the physical experiences that reflect the categorization and rationalization of reality. An analysis of the linguistic associations among the senses is not sufficient to answer these questions. We also need to examine the conceptual common denominator among the different senses, or the sensory category. In the next chapter I will present the main components of this category. As described above, these components will include the repeated reflection of ideas regarding the senses and their essence;[181] and use of a vocabulary of the different senses for similar images and contexts.[182] Only after examining the definition of the category, and the level of agreement for each of the seven mentioned modalities to the category, will we be able finally to decide regarding the existence of a *septasensory* model in biblical epistemology.

181. Mainly the Somatic aspect of the sensorium, and its divine source.
182. Mainly the common metaphors to the various senses.

Chapter 3

THE SENSORIUM: DEFINITION

In the previous chapter I discussed the sensorium as reflected in the Hebrew Bible, and identified seven associatively linked senses. I also established a need to explore the contextual patterns[1] in which these senses are mentioned, and for which they serve as metaphors and idioms in order to establish a septasensory model for biblical epistemology. The current chapter will, therefore, answer several questions: What are the common contextual patterns to the seven mentioned modalities? Do these contextual patterns confirm the septasensory model? And, finally, what is the definition of the sensory category in the Hebrew Bible? As I pointed out earlier, there is no general term in the Hebrew Bible to describe the sensorium, nor is there any consistent reflective writing about the senses.[2] However, as I hope to demonstrate in the following pages, a sense-like category did exist, albeit intuitively, in the culture reflected in the Hebrew Bible. The description of the contextual patterns, alongside some common knowledge associative models, will help us arrive at a dictionary definition of the word "sense," if it had existed in Biblical Hebrew.

The following discussion focuses on two main characteristics that I have observed. The first section, "Sense and Soma," shows how the actions of the different senses, actions that depend on bodily organs, are described in the Hebrew Bible. I will show how in its biblical meaning, sense is primarily a somatic experience. I will examine each sensory organ separately, and show how these organs are similarly linked to their respective senses. The second part, "Sense and Sovereignty," presents a number of contexts in which metaphors and imagery related to the vocabulary of the different senses is present; the power to help and to harm, the ability to learn, understand, and know, the sensory aspect of

1. For a definition, see pp. 60–62, above.
2. Namely, literature which is intended to write about epistemology of the senses, as found in some ancient Greek philosophical writings.

emotional experience, and sensory idioms for moral judgment.[3] I will also suggest that all these contexts point to a biblical perception of sensation as experience, ability, and sovereignty. The chapter will conclude with a demonstration of how the accumulated data can be used to define the biblical category of senses and its content. A third aspect of the sensorium will be dealt with in the next chapter, "Theology of the Senses." The notion that the senses are a divine creation will expand our understanding of the biblical sensorium and its definition. To clarify: the topic in the next chapter is separated from the present discussion for the sake of the logical argument, rather than because of methodological reasons.

Sense and Soma

An examination of the linguistic evidence associated with the senses presents several challenges, quite apart from the lack of a linguistic term for "sense." In fact, the Hebrew Bible offers no nouns that relate to the senses, such as "sight" or "smell,"[4] nor does it offer any general terms that describe the sensorium. When we do find a phrase that could be interpreted as a general statement about the character of the senses, the focus is on the sensory organs: "The hearing ear and the seeing eye—the Lord has made them both" (Prov 20:12). This proverb could easily be rephrased as "God has created sight and hearing," but, indeed, in the Hebrew Bible sensory experience is described through sensory verbs and bodily organs. The link between the senses and the organs indicates that in the perception reflected in the Hebrew Bible, sensation is seen as a somatic experience, an embodied experience.

---

3. Any choice of contextual pattern is modelled by the scholar, and not only by the data. Semantic fields are influenced by the scholar, as well as by the data; see T. Sovran, *Semantic Fields: A Linguistic-Philosophical Study of Meaning Relations* (Jerusalem: Magnes, 2000), 15–28. For a similar discussion of the senses within three overlapping semantic fields: knowledge, control, and sexuality, see *MKCS*. The current dissection is different and does not follow only semantic reasoning.

4. The exemptions are "the seeing (ראותה) of the eyes" (Qoh 5:10), and "walking" (הליכה, Nah 2:6). Generally, using the infinitive to express gerundive in Biblical Hebrew is limited (see Gesenius §113). It seems that this phenomena should be explained by contextual reasoning (the various genres in the Hebrew Bible do not require such usage), rather than by cultural reasoning (as if there is no abstract perception of action in biblical thought). And see also Barr, *Semantics*, 15; A. Gibson, *Biblical Semantic Logic: A Preliminary Analysis* (New York: St. Martin's, 1981), 13–16.

In the following pages I will show how each of the senses identified in the previous chapter is associated with a bodily organ that controls the sensory ability. These organs appear as agents of action, as the subject in grammatical terms, in verses that incorporate sensory verbs. These same organs are also described as agents of sensory actions, even in the absence of specific sensory verbs. At first glance, the question of the correlation between sense and organ seems redundant. Isn't it clear that the eye sees, the nose smells, and the ear hears? Nevertheless, in fact, this question is far from simple. The tongue, which is perceived as a taste organ in modern thought, indicates speech in the Hebrew Bible. The mouth serves to indicate two sensations: taste and speech. The senses of touch, posture, and mobility would appear to belong to the whole body, but the biblical text makes a direct correlation between these sensations and specific organs: the hand and the foot. And so, even if some sensations are experienced through the whole body, their verbalization is markedly related to a specific organ. Furthermore, the mentioned sensory organs are all used as synecdoche to the actor, be it human or divine, in a way similar to the mind and the soul.[5]

The Eye
An examination of many biblical verses makes it clear that the eye is described in the Hebrew Bible as the sight organ.[6] There is a frequent combination of the noun "eye" (עין) and the verb "to see" (ראה): "Look, my eye has seen all this, my ear has heard and understood it" (Job 13:1). These two words occur together in various phrases: נשא עיניו וירא: "...Abraham raised his eyes and saw the place far away" (Gen 22:4, my translation), already discussed;[7] הרואות pron. suffix + עינים: "...your own eyes have seen everything that the Lord your God has done..." (Deut 3:21), a phrase which denotes personal testimony; and מראה עינים, "...because of the dread that your heart shall feel and the sights that your eyes shall see..." (Deut 28:67).[8] In addition to ראה, the eye also appears parallel to the verb נבט ("to look down"): "Lift up your eyes to the heavens, and look (והביטו) at the earth beneath..." (Isa 51:6). Even in verses where the eye is not mentioned as the subject of an action, there is an assumption of a seeing organ, in particular when the noun gets a

---

5. See pp. 175–82, below.
6. F. J. Stendebach, "עֵין *ʿayin*," *TDOT* 11:28–45 (29).
7. See pp. 58–59, above.
8. These terms and phrases are quite common, hence the lack of further reference.

complement preposition and object: "For my eyes are on (עיני על) all their ways; they are not hidden from my presence, nor is their iniquity concealed from my sight (עיני)" (Jer 16:17);[9] "A land that the Lord your God looks after (דרש). The eyes of the Lord your God are always on it (עיני...בה), from the beginning of the year to the end of the year" (Deut 11:12); "But you, my lord the king—the eyes of all Israel are on you (עיני...עליך) to tell them who shall sit on the throne of my lord the king after him" (1 Kgs 1:20). As these verses show clearly, the eye marks seeing, but also any act for which seeing serves as an idiom, such as providence and authority. As Stendebach points out, the concrete use of the eye as a sensory and sight organ appears in only a small proportion of the verses, while derived meanings are the majority.[10]

To supplement Stendebach—it seems that the semantic expansion of the eye as the seat of the personality, thought, and knowledge, the source of emotions and judgment,[11] is closely linked, and fundamentally based on similar derived meanings for sight verbs. All these images are effectively based on sight as the central sense in biblical perception.[12] The eye represents the sight action so frequently that there is no real differentiation between the derived meanings associated with the word eye, and the derived meanings of sight verbs, the most important of which is the verb "to see" (ראה). An example of a derived meaning, where sight is not to be taken literally, is the meaning of desires, particularly sexual desires, which is associated with the semantic field of sight. This meaning can be expressed in the Hebrew Bible using the verb "to see" (ראה), or the phrase "to lift the eye towards (someone)."[13] This is just one of many examples of a close eye–sight parallel in biblical perception. Finally, it is worth noting that phrases such as "open his eye" (פתח/פקח עין), which mean "to see," highlight the somatic element of sensory perception in biblical epistemology.[14]

9. Cf. Job 24:23.
10. Stendebach, *TDOT* 11:31.
11. Ibid., 11:31–33.
12. For more on this matter, see Chapter 5.
13. For ראה, see Gen 34:1–2; 38:2; Judg 14:1–2; 16:1 and elsewhere. For נשא עין אל, see Gen 39:7; Ezek 23:27. See also S. M. Paul, "Euphemistically 'Speaking' and a Covetous Eye," *HAR* 14 (1994): 193–204 (198–200).
14. Gen 21:19; 2 Kgs 6:17; Isa 42:7; Jer 32:19; Zech 12:4; Job 14:3 and many more. Cf. pp. 71–72, above.

The Ear

Like the eye–sight correlation, the ear–hearing correlation would seem to be self-evident. In the Hebrew Bible, the ear is a hearing organ,[15] and only in a small number of biblical verses does the ear appear as an organ unconnected with hearing.[16] The root "to hear" (שמע) is frequently used as a description of the action of the ear (אזן): "But to this day the Lord has not given you a mind to understand, or eyes to see, or ears to hear" (Deut 29:3); "… according to all that we have heard with our ears" (2 Sam 7:22). In other verses, the root שמע is parallel to the ear, so that the meaning of the ear as a hearing organ is expressed via parallelism: "Hear (שמעת) my plea; Do not shut your ear (תעלם אזנך) to my groan, to my cry!" (Lam 3:56, JPS).[17] Similarly, the hearing ear parallels "to listen" (קשב): "…the ears of those who have hearing will listen" (תקשבנה, Isa 32:3);[18] "My child, be attentive (הקשיבה) to my wisdom; incline your ear (הט־אזנך) to my understanding" (Prov 5:1).[19] Finally, the denominative verb "to hear" (אזן Hiphil) is derived from the noun "ear" (אֹזֶן): "they have ears (אזנים), but they do not hear (יאזינו)…" (Ps 135:17). The hearing organ is becoming the hearing experience.[20]

Another example where the ear is primarily perceived as a hearing organ (without a hearing verb) is the phrase "in the ears of" (pron. suffix + אזן + ב), used to describe a hearing agent. Speaking is addressed to the ear.[21] Speaking into the ears appears in such phrases as: "When Samuel had heard (וישמע) all the words of the people, he repeated (וידברם) them in the ears of the Lord (באזני יהוה)" (1 Sam 8:21);[22] "Go and proclaim

15. Shupak, *Where Can Wisdom Be Found?*, 277–78; Wolff, *Anthropology of the Old Testament*, 75–76.

16. BDB, 23 counts 15 out of 157: Gen 35:4; Exod 21:6; 32:2, 3; Lev 8:23, 24; 14:14, 17, 25, 28; Deut 15:17; Ezek 16:12; 23:23; Amos 3:12; Prov 26:17. For a discussion of the difference between sight and hearing, cf. Carasik, *Theologies of the Mind*, 36–40.

17. There are many more examples. Note how shutting the ear is expressed by the verb עלם, "to make hidden," which associates the phrase with sight.

18. Cf. Pss 10:17; 130:2; Prov 2:2; Neh 1:6, 11; 9:34; 2 Chr 6:40; 7:15.

19. Cf. Jer 6:10.

20. In contrast to other denominative verbs, such as רגל Piel (from "foot"), or עין (from "eye"), which go further away from the original, concrete meaning of everyday usage of the specific organ. For אזן Hiphil as denominative (from "ear"), see BDB, 24; *HALOT* 1:27.

21. Cf. לעיני, and the discussion on pp. 258–62, below.

22. Cf. Gen 20:8; 23:13, 16; 44:18; 50:4; Exod 11:2; Num 14:28; Deut 5:1; 31:28, 30; 32:44; Josh 20:4; Judg 2–3; 1 Sam 11:4; 18:23; 25:24; 2 Sam 3:19; 2 Kgs 18:26; Isa 37:17; Jer 26:11, 15; 28:7.

(וּקְרָאתָ) in the hearing (בְּאָזְנֵי) of Jerusalem…" (Jer 2:2).[23] In addition to the verbs "to talk" (דבר) and "to proclaim" (קרא), the phrase "in the ears of" describes the target of "to say" (אמר)[24] and "to command" (צוה).[25]

We saw how the eye is an organ for concrete sight, yet also has meanings derived from the field of sight. Similarly, the ear, the hearing organ, becomes a symbol for understanding based on a derived meaning of hearing. To make something known, it should be revealed to the ears, even when actual hearing is not involved: "Because you, O Lord of Hosts, the God of Israel, have revealed (גָּלִיתָה אֶת־אֹזֶן) to your servant that you will build a house for him…" (2 Sam 7:27).[26] Lastly, an open or closed ear denotes hearing (or lack of it) without any hearing verbs. The ear can be "open" (פקח, פתח), or "inclined" (כרה) when it hears, or "shut" (אטם), "heavy/dull" (כבד), or uncircumcised (ערל) when it does not hear.[27] In sum, unlike the eye, the ear in the Hebrew Bible is nearly always portrayed as the organ of physical hearing. It almost never has other derived connotations, apart from understanding: "Look, my eye has seen all this, my ear has heard and understood it" (Job 13:1).[28]

The Foot/Leg

An examination of the verbs used with "foot" as the subject, or parallel to foot, shows how the foot indicates the means of mobility and posture in the Hebrew Bible.[29] Three verbs recur in conjunction with the foot. The first is "to walk" (הלך), as in: "My child, do not walk (תלך) in their way, keep your foot (רַגְלְךָ) from their paths" (Prov 1:15)[30]—here הלך parallels the foot, and they are both an idiom for im/moral behaviour. The second verb is "to step" (דרך), as in: "Every place that the sole of your foot will tread upon (תִּדְרֹךְ כַּף־רַגְלְכֶם) I have given to you, as I

---

23. Cf. Exod 24:7; Deut 31:11; Judg 7:3; 2 Kgs 23:2; Jer 29:29; 36:10, 13, 14, 15, 21; Ezek 8:18; 9:1; Neh 8:3; 13:1; 2 Chr 34:30.

24. Judg 17:2; Isa 49:20; Ezek 9:5; Job 33:8.

25. 2 Sam 18:12.

26. Cf. 1 Sam 9:15; 20:2, 12, 13; 22:8, 17; Job 33:6; 36:10, 15; Ruth 4:4; 1 Chr 17:25. The parallel heart/mind–ear–eye, will be dealt with below, pp. 129–30.

27. "To open the ear" (פתח, Isa 35:5; 48:8; 50:5; פקח, Isa 42:20; כרה, Ps 40:7); "to seal the ear" (אטם, Isa 33:15; Ps 58:5; Prov 21:13); "make the ear dull" (כבד, Isa 6:10; 49:1); "blocked/uncircumcised ear" (ערל, Jer 6:10), see Malul, "Piercing a Slave's Ear," 153–55. Also compare to "sealing the lips" (אטם, Prov 17:28).

28. See n. 16.

29. See also F. J. Stendebach, "רֶגֶל *regel*; רָגַל *rāgal*; מַרְגְּלוֹת *margelôt*; רַגְלִי *raglî*; רְגָלִים *regālîm*," *TDOT* 13:309–24 (314).

30. Cf. Deut 29:4; Isa 3:16; Pss 56:14; 115:7; Prov 3:23.

promised to Moses" (Josh 1:3)[31]—here stepping is what the foot does, and had both a literal meaning (i.e. to walk over the land) as well as symbolic meaning (to gain control over it). The third verb is "to go" (עבר), as in: "He turned the sea into dry land; they passed through the river on foot (יעברו...ברגל)..." (Ps 66:6).[32]

Interestingly, the foot also indicates posture and standing. Portrayals of the foot must also be understood in conjunction with verbs that at first glance would seem to indicate stopping. In particular, we think of the verb "to stand": "Our feet are standing (עמדות היו רגלינו) within your gates, O Jerusalem" (Ps 122:2).[33] The Psalter expresses presence as standing feet, and it is clear from the last words of v. 1—"we are going" (נלך)—that it was movement which led to the presence. Another "stopping" verb which describes the foot is "to rest" (נוח): "When the soles of the feet (כפות רגלי) of the priests who bear the ark of the Lord, the Lord of all the earth, rest (נוח) in the waters of the Jordan, the waters of the Jordan flowing from above shall be cut off..." (Josh 3:13).[34] Here again, it is the stopping of movement that matters, and that is described as the stopping of the feet. Lastly, the legs also "stand up" (קום): "Then King David rose to his feet and said..." (1 Chr 28:2).[35] The verb קום, which can mean "to stand up" or "to stand," in relation to the feet can also mean "to stop."

Like the eye and the ear, the foot too can bear the metaphorical load of its related sensory experience, kinaesthesia. For example, the metaphor mentioned above, "walking over is control," can be expressed using the foot, without any movement verb: "He bowed the heavens, and came down; thick darkness was under his feet (תחת רגליו)" (2 Sam 22:10; Ps 18:10). The physical foot gets here the abstract meaning attached to walking, and appears as an agent of action. Such a description is not reserved for God: "He subdued peoples under us, and nations under our feet" (Ps 47:4 [3]).[36] In the Hebrew Bible, we see body mobility and posture described as a physical ability of the feet, not of the whole body.

---

31. Cf. Deut 2:5; 11:24; Josh 14:9; Prov 3:23; 4:26.

32. Cf. Num 20:19; Deut 2:28; Ezek 29:11. So also "to lift" (נשא, Gen 29:1; רום Hiphil, Gen 41:44); "to ascend" (עלה, Judg 4:10); "to flee" (נוס, Judg 4:15, 17); "to come" (בא, 1 Kgs 14:6, 12; Isa 41:3); "to run" (רוץ, Isa 59:7; Prov 1:16; 6:18); "to move" (נוע, Jer 14:10; נוד, 2 Kgs 21:8). All these roots are motion roots.

33. Cf. Exod 3:5; Josh 5:15; 2 Sam 22:34; Ezek 2:1; 3:24; 37:10; Zech 14:4, 12; Pss 18:34; 26:12; 31:9; 2 Chr 3:13.

34. Cf. Gen 8:9; Deut 28:65.

35. Cf. 2 Kgs 13:21; Ps 40:3.

36. Cf. 1 Kgs 5:17; 2 Kgs 29:39; Ps 18:39. On the foot as a symbol of control in the Bible and the ancient Near East, see Stendebach, *TDOT* 13:319–21.

When the legs or feet do not function, it is the type of walking/movement which is described; the lame (פסח) is the one who limps. The harmed foot is describes through its main sensory experience, kinaesthesia. The following verse demonstrates this: "I was eyes to the blind, and feet to the lame" (Job 29:15). The lame have feet, but what they do not have is (proper) walking. The feet here, therefore, are more than a limb.

The Mouth (Including Tongue, Lips, and Palate)

The tongue as the organ of speech is the most prevalent of the organs of the mouth: "The spirit of the Lord speaks through me, his word (מלתו) is upon my tongue (לשוני)" (2 Sam 23:2). The tongue appears together with verbs that portray speech and verbal communication such as "to speak" (דבר Piel): "They all deceive their neighbours, and no one speaks (ידברו) the truth; they have taught their tongues (לשונם) to speak lies (דבר שקר); they commit iniquity and are too weary to repent" (Jer 9:4).[37] Out of all possible mouth parts, the tongue is mentioned as the agent of speech. This choice repeats with other verbs, such as "to utter" (הגה): "Then my tongue shall tell (לשוני תהגה) of your righteousness and of your praise all day long" (Ps 35:28).[38] The tongue also appears in combination with the verb "to take an oath" (שבע Niphal, Isa 45:23), with the verb "to sing a praise" (רנן Piel, Ps 51:16), and with the verb "to answer" (ענה, Prov 16:1).[39]

The tongue as the organ of speech is further expressed in the fact that dumbness is described as a disability in the functioning of the tongue: "And I will make your tongue cling to the roof of your mouth, so that you shall be speechless..." (ולשונך אדביק לחכך ונאלמת, Ezek 3:26).[40] Similarly, speech is described as opening the mouth, alongside the speech of the tongue: "See, I open my mouth; the tongue in my mouth speaks" (פתחתי פי דברה לשוני בחכי, Job 33:2). In contrast to the image of the open mouth, we also find the closed mouth as an image for dumbness: "But I am like the deaf, I do not hear; like the mute, who cannot speak" (אלם לא יפתח פיו, Ps 38:14).[41] Just as the physical inability to speak is described as a "mute tongue" or "closed mouth," so other speech defects that are not dumbness make use of mouth vocabulary: "but Moses said to the Lord, 'O my Lord, I have never been eloquent (איש דברים), neither in the past nor even now that you have spoken (דברך) to your servant; but I

---

37. Cf. Jer 9:7; Mic 6:12; Zeph 3:13; Pss 14:4; 39:4; 109:2.
38. Cf. Isa 59:3; Ps 71:24; Job 27:4.
39. Cf. Ps 119:172.
40. Cf. Isa 38:6; Ps 137:6; Job 29:2.
41. Cf. Prov 31:8.

am slow of speech (כבד־פֶּה) and slow of tongue (כבד לשון)'" (Exod 4:10).[42] In this famous denial, Moses claims that he cannot speak properly, and whatever the exact nature of his difficulty is, it has to do with words, as the use of the word דבר in the verse indicates. In his response, God asks, "who gives speech (lit. mouth, פה) to mortals?" (v. 11).

The last few examples demonstrate how the mouth, and not only the tongue, symbolizes speech. And indeed, the mouth reappears as the subject of speech verbs, such as "to speak" (דבר Piel): "...you shall see the king of Babylon eye-to-eye and speak with him mouth-to-mouth (פיהו את־פיך ידבר) and you shall go to Babylon" (Jer 34:3).[43] Note how the speaking mouth (הגה) parallels the speaking (דבר) tongue in the following example: "The mouths (פי) of the righteous utter (יהגה) wisdom, and their tongues speak (ולשונו תדבר) justice" (Ps 37:30). Other verbs from the field of speech that describe the action of the mouth include "to inquire" (שאל);[44] "to answer" (ענה, 2 Sam 1:16); "to announce" (נגד Hiphil);[45] and "to command" (צוה Piel, Isa 34:16).

The common verb "to say" (אמר) does not appear in combination with the mouth or tongue to represent the speaker. It seems that this verb denotes the content of speech, rather than the act itself. The nominal form "words" (*אֵמֶר), which describes the content of speech, is found in the expression "words of the mouth" (אמרי פה), that is, the consequence of speech, the words themselves, their meaning, and not the action.[46] The shift here from the organ of speech to the content of it is quite prevalent. Typically the word "tongue" (לשון) describes the content of speech, the words: "You love all pernicious words (דברי), treacherous speech (לשון)" (Ps 52:6, and elsewhere). Note how tongue is parallel to words in this verse. The semantic shift speech–content of speech is further shifted and the tongue can also describe "language" or "the ability of speech."[47] The words of Isaiah serve as an example for this shift: "I am going to bring upon you a nation from far away, O house of Israel, says the Lord. It is an enduring nation, it is an ancient nation, a nation whose language

42. Cf. Ezek 3:6–7, see J. H. Tigay, "'Heavy of Mouth' and 'Heavy of Tongue' on Moses' Speech Difficulty," *BASOR* 231 (1978): 56–67.

43. Cf. Gen 45:12; Num 12:8; Isa 1:20; 40:5; 58:14; Jer 9:11; 32:4; 34:3; Mic 4:4; Pss 49:4; 63:12; 66:14; 114:8, 11; 145:21, as well as combined with "word" (דבר). For more details, see F. Garcia-López, "פֶּה *peh*," *TDOT* 11:490–503 (495).

44. Gen 24:57; Josh 9:14; Isa 30:2.

45. Gen 43:7; Ps 51:17.

46. See Deut 32:1; Hos 6:5; Pss 19:15; 54:4; 78:1; 138:4; Prov 4:5; 5:7; 6:2; 7:24; 8:8; Job 8:2; 23:12.

47. See Wolff, *Anthropology of the Old Testament*, 77.

(לשנו) you do not know, nor can you understand (תשמע) what they say (ידבר)" (Jer 5:15).[48]

Finally, the lips also speak: "My lips (שפתי) will not speak (תדברנה) falsehood, and my tongue (לשוני) will not utter (יהגה) deceit" (Job 27:4). Similar to the tongue, the lips as the speech organ also have the abstract meaning "speech," "language": "Truly, as one who speaks (ידבר) to that people in a stammering jargon (שפה) and an alien tongue" (לשון, Isa 28:11).[49] Lastly, the lips can symbolise speech, in descriptions of speech difficulty. When Moses refuses his mission the second time, he claims to have a "heavy mouth" and a "heavy tongue" (Exod 4:10),[50] but also "uncircumcised lips": "But Moses spoke to the Lord, 'The Israelites have not listened to me (שמע); how then shall Pharaoh listen (ישמע) to me, poor speaker (ערל שפתים) that I am?'" (Exod 6:12; cf. v. 30). To sum up, the mouth, the lips, and the tongue are all considered the organs of speech, in its concrete meaning, but also in derived meanings, such as speech, words, and language.

In the Hebrew Bible, the mouth is also the organ of eating and drinking.[51] For example, it appears with the verb "to eat" (אכל): "...O mortal, eat (אכול) what is offered to you; eat (אכול) this scroll, and go, speak (אכול ולך דבר) to the house of Israel. So I opened my mouth (ואפתח את־פי), and he gave me the scroll to eat (ויאכילני)" (Ezek 3:1–2).[52] The phrase "to open the mouth" which we encountered above, means here "to eat" and not "to speak." At the same time, this prophecy demonstrates the associative pattern eating–speech, and its core image—the mouth.[53] Clearly, thirst and hunger can also be expressed using the mouth and its parts as images: "The tongue (לשון) of the infant sticks to the roof of its mouth for thirst (בצמא, Lam 4:4). Here too, the same phrase "a tongue stuck to the roof of the mouth" (דבק לשון לחך) is used to describe dumbness (above) and thirst—the opposites of speech and eating.

Another phrase that describes both eating and speech is "to open the mouth/lips wide" (פצה פה/שפתים). This physical description denotes speech: "...I will pay you my vows, those that my lips uttered (פצו שפתי) and my mouth promised (דבר פי) when I was in trouble" (Ps 66:14).[54] A

---

48. Cf. Isa 33:19; Ezek 3:5; Zech 8:23; Est 1:22; 3:12; 8:9; Dan 1:4; Neh 13:24.

49. Both meanings are frequent.

50. See n. 42.

51. Garcia-López, *TDOT* 11:493. See Judg 7:6; Prov 19:24; Neh 9:20.

52. Cf. Ezek 2:8; 4:10; Nah 3:12; Ps 78:30; Prov 30:20 (figuratively); Dan 10:3.

53. See pp. 93–94, above.

54. As well as Judg 11:35, 36; Lam 2:16; 3:46; Isa 10:14; Job 35:16. Opening the mouth as speech is most prominent in the root פנה ('to talk," "to open").

similar phrase is used to describe eating in Ezek 2:8 ("open your mouth and eat," פצה פיך ואכל). In at least one verse, this phrase incorporates a dual meaning: "Many bulls encircle me, strong bulls of Bashan surround me; they open wide their mouths (פצו פיהם) at me, like a ravening (טרף) and roaring (שאג) lion" (Ps 22:12–13 [13–14]). The imagery of harming speech, and of eating as a harmful act, occurs frequently in biblical poetry.[55] In this verse, it is jointly through the physical act of opening the mouth.

Another organ of the mouth linked to taste is the palate: "Does not the ear test words as the palate tastes (חך יטעם) food?" (Job 12:11; cf. 34:3). Similarly, "...and his fruit was sweet to my taste (lit. 'palate,' חכי)" (Song 2:3; cf. Prov 24:13). The last example demonstrates how the palate as an organ for tasting gets the more abstract meaning "taste." Again we find that the sensory organ is identified with the sensory experience. As we saw before, the palate also appears frequently in association with speech, parallel to the tongue (Job 31:30; 33:2), and in conjunction with the verb "to utter" (הגה): "for my mouth (חכי) will utter (יהגה) truth; wickedness is an abomination to my lips (שפתי)" (Prov 8:7).[56] In a similar phrase of the speaking palate, we find again the proximity between speech and taste. In Proverbs, the son is warned of the words of the foreign woman, "For the lips (שפתי) of a loose woman drip honey, and her speech (lit. 'palate,' חכה) is smoother than oil" (Prov 5:3). Speech, which serves as an idiom for behaviour, is here described using terms associated with taste and the outcome of the distasteful words is bitter (v. 4).

Examination of biblical verses that make an explicit literal link between the organs of the mouth and eating, stresses the role of taste in the eating process, and displays the semantic proximity between eating and speech:

> Though wickedness is sweet in their mouth (תמתיק בפיו),
> though they hide it under their tongues (לשונו),
> though they are loath to let it go,
> and hold it in their mouths (lit. "palate," חכו),
> yet their food is turned in their stomachs (מעיו);
> it is the venom of asps within them (קרבו). (Job 20:12–14)

These words of Zophar demonstrate how words, or even thoughts (= silent speech), are located in the mouth, tongue, and palate. They also give another example of how sensory organs are attached to the inwards.

---

55. See pp. 146–49, below.
56. Cf. Wolff, *Anthropology of the Old Testament*, 77.

Thirdly, they demonstrate yet again the proximity in imagery between speech and eating, as the words become the food of the wicked. To use a more positive example: "How sweet are your words to my taste (חֵךְ), sweeter than honey to my mouth (פִי)!" (Ps 119:103). Again, the words have a taste, described physically in the mouth and palate.

To summarize, both physically and semantically, eating/taste and speech are associated with the use of the mouth and its organs. It is noteworthy that the imagery of the speaking mouth is much more prevalent than the imagery of the eating and tasting mouth.[57] One example is the portrayal of God's mouth, which often appears as an agent of speech, but never in conjunction with eating. Even in those verses that compare divine harm to eating, it is not God's eating mouth but another agent, such as "his tongue is like a devouring fire" (Isa 30:27). As we saw, descriptions that combine the sense of taste with the sense of speech, show a semantic proximity between these experiences, sprouting from the fact that both are performed/experienced through the mouth.[58]

The Nose

The correlation between the nose and the sense of smell is practically self-evident, and yet it occurs infrequently in the Hebrew Bible. The description of the nose as a smelling organ appears explicitly only once: "They have ears, but do not hear; noses (אַף), but do not smell (יְרִיחוּן)" (Ps 115:6). Other verses only hint at this link. Amos describes the stench of the camp that enters the nose (4:10). In the blessing of Moses, when the incense offered by the Levites reaches the nose of God, we read: "They shall teach Jacob your ordinances, and Israel your law; they shall place incense before you (lit. 'your nose,' אַפֶּךָ), and whole burnt offerings on your altar" (Deut 33:10).[59] But as with the mouth, the nose does more than just smell. In many biblical verses, it explicitly refers to the breathing organ, with its connotation of life itself. When man was created, God "breathed into his nostrils (בְּאַפָּיו) the breath of life" (Gen 2:7). Elsewhere the breath in the nostrils, or nose, is used to express life:

57. Cf. ibid.

58. Wasserman, "Sweeter than Honey," 194. Similar context is found in OB: "Mama—her praise in sweeter than honey and wine" (*^dMamma zamāršama eli dišpim u karānim ṭābu*); "Your name fills the mouth like cake, oil and cream" (*šumki kīma kukki šamni u lildu pīam malu*) and more examples (p. 196). The image of eating as a source of words (Ezek 3:1–3 [p. 185] and cf. Ezek 2:8) parallels the image of touch as a source of words: "The Lord put out his hand and touched (וַיַּגַּע) my mouth, and the Lord said to me: Herewith I put My words into your mouth" (Jer 1:9, JPS). For more on eating and speech, see pp. 93–94, and Chapter 2, n. 130.

59. For more on these texts, see my "The Sensorium," 165–67.

"As long as my breath (נשמתי) is in me and the spirit (רוח) of God is in my nostrils (באפי), my lips will not speak..." (Job 27:3).[60] The nose recurs as an organ containing the spirit (i.e. breath) in descriptions of God: "Then the channels of the sea were seen, and the foundations of the world were laid bare at your rebuke, O Lord, at the blast of the breath of your nostrils (נשמת רוח אפיך)" (Ps 18:16 [15]). The breath coming out of the nostrils, is in the backdrop of the semantic blur between אף as nose, and as anger.[61] We find such images in the same psalm, and quite often elsewhere: "Smoke went up from his nostrils (באפו), and devouring fire from his mouth" (v. 9 [8]).[62]

The dual function of the nose as the smelling and breathing organ, together with the physiological basis of smelling as intake of air, is strongly reflected in the interchange of meanings of the root ריח/רוח and its derivatives.[63] This root is used for smell, wind, breath, to name only three. See, for example, the following verse: "I say I will climb the palm tree and lay hold of its branches. Oh, may your breasts be like clusters of the vine, and the scent of your breath (ריח אפך) like apples" (Song 7:9). The phrase ריח אף in this translation interprets ריח as scent, and the nose (אף) as breath, that is, standing in place of breath as the breathing organ. Yet a closer look shows that this dual meaning belongs solely to the word ריח, meaning either breath or scent. And both are related to the nose.[64] This allows us to establish a correlation not just between breathing and smelling, but between exhalation and spreading a smell. To sum, the nose in the Hebrew Bible is both the organ of smelling and of breathing, and the borders between both experiences are not always easily discerned.

The Hand

In the Hebrew Bible, the hand symbolizes the feeling limb, as we see in the verse: "They have hands (ידיהם), but do not feel (ימישון); feet, but do not walk..." (Ps 115:7).[65] We see from other verses as well that even

60. Cf. Isa 2:22; 7:22; Lam 4:20.

61. See B. Kedar-Kopfstein, "On the Decoding of Polysemantic Lexemes in Biblical Hebrew," *ZAW* 7 (1994): 17–25.

62. Cf. 2 Sam 22:9, 16; Job 4:9, and see my ""The Sensorium," 173–79.

63. See also T. Kronholm, "רוח *rwḥ*; רֵיחַ *rêaḥ*," *TDOT* 13:361–65 (365); Wolff, *Anthropology of the Old Testament*, 37.

64. Y. Zakovitch, *The Song of Songs: Introduction and Commentary* (Mikra Le'Israel; Tel Aviv: Am Oved, 1992 [Hebrew]), 125. The next verse contains a similar double meaning, in the context of taste: "...your palate (חכך) like the best wine" (Song 7:10).

65. Cf. Judg 16:26.

though touch is facilitated by all of the body's limbs and organs, the hand symbolizes touch more than any other organ. For example, the verb "to touch" (נגע) often describes the action of the hand, even when the meaning does not actually refer to manual touching: "You shall set limits for the people all around, saying, 'Be careful not to go up (עלות) the mountain or to touch (נגע) the edge of it. Any who touch (נגע) the mountain shall be put to death. No hand (יד) shall touch (תגע) them, but they shall be stoned or shot with arrows; whether animal or human being, they shall not live. When the trumpet sounds a long blast, they may go up on the mountain'" (Exod 19:12–13). In this warning previous to the revelation in Sinai, the people are warned not to touch the mountain. Their death penalty cannot involve touching either, and although it is clear that in both cases it is forbidden to touch with any body part, the hand is mentioned explicitly.

The idiom "hand touches" (נגע יד), indicating harm, is not unique to the book of Exodus: "Have pity on me, have pity on me, O you my friends, for the hand (יד) of God has touched (נגעה) me!" (Job 19:21; cf. 1 Sam 6:9). In many other places, the touch of a hand appears in the phrase "the hand was in" (היתה יד ב), and the meaning of tactile experience is marked by the hand only, and embedded in the phrase.[66]

The last phrase demonstrates how the hand becomes an agent of action, based on its tactile context. As such, the hand can express the means of support, and not only harm, whether that is the hand of God— "Now the hand (יד) of the Lord had been (היתה) upon me the evening before the fugitive came…" (Ezek 33:22)—or the hand of a human being—"But the hand of Ahikam son of Shaphan was with Jeremiah so that he was not given over into the hands of the people to be put to death" (Jer 26:24).[67] The hand, being "on" someone, clearly a tactile idiom, is a metaphor for support. Interestingly, the hand can express this meaning even without any verb at all.[68] In addition to the verbs נגע and היה, the hand is often mentioned alongside the verbs "to grasp" (תפש), and "be given" (Niphal נתן): "And you yourself shall not escape from his hand (מידו), but shall surely be captured (תפש תתפש) and handed (בידו תנתן) over to him…" (Jer 34:3).[69] Again, it is not the actual hand that is

66. See Gen 37:27; Exod 9:3; Deut 2:15; 17:7; Josh 2:19; Judg 2:15; 1 Sam 18:17, 21; 24:13, 14; Ezek 13:9; 1 Chr 21:1.

67. In the phrases "the hand was/is + on" (אל, 1 Kgs 18:46; Ezek 33:22; על, Ps 80:18; Ezra 8:31; את, Jer 26:24); + with (עם, 1 Chr 4:10); without a verb (2 Sam 14:19; Neh 2:18).

68. See pp. 138–39, below.

69. Cf. Jer 38:23; Ezek 29:9; Prov 30:28.

involved, but the tactile image that requires the hand to be the chosen synecdoche to the person. The verb "to grasp" (תפש) is found also with "palm" (כף): "The sword is given to be polished, to be grasped in the hand (לתפש בכף)" (Ezek 21:16; cf. 29:7). Other common verbs that describe the act of the hand are "to take" (לקח)[70] and "to hold" (אחז, Deut 32:41; 2 Sam 20:9). The hand is the agent of multiple acts and experiences that are tactile, and becomes representative of the tactile even in expressions that are not explicitly related to touch.

Summary

In our modern perception, we imagine the senses as figurative abilities that are differentiated from the sensory body organs and limbs. Yet in the biblical perception, where the embodiment is taken for granted, there is no real differentiation between touching and holding—both of which are associated with the hand. There is no real differentiation between mobility and posture—both of which are actions associated with the foot. Smell and spirit (breath) are performed through the nose, while speech, eating, and taste have shared symbolic meanings associated with the mouth. In the present discussion of the senses, we find biblical references to seven senses, or to seven experiences of feelings that belong to a single category. But we must also entertain the hypothesis that in terms of biblical categorization, the Hebrew Bible does not treat the senses as abilities, a perception that we first find explicitly only in the Apocrypha. Instead, the Hebrew Bible treats the senses as a category of experiencing the world through body organs, a category that incorporates six elements, six experiential organs: the eye, the ear, the nose, the mouth, the hand, and the foot. These are external organs, out of which the ones found in the head are linked to internal organs (נפש, לב).

This association between a particular organ and a sensory ability is also evident in descriptions of the functioning or non-functioning of the sensory organs. Apart from the portrayal of damaged organs through the use of the verbs כבד and ערל, we find the proper functioning of the sensory organs portrayed as the opening of the organ, with malfunctioning organs portrayed as the closing of the organ.[71] This holds both for the direct and derived meanings. Seeing eyes are open eyes,[72] as is also

---

70. Gen 3:22; 8:9; 43:15; Judg 15:15; Josh 9:11; 1 Sam 21:9; 2 Sam 23:6; 1 Kgs 14:3; 2 Kgs 6:7; Amos 9:2; Jer 36:14.

71. Cf. "to open (פתח) the womb" (Gen 29:31; 30:22), vs. "to close (סגר) the womb" (1 Sam 1:5–6; cf. Job 3:10).

72. 1 Kgs 8:29, 52; 2 Chr 6:20, 40; 7:15; Neh 1:6.

evident from the root "to open" (פקח) that usually serves as a description of sight;[73] this is opposed to eyes that do not see, because they are closed (Isa 33:15). This imagery is based on a physical portrayal of the organ. But we also find it being used regarding the ears, which do not open or close physically. The hearing ear is described as open,[74] while the ear that does not hear is closed.[75] The hand that helps and supports is open,[76] but when it cannot function it is closed (Deut 15:7). The speaking mouth is open, as opposed to a dumb mouth: "I am like the deaf, I do not hear; like the mute, who does not open his mouth" (Ps 38:14, my translation).[77] Silence is described as a closed mouth.[78] Open lips are lips that speak,[79] while closed lips express silence (Prov 17:28). Opening the mouth in speech is also reflected in the verb "to answer" (ענה), which has the root meaning "to open." Finally, I should mention the unnoticed description of the nose as flowing (with air, and smelling properly), or as a shut nose, and therefore a nose that breathes abruptly, or does not smell. Such descriptions are found mostly with regard to the divine nose, which, when angry, does not smell (= accept) sacrifice. God is, in times of anger, described as having a "cringed nose."[80]

Two biblical verses provide detailed descriptions of the sensory category. Both verses list sensory abilities (or lack thereof) attributed to idols, and both verses describe the senses as linked with the sensory organ:

> A. Their idols are silver and gold, the work of human hands.
>   They have *mouths*, but do not speak; *eyes*, but do not see.
>   They have *ears*, but do not hear; *noses*, but do not smell.
>   They have *hands*, but do not feel; *feet*, but do not walk.
>   They make no sound in their *throats*. (Ps 115:4–7)

73. Besides Isa 42:20, where the same root describes ears/hearing.

74. Isa 48:8; 50:5 (פתח); see also 42:20 (פקח).

75. Isa 33:15; Ps 58:5; Prov 21:13.

76. Deut 15:8, 11; Pss 104:28; 145:16.

77. Cf. Num 22:28; Ezek 3:27; 21:27; 24:27; 33:22; Isa 53:7; Pss 78:2; 109:2; Job 3:1; 33:2; Prov 24:7; 31:8, 9; Dan 10:16. The opening of the mouth in Ezek 3:2 is meant for eating, but leads to speech. Besides this example the only other verse where opening of the mouth is attested for eating is metaphorically, in the mouth of the ground (Num 15:32; 26:10, cf. פצה).

78. Isa 52:15; Ps 107:42; Job 5:16.

79. Job 11:5; 32:20; Ps 51:27.

80. The idea cannot be fully developed here, some discussion is found in Chapter 2, n. 158, and hopefully will be further developed in a separate article.

B. The idols of the nations are silver and gold, the work of human hands.

They have *mouths*, but they do not speak; they have *eyes*, but they do not see;

They have *ears*, but they do not hear, and there is no breath in their *mouths*. (Ps 135:15–17)

As we saw earlier, this phenomenon recurs with each of these organs. Just as a sensory ability is associated with a specific organ, so a sensory disability is associated with damage to that same organ. Such phraseology assumes that each ability is inherent in and originates from a particular organ, thus reflecting the embodied way in which the Hebrew Bible perceives the senses.

The biblical text also uses other organs whose actions are portrayed through sensory verbs. The heart/mind (לב) is the most obvious example. The heart hears (1 Kgs 3:9), walks,[81] speaks,[82] and touches.[83] There are also many biblical verses where the heart is parallel to the ear and the eye.[84] Like the other organs, the heart is also associated with a particular action, as we see in the following parallel: "But to this day the Lord has not given you a mind to understand (לב להבין), or eyes to see, or ears to hear" (Deut 29:3). As this parallel clearly shows, the heart is the knowing organ, based on the perception of the heart as the centre of human consciousness.[85] The character of the knowledge attributed to the heart is sometimes portrayed as what we would today call abstract understanding, and sometimes portrayed as what we would call a skill. For example, Bezalel, Oholiab, as well as any craftsman of the tabernacle, are described as "wise of heart."[86] The correlation between the heart and the sensory organs is clearly related to the contextual pattern of knowledge

---

81. 2 Kgs 5:26; Ezek 11:12; 20:16; 33:31; Job 31:7.

82. The speech of the heart/mind is expressed through the roots אמר (Ps 27:8), and הגה (Prov 15:28; 27:2). These expressions are part of the image of thinking as inward talking. See pp. 159–60, below, and references there.

83. The touching of the heart/mind is found together with the root לקח (Hos 4:11; Job 16:12).

84. For the parallel heart‖ear, see Deut 29:3; Isa 6:10; 32:3–4; Jer 5:21; Ezek 3:10; 40:4; 44:5; Ps 10:17; Prov 2:2; 18:15; 22:17; 23:12. For the parallel heart‖eye see Num 15:39; Deut 4:9; 28:65, 67; 29:3*; 1 Kgs 9:3; 2 Kgs 10:30; Isa 6:10*; 10:12; 44:18; Jer 5:21*; 22:17; Ezek 6:9; 40:4*; 44:5*; Pss 19:9; 36:2; 38:11; 101:5; 131:1; Prov 21:4; 23:16, 33; Job 15:12; Lam 5:17; Qoh 11:9; 2 Chr 7:16; 16:9. References marked with an asterisk include triple parallelism eye‖heart‖ear.

85. See also Wolff, *Anthropology of the Old Testament*, and specifically "the heart as the centre of the consciously living man" (p. 55).

86. Exod 31:6; 35:10, 25; 36:1, 2, 8.

and understanding in which the senses are characteristically mentioned in the Hebrew Bible.[87] As we will see below, there are other contexts of the biblical sensorium, and we will have to analyse these contexts to better understand the place of the hear/mind and the sensorium.

Sense and Sovereignty

Anyone exploring the vocabulary associated with the senses in the Hebrew Bible will find that this vocabulary is not limited to a description of concrete sensory experiences. The verbs and nouns mentioned above often serve to portray derived meanings and metaphors. We can demonstrate this through the use of the roots "to see" and "to hear," which express not only sight of objects and hearing of voices, but also understanding. An examination of the vocabulary associated with the seven senses shows several examples of derived use and imagery. We often find that the derived meaning associated with one sense is found as a derived meaning in the vocabulary of the other senses. In other words, the different senses belong to overlapping (but not always identical) contexts, so that these contexts become contextual patterns. I regard these contextual patterns as a major part of the definition of the sensory category. Below, I will examine the main contextual patterns: help and harm; learning, understanding and knowledge; emotional experience; moral judgment; and life, experience, and ability. These contextual patterns were divided for the sake of convenience; yet one should note that at times these contexts overlap. As we will see, sensory images such as help are closely associated with sensory images such as understanding, and so on. In their whole, these contextual patterns share a fundamental image—that of the sensory experience as the mark of personal, sovereign, act of the person.

The Power to Help

One of the most prevalent uses of metaphors in relation to the senses occurs in the context of expressions for help, particularly divine help. God's responsiveness to appeals from the people or from the individual worshipper is expressed in looking, hearing, smelling, speaking, and maybe even touching. These metaphorical expressions mediate the abstract responsiveness, support, and help of God, through physical-concrete idioms.

---

87. See pp. 157–62, below.

In the field of hearing, we frequently find the phrase "to direct the ear" (נטה אזן Hiphil), which expresses the idea that God pays special attention, particularly in the context of prayer: "Do not hide your face from me in the day of my distress. Incline your ear (הטה אזנך) to me; answer me (ענני) speedily in the day when I call" (Ps 102:3).[88] Lending an ear, unlike hearing, incorporates an element of mobility, an intimation that this concerns active, intentional listening.[89] This phrase recurs together with other combinations that denote turning in the direction of the recipient of the help. In this last verse, this means the revelation of the face and the response. The turning the ear metaphor, as an indicator of help, is a physical description that expands the basic meaning of passive hearing, and incorporates an element of response. In this verse, the response is reflected through the verb ענה, "to reply," which indicates the answering of the request. This theme recurs in many other passages involving divine help.

Such use of the verb "to answer" (ענה) appears both in biblical prose and in biblical poetry. In prose, see the words of Jacob's description of the divine help he has received: "then come, let us go up to Bethel, that I may make an altar there to the God who answered (הענה) me in the day of my distress and has been with me wherever I have gone" (Gen 35:3). In the poetry, the verb reoccurs in pleas for divine help: "The Lord answer (יענך) you in the day of trouble! The name of the God of Jacob protect you! May he send you help from the sanctuary, and give you support from Zion" (Ps 20:2–3 [1–2]).[90] In many biblical passages, God's answer as an image of his help appears as a response to an appeal, creating a dialogue metaphor—the help is an answer to a question or a concrete request.[91] A fine example is found in the story of the prophet Elijah and the priests of Baal. The main condition of the trial is the following: "'Then you call (וקראתם) on the name of your god and I will call (אקרא) on the name of the Lord; the god who answers (יענה) by fire is indeed God.' All the people answered, 'Well spoken!'" (1 Kgs 18:24). Even though the requested response in this episode is a visual and maybe

---

88. Cf. 2 Kgs 19:16; Isa 37:17; Pss 17:6; 31:3; 71:2; 86:1; 88:3; 116:2; Dan 9:18. All theses verses are part of explicit prayer and plea for help. The expression repeats with the meaning "obedience" when the subject is human. More on the matter below. For the phrase "hide the face" in this verse and elsewhere, see Balentine, *The Hidden God*, 49–64.

89. The structure נטה Hiphil + sensory organ can express help or harm, and in any case denotes attention (H. Ringgren, "נָטָה *nāṭâ*," *TDOT* 9:381–87 [384–86]); cf. *HALOT* 2:92–693).

90. Cf. Isa 65:24; Jonah 2:3; Ps 13:4 and many others.

91. Pss 4:2; 27:7; 55:3; 86:1; 102:3; 119:145, and many others.

thermal symbol, fire, it is described in terms of vocal response, a kind of dialogue. This theme continues as the story unfolds:

> So they took the bull that was given them, prepared it, and called (ויקראו) on the name of Baal from morning until noon, crying, "O Baal, answer us (ענו)!" But there was no voice (קול), and no answer (ענה). They limped about the altar that they had made. At noon Elijah mocked them, saying, "Cry aloud (קראו בקול גדול)! Surely he is a god; either he is meditating, or he has wandered away, or he is on a journey, or perhaps he is asleep and must be awakened." Then they cried aloud (ויקראו בקול גדול) and, as was their custom, they cut themselves with swords and lances until the blood gushed out over them. As midday passed, they raved on until the time of the offering of the oblation, but there was no voice (קול), no answer (ענה), and no response (קשב). (vv. 26–29)

The stress of the vocal-aural dialogue here is a clear satire on behalf of the Baal prophets, yet when Elijah calls Yahweh, he uses similar vocabulary: "Answer me (ענני), O Lord, answer me (ענני), so that this people may know that you, O Lord, are God..." (v. 37). The difference between the "dialogue" with Baal and that with Yahweh is a matter of quantity, not quality. God's response is described using the verb "to answer" (ענה), and the whole narrative highlights the imagery of conversation as a description of God's responsiveness and his response to the request of the worshipper/sacrifice, an image that is expanded in other passages to describe actual help.

Notably, despite the oral/aural dimension of ענה, it also appears parallel to sight: "Look at me (הביטה), answer me (ענני), O Lord, my God!..." (Ps 13:4, JPS); "It is I who answer (עניתי) and look after you (ואשורנו)" (Hos 14:9).[92] The above examples demonstrate how descriptions of God's attentive ear are expanded into descriptions of his response (i.e. help) as part of the conversation metaphor. God answers what he hears, thereby responding to the request and giving help. The root ענה is a metaphor for God's responsiveness, and it repeats together with hearing, sight,[93] as well as on its own: "When the poor and needy

---

92. For the problem of ואשורנו in this verse, see H. W. Wolff, *Hosea: A Commentary on the Book of the Prophet Hosea* (trans. G. Stansell; Hermeneia; Philadelphia: Fortress, 1974), 233. It seems to me that the meaning of sight is the proper one, and see Job 33:14: "For God speaks in one way, and in two, though people do not perceive it (ישורנה)." The meaning is that God speaks, but people do not see (perceive) it; see N. C. Habel, *The Book of Job* (OTL; London: SCM, 1985), 455; J. E. Hartley, *The Book of Job* (NICOT; Grand Rapids: Eerdmans, 1988), 441; BDB, 1003. Comparing the two verses (Job 33:14 and 35:13–14) demonstrates an associative link between speech and sight.

93. For sight as metaphor for divine help, see below.

seek water, and there is none, and their tongue is parched with thirst, I the Lord will answer them (אענם), I the God of Israel will not forsake them (אעזבם)" (Isa 41:17).[94]

In addition to the metaphor of conversation, the phrase "to direct the ear" (נטה אזן) recurs in conjunction with a visual phrase "to open the eye" (פקח עין), denoting attentiveness: "Incline your ear (הטה אזנך), O Lord, and hear (ושמע); open your eyes (פקח עיניך), O Lord, and see (וראה); hear (ושמע) the words of Sennacherib, which he has sent to mock the living God" (2 Kgs 19:16).[95] Opening the eye can describe attentiveness as in the above verse, and more particularly divine help and providence, as we see in the following: "On that day, says the Lord, I will strike every horse with panic, and its rider with madness. But on the house of Judah I will keep a watchful eye (אפקח את-עיני), when I strike every horse of the peoples with blindness (עורון)" (Zech 12:4). God's *watching* over Judah is further stressed when the enemies are punished with blindness. A similar expression is "to set eyes on" (שים עין), which has the same basic meaning of providence. Joseph's promise to watch over Benjamin is so described: "…Bring him down to me, so that I may set my eyes on him (ואשימה עיני עליו)" (Gen 44:21).[96] Here too, the basic meaning is attentiveness, and this attentiveness can be positive (watching over), or negative (hurting). Such differentiation is explicitly found in the words of Amos: "And though they go into captivity in front of their enemies, there I will command the sword, and it shall kill them; and I will fix my eyes on them (ושמתי עיני עליהם) for harm and not for good (לרעה ולא לטובה)" (Amos 9:4; cf. Jer 24:6). The combination "set eyes on" thus expresses relating and attention. Taken positively, this can be interpreted as help or protection. Taken negatively, this can be interpreted as punishment. I shall return to this theme below in my discussion of "to see in" (ראה ב).

In addition to the above combination of phrases, we find the two phrases "attentive ear" (אזן קשבת) and "open eye" (עין פתוחה) together as expression of divine guard and aid: "let your ear be attentive (אזנך קשבת) and your eyes open to hear (עיניך פתוחות לשמע) the prayer of your servant that I now pray before you day and night…" (Neh 1:6).[97] As shown above with regard to ענה and נטה אזן, the focus on paying attention and hearing is linked to the request for help in prayer: "Lord, hear (שמעה)

94. We find in this verse again the overlap between eating and speech, and see the discussion above, pp. 93–94.
95. Cf. Isa 37:17; Dan 9:18.
96. Cf. Jer 39:12; 40:4; Ezra 5:12.
97. Cf. 2 Chr 6:40; 7:15.

my voice! Let your ears be attentive (אָזְנֶיךָ קַשֻּׁבוֹת) to the voice of my supplications!" (Ps 130:2). Even when the roots "to listen" (קשב) or "to hear" (שמע) do not appear in these phrases, and outside explicit prayer contexts (and genre), hearing clearly refers to divine help as a response to a vocal plea, such as groan (נאקה, Exod 2:24), voice, shout (קול צעקה, Num 20:16; זעקה, 2 Chr 20:9), and prayer or supplication (תפילה, תחינה, 2 Chr 33:13).[98]

Hearing a supplication indicates divine help, because it is an attentive, deliberate hearing. Often, the intention of hearing is described physically, such as in the expression נטה אזן mentioned above. God's responsiveness is listening: "I waited patiently for the Lord; he inclined (ויט) to me and heard (וישמע) my cry" (Ps 40:2); "For the Lord listens (שמע) to the needy, and does not spurn (בזה) his captives" (Ps 69:34, JPS).[99] The metaphor "hearing is (divine) help" is, therefore, based on different meanings attributed to the hearing modality. Some of the meanings are concrete/physical, such as hearing a vocal appeal and responding to it. At other times, the vocal response likens help to answering a question, creating an image of speech as proffering help. Another physical image is the description of listening (i.e. deliberate hearing) through the metaphor of direction: inclining the ear towards the recipient of help, as opposed to turning the ear away to signify a refusal to help. But the metaphor of hearing as divine help is also based on the derived meanings of the hearing action, such as judgment: "then hear (תשמע) in heaven, and act, and judge your servants, condemning the guilty by bringing their conduct on their own head, and vindicating the righteous by rewarding them according to their righteousness" (1 Kgs 8:32). Here, hearing is a metaphor for divine justice, yet the blur between divine justice and delivery is self-evident. Hearing as judgment is found also in descriptions of the human agent, the king-judge. It seems that this metaphor has its origin in the judicial reality of the biblical culture.[100]

Another important figurative meaning of hearing, on which the divine help metaphor is based, is understanding and agreement. This is evident from the use of identical expressions to portray both divine help and human learning and obedience. The phrases "to listen to" (שמע אל/ל), "to listen to the voice of" (שמע בקול/לקול), and "to incline the ear" (נטה אזן)

---

98. And many others.

99. For the physical meaning of distance in the root בזה, see my "Honour and Shame in the Hebrew Bible" (M.A. diss., The Hebrew University of Jerusalem, 2002 [Hebrew]), 71.

100.   See 2 Sam 14:16–17; 19:3, and Malul, "Ceremonial and Juridical Background," section b.

all portray understanding and agreement, not just hearing. As part of the Hebrew Bible's description of the asymmetrical relationship between God and humans, hearing God's voice means obeying him. When God hears a person's voice or the people's (collective) voice, he responds to it and gives help.[101]

I have briefly mentioned the use of sight imagery to describe divine help—in particular, in the phrases "open the eyes of" (פקח עין) and "to place an eye on" (שים עין), which appear in parallel to hearing. But the image of the seeing God as a helper recurs in many biblical passages, as I will now detail. One widespread expression is "to see the affliction" (ראה עני): "Look on my misery (ראה עניי) and rescue me, for I do not forget your law" (Ps 119:153).[102] In some verses, this phrase explicitly parallels other help expressions, such as "to give heed" (פקד, Exod 4:31),[103] and "to help" (עזר, 2 Kgs 14:26). As we saw with hearing images, the very sight and recognition of evil creates the help. We see how God's look signifies his attentiveness, and lack of it leads to harmful results: "The Lord himself has scattered them, he will regard (lit. 'look,' להביטם) them no more; no honour was shown to the priests, no favour to the elders" (Lam 4:16; cf. Amos 5:22).

In other passages, the phrase "to look at" (ראה ב) describes divine help and responsiveness. Sometimes, this phrase is used in conjunction with "affliction" (עני), similar to what we saw earlier: "Leah conceived and bore a son, and she named him Reuben; for she said, 'Because the Lord has looked on my affliction (ראה בעניי); surely now my husband will love me'" (Gen 29:32). At other times, ראה ב occurs by itself: "When he saw that they were in distress (וירא בצר להם), when he heard (בשמעו) their cry, he was mindful of his covenant and in his great faithfulness relented" (Ps 106:44–45). Sight (and hearing) in these verses demonstrate(s) not only God's awareness of the problem, but also his actual help. A clear example is found in the words of Hannah: "…O Lord of Hosts, if you will look upon the suffering (תראה בעני) of your maidservant and will remember me and not forget your maidservant, and if you will grant your maidservant a male child, I will dedicate him to the Lord for all the days of his life" (1 Sam 1:11).[104]

---

101. A similar semantic specification repeats in human asymmetrical relationships, such as a covenant.

102. Cf. Pss 31:8; 9:14; 2 Kgs 14:26; Neh 9:9.

103. See *HALOT* 3:956. Meaning 2 of פקד is "to look at, see to something," assuming a visual meaning to the root, and including a discussion and reference there.

104. Cf. Exod 2:11, for similar meaning, when describing Moses' actions.

According to Menahem Zevi Kaddari, the basic meaning of ראה ב, "to see," is experience and empathy. Kaddari shows how this phrase uniquely describes emotional experience, in contrast to "to see" + accusative marker (ראה את), which describes cognitive experience.[105] Use of sight as a metaphor for empathetic experience has no intrinsic positive or negative connotation. Sometimes a positive emotional experience is interpreted as help, as we saw earlier. At other times, the very same phrase (ראה ב) can describe a negative emotional experience. When Moses was brought low by the burden of the ever-complaining Israelites, he begs: "If this is the way you are going to treat me, put me to death at once—if I have found favour in your sight—and do not let me see my misery (אל אראה ברעתי)" (Num 11:15). The words of reproach to Shemaiah the priest demonstrate the meaning once again: "...he shall not have anyone living among this people to see the good (יראה בטוב) that I am going to do to my people, says the Lord, for he has spoken rebellion against the Lord" (Jer 29:32). In these examples, derived (not concrete) sight describes experience, involvement, or presence. Interestingly, though, when God is the subject of ראה ב, the phrase is only used to describe positive empathy, that is, help.[106]

The use of terms from the semantic field of sight, especially the root "to see" (ראה), to denote experience in general is not limited to the phrase ראה ב alone; rather, it appears in other expressions and phrases: "...If the people face (lit. 'see,' בראתם) war, they may change their minds and return to Egypt" (Exod 13:17).[107] Sight describes not only concrete experience as in the cited verse, but also the experience of life, or existence in general. In the following example, three occurrences of ראה have nuances, yet all embed some aspect of experience in them:

> Consider (ראה) the work of God; who can make straight what he has made crooked? In the day of prosperity be (היה) joyful, and in the day of adversity consider (ראה); God has made the one as well as the other, so that mortals may not find out anything that will come after them. In my vain life I have seen (ראיתי) everything; there are righteous people who perish in their righteousness, and there are wicked people who prolong their life in their evil-doing. (Qoh 7:13–15)[108]

---

105.   Kaddari, "What is the Difference?," 69–70.

106.   For ראה ב/נבט ב, see ibid., 73–75, and pp. 151–54, below.

107.   Cf. Num 4:23; Deut 1:36 and many others.

108.   Cf. Jer 20:18; Ps 16:10. Note the shared semantic shift (not etymological) in Biblical Hebrew and Akkadian. The verb "to see" (ראה, *amāru*) can mean also "to experience" (*CAD* 1/II, 6–12). See also pp. 251–54, below.

This short review of sight terms offers a somewhat different explanation for the use of sight as opposed to hearing as a metaphor for divine help. Experience or empathy seem to lie at the core of the sight descriptions of God as a divine helper and saviour, while understanding and judgment lie at the core of hearing descriptions. Both metaphors perceive the senses as a medium for understanding and getting to know the world, but also imply a range of other meanings.[109] Importantly, neither metaphor differentiates between emotional or cognitive understanding, which fits with the perception of the senses as reflected in the Hebrew Bible.[110] In fact, one could say that the experience of knowledge is perception, and that perception can be experienced through emotions, such as empathy: "Let me exult and rejoice in your steadfast love, because you have seen (ראית) my affliction; you know (ידעת) of my distress" (Ps 31:8, my translation).[111]

Another difference between sight- and hearing-help metaphors is the context in which they appear. The hearing and speaking God appears mainly in the context of prayer, while the seeing God appears in the context of general help, as well as in biblical passages that contain no direct appeal for help. The discussion on sight adds a further physical dimension to our understanding of God as a helper. The physical metaphor of hearing as help is associated with mobility, or inclining the ear. The physical metaphor of sight is associated with opening the eyes.[112]

This notion is even more evident in passages that describe a refusal to help, using expressions such as "to close an eye" (עצם עין, Isa 33:15) or "to close an ear" (אטם אזן, Isa 33:15; Prov 21:13). These expressions also reinforce the correlation between help and judgment. Another combination that describes a refusal of help is "to hide the eye" (עלם עין): "When you stretch out your hands, I will hide my eyes (אעלים עיני) from you; even though you make many prayers, I will not listen (שמע); your hands are full of blood" (Isa 1:15).[113] Here too, the phrase is not unique for the description of God's attitude to his people; the same phrase can describe human behaviour: "Her priests have violated my teaching: they have profaned what is sacred to me, they have not distinguished between the sacred and the profane, they have not taught the difference between the unclean and the clean, and they have closed their eyes (העלימו עיניהם) to my sabbaths. I am profaned in their midst" (Ezek 22:26).[114] Note how

---

109. On the dissimilarity between sight and hearing, see pp. 248–51, below.
110. See pp. 183–88, below.
111. Cf. Exod 2:25.
112. See Chapter 2, n. 188, for שעה.
113. Cf. העלים אזן in Lam 3:56.
114. Cf. Lev 20:4; 1 Sam 12:3; Prov 28:27.

"hiding the eyes" is understood as avoidance of help when God is the agent, while it is understood as lack of obedience when it is a human one. This difference between the meanings involves the asymmetric balance of power between God on the one hand, and the people or an individual on the other, as already evident in hearing metaphors.[115]

Thus far, I have presented images of divine help derived from attention and understanding metaphors. But help described as sight is also derived from forgiveness and mercy images, such as the combination "to spare an eye" (חוס עין): "Therefore I will act in wrath; my eye will not spare (לא־תחוס עיני), nor will I have pity; and though they cry in my hearing (באזני) with a loud voice, I will not listen (אשמע) to them" (Ezek 8:18).[116] In this phrase, which uses the eye to represent the subject of the action, God's eye has the capacity for forgiveness or anger. This perception correlates with the image of sight as empathy. A similar response of God to his people appears in images associated with the sense of smell, where the actions of the people could produce a reaction of forgiveness (ארך אפיים) or anger (אף, חמה).[117] The reaction of God to what he sees or smells, which can be either a positive or negative reaction, involves a mindful sensory perception, whether through sight, hearing, or smell. Appealing for God's help through sacrifices can be accepted or rejected: "I will lay your cities waste, will make your sanctuaries desolate, and I will not smell (לא אריח) your pleasing odours" (Lev 26:31).[118] In this example, God's responsiveness is expressed in his attentive sight and smell, just as an appeal to God in prayer is answered by listening and response. Finally, the image of sight as aid and protection sprouts from the widespread ancient Near Eastern (including the Hebrew Bible) demand to be seen in the sanctuary, to be present before God, a matter on which I will not expand here.[119]

In addition to the idioms and metaphors already discussed, there is widespread use of touch as a description of God's help, particularly when the hand of God represents his strength and abilities:[120] "do not fear, for I am with you, do not be afraid, for I am your God; I will strengthen you

115.   See Chapter 2, n. 105.
116.   Cf. Jer 21:7; Ezek 9:10; 20:17; Joel 2:17; Neh 13:22.
117.   For the use of the senses to hurt or punish, see below.
118.   Cf. Amos 5:21–22.
119.   See, however, M. Elat, *Samuel and the Foundation of Kingship in Ancient Israel* (Jerusalem: Magnes, 1998 [Hebrew]), 19–20; M. Malul "Some Idioms and Expressions in Biblical Hebrew Originating in Symbolic Acts in the Realm of Treaty-Making" (Hebrew), *HaIvrit WeAhyoteha* 4–5 (2004–2005): 189–208 (196–98).
120.   As will be shown below, the "hand of God" is also a source of hurt and punishment.

(אמצתיך), I will help you (עזרתיך), I will uphold you (תמכתיך) with my victorious right hand (ימין)" (Isa 41:10). The verb "to uphold" (תמך), which belongs to the semantic field of touch, is used as an idiom for help quite often: "for you have been my help, and in the shadow of your wings I sing for joy. My soul clings to you; your right hand upholds (תמכה ימינך) me" (Ps 63:8–9).[121] A similar meaning is found in the verb "to uphold" (סמך), even when the hand is not explicitly mentioned: "But surely, God is my helper; the Lord is the upholder of my life (סמכי נפשי)" (Ps 54:6).[122] In fact, there are many verbs that have a concrete meaning of tactile experience which serve to describe abstract aid and support: the verb "to grasp" (אחז), for instance, is used to denote divine aid— "even there your hand (ידך) shall lead me, and your right hand (ימינך) shall hold me fast (תאחזני)" (Ps 139:10; cf. Ps 73:23). The verb "to strengthen" (חזק Piel) also belongs to the tactile semantic field and appears in similar contexts. Its literal meaning is to strengthen, and it could express help and support. The following verse demonstrates a concrete strengthening: "I will strengthen (חזקתי) the arms of the king of Babylon, and put my sword in his hand..." (Ezek 30:24). In the description of Job, we find abstract strengthening, meaning help and support: "See, you have instructed many; you have strengthened (תחזק) the weak hands. Your words have supported those who were stumbling, and you have made firm (תאמץ) the feeble knees" (Job 4:3).[123]

The concrete meaning of all the mentioned verbs is related to touch, and their derived meaning is help and support. We saw that often these verbs describe the act of the hand, and indeed, the same meaning is given to the hand without explicit tactile verbs, most commonly, God's right hand (ימין): "That those whom you love might be rescued, deliver with your right hand (ימינך) and answer me (וענני)" (Ps 60:7).[124] The implicit act of the hand is parallel to ענה, the verbal image of help, yet just as the eye can represent positive or negative attention, so the hand can represent positive or negative "touch." In some cases, the narrator clarifies what kind of influence the hand has: "For I failed[125] to ask the king for a band of soldiers and cavalry to protect us against the enemy on our way, since we had told the king that the hand of our God is gracious

---

121. Cf. Isa 42:1; Pss 16:5; 41:13; Prov 28:17.
122. Cf. Isa 63:5; 59:16; Pss 37:17, 24; 145:14.
123. Cf. Deut 1:38; 1 Sam 23:16; Ezek 30:24; Hos 7:15; Nah 2:2; 2 Chr 11:17; Neh 3:19 and many more.
124. Cf. Ps 108:6, as well as Ps 44:4, together with "arm" (זרוע).
125. My translation. See further my "בוש in the Psalms—Shame or Disappointment?," *JSOT* 34 (2010): 294–313 (311).

(עזו...על...לטובה) to all who seek him, but his power and his wrath (עזו ואפו) are against all who forsake him" (Ezra 8:22; cf. Neh 2:18). The phrase "the hand on" (יד על) elsewhere denotes a harmful divine act (punishment), and appears to be a neutral phrase that can describe either positive or negative divine intervention, like the parallel expression "the eye on" (עין על). Both expressions assume sensory experience at the base of the idiomatic meaning.

To summarize, we found that metaphors of divine help are described through the senses of hearing, speech, sight, smell, and touch, indicating God's responsiveness to requests and his help. At times, these metaphors are associated with human help, providence, or judgment. At other times, they exclusively describe divine help. We also found that when it is God who is using the senses, they can also be interpreted as harm and punishment, with the meaning attached to a sensory experience changing according to the subject of the action. Hearing has one meaning when God (or the dominant partner in a relationship) hears—help, attentiveness; it has another meaning when the weaker party hears—obedience.[126] Similarly, sight can mean judgment, empathy, and help when God sees, and expectation when humans see. On its own, the kinaesthetic sense does not necessarily indicate responsiveness to a request and help. However, characteristics of kinaesthesia and orientation are often used to describe the use of the different senses. Turning towards the supplicant is described through the verbs "to incline" (שעה, נטה)[127] and indicates help. Turning away from the supplicant, which is described through the verbs "to hide" (עלם Hiphil) and "to reject" (מאס), indicates refusal to give help and even punishment. The imagery of conscious opening/closing of the senses also indicates a voluntary use of the senses. In his desire to help, God hears, smells, answers, and sees.[128] In his refusal to help, God closes his ears, refuses to smell, is silent, and diverts his eyes.

The use of the phrases and idioms examined above creates a contextual pattern in which the various modalities appear in a similar context, albeit with variance in specific semantic reasoning. Like other sensory contextual patterns in the Hebrew Bible, the context of help—including divine help—involves a perception of the use of the senses as indicators of the ability to act: "See, the Lord's hand (יד) is not too short to save, nor his ear too dull to hear (כבדה אזנו משמוע)" (Isa 59:1). A summary of the phrases and metaphors mentioned in this section appears

---

126.   For the ambivalence of hearing and obedience, see *MKCS*, 155.

127.   See Chapter 2, n. 188.

128.   On the meaning "to open" in the root "to answer" (ענה), see Levine, "Biblical Women's Marital Rights," 103.

in Table 3, below. It demonstrates how the biblical sensorium reappears in the context of help and support, based on a range of meanings including dialogue, responsiveness, judgment, understanding, providence, empathy/identification, and mercy.

Table 3. *Sensory Phrases and Metaphors for Help and Support*

Sight	Hearing	Kinaesthesia	Speech	Taste[129]	Smell	Tactile
נבט Hiphil	שמע	לא בזה	ענה		ריח Hiphil	תמך
ראה ב	שמע אל/ל	שעה			ארך אפיים	סמך
ראה את עני	שמע בקול/לקול	נטה				אחז
שום עין	קשב					נשא
פקח עין	אזן קשבת					שלח
עינים פתוחות	אזן Hiphil נטה					חזק Piel
חוס עין						לא עזב
						יד
Hiphil עין [130] עלם	אטם אזן[130]	מאס[130]				יד אל/על
עצם עין[130]						ימין
						זרוע

The Power to Harm

As is clear from the previous paragraphs and the summary table, various sensory experiences offer evidence of a widespread metaphor for describing a God who helps his people as a whole as well as individuals. This group of metaphors was partially based on the actions performed as part of the juridical and the ritual systems (i.e. the metaphor has a concrete base), and partially on derived meanings attributed to the different senses and sensory organs (i.e. the metaphor is based on another metaphor). These metaphors are commonly used to portray both human and divine help, even though most of the examples in the biblical text relate to divine help alone. We also saw how the use of the different senses could denote help and support in some cases, and harmful action in others. In the following paragraphs, I will examine idioms and phrases, concrete

---

129. The absence of one sense from a specific contextual pattern is detailed in Table 10 and the subsequent discussion.

130. These phrases express unwillingness to help, and provide evidence by way of negation.

and metaphoric, that describe sensory experience as harm and damage. Such idioms and phrases describe both divine and human acts. Moreover, the following paragraphs will demonstrate how using the senses to harm, just like using the senses to help, is based on the perception of sensory experience as a symbol of strength and ability.[131]

Most idioms and phrases discussed below are associated with control,[132] and more specifically, they are derived from the field of warfare and conquest. That is most obvious when kinaesthetic experience is involved, as well as the foot as the representing kinaesthetic organ.[133] The metaphor "walking is control" most probably has its origin in legal symbolic acts that express control and conquest. See, for example, the grand finale of the fight over the five kings: "When they brought the kings out to Joshua, Joshua summoned all the Israelites, and said to the chiefs of the warriors who had gone with him, 'Come near, put your feet (שימו את־רגליכם) on the necks of these kings.' Then they came near and put their feet (וישימו את־רגליהם) on their necks" (Josh 10:24). Publicly stepping on the enemy, here expressed by the phrase "to put the feet on" (שים רגל על), is a widespread ancient Near Eastern sign of control. In addition to it, stepping and walking in the Hebrew Bible (and the ancient Near East) symbolize conquest and control over a land. When Yahweh warns the Israelite not to conquer the land of the descendants of Esau, he uses the following words: "Do not engage in battle with them, for I will not give you even so much as a foot's length (מדרך כף־רגל) of their land, since I have given Mt. Seir to Esau as a possession" (Deut 2:5).

Another example of how the foot symbolizes control is bowing down before the ruler (or before God). The future status of Zion is thus described: "Kings shall be your foster fathers, and their queens your nursing mothers. With their faces to the ground they shall bow down to you (לך), and lick the dust of your feet (רגליך)…" (Isa 49:23). Meir Malul comments on these multiple expressions of power, and points out that they have their origins in walking/stepping as a symbolic legal act, and not just an act of humiliation.[134] And hence, even when the walking

---

131. See pp. 175–82, below, for further discussion.

132. See, at length, *MKCS*, 155–231. Control is not always harm. In the current discussion, the field of control is represented in a few different fields. It seems that the association of control in sensory perception is deeply rooted in the perception of sensory perception as ability (see pp. 175–82, below).

133. For the foot as the organ representing movement, see Stendebach, *TDOT* 13:314, as well as pp. 125–26, above.

134. *MKCS*, 146–47. For this idiom as shaming act, see M. L. Bechtel, "Shame as Sanction of Social Control in Biblical Israel: Judicial, Political and Social Shaming," *JSOT* 49 (1991): 47–76 (72–74).

act and the foot do not represent an actual legal act, they indicate the balance of power between the two parties, which in the Hebrew Bible is often portrayed through the spatial image of tall vs. short. This is expressed symbolically in legal actions surrounding ownership, and in other symbolic actions such as bowing down. The stepping and walking actions definitely belong in the kinaesthetic field, as is clear from the use of the root "to move" (נוע) that describes both walking and control. A fine example is found in the parable of Jotham. When the trees ask the olive tree to rule over them, the olive tree gives the following response: "Shall I stop producing my rich oil by which gods and mortals are honoured, and go to sway (לנוע) over the trees?" (Judg 9:9).[135]

All these examples for stepping, walking, and the leg as a means of control are set in the backdrop of kinaesthetic harming expressions. Here too the leg can occur on its own, without kinaesthetic verbs, to denote this meaning. See the victory song of David: "I pursued my enemies and destroyed them, and did not turn back until they were consumed. I consumed them; I struck them down, so that they did not rise (לא יקומון); they fell under my feet (תחת רגלי). For you girded me with strength for the battle; you made my assailants sink under me" (2 Sam 22:38–40). Note how the speaker's control, having his feet on top, is contrasted to the lack of mobility imposed on his enemies—they are unable to stand up. Similar notions are expressed using other words for feet, such as פעם. The power of Yahweh (in contrast to the king of Assyria and the idols) is described thus: "I dug wells and drank foreign waters, I dried up with the sole of my foot (בכף־פעמי) all the streams of Egypt" (2 Kgs 19:24; Isa 37:25).

Notably, conquering territory on foot, as well as other symbolic actions that constitute a metaphor of control and harm, are all based on kinaesthesia, as the roots describing conquest demonstrate.[136] The semantic correlation between control, conquest, and harm is evident from the different verbs from the kinaesthetic field used to describe these actions. The verb "to step" (דרך) denotes control, conquest, and harm. The control of God is clear from Job 9:8: "Who alone stretched out the heavens and trampled (דורך) the waves of the Sea."[137] The conquest of Canaan is described in Deut 11:24: "Every place on which you set foot (תדרך כף־רגלכם) shall be yours; your territory shall extend from the wilderness to the Lebanon and from the river, the River Euphrates, to the

---

135. Cf. vv. 11, 13.

136. For example, "to conquer" (כבש) belongs to the field of movement. See *MKCS*, 147.

137. Cf. Amos 4:13; Mic 1:3.

Western Sea."[138] And, finally, harm is evident in the wine press prophecy: "I have trodden (דרכתי) the wine press alone, and from the peoples no one was with me; I trod them in my anger (אדרכם באפי) and trampled them in my wrath (ארמסם בחמתי)..." (Isa 63:3, cf. v. 6). The last verse demonstrates both concrete stepping, and derived meaning of harm in the verb דרך. It also parallels the verb רמס, which has the same concrete meaning (to step over), but serves only to describe the derived meaning—trampling that leads to destruction: "And among the nations the remnant of Jacob, surrounded by many peoples, shall be like a lion among the animals of the forest, like a young lion among the flocks of sheep, which, when it goes through (עבר), treads down (רמס) and tears in pieces (טרף), with no one to deliver" (Mic 5:7).[139] The cluster of verbs that denote harm in this verse includes kinaesthetic verbs רמס and עבר,[140] and an eating verb (טרף, see below).

These kinaesthetic expressions associated with harm and punishment actions are frequently correlated with conquest and warfare, a correlation that we shall return to below. For now, note that the verb "to spy" (רגל Piel) is also a kinaesthetic verb, one that can describe harm, albeit indirectly. The derived meaning of the root and its shift to denote speech, can describe actual harm. The righteous "...do not slander (רגל) with their tongue, and do no evil to their friends, nor take up a reproach (חרפה) against their neighbours" (Ps 15:3).[141] The unique phrase found in this verse, "to slander with the tongue" (רגל על לשונו), parallels causing harm and reproaching (also a verbal act). Speech can indeed be harmful, as the proverb goes, "Death and life are in the power of the tongue..." (Prov 18:21).[142] Harming speech recurs in different expressions and phrases that denote negative, lying, or hurtful speech. The tongue seems to be particularly endowed with the power to cause damage.[143] The wrongdoers have "haughty eyes, a lying tongue, and hands that shed innocent blood" (Prov 6:17). Interestingly, the tongue as a vehicle for hurtful speech is often described as a sharp weapon, such as the sword, the arrow, and the bow. The wicked are those "who whet their tongues like swords, who

---

138. Cf. Deut 11:25; Josh 9:3.

139. This is the meaning in all occurrences of רמס (2 Kgs 7:17, 20; 9:33; 14:9; Isa 1:12; 16:4; 26:6; 28:3; 41:25; 63:3; Ezek 26:11; 34:18; Mic 5:7; Nah 3:14; Pss 7:6; 91:13; Dan 8:7, 10; 2 Chr 25:18).

140. Cf. Exod 12:23. Another walking verb that denotes control and harm is צעד; see Judg 5:4; Ps 68:8.

141. Here the verb is רגל Qal, yet similar meaning in Piel is found in 2 Sam 19:28, see pp. 83–84, above.

142. Cf. Prov 12:18; 15:4.

143. Shupak, *Where Can Wisdom Be Found?*, 282.

aim bitter words like arrows, shooting from ambush at the blameless; they shoot suddenly and without fear" (Ps 64:4).[144] The Judean traitors are similarly portrayed: "They bend their tongues like bows; they have grown strong in the land for falsehood, and not for truth; for they proceed from evil to evil… Their tongue is a deadly arrow; it speaks deceit through the mouth. They all speak friendly words to their neighbours, but inwardly are planning to lay an ambush" (Jer 9:2, 7 [3, 9]).[145] The tongue, which symbolizes speech, can be used as a sword, an arrow, a bow, it is even possible to strike (נכה Hiphil) with the tongue (Jer 18:18). Such description of the tongue is stressed when the "man of tongue" (איש לשון) parallels the "man of wrongdoing" (איש חמס רע, Ps 140:12), as well as in the parallel between deceiving speech and evil deeds: "Keep your tongue from evil, and your lips from speaking deceit" (Ps 34:14).[146]

As these examples demonstrate, lying is a supreme example of causing harm, and lying speech is compared to harming with a sharp weapon. This metaphor is not exclusively used with the tongue. It also appears in correlation with the mouth: "you devote your mouth (פיך) to evil, and yoke your tongue (לשונך) to deceit" (Ps 50:19, JPS).[147] The power of speech can be produced by the lips as well: "…he shall strike the earth with the rod of his mouth (שבט פיו), and with the breath of his lips (רוח שפתיו) he shall kill the wicked" (Isa 11:4). In this verse, the real power of words in the juridical system is extended to describe an immediate physical outcome of speech. The image of the "rod of the mouth" is yet another example of harmful speech as a weapon.

Sharpness of speech is also embedded in the root "to reproach" (חרף), already mentioned above as a parallel to רגל. In the Hebrew Bible, this root in its verbal form is used to describe harmful or insulting speech in a military context.[148] In Mishnaic Hebrew, as well as other Semitic languages, such as Aramaic, the meaning of this root is "sharp."[149] It seems that the images of sharp speech are at the background of this enigmatic

144. Cf. Ps 57:5, the association between taste and speech was discussed above, pp. 120–23.

145. Cf. Hos 7:16. Another image is of the tongue as a whip (שוט, Job 5:21, see *HALOT* 4:1440 for interpretation) and as a razor (תער, Ps 52:4).

146. Cf. Ps 50:19; Job 20:12. See Malul, "Ceremonial and Juridical Background" (part b III) for the juridical background, and more specifically the phrase "to stab (לטש) with the eye" (Job 16:9), which images sight as a sharp object.

147. Cf. Job 20:12; Ps 34:14.

148. See my "Honour and Shame," 29–32.

149. BDB, 357; *HALOT* 1:355; E. Kutsch, "חרף ḥrp II," *TDOT* 5:209–15 (209–10).

semantic shift.[150] At least in one verse where this root appears in the context of harm, we find again the associative pattern speech-eating, to which we will return below: "It is zeal for your house that has consumed me (אכלתני); the insults of those who insult you (חרפות חורפיך) have fallen on me" (Ps 69:10).

To sum up, although the background to metaphors of hurtful speech appears to be the legal and social field,[151] a large number of metaphors is associated with military weaponry. There are many examples of hurtful words expressed as a sharp weapon, and there is a correlation between the root חרף and military narratives. Hurtful tongue images therefore belong in a similar context as the stepping and trampling foot. Like other sensory expressions, the capacity for hurtful speech is associated with power and ability—speech can have a positive *or* negative impact, and is not necessarily harming or helping.[152]

We saw in the previous verse from Psalms that hurtful speech is compared to consumption (eating). The verse is not unique, and eating is often used to describe hurtful acts: "Assuredly, thus said the Lord, the God of Hosts: 'Because they said that (דברכם את־הדבר), I am putting my words (דברי) into your mouth (בפיך) as fire, and this people shall be firewood, which it will consume (ואכלתם)'" (Jer 5:14, JPS).[153] Descriptions of consumption as a metaphor for destruction appear several times in the military context of control and conquest, sometimes as concrete (real), at other times metaphoric.[154] An example of the concrete description is the image of an animal with its prey (e.g. Gen 37:33), or an animal consuming a carcass (e.g. 1 Kgs 14:11), which then becomes a figurative image for killing and harm: "Mark this, then, you who forget God, or I will tear you apart (אטרף), and there will be no one to deliver" (Ps 50:22).[155] A similar figurative phrase describes death by the sword:

150.   For discussion of the enigma, see J. K. Aitken, *The Semantics of Blessing and Cursing in Ancient Hebrew* (ANESSup 23; Leuven: Peeters, 2007), 174.

151.   Malul, "Ceremonial and Juridical Background," n. 80, for eating as slander.

152.   See also "I have killed them by the words of my mouth" (Hos 6:5, NRSV), and the opposite: "…one does not live by bread alone, but by every word that comes from the mouth of the Lord" (Deut 8:3, NRSV).

153.   Cf. the parallel eating–speech, in the root בלע: "The words from the mouth of the wise are favour, but the lips of the fools consume them (תבלענו)" (Qoh 10:12, my translation); "You love all words of slander (בלע), deceitful tongue" (Ps 52:6, my translation—this verse can only fit in the scheme if we assume a pun: II בלע, "slander," has a homonym, I בלע, "something that was swollen").

154.   Idioms of eating are related but are not identical with the sense of taste. For the sense of taste and control, see *MKCS*, 130–34.

155.   Cf. Amos 1:11; Mic 5:7.

"…Your own sword devoured (אכלה חרבכם) your prophets like a ravening lion" (Jer 2:30). The image of the consuming sword is, in fact, quite common, as clear from David's comment on the death of Uriah: "…Do not let this matter trouble you, for the sword devours (תאכל החרב) now one and now another; press your attack on the city, and overthrow it…" (2 Sam 11:25).[156] These images also throw light on the term "by the mouth of the sword" (לפי חרב) which can be understood as a metaphor of the consuming sword: "Then the people of Judah fought against Jerusalem and took it. They put it to the sword (lit. 'to the mouth of the sword,' לפי חרב) and set the city on fire" (Judg 1:8).[157]

Similar to destruction by sword, destruction by fire too originates from concrete description and evolved into a figurative description of consumption. The past destruction of Moab is thus described: "For fire came out from Heshbon, flame from the city of Sihon. It devoured (אכלה) Ar of Moab, and swallowed up the heights of the Arnon" (Num 21:28).[158] Although real fire could have been part of warfare, in this song it is an idiom for swift conquest. When the fire is the fire of God, it can be a real fire, and it can be a metaphor for God's revelation as harmful and destructive power:[159] "Now when the people (וישמע) complained in the hearing (באזני) of the Lord about their misfortunes, the Lord heard it and his anger was kindled (ויחר אפו). Then the fire of the Lord burned (ותבער אש) against them, and consumed (ותאכל) some outlying parts of the camp" (Num 11:1, actual fire); "For the Lord your God is a devouring fire (אש אכלה), a jealous God" (Deut 4:24, metaphoric fire).[160] The harmful action of God as consuming fire parallels his harming voice and arm, and thus demonstrates the multisensory aspect of the harm context:

156. See also 2 Sam 18:8; Isa 1:19–20; 31:8; Jer 12:12; 46:10, 14; Nah 2:14; 3:15.

157. Cf. Josh 6:21; 8:24; Judg 4:15; 18:27; 1 Sam 22:19; 2 Sam 15:14; 2 Kgs 10:25. Yet some scholars understand the lexeme פה to mean "edge" (similar to "lips" [שפה]; see, e.g., Garcia-López, *TDOT* 11:493). Ancient Near Eastern iconography seems to support our view. Teeth and tongues were common decorative motifs used on swords and axes in Mesopotamia. See C. Wilcke, "A Riding Tooth: Metaphor, Metonymy and Synecdoche, Quick and Frozen in Everyday Language," in *Figurative Language in the Ancient Near East* (ed. M. Mindlin, M. J. Geller, and J. E. Wansbrough; London: School of Oriental and African Studies, 1987), 77–102 (79–81).

158. See also Judg 9:15, 20; Isa 5:24; 26:11; 33:14; Jer 23:25; 48:35 and many others where burning fire "eats."

159. E.g. Lev 9:24, and many more. Note the danger in fire theophany, expressed in Deut 5:21.

160. See also Lev 10:2; Num 16:35; 26:10; Deut 9:3; 2 Sam 22:9; 2 Kgs 1:10–14; Isa 8:17; 29:6; 30:27; Zeph 3:8; Pss 18:9; 21:10.

"And the Lord will cause his majestic voice to be heard (הֹשְׁמִיעַ...קוֹלוֹ) and the descending blow of his arm to be seen (זְרוֹעוֹ יַרְאָה), in furious anger (אַף) and a flame of devouring fire (אֵשׁ אוֹכְלָה), with a cloudburst and tempest and hailstones" (Isa 30:30).[161] Nevertheless, we should note that the description of a devouring God is not limited to harm by fire, but also appears as an image of destruction by ingestion: "God who brings him out of Egypt, is like the horns of a wild ox for him; he shall devour (יֹאכַל) the nations that are his foes and break (יְגָרֵם) their bones. He shall strike with his arrows" (Num 24:8).

Thus far, we have seen destruction by the sword and by fire compared to consumption. Both these images are correlated with conquest and war. We also find descriptions of "consuming" the enemy's loot: "You may, however, take as your booty the women, the children, livestock, and everything else in the town, all its spoil. You may enjoy (lit. 'eat,' וְאָכַלְתָּ) the spoil of your enemies, which the Lord your God has given you" (Deut 20:14). Such portrayals appear to refer not just to the looting of food, but to looting in general, so the eating idiom is expanded beyond the concrete.[162] Concrete actions of death by sword, fire, and looting are all described as consumption that evolves into metaphors for conquest: "You shall devour (וְאָכַלְתָּ) all the peoples that the Lord your God is giving over to you, showing them no pity..." (Deut 7:16). Furthermore, the root "to eat, to devour" (אכל) can also describe harm in the general sense, as in the expression "a land that consumes its inhabitants" (אֶרֶץ אֹכֶלֶת יוֹשְׁבֶיהָ, Num 13:32). It can also be used to describe harm by disease: "The sword is outside, pestilence and famine are inside; those in the field die (יָמוּת) by the sword; those in the city—famine and pestilence devour them (יֹאכְלֶנּוּ)" (Ezek 7:15). Here the root אכל parallels מוּת, "to die."[163] We find אכל is used in an abstract, derived way, to describe different kinds of offence. The images of sword, fire, wild beasts, and disease give this verb an implicit hue of excessive eating, which is wrong eating. The enemies are the ones eating excessively in ritual context, moral context, and finally, military context: "Therefore all who devour you shall be devoured (אֹכְלַיִךְ יֵאָכֵלוּ), and all your foes, everyone of them, shall go into captivity; those who plunder you shall be plundered, and all who prey on you I will make a prey" (Jer 30:16).[164]

161.   Cf. Isa 10:17.

162.   Cf. Isa 1:7; 62:8–9; Jer 3:24.

163.   See also the use of אכל as slander: "When evildoers assail me to devour my flesh (לֶאֱכֹל אֶת־בְּשָׂרִי)—my adversaries and foes—they shall stumble and fall" (Ps 27:2; cf. Ps 53:6). For a detailed explanation, see Malul, "Ceremonial and Juridical Background," nn. 22, 67.

164.   See n. 153, above.

As we saw with roots in the field of mobility, there are several roots in the consumption field that are unique to harmful consumption, such as "to devour" (טרף), "to swallow" (בלע), "to gnaw" (גרם), and "to chew" (גרס), alongside the more common root "to eat" (אכל), which can describe positive and negative consumption. We also saw that "devouring" as a harmful act can be the result of God's fiery fury: "You will make them like a fiery furnace when you appear (לעת פניך). The Lord will swallow them up (יבלעם) in his wrath (באפו), and fire will consume them (תאכלם)" (Ps 21:10). God's harmful acts in this verse are derived from his אף, literally, "nose," and are more commonly translated and interpreted as wrath or anger.[165] The polysemantic nature of the word אף raises the question of a correlation between the sense of smell and harm. In many verses where אף is mentioned, it is difficult categorically to determine which of the meanings is appropriate, since descriptions of God's anger relate both to the nose as an organ, and to his anger.[166] Thus we find the consuming fire described as emerging from God's nose: "For a fire is kindled by my anger (alternatively, 'in my nose,' באפי), and burns to the depths of Sheol; it devours (ותאכל) the earth and its increase, and sets on fire the foundations of the mountains" (Deut 32:22).[167] It seems that the polysemantic nature of the word should be explained on a syntagmatic basis. The common phrases חרה/חרון/חרי אף mean "to be angry," "anger," either since while angry the nose is hot, or because it is "cringed."[168] When אף appears on its own, it can bear the meaning of the whole phrase, because of syntagmatic association. The physical aspect of the phrase, thought, is not lost: "Then the earth reeled and rocked; the foundations also of the mountains trembled and quaked, because he was angry (חרה). Smoke went up from his nostrils (אפו), and devouring fire from his mouth (פיו); glowing coals flamed forth from him" (Ps 18:9 [8]).[169] The nose here is a source of divine harm, and as we saw earlier the smelling nose denotes God's acceptance of sacrifice, and inevitably his help. The link to smell, and particularly smelling sacrifice, is

---

165. The anger (lit. "nose") of Yahweh is described as consuming fire in 2 Sam 22:9; Isa 30:20, 27; Zeph 3:8; Pss 18:9; 21:10.

166. Kedar-Kopfstein, "Decoding of Polysemantic Lexemes," 19–20.

167. Cf. Jer 15:14; 17:4; Isa 30:27; 65:5.

168. Anger is the contextual meaning of the phrase, the etymology and semantic reasoning for the phrase is debatable. See pp. 104–6, 128, above, and Kotzé, "A Cognitive Linguistic Methodology," for a recent summary of opinions. See also the verb אנף, which describes divine anger and is a denominative verb derived from אף (see *HALOT* 1:72 for this and other opinions).

169. Cf. Ps 74:1; Job 41:12.

therefore part of the idiom of the angry nose. Notably, unlike the other sensory organs, the nose is not a source of harm in a military context.

So far, I have discussed kinaesthetic, speech, eating, and olfactory images of harm that sprout from contexts of war, slander, and sacrifice. I will now turn to phrases and idioms related to sight as harm.

The power of sight is based on the metaphor "sight is control/ownership," as we find in the descriptions of the promise of the land to Abraham and to Moses.[170] In the description of Balaam's prophecy, sight also reflects a position of power and control. Balak assumes that seeing the Israelites will make the curse possible, and states: "…Come with me to another place from which you may see them (תראנו); you shall see (תראה) only part of them, and shall not see (לא תראה) them all; then curse them for me from there" (Num 23:13). The similarity to kinaesthetic expressions of control and ownership mentioned above is notable. In addition, control is expressed by the spatial image of height which enables watching from above. The power of Yahweh is that "he rules forever in his might; His eyes scan (עיניו...תצפינה) the nations…" (Ps 66:7, JPS). Being high is an image for control as it enables one to see, and hence to know more than others. The ability to see all can cause help (as demonstrated above), or harm, and is neutral by itself: "The Lord looks down (הביט) from heaven; he sees (ראה) all humankind. From where he sits enthroned he watches (השגיח) all the inhabitants of the earth—he who fashions (יצר) the hearts of them all, and observes (מבין) all their deeds" (Ps 33:13–15).[171]

Understanding the fundamental metaphor "sight is control" leads us to images and phrases of sight as harm, prominent but not reserved to the military context. The root "to look at" (שור) is used alongside "to see" (ראה): "Look at the heavens and see (ראה); observe (שור) the clouds, which are higher than you" (Job 35:5; cf. 7:8). In several verses we find that the participle שורר does not serve as a neutral adjective to describe a person who is looking, but rather an enemy, someone who lies in wait: "He will repay the evil of my watchful foes (שררי)" (Ps 54:7).[172] The noun שור, also describes the enemy: "My eyes have seen (תבט עיני) the defeat of my adversaries (שורי); my ears have heard (תשמענה) the rout of my wicked foes" (Ps 92:12, NIV). The pun embedded in the verse is the reversal of fate, the "watchful foes" (JPS) will be seen. It seems that the

---

170.   Gen 13:14–15; Num 27:12–13; Deut 32:49. See Malul, "Holistic-Integrative Investigation," 148–50; Stendebach, *TDOT* 11:35.

171.   Cf. Ps 128:6; Prov 15:6.

172.   Cf. Job 36:24; Pss 5:9; 27:11; 56:3; 59:11.

correlation between the meaning "to see" and the meaning "to harm" in the root שור, is polysemantic, rather than homonymic, and that it is linked to the spatial image of sight.[173]

Another sight-related root which is frequently used in military context is "to watch" (צפה), which can describe neutral sight or lurking: "The wicked watch (צופה) for the righteous, and seek to kill them" (Ps 37:32). Again, the negative sight is born out of neutral metaphor "sight is waiting/expectation" (cf. ראה עין על, which can have the same meaning as קוה), and the verb צפה includes these meanings too. Hence, watching in expectation can be positive (hope) or negative. Interestingly, the root צפן, which has a similar euphony, describes a hidden thing, but also hiding in order to watch and harm: "...Come with us, let us lie in wait (נארבה) for blood; let us wantonly ambush (נצפנה) the innocent" (Prov 1:11; cf. v. 18). Apart from the similar sound of the roots, צפה and צפן share the meaning of secretly seeing in an attempt to harm.

As we have seen, sight-related metaphors of understanding and control usually describe help situations: "The eyes of the Lord are on (עיני...אל) the righteous, and his ears are open to their cry" (Ps 34:16).[174] Sight seems to be positive unless otherwise mentioned. This is the case unless stated differently: "and though they go into captivity in front of their enemies, there I will command the sword, and it shall kill them; and I will fix my eyes" (שמתי עיני) on them for harm and not for good (Amos 9:4). At times, only a careful analysis of the parallelism reveals an idiom of harmful sight: "You deliver a humble people, but your eyes are upon (עיניך על) the haughty to bring them down" (2 Sam 22:28). Nevertheless, when it comes to the denominative verb "to set an eye on" (עין Piel) it is reserved to negative sight, which implies jealousy and harming

173.   See also the word "wall" (שור, Gen 49:22; 2 Sam 22:30; Ps 18:30; and in Aramaic Ezra 4:12, 13, 15) that has the same polysemantic sense. I reject the division into homonymic roots in this case. See Palache, *Semantic Notes*, 27–28, for the links between sight verbs and circling, including שור. According to BDB, 1003, the root שור in Isa 57:9 means movement, and not sight, similar to the noun תשורה (1 Sam 9:7), meaning present/merchandise. Thus BDB (1004) distinguished II שור ("to relate > to see") and III שור ("to be high > wall"). This distinction is not grounded etymologically or semantically. In fact, a similar semantic shift "to see someone > gift" is found in Akkadian. The word *tāmartu* ("gift") is derived from the root *amāru* ("to see"). The semantic shift is based on the obligation to see the face of the covenant-lord each year; see Malul, "Some Idioms," 197; H. R. Cohen, *Biblical Hapax Legomena in the Light of Akkadian and Ugaritic* (SBL Dissertation Series; Atlanta: Scholars Press, 1978), 24–30. Furthermore, we should consider the etymological link between שור/שרר and צרר.

174.   Cf. 33:18 and the examples given above, pp. 132–37.

intentions. Saul's attitude towards David, is so described: "So Saul eyed (ויהי...עוין) David from that day on" (1 Sam 18:9). Lifting the eyes can also be interpreted as an attack: "Whom have you mocked and reviled? Against whom have you raised your voice and haughtily lifted your eyes (ותשא...עיניך)? Against the Holy One of Israel!" (2 Kgs 19:22; Isa 37:23). Verbal attack is parallel in this verse to some kind of an inappropriate look, and both have the spatial aspect of (the attempt to gain) height. Clearly, in this verse the attempt to harm through speech or sight is unrealistic, as the power of the offender (king of Assyria) is less the offended (Yahweh). Height metaphors in the Hebrew Bible, whether associated with the eye, the heart, or any other action, have a dual meaning: they can indicate control (honour), but can also indicate a deceiving attempt to achieve such control (i.e. pretending to be an honourable person).[175] The following parallel demonstrates similar imagery: "haughty (lit. 'high,' רמות) eyes, a lying tongue..." (Prov 6:17).[176]

Thus far, we have seen that sight denotes control, and such control is expanded to harmful deeds in the concrete realm of spying, as well as the abstract realm of harming. Another phrase that deserves attention is "bad/to bad with the eye" (עין רע/רעע עין). John Elliott claims that this combination is associated with the "evil eye" phenomenon in the Hebrew Bible, based on a belief in the power of the eye to cause harm and to sow destruction.[177] In fact, it is difficult to determine whether belief in the evil eye was widespread during the biblical period,[178] and Elliott presents very few biblical passages to support his statement. The "evil eye" combination only appears twice in the book of Proverbs, and seems to

---

175. See my "Honour and Shame," 74–76, 88–89.

176. For the legal background of these phrases, see part B in Malul, "Ceremonial and Juridical Background."

177. J. H. Elliott, "The Evil Eye in the First Testament: The Ecology and Culture of Pervasive Belief," in *The Bible and the Politics of Exegesis* (Festschrift Norman K. Gottwald; ed. D. Jobling, P. L. Day, and G. T. Sheppard; Cleveland, Ohio: Pilgrim, 1991), 147–59.

178. For the belief in the evil eye in Mesopotamia, Thomsen claims that it is quite rare, and that magic was more often described as evil tongue or mouth (speech), than eye (sight); see Thomsen, "The Evil Eye," 28, vis-à-vis Stendebach, *TDOT* 11:30. Note that Middle Hebrew also parallels the "evil eye" to "the evil tongue." Malul reaches a different conclusion, and finds that the biblical and ancient Near Eastern belief in the evil eye was quite widespread, based on the model that the eye sends out "rays" or "powers." Malul further claims that this model explains the legal symbolic act of the open eye; see Malul, "Ceremonial and Juridical Background," n. 67; *MKCS*, 208–9, 267–68, see also Ford, "Ninety-Nine by the Evil Eye," for Ugarit.

denote a stingy person: "A miserly (רע עין) man runs after wealth; He does not realize that loss will overtake it" (Prov 28:22, JPS; cf. 23:6). A comparison with the contrasting expression "good eye" (טוב עין) hints at the same meaning: "The generous (טוב עין) man is blessed, for he gives of his bread to the poor" (Prov 22:9). The phrase "evil eye" is therefore less a metaphor of harm than a metaphor of refraining from help. This is similar to the mentioned phrases "hide the eye" (עלם עין) and "eye without mercy" (לא חסה עין):[179] "Whoever gives to the poor will lack nothing, but one who turns a blind eye (מעלים עיניו) will get many a curse" (Prov 28:27). While it might be possible to assume indirectly that refraining from help is equivalent to harm, this cannot be inferred directly from the meaning of the phrase or its contextual usage.

The verb "to do bad" (רעע) also appears together with the eye in three verses: "Be careful that you do not entertain a mean thought, thinking, 'The seventh year, the year of remission, is near,' and therefore *view* your needy neighbour with *hostility* (רעה עינך) and give nothing; your neighbour might cry to the Lord against you, and you would incur guilt" (Deut 15:9). This phrase, like the "evil eye," indicates refraining from help, and is sometimes interpreted as jealousy.[180] The same phrase appears in the covenant curse: "He who is most tender and fastidious among you shall be too mean (תרע עינו) to his brother and the wife of his bosom and the children he has spared (Deut 28:54; cf. v. 56). In short, the root רעע (as adjective or verb) describes the eye in those biblical passages in which the rich and poor are contrasted.[181] Having an evil eye indicated refraining from help, especially stinginess, rather than actual harm. It is possible that having a "good eye" (עין טוב) is to be paralleled to having a "satisfied eye" (עין שבע),[182] a phrase which appears three times in the Hebrew Bible, describing satisfaction, in contrast to metaphors of jealousy and stinginess.[183]

We have already seen that most harm metaphors originating in the field of speech, eating, smell, and sight are associated with the semantic

---

179. Refraining from sight is expressed in the phrases "to hide the eye" (העלים, Josh 13:14; Isa 1:15); "his eye did not show mercy" (חסה, Ezek 5:11; 7:4, 9; 8:18; 9:10). These phrases are negated to help images, see Stendebach, *TDOT* 11:41.

180. Elliott, "The Evil Eye," 151, but see Tigay, who explains the phrase רעה עין ("the eye is mean"), as a simple synecdoche, "you are mean"; see J. H. Tigay, *Deuteronomy: The Traditional Hebrew Text with the New JPS Translation* (JPS Torah Commentary; Philadelphia: Jewish Publication Society, 1996), 147.

181. Elliott, "The Evil Eye," 149.

182. See Chapter 1, n. 165.

183. Qoh 1:8; 4:8; Prov 27:20. Cf. the usage of hunger idioms to describe desire (Ps 78:29–30).

field of war and conquest. There is also widespread use of tactile images to describe harm, as we will show below. Just like in the field of kinaesthesia and eating, there are roots in the field of touch that exclusively mean harmful touch, such as "to trap" (לכד) and "to conquer" (כבש). We also find that the verbs נגע and פגע ("to touch"), which are tactile verbs, most often are used to describe violent touch. It is hard to determine whether a negative tone is part of the basic meaning of these roots, yet contextual examination shows that such a tone is present.[184] A fine example is found in a warning to Israel's enemies: "Do not touch (תגעו) my anointed ones; do my prophets no harm (תרעו)" (Ps 105:1; Chr 16:22). In this parallel, it is clear that פגע means "to harm." Similar is Abimelech's warning: "Whoever touches (הנגע) this man or his wife shall be put to death" (Gen 26:11).[185] In a few cases, we find a negative indicator to stress the type of touch involved: "He will deliver you from six troubles; in seven no harm shall touch you (לא־יגע בך רע)" (Job 5:19). Here, a "bad" touch is opposite to deliverance (נצל Hiphil), and the specification of the type of touch hints that it is possible to have a positive touch too. However, in many biblical passages this root is used to describe a specific case of harming someone's legal rights, and not just harm in general, and its negative tone is self-evident. When Isaac bargains with the shepherds of Gerar, here is what they say: "We see plainly that the Lord has been with you; so we say, let there be an oath between you and us, and let us make a covenant with you so that you will do us no harm (רעה), just as we have not touched you (נגענוך) and have done to you nothing but good (טוב) and have sent you away in peace. You are now the blessed of the Lord" (Gen 26:29).[186]

In this context, we should note the root in the noun form (נֶגַע) that bears the meaning of illness and crime. In the legal context, the Deuteronomic legislator gives a fine example:

> If a judicial decision is too difficult for you to make between one kind of bloodshed and another, one kind of legal right and another, or one kind of assault and another (בין נגע לנגע)—any such matters of dispute in your towns—then you shall immediately go up to the place that the Lord your God will choose, where you shall consult with the levitical priests and the judge who is in office in those days; they shall announce to you the decision in the case. (Deut 16:8; cf. 21:5)

184. On the debate, see Schwienhorst, *TDOT* 9:204.
185. Cf. 2 Sam 14:10; Jer 12:14; Zech 2:12.
186. Cf. Josh 9:19; 2 Sam 14:10; and similarly 1 Sam 25:7. See Schwienhorst, *TDOT* 9:205.

In many other cases נגע parallels other forms of harm and specifically physical harm (e.g. "Then I will punish their transgression with the rod and their iniquity with scourges [נגעים]," Ps 89:33),[187] and also a more positive note (e.g. "no evil shall befall you, no scourge [נגע] come near your tent," Ps 91:10). It is often used to denote harm through disease rather than through other calamities, and is also associated with divine punishment.[188] For example, this is how Pharaoh is punished for having taken Sarah into his house: "But the Lord afflicted Pharaoh and his house with great plagues (נגעים) because of Sarai, Abram's wife" (Gen 12:17).[189]

Divine harm is also described through the root נגע in various contexts, such as military (Judg 20:34), death (1 Sam 6:9), and leprosy (2 Kgs 15:5; 2 Chr 26:20). It is also correlated to God's power and control in the world: "who looks (מביט) on the earth and it trembles, who touches (יגע) the mountains and they smoke" (Ps 104:32). In other verses, God's touch describes harm in general, and is correlated directly to God's hand as a means for action: "Have pity on me, have pity on me, O you my friends, for the hand (יד) of God has touched (נגעה) me!" (Job 19:21).[190] As we see below, the image of God's hand as doing harm is a recurring theme, yet before returning to the matter, a word must be said on another root, the root פגע. Both roots, נגע and פגע, have a common meaning at several levels. Their core meaning is associated with touch, their derived meaning is associated with harm, their meaning in the Hiphil indicates arriving, and the noun derived from both roots exclusively describes negative occurrences. The root פגע describes harm through disease, war, death or general harm by humans or by God: "...The God of the Hebrews has revealed himself to us; let us go a three days' journey into the wilderness to sacrifice to the Lord our God, or he will fall upon us (יפגענו) with pestilence or sword" (Exod 5:3); "Naomi said to Ruth, her daughter-in-law, 'It is better, my daughter, that you go out with his young women, otherwise you might be bothered (יפגעו־בך) in another field'" (Ruth 2:22).[191]

187. Cf. 2 Sam 7:14.

188. See Gen 12:17; Exod 11:1; Deut 24:6; 1 Kgs 37–38; 2 Chr 6:28–29, and all references to skin disease נגע הצרעת in Leviticus (see Schwienhorst, *TDOT* 9:208–9).

189. For the associative pattern touch–speech, see also "He will meet with disease (נגע) and disgrace; His reproach (חרפה) will never be expunged" (Prov 6:33, JPS), see n. 148, above.

190. Cf. Job 1:11; 2:5; Isa 53:4.

191. As well as Num 35:19, 21; Judg 8:21; 15:12; 18:25; Josh 2:16; 1 Sam 22:17, 18; 2 Sam 1:15; 1 Kgs 2:25, 29, 31, 32, 34, 46; Isa 47:3; Ruth 2:22. The noun פֶּגַע has the same range of meanings (1 Kgs 5:18; Qoh 9:11).

As has been shown, in some verses harmful divine touch is sometimes associated with God's hand to represent God's strength. Here too, God's harm can be linked either to disease, as in the pestilence plague: "the hand (יד) of the Lord will strike with a deadly pestilence your livestock in the field..." (Exod 9:3); or unnatural death: "Indeed, the Lord's own hand was against them (יד...היתה בם), to root them out from the camp, until all had perished" (Deut 2:15).[192]

Portraying God's hand as causing harm comes from the neutral perception of the hand as representing God's power, whether to help or to harm: "Your right hand (ימינך), O Lord, glorious in power—your right hand (ימינך), O Lord, shattered the enemy" (Exod 15:6).[193] God's harm can be indicated by kinaesthetic direction, using the verb "to stretch out" (נטה), which we saw before in the context of hearing: "Their houses shall be turned over to others, their fields and wives together; for I will stretch out my hand (אטה ידי) against the inhabitants of the land, says the Lord" (Jer 6:12).[194] The outreaching arm of God represents his strength in general, and his ability to harm in particular.[195] However, the hand as a symbol of strength and sovereignty also appears in human contexts. Similar to the other senses, here too images from the field of warfare and conquest predominate, especially the combination "to give/be given in the hand" (נתן ביד Qal/Niphal): "I will bring the sword against you, executing vengeance for the covenant; and if you withdraw within your cities, I will send pestilence among you, and you shall be delivered (ונתתם ביד) into enemy hands" (Lev 26:25). In some cases, it is the meaning of control that dominates the phrase. When David avoids hurting Saul, he says: "The Lord rewards everyone for his righteousness and his faithfulness; for the Lord gave you into my hand today (נתנך ב...ביד), but I would not raise my hand (לשלוח ידי) against the Lord's anointed" (1 Sam 26:23).[196] At times, the hand appears on its own, without an accompanying verb, with the exact same meaning—as Moab is subdued "under the hand of Israel" (יד ישראל, Judg 3:30), and David is potentially to be harmed by the hand of the Philistines (יד פלשתים), and not by the hand of Saul (1 Sam 18:17).[197]

192. Cf. Judg 2:15; Josh 4:24 and many more.
193. Cf. Job 12:10; Ps 21:9 and many more.
194. As well as Jer 15:6; 51:25; Ezek 6:14; 14:9, 13; 16:27; 25:7, 13, 16; 35:3; Zeph 1:4. See also "to raise a hand" (נוף Hiphil, Zech 2:13); "to turn the hand" (שוב Hiphil, Amos 1:8); and "to lay a hand" (שים, Ezek 39:21).
195. Exod 9:3; Josh 4:23; 1 Sam 5:9; Isa 19:16 and many more.
196. Cf. 1 Sam 14:37; Jer 20:5; Ps 78:61; Lam 1:7 and many more.
197. For more on the hand as a symbol of sovereignty and power, see pp. 125–27, 138–39, above, as well as Malul, *Society, Law, and Custom*, 164–65.

To summarize, both harm and help metaphors are based on the actions of the senses, particularly on the perception that the senses can express the strength and sovereignty of the person implementing the action. Nevertheless, these idioms, figures, and metaphors are taken from different fields. Most harm metaphors are taken from the field of war and conquest, which is why they are so closely correlated with the metaphor "sensory perception is control." The various senses that belong to the contextual pattern of harm are summarized in the table below. Note that the words and phrases belonging to this context are describing a spectrum of meanings, including: control, conquest, punishment, slander, miserliness, refraining from help and diseases.

Table 4. *Sensory Phrases and Metaphors for Harm*

Sight	Hearing[198]	Kinaesthesia	Speech	Taste	Smell	Tactile
ראה		דרך	חרף Piel	אכל	אנף	נגע
עין (verb)		רמס	נשא חרפה על	טרף	אף	פגע
שור Polel		כבש	רגל Piel	בלע		לכד
צפה		עבר	קול Hiphil רום	גרם		כבש
נשא עין		צעד	רגל על לשון	גרס		יד
שם עין		רגל Piel	לשון	פה		נטה יד
עין על		קום על	לשון שקר	פי חרב		יד נטויה
		שים רגל	שלח פה	אש אכלה		נתן ביד
		מדרך כף רגל	שפתים			זרוע
		תחת רגל				פגע
		כף פעם				נגע

Learn, Understand, Know

One of the main contextual patterns in which sensory experience is mentioned in the Hebrew Bible is that of epistemology, that is, the senses serve as a medium through which people learn about and think about the world. The semantic field of knowledge is explored at length in *MKCS*[199] and therefore will receive a briefer discussion below. The contextual pattern of judgment will be included in the following paragraph, as part of moral judgment. Naturally there is some overlap between understanding, study, thought, and judgment, and these are separated for the sake of clarity.

198. The absence of one sense from a specific contextual pattern is detailed in Table 10 and the subsequent discussion.

199. *MKCS*, mainly 130–51.

In numerous biblical passages, eyes and ears are parallel to the heart/mind (לב), particularly when the heart is mentioned as the thought organ: "But to this day the Lord has not given you a mind to understand (לב לדעת), or eyes to see (עינים לראות), or ears to hear (אזנים לשמע)" (Deut 29:3 [4]).[200] This parallel recurs to express knowledge and understanding: "Make the mind of this people dull (השמן לב), and stop their ears (אזניו הכבד), and shut their eyes (עיניו השע), so that they may not look with their eyes (יראה בעיניו), and listen with their ears (באזניו ישמע), and comprehend with their minds (לבבו יבין), and turn and be healed" (Isa 6:10). More specifically, when hearing is involved, the parallel to the heart/mind expresses learning: "An intelligent mind (לב נבון) acquires knowledge (דעת), and the ear (אזן) of the wise seeks knowledge (דעת)" (Prov 18:15).

Sight and hearing express knowing and learning even when they are not parallel to the heart/mind. Moreover, both sight and hearing bring about knowledge which leads to action: "When the Israelites saw (ויראו) that Abimelech was dead, they all went home" (Judg 9:55). Another example is: "As soon as Ahab heard (כשמע) that Naboth was dead, Ahab set out to go down to the vineyard of Naboth the Jezreelite, to take possession of it" (1 Kgs 21:16). Another example can be found in the words of the shepherds to Isaac: "We see plainly (ראה ראינו) that the Lord has been with you; so we say, let there be an oath between you and us, and let us make a covenant with you" (Gen 26:28). Note too the words of the Gibeonites to Joshua: "Your servants have come from a very far country, because of the name of the Lord your God; for we have heard a report of him (שמענו שמעו), of all that he did in Egypt" (Josh 9:9). At first glance, hearing and sight in these two verses are both an exposure to new knowledge, yet the difference between the two is an important one; the shepherds "saw," that is, their knowledge was based on their personal experience, while the Gibeonites "heard," in other words they acquired their knowledge second hand.[201] Despite this difference in meaning, both the verbs "to hear" (שמע) and "to see" (ראה) appear in parallel to the verb "to know" (ידע): "Have you not known (ידעת)? Have you not heard (שמעת)? The Lord is the everlasting God, the creator of the ends of the earth..." (Isa 40:28).

Two further important subtleties are correlated with sight as a thought image. The first is sight as analysis and choice, reflected in the expression "know and see" (דע וראה): "So Gad came to David and told him; he

---

200.   Cf. n. 84, above.
201.   See below, pp. 248–51.

asked him, 'Shall three years of famine come to you on your land? Or will you flee three months before your foes while they pursue you? Or shall there be three days' pestilence in your land? Now consider, and decide (דע וראה) what answer I shall return to the one who sent me'" (2 Sam 24:13).[202] The second subtlety is the parallel between sight, thought, and ability: "The makers of idols all work to no purpose; and the things they treasure can do no good (בל־יועילו), as they themselves can testify. They neither look (בל־יראו) nor think (בל־ידעו), and so they shall be shamed" (Isa 44:9, JPS). This parallel demonstrates how different sensory metaphors are based on the perception of sense as an ability, whether the ability to think or any other ability.

Speech is another sense that serves as a metaphor for thought. This is particularly strong in the image of speech within the heart: "Then Jeroboam said to himself (ויאמר...בלבו), 'Now the kingdom may well revert to the house of David'... So the king took counsel and made two calves of gold..." (1 Kgs 12:26, 28). In this verse, internal speech is an image for thought. More specifically, this image is also used to describe planning: "Now Esau hated Jacob because of the blessing with which his father had blessed him, and Esau said to himself (ויאמר...בלבו), 'The days of mourning for my father are approaching; then I will kill my brother Jacob'" (Gen 27:41). As noted above, the heart is the organ of thought and knowledge, and thus speech in the heart is an image for thought. However, the verb "to say" (אמר) refers to thought even when the heart is not mentioned: "Abraham said, 'I did it because I thought (lit. 'say,' אמרתי), there is no fear of God at all in this place, and they will kill me because of my wife'" (Gen 20:11). Just as thought leads to planning when sight is the main idiom, so it does when speech is. When the Hebrew man fighting reproached Moses, "he says: 'Who made you a ruler and judge over us? Do you mean (lit. "say," אמר) to kill me as you killed the Egyptian?' Then Moses was afraid and thought (lit. 'say,' ויאמר), 'Surely the thing is known'" (Exod 2:14).[203] The language of the Hebrew Bible thus portrays thoughts as a verbal, rather than abstract process, and speech can be both the thought process, and its expression.[204]

As Malul points out, many verbs that are used to portray sensory discernment have their origin in the meaning of physical/tactile discernment, and particularly "to be wise" (חכם), "to plan" (חשב, זמם), and "to

---

202. And at times "see and know" (ראה ודע); cf. 1 Sam 12:17; 14:38; 23:22, 23; 24:13; 25:17; 1 Kgs 20:7, 22; 2 Kgs 5:7; Jer 2:19, 23.

203. *HALOT* 1:66; S. Wagner, "אָמַר *ʾāmar*; אֹמֶר *ʾōmer*; אֵמֶר *ʾēmer*; אִמְרָה *ʾimrāh*; אֶמְרָה *ʾemrāh*; מַאֲמָר *maʾamār*; מֵאמָר *mēʾmar*," *TDOT* 1:328–45 (333).

204. See Carasik, *Theologies of the Mind*, 93ff. and pp. 84–92, above.

understand" (שכל).[205] The correlation between the tactile sense and thought is not merely etymological. As we observe with other senses, tactile images are used to portray knowledge. A fine example is the way in which the verb "to grasp" (תפש) is used to describe a profession, such as a player, who is "the holder of lyre and pipe" (תפש כנור ועוגב, Gen 4:21), and the mariner, who is "the holder of oar" (תפש משוט, Ezek 27:29). While these two professions indicate the actual holding and playing of an instrument, the use of תפש to describe a professional skill is used figuratively as well, as in the phrase "holders of Torah" (תפשי התורה, Jer 2:8)—the priests. In Biblical Hebrew, "to grasp" (תפש) demonstrates that skill and knowledge are not far apart. The term "sword holders" (תפשי חרבות, Ezek 38:4; אחזי חרב, Song 3:8), which has to do with military skill, expresses the learning process of training. Mighty man are "all equipped with swords (אחזי חרב) and expert in war (מלמדי מלחמה), each with his sword at his thigh because of alarms by night" (Song 3:8). "To hold" (אחז) and "to be learnt" (למד Pual) are similar in a culture where all learning is by way of apprenticeship and participation. Abstract and material knowledge and skill are both expressed through tactile (concrete) idioms, as well as idioms of thought (abstract), as we saw before.[206]

The kinaesthetic sense also includes imagery of knowledge and learning, particularly images associated with investigation. These images are based on concrete portrayals of spatial mobility in order to gather information. For example, "to roam" (שוט): "One day the heavenly beings came to present themselves before the Lord, and Satan also came among them. The Lord said to Satan, 'Where have you come from?' Satan answered the Lord, 'From going to and fro (שוט) on the earth, and from walking up and down (התהלך) on it'" (Job 1:6–7).[207] The verb "to walk around" (הלך Hithpael) is used elsewhere to describe geographical exploration: "So the men started on their way; and Joshua charged those who went to write the description (ההלכים לכתב) of the land, saying, 'Go throughout the land (לכו והתהלכו) and write a (וכתבו) description of it, and come back to me; and I will cast lots for you here before the Lord in Shiloh'" (Josh 18:8).[208] Note, however, that the verb "to roam" (שוט), which expresses mobility, is also used to portray searching without actual movement: "For the eyes of the Lord range throughout (משטטות)

---

205. *MKCS*, mainly 103–6.
206. See p. 139, above.
207. Cf. Job 2:2; 2 Sam 24:2. 8.
208. Cf. Gen 13:17; Zech 1:10; Job 1:7; 1 Chr 21:4 and more.

the entire earth…" (2 Chr 16:9).[209] Finally, this root also has a figurative connotation of learning: "But you, Daniel, keep the words secret, and seal the book until the time of the end. Many will range far and wide (ישטטו) and knowledge will increase" (Dan 12:4).[210]

The verb "to scout," תור, undergoes a similar semantic process: its original meaning is associated with movement, especially circular or cyclical mobility.[211] In many biblical passages, however, this verb is used to portray mobility and walking in order to search: "…the Lord your God, who goes (ההלך) before you on the way to seek out (לתור) a place for you to camp, in fire by night, and in the cloud by day, to show you (לראתכם) the route you should take" (Deut 1:32–33).[212] In other passages, the meaning is closer to espionage:

> Moses sent them to spy out (לתור) the land of Canaan, and said to them, "Go up there into the Negeb, and go up into the hill country, and see (וראיתם) what the land is like, and whether the people who live in it are strong or weak, whether they are few or many, and whether the land they live in is good or bad, and whether the towns that they live in are unwalled or fortified." (Num 13:17–19)[213]

As these verses show, the concrete meaning of spatial mobility extends to mean study and investigation in general. This is expressed in the

209.   Cf. Zech 4:10. This verse can also be understood as a description of angel-spies that walk through the land; see the detailed discussion in N. H. Tur-Sinai, *The Book of Job: A New Commentary* (Jerusalem: Kiryat Sefer, 1957), 38–45.

210.   There is no agreement regarding the translation on the last part of the verse, ישוטטו רבים ותרבה הדעת…. Mostly, its first half is understood as referring to walking back and forth, or running around in a way which reflects helplessness; see E.-J. Waschke, "שוט *šûṭ*; שוֹט *šôṭ*; שיט *šayiṭ*; מְשוֹט/מָשוֹט *miššôṭ/mašôṭ*; שְׁאָט *šeʾāṭ*," *TDOT* 16:528–32 (528); J. J. Collins, *Daniel: A Commentary on the Book of Daniel* (Hermeneia; Minneapolis: Fortress, 1993), 369. A. Lacocque, *The Book of Daniel* (trans. D. Pellauer; Atlanta: John Knox, 1979), 240–41, and comparison to Amos 8:12 on p. 246. The first part of the verse, therefore, negates the second part: "*but* knowledge will increase" (p. 240). The problematic meaning of such translation leads to emendations that make the two parts of the stanza parallel. Most commonly, the suggestion to read "evil" (רעה) instead of knowledge (דעה): "Many will run to and fro, and evil will increase" (Collins, *Daniel*, 369; cf. NRSV, *BHS*). I accept the JPS translation cited above. It seems that walking back as searching for knowledge is the meaning here, like elsewhere in the Hebrew Bible, and such interpretation demonstrates the link movement–learning.

211.   *HALOT* 4:1708; and Liwak, who doubts the link between these two meanings. R. Liwak, "תור *twr*," *TDOT* 15:604–8 (605–6).

212.   Cf. Num 10:33.

213.   Cf. Num 13:2, 21, 25, 32, 38; 14:7, 38.

figurative use of the root תור in the words of Qohelet: "I turned (סבותי)
my mind to know (לדעת) and to search out (לתור) and to seek (בקש)
wisdom and the sum of things, and to know that wickedness is folly and
that foolishness is madness" (Qoh 7:25; cf. 1:13). Finally, walking and
mobility as investigation, specifically as espionage, is expressed through
the root רגל: "So the Danites sent five valiant men from the whole
number of their clan, from Zorah and from Eshtaol, to spy out (לרגל) the
land and to explore it (לחקרה); and they said to them, 'Go, explore
(לכו חקרו) the land.' When they came to the hill country of Ephraim, to
the house of Micah, they stayed there" (Judg 18:2).[214] We thus find that
roots portraying mobility, such as שוט, תור, רגל, and הלך indicate a
physical examination and analysis of a space. By extension, this means
an examination and analysis of the space's qualities, giving rise to the
derived meaning of examination and knowledge in general.

Finally, we must mention the taste sense. Although taste is clearly
perceived as a judgmental sense, to be discussed in the next section, it
only appears rarely in the specific context of knowledge. Two verses are
an exception to this. One verse describes the learning and investigation
process: "apart from him who can eat or who can perceive?" (Qoh 2:25,
my translation).[215] The second verse describes discernment and knowledge: "O taste and see that the Lord is good; happy are those who take
refuge in him" (Ps 34:9). We also find metaphors associated with
judgment and learning, indicating that in biblical perception, the taste
sense also belongs to the cognitive space.

To summarize, different senses are repeated in the context of understanding the world, or knowledge. However, the different tools of
understanding, such as learning, thought, investigation, or choice, are
correlated with different senses. Learning appears largely in correlation
with hearing and mobility.[216] Analysis and choice are associated with
sight, and occasionally with taste.[217] Planning is portrayed as speech and
sight. Investigation is portrayed using mobility and sight metaphors.
Together, the different senses create a spectrum of meanings that com-
pletes the perceptive picture of the world, making the sensorium the
main epistemological tool in biblical perception. The expressions and
phrases discussed can be summarized in the following table:

214. Cf. Num 21:32; Deut 1:24; Josh 6:25; 7:2; 14:7; Judg 18:14, 17; 2 Sam
10:3; 1 Chr 19:3.
215. For this verse, see also Chapter 2, n. 10.
216. Carasik, *Theologies of the Mind*, 219.
217. See Chapter 1, n. 130.

Table 5. *Sensory Phrases and Metaphors for Thought and Learning*

	Hearing	Kinaesthesia	Speech	Taste	Smell[218]	Tactile
ראה	שמע	נוע	אמר	אכל		אחז
דע וראה		הלך	אמר בלב	טעם		תפש
עין	אזן	רגל				חכם[219]
		שוט				חשב[216]
		תור				שכל[216]
						זמם[216]

Sensory Emotions

We have already seen that the biblical perception of sensory perception is not restricted to mental awareness alone, but also to embodied and emotional awareness. In fact, the Hebrew Bible does not make a strict differentiation between these types of experience. Below, I will demonstrate how sensory images and phrases portray emotional experience, especially enjoyment and suffering.[220]

A note before proceeding: this section is not intended to provide an in-depth discussion of emotions in the Hebrew Bible, or to discuss the biological difference between emotions and the senses or sensory organs. Instead, my purpose is to demonstrate how emotional experience is portrayed through vocabulary taken from the semantic fields of the various senses. I will focus on two pairs of emotions, which are prominent with sensory imagery, happiness and sadness, and joy and suffering. In addition, we find expressions of anger and mercy where olfactory idioms are commonly employed;[221] expressions of fear, which reflect disability of various senses;[222] and sensory images, especially those derived from the field of sight, that indicate the experience of identification or empathy.[223]

The expressions and phrases in this section represent two facets of emotion: what causes the emotional experience, and the emotional experience itself. An example of a visual idiom is needed. I noted earlier that in the Hebrew Bible the eyes represent the seat of will and desires. Satisfaction, which in biblical sources is portrayed as a satisfied eye,

218. The absence of one sense from a specific contextual pattern is detailed in Table 10 and the subsequent discussion.

219. *MKCS*, 103–6.

220. See the "blessings of enjoinment" (ברכות הנהנין) in Jewish tradition, which include four sensory experiences: taste, sight, hearing, and smell.

221. See pp. 151–54, above.

222. See pp. 212–19, above.

223. See pp. 135–37, above, and p. 251, below.

leads to joy and enjoyment: "Whatever my eyes desired (שאלו עיני) I did not keep from them; I kept my heart from no pleasure (שמחה), for my heart found pleasure (שמחה) in all my toil, and this was my reward for all my toil" (Qoh 2:10); "The light of the eyes (מאור-עינים) rejoices (ישמח) the heart, and good news (שמועה) refreshes the body" (Prov 15:30). In both verses, satisfying or lightning the eye leads to the emotional experience of enjoyment and happiness; elsewhere a state of the eyes can describe this emotional experience itself. The parallel in the next verse demonstrates the point: "the precepts of the Lord are right, rejoicing the heart (משמחי-לב); the commandment of the Lord is clear, enlightening the eyes" (מאירת עינים, Ps 19:9). In this verse, sight itself is parallel to happiness. Both causing happiness and happiness itself are described using similar phrases (מאור עינים for the first, and אור עינים Hiphil for the second). In other biblical passages, the metaphor of lightened eyes indicates sight in its derived meanings—understanding, ability, and life. Here, it appears in correlation with happiness and satisfaction. The description of sight as happiness recurs in correlation with the description of life in Qohelet, where eating, drinking, and seeing good things are parallel to enjoyment/happiness:

> This is what I have seen (ראיתי) to be good: it is fitting to eat and drink (לאכול-ולשתות) and find enjoyment (לראות טובה) in all the toil with which one toils under the sun the few days of the life God gives us; for this is our lot. Likewise all to whom God gives wealth and possessions and whom he enables to enjoy (lit. "to eat," לאכל) them, and to accept their lot and find enjoyment (לשמח) in their toil—this is the gift of God. (Qoh 5:17–18)

Elsewhere too, Qohelet highlights eating and drinking as a source of enjoyment: "So I commend enjoyment (שמחה), for there is nothing better for people under the sun than to eat, and drink, and enjoy themselves (לאכול ולשתות ולשמוח), for this will go with them in their toil through the days of life that God gives them under the sun" (Qoh 8:15). Eating and drinking as a source of enjoyment are not restricted to Qohelet. Similar to the phrase "to see good" (ראה טוב/ה),[224] the phrase "to eat good" (אכל בטובה) symbolizes a positive life experience: "...Another dies in bitterness (מרה) of soul, never having tasted of good (אכל בטובה)" (Job 21:25).[225] The contrast in this verse between bitter and good resembles the contrast between bitter and sweet, derived from the sense of taste, to portray experiences that do not involve eating.[226] The use of the word

---

224. Jer 29:32; Ps 34:13; Job 7:7; Qoh 2:1; 3:3; 5:17; 6:6.
225. Cf. Qoh 5:17–18; 10:13.
226. See "to be sweet" (מתק, Ps 55:15; Job 20:12); "sweetness" (מתק, Prov 16:21; 27:9) and "honey" (דבש, Pss 19:11; 119:103; Prov 16:24).

bitter to describe an experience of sadness or suffering recurs in many
biblical passages: "Moan therefore, mortal; moan with breaking heart
and bitter grief (מריריות) before their eyes" (Ezek 21:11).[227]

Several other verses portray eating and drinking as a source of
happiness and enjoyment, in a more concrete way,[228] such as "wine that
cheers the hearts of men" (Ps 104:15, JPS), and eating as part of ritual
celebrations, as highlighted in Isaiah's rebuke: "...there was rejoicing
and merriment (ששון ושמחה), killing of cattle and slaughtering of sheep,
eating (אכל) of meat and drinking (שתות) of wine: 'Eat and drink (אכול
ושתו), for tomorrow we die!'" (Isa 22:13). Another verse in Isaiah
equates eating and drinking with joy in a clearer parallelism: "Assuredly,
thus said the Lord God: My servants shall eat (יאכלו), and you shall
hunger (תרעבו); my servants shall drink (ישתו), and you shall thirst
(תצמאו); my servants shall rejoice (ישמחו), and you shall be shamed
(תבשו)" (Isa 65:13). This last example shows how eating and enjoyment
are part of a broader dichotomous whole, with the absence of eating (=
fasting) equated with suffering and sadness.[229] Fasting is portrayed in the
Hebrew Bible as "affliction of the soul/throat" (ענה נפש), a description
originating in the perception of the נפש as the seat of hunger.[230] Not
eating therefore portrays the suffering and sadness of the one fasting.
Biblical characters such as Ahab and Hanna are so sad that they refuse to
eat.[231]

Another description of the enjoyment of eating is found in Barzillai's
words to David: "Today I am eighty years old; can I discern (אדע) what
is pleasant and what is not? Can your servant taste (אטעם) what he eats or
what he drinks? Can I still listen (אשמע) to the voice of singing men and
singing women? Why then should your servant be an added burden to
my lord the king?" (2 Sam 19:36). In describing his inability to enjoy life
in the king's court, Barzillai mentions food, drink, and music. It is not
the only reference to the enjoyment of vocal experience—the words of
wisdom are described: "My soul (כליותי) will rejoice when your lips

227. Cf. 1 Sam 15:32; Isa 33:7; Ezek 27:30; Amos 8:10; Job 11:25 and many
more. See also H.-J. Fabry and H. Ringgren, "מרר *mrr*; מַר *mar*; מֹרָה *mōrâ*; מָרוֹר
mārôr; מְרִירוּת *merîrût*; מְרֵרָה *merērâ*; מְרוֹרָה *merôrâ*; מֶמֶר *memer*; מַמְרֹרִים
mamrōrîm; תַּמְרוּרִים *tamrûrîm*," *TDOT* 9:15–19 (17–19).
228. For the ceremonial, rather than experience aspect, see G. A. Anderson, *A
Time to Mourn, a Time to Dance: The Expression of Grief and Joy in Israelite
Religion* (University Park: Pennsylvania State University Press, 1991).
229. For the double contrasts happiness–sorrow‖honour–shame, found in Isa
65:13, see my "Honour and Shame," 47–48.
230. See pp. 96–98, above.
231. 1 Sam 1:7–9 (Hannah); 1 Kgs 21:4–5, 7 (Ahab).

speak what is right" (Prov 23:16). Just as listening to a song (2 Sam 19:36), speech (Prov 23:16), or good tidings (Prov 15:30) denotes enjoyment and happiness, so evil tidings denote sadness and pain: "I hear (שמעתי), and I tremble (ותרגז בטני) within; my lips quiver at the sound. Rottenness enters into my bones, and my steps tremble beneath me. I wait quietly for the day of calamity to come upon the people who attack us" (Hab 3:16).[232] This verse demonstrates how the emotional response is experienced by the entire body, and is similar to the following description: "Be gracious to me, O Lord, for I am in distress; my eye wastes away from grief, my soul and body also" (Ps 31:10).

Expressions of joy recur in several psalms where verbal actions are described, such as singing (זמרה), laughter (זמרה), and joyful shouts (רינה): "Then our mouth was filled with laughter, and our tongue with shouts of joy then it was said among the nations, 'The Lord has done great things for them.' The Lord has done great things for us, and we rejoiced" (היינו שמחים)" (Ps 126:2–3); "My lips will shout for joy when I sing praises to you; my soul also, which you have rescued" (Ps 71:23). In these verses, the verbal response is a result of the emotion of happiness and relief. But in other verses, it is speech that creates this emotion: "I must speak, so that I may find relief (וירוח); I must open my lips and answer" (Job 32:20).[233] Sadness and pain are also expressed verbally or vocally in descriptions of weeping: "...A voice (קול) is heard in Ramah, lamentation (נהי) and bitter weeping (בכי תמרורים). Rachel is weeping for her children... Keep your voice from weeping (קולך מבכי), and your eyes from tears (עיניך מדמעה)..." (Jer 31:15). As we see in this verse, sadness is often associated with the eye, where tears originate.[234]

Enjoyment or aesthetic rejection caused by the different senses is, in fact, present in every judgmental description:[235] good, evil, beautiful, bitter, and sweet are just some of the adjectives that signify these experiences. As we have seen, these physical experiences are developed in a culture through different customs, such as eating and singing. The enjoyment of fragrances is another example, and it is found particularly in the Song of Songs: "While the king was on his couch, my nard gave forth its fragrance (ריחו)" (Song 1:12). This verse describes how the fragrance of the beloved's perfume reaches the king as he reclines on his throne.[236] The beloved's words appear against a background of smelling

232. Cf. Jer 51:51.
233. Cf. Ps 39:2–4.
234. Cf. Jer 8:23; 9:17; 13:17; 14:17.
235. See the next section, pp. 167–74.
236. Zakovitch, *The Song of Songs*, 56.

perfume, a popular custom in royal households and high society in biblical times.[237] Enjoyment of the sense of smell is also highlighted in the description (which includes aesthetic judgment) of the beloved in another passage in the Song of Songs: "How sweet (יָפוּ) is your love, my sister, my bride! How much better is your love than wine, and the fragrance (רֵיחַ) of your oils than any spice! Your lips distil nectar, my bride; honey and milk are under your tongue; the scent (רֵיחַ) of your garments is like the scent (רֵיחַ) of Lebanon" (Song 4:10–11). In this description, consisting mainly of metaphors from the field of smell and taste, we see the adjectives "beautiful" (יָפֶה) and "good" (טוֹב) used to reflect enjoyment through these senses. Sensory pleasure (and displeasure) is closely linked, therefore, to moral judgment, as will be discussed in the next paragraph.

In summary, the experiences of enjoyment and happiness are described in the Hebrew Bible as originating from a sensory experience, and are also expressed through the senses. Similarly, we find that the experiences of suffering and pain are caused by the senses, and are also experienced through them. The words and metaphors relating to this contextual pattern are presented in the table below:

Table 6. *Sensory Phrases and Metaphors for Emotional Experience (Pleasure/Suffering)*

Sight	Hearing	Kinaesthesia	Speech	Taste	Smell	Tactile[238]
ראה	שמע	מתניים	דבר Piel	טעם	ריח	
עין	שמועה		ענה	אכל		
עינים Hiphil אור	שרים ושרות		זמר	שתה		
מאור עינים			קול	סער		
			רנן Piel	מר		
			פתח שפתים	מרירות		
			שחוק	מתוק		
			פה	דבש		
			לשון			

Moral Judgment

I have already discussed the way that the senses appear in the contextual pattern of learning and knowledge. In this section, I will show how the general perception of the senses as means for discernment is extended to

237. Bachar, "Perfume in the Song"; see also my "The Sensorium," 162–67.
238. The absence of one sense from a specific contextual pattern is detailed in Table 10, below, and the subsequent discussion.

mean subjective discernment, using juridical metaphors in general, and moral decisions in particular. An important aspect of moral judgment in the Hebrew Bible is the awareness to subjective perception of reality, as demonstrated in metaphors of sensory discernment in both a juridical and a general context. In the juridical context, hearing is an eminent vehicle for judgmental and analysis. Note the description of David as a supreme judge, spoken via the mouth of the wise woman of Tekoa: "The word of my lord the king will set me at rest; for my lord the king is like the angel of God, discerning good and evil (לשמע הטוב והרע). The Lord your God be with you!" (2 Sam 14:17). Here and elsewhere, distinguishing between good and evil (טוב ורע) is not only the source of knowledge (cf. Gen 3:10, 22), but also the ability to judge. David's ability to judge in the above verse is described as "hearing" (שמע). Solomon's wish for judging capacity is similarly described: "Grant, then, your servant an understanding mind (לב שמע) to judge (לשפט) your people, to distinguish between good and bad; for who can judge (יוכל לשפט) this vast people of yours?" (1 Kgs 3:9, JPS). Here too, discernment between good and bad is described as hearing, the hearing of the heart. We already see how the pair good/evil can mean correct/incorrect. As will be shown below, this pair can also describe aesthetics, mainly when "good" means beautiful. These multiple meanings are an expression of the multifaceted nature of sensory experience, which includes knowledge, enjoinment, and judgment, which all lead to moral opinion expressed through the senses.

Judgment is not only described as hearing, but also as sight: "...He shall not judge (ישפוט) by what his eyes see, or decide (יוכיח) by what his ears hear" (Isa 11:3).[239] There are several phrases where sight describes the ability critically to discern reality.[240] Thus, for example, the expression "to see that" (ראה כי) indicates an evaluation of the situation, and not just sight or consciousness, especially with the complement "good" (ראה כי טוב); this phrase describes God's evaluation of each day of creation,[241] and can also describe moral evaluation, as in the flood narrative: "The Lord saw that the wickedness of humankind was great (וירא...כי רבה רעת האדם) in the earth, and that every inclination of the thoughts of their hearts was only evil continually" (Gen 6:5; cf. v. 12). Lastly, the phrase describes aesthetic evaluation, as expressed in the story of the sons of God and the human daughters: "the sons of God saw

239.   The verse assumes the conventional way of judgment, through sight and hearing.
240.   For a more detailed discussion, see pp. 248–51, below.
241.   Gen 1:4, 10, 12, 18, 21, 25; 49:15.

that they were fair (וירא...כי טבת); and they took wives for themselves of all that they chose" (Gen 6:2). The interplay of meanings for ראה כי טוב/רע in these verses hints at various types of judgment, and for the shared aspects of types of judgment.

The correlation between moral and aesthetic evaluation is evident in the paradigmatic parallel between good (טוב) and beautiful (יפה). An example for the parallel is found in the portrayals of the matriarchs. In the two different wife–sister narratives, these two adjectives are interchanged. When Abram neared Egypt, "...he said to his wife Sarai, 'I know well that you are a woman beautiful in appearance (יפת־מראה)'" (Gen 12:11); "When Isaac lived in Gerar, he said, 'She is my sister'; for he was afraid to say, 'My wife,' thinking, 'or else the men of the place might kill me for the sake of Rebekah, because she is attractive in appearance (טובת מראה)'" (Gen 26:7).[242] This parallel between good and beautiful constitutes the basis for moral aesthetics.[243]

A further correlation between visual aesthetics and morals is the distinction between good appearance (טוב מראה) and bad appearance (רע מראה), which can also indicate a state of health as opposed to a state of illness, as found in the description of the cows in Pharaoh's dream (Gen 41:4, 20). This correlation originates in the perception that physical disabilities were a sign of divine punishment, the result of negative behaviour.[244] The importance of physical perfection is further demonstrated by the description of Daniel's professional point of departure:

> Then the king commanded his palace master Ashpenaz to bring some of the Israelites of the royal family and of the nobility, young men without physical defect (מום) and handsome (טובי מראה), versed in every branch of wisdom (משכילים בכל־חכמה), endowed with knowledge and insight (ידעי דעת ומביני מדע), and competent to serve (כה...לעמד) in the king's palace; they were to be taught the literature and language of the Chaldeans. (Dan 1:4)[245]

---

242. Cf. 2 Sam 11:2; Est 1:11; 2:2, 3, 7. A similar parallel of "good" (טוב) and "beautiful" (יפה) is found in 1 Sam 16:12.

243. Similar polysemy is found in the Akkadian verbs *ṭābu*, "to be sweet" (smell or taste) or "to be good" (*CAD* 19:19ff.), and *damqu*, "to be beautiful," "to be good" (*CAD* 3:68ff.).

244. See further below, pp. 248–51, and J. H. W. Dorman, "The Blemished Body: Deformity and Disability in the Qumran Scrolls" (Ph.D. diss., Rijksuniversiteit Groningen, 2007).

245. This is similar to the demand for the priests and the offerings to be blameless (Lev 21:18–20; 22:22–24; Deut 15:21). See also pp. 205–6, below.

The demand for "good" physical appearance, alongside wisdom, is only rarely negated in biblical literature. There are two additional meanings derived from the correlation between good and beautiful: the use of the word good to indicate something correct,[246] and the parallel between good and life: "See, I have set before you today life and prosperity (טוב), death and adversity (רע)" (Deut 30:15). This transition from the field of visual and aesthetic preference to the field of moral preference is not limited just to the expression "to see that," or to the interchangeability of good and beautiful. It recurs in the phrase "good/evil in the sight of my eyes" (טוב/רע בעיני), which will be discussed in the Chapter 5.[247]

In addition to hearing and sight, taste is also a means of distinguishing and weighing up good and evil: "O taste and see (טעמו וראו) that the Lord is good (כי־טוב); happy are those who take refuge in him" (Ps 34:9). This correlation between appearance and substance, which lies at the core of the parallel between physical perfection and moral perfection, also appears in the parallel between visual appearance and taste: "Out of the ground the Lord God made to grow every tree that is pleasant to the sight (נחמד למראה) and good for food (טוב למאכל), the tree of life also in the midst of the garden, and the tree of the knowledge of good and evil" (Gen 2:9). The imagery of tasting or eating, when correlated with the distinction between good and evil, also appears in Barzillai's words, mentioned before: "I am now eighty years old. Can I tell the difference between good and bad (טוב לרע)? Can your servant taste (יטעם) what he eats and drinks? Can I still listen (אשמע) to the singing of men and women? Why then should your servant continue to be a burden to my lord the king?" (2 Sam 19:36, JPS); and see also Isaiah's words: "Butter and honey shall he eat (יאכל), that he may know to refuse the evil (רע), and choose the good (טוב)" (Isa 7:15, KJV).[248] Similar to the interchangeable meaning of beautiful and good/healthy, we find examples in the Hebrew Bible of a correlation between sweet taste and good/healthy: "My child, eat (אכל) honey, for it is good (כי־טוב), and the drippings of

---

246. See Gen 40:16; Num 24:1; 2 Sam 15:3.

247. According to Stendebach, a similar semantic shift appears in נשא חן בעיני (*TDOT* 11:37; cf. Johnson, *The Vitality of the Individual*, 47–48), yet according to Zedaka, this is not a case where בעיני describes judgment; see Y. Zedaka, "'And Noah Found Favour in the Eyes of the Lord' (Semantic and Syntactic Analysis)" (Hebrew), *Bikoret u Parshanut* 24 (1988): 133–40.

248. These two verses might mark (1) an ability for moral judgment, (2) an ability to enjoy life, as discussed before, or (3) an ability to discern between beneficial and harming acts; see J. N. Oswalt, *The Book of Isaiah: Chapters 1–39* (NICOT; Grand Rapids: Eerdmans, 1986), 213–14.

the honeycomb are sweet (מתוק) to your taste" (Prov 24:13); "Pleasant words are like a honeycomb (צוּף־דבשׁ), sweetness to the soul (מתוק לנפשׁ) and health to the body (מרפא לעצם, Prov 16:24). This correlation is further reinforced by the correlation between the word "good" and satiation.[249] We thus find that a derived meaning of the sense of taste is judgment, a subjective understanding of the situation. In regular use, this is also used to describe the ability for good judgment:[250] "He deprives of speech (שׂפה) those who are trusted, and takes away the discernment (טעם) of the elders" (Job 12:20).[251]

In addition to examples where the sense of taste serves as moral judgment, adjectives from the field of taste serve to describe moral essence. Just as the taste of food or wine characterizes their essence, so the taste of a person or a group characterizes the essence and behaviour of that man or group.[252] Tastes that are used as an idiom for essence include different adjectives. "Sweet" normally describes a positive value:[253] "The wise of heart is called perceptive, and pleasant (lit. 'sweet,' מתק) speech increases persuasiveness" (Prov 16:21; cf. v. 24). It is clear in this verse that sweetness describes valuable speech. We find a similar use of this description in the word "honey": "I do not turn away from your ordinances, for you have taught me. How sweet (נמלצו) are your words to my taste, sweeter than honey (מדבשׁ) to my mouth!" (Ps 119:102–3).[254] The description of pleasant speech as something sweet recurs in combinations with the words "secret" (סוד, Ps 55:15) and "advice" (עצה, Prov 27:9). Just as the adjective "sweet" is used to describe positive behaviour or speech, so the adjective "bitter" describes negative values or behaviour: "Your wickedness will punish you, and your apostasies will convict you. Know and see (דעי וראי) that it is evil and bitter (רע ומר) for you to forsake the Lord your God…" (Jer 2:19; cf. 4:18). The quality of food as a metaphor for moral behaviour is not restricted solely to sweet and bitter adjectives. It also appears in phrases describing good and bad. In the parable of the figs, Jeremiah describes them thus:

---

249. See Chapter 1, n. 165.

250. J. Schüpphaus, "טָעַם *ṭāʿam*; טַעַם *ṭaʿam*; טְעֵם *ṭeʿēm*; מַטְעַמִּים *maṭʿammîm*," *TDOT* 5:345–47 (346).

251. Cf. 1 Sam 25:33; Prov 11:22; Ps 119:66. Similarly, "change of taste" (שׁנה טעמו, 1 Sam 21:14; Ps 34:1) means the lost of judgment.

252. B. Kedar-Kopfstein, "מָתַק *māṯaq*; מָתוֹק *māṯôq*; מֹתֶק *mōṯeq*; מֶתֶק *meṯeq*; מַמְתַקִּים *mametaqqîm*," *TDOT* 9:103–7 (105); Fabry and Ringgren, *TDOT* 9:18. The same concept is found in smell vocabulary.

253. Kedar-Kopfstein, *TDOT* 9:107.

254. Cf. Ps 19:11. For more on taste and speech, see pp. 157–62 and 93–103.

"One basket had very good (טבות) figs, like first-ripe figs, but the other basket had very bad figs (רעות), so bad that they could not be eaten" (Jer 24:2). As the subsequent verses reveal, the good, edible figs symbolize the man of Judah, while the bad, inedible figs symbolize Zedekiah and his courtiers.

A similar phenomenon appears with smell metaphors. While we find no examples of the sense of smell being used for moral judgment,[255] we do find foul smell being used as a metaphor for negative behaviour. After Simon and Levi kill the Shechemites, Jacob reproves: "You have brought trouble (עכרתם) on me by making me odious (להבאישני) to the inhabitants of the land, the Canaanites and the Perizzites..." (Gen 34:30).[256] In this verse, as elsewhere, the root באש does not only describe a bad odour, but also has the derived meaning of holding a subjective opinion about the behaviour of a person or group, just as we found with judgment imagery.[257] The examples from the olfactory field further strengthen the correlation between moral judgment and subjective opinion expressed through the sensory images, as well as the parallel between the substance of sensory experience and moral essence.

Similar meanings are found within kinaesthetic imagery. While there are no examples of moral judgment expressed through kinaesthetic sensation, we do find metaphors of the way someone walks and moves as an indication of that person's moral behaviour. Normative behaviour is described in the Hebrew Bible as following a path, or walking straight: "Folly is a joy to one who has no sense (לב), but a person of understanding walks straight ahead (יישר לכת)" (Prov 15:21); "Today you have obtained the Lord's agreement: to be your God; and for you to walk in his ways (ללכת בדרכיו), to keep his statutes, his commandments, and his ordinances, and to obey him (lit. 'to hear,' לשמע בקלו)" (Deut 26:17).[258] This last example highlights the parallel with hearing as an indicator of obedience, and, by extension, appropriate behaviour, and walking as appropriate behaviour. Similarly, a refusal to listen, alongside crooked walking, can describe negative or immoral behaviour: "Yet they did

---

255. Isa 11:3 talks about moral judgment using the sense of smell, yet this verse describes a future, utopic usage of smell. See Chapter 1, n. 73.

256. Cf. Exod 5:21; 1 Sam 13:4; 2 Sam 10:6; 16:21; Prov 13:5; 1 Chr 19:6 and my "The Sensorium," 180–85.

257. For more on moral judgment and smell in other cultures, see A. Synnott, "A Sociology of Smell," *Canadian Review of Sociology and Anthropology* 28, no. 4 (1991): 437–59. On the negative tone of באש, see also P. R. Ackroyd, "A Note on the Hebrew Roots באש and בוש," *JTS* 43 (1942): 160–61.

258. Cf. Deut 19:9; Josh 22:5; 2 Chr 17:3; Ezek 5:7 and many more.

not obey (lit. 'hear,' שמעו) or incline their ear (הטו אזנם), but, in the stubbornness of their evil will (לבם הרע), they walked (ילכו) in their own counsels, and looked backward rather than forward" (Jer 7:24).[259]

A similar semantic load is associated with speech, particularly speaking slander, which reflects immoral behaviour: "For your hands are defiled with blood, and your fingers with iniquity; your lips have spoken lies (שפתותיכם דברו־שקר), your tongue mutters wickedness (לשונכם עולה תהגה)" (Isa 59:3). In this passage, we see evidence of the real damage that slander can cause, already discussed above,[260] yet false speech is not only harming, but immoral, as the parallel between "lie" (שקר) and "crime" (פשע) demonstrates: "Whom are you mocking? Against whom do you open your mouth wide and stick out your tongue? Are you not children of transgression (ילדי־פשע), the offspring of deceit (זרע שקר)?" (Isa 57:4). Moreover, slander becomes a symbol of unseemly behaviour even in the general context of appropriate behaviour: "...I will guard my ways (דרכי) that I may not sin with my tongue (חטוא בלשוני); I will keep a muzzle on my mouth (פי) as long as the wicked are in my presence" (Ps 39:2). This verse also demonstrates the parallel between speech and following a path, which itself serves as a metaphor for behaviour. A similar parallel exists between true speech and walking a straight path, as in the description of the Levite: "True (אמת) instruction was in his mouth (פיהו), and no wrong (עולה) was found on his lips (שפתיו). He walked (הלך) with me in integrity and uprightness (בשלום ובמישור), and he turned many from iniquity" (Mal 2:6). Falsehood and truth are thus presented as verbal entities, but also as spatial entities, whereby straight, or upright walking indicates appropriate behaviour. Furthermore, the content of speech is the substance of a person: "For Jerusalem has stumbled (כשלה) and Judah has fallen (נפלה), because their speech (לשונם) and their deeds (מעלליהם) are against the Lord, defying his glorious presence" (Isa 3:8). We found that the substance of speech—positive or negative—just like taste, smell, appearance, and the way of walking, appears in the context and as the description of moral or immoral behaviour.

When it comes to subjective judgment through the senses, Antony Synnott has an interesting perspective on the sense of smell. He states that the essence of smell symbolizes a person or a group, and that positive or negative smell is evidence of the moral quality and behaviour of that same person or group:

---

259. See typologically similar phenomenon in Guerts, *Culture and the Senses*, 51, 69.

260. Cf. pp. 145–48, above.

The fundamental hypothesis is simple: what smells good, is good. Conversely, what smells bad, is bad... [W]hat I am attempting to demonstrate is how people think about odours, i.e. in metaphorical and symbolic terms, not the odours themselves. The odours themselves are intrinsically meaningless... We may describe someone as smelling "divine" or "beautiful," "lovely" or just plain "good"; yet all these adjectives are also evaluations and moral judgments. Description is prescription. The aromas are converted from physical sensations to symbolic evaluations.[261]

Phenomenologically, the olfactory sense discriminates between good and bad odours,[262] yet there is almost no such thing as a good or bad smell. Smells carry whatever symbolic meaning a particular culture allocates to them. The examples above demonstrate how this logic effectively underpins every derived use of the senses to describe moral judgment, and every use of discernment to describe moral character. There are very few universal good and bad tastes, pleasant and unpleasant sounds, beautiful and ugly appearances. Just as beauty is in the eye of the beholder, so aroma is in the nose of the beholder, and so forth; sensory perception is both judgment and pleasure, and thus pleasurable impressions are compared to correct impressions. Inevitably, the attribution of aesthetic qualities to moral evaluation is found throughout the biblical sensorium.

Such a semantic shift occurs in idioms and phrases related to sight, hearing, taste, smell, and even mobility. The opposites good/evil, which are sometimes used judgmentally to describe behaviour in the Hebrew Bible, are often portrayed by alternative terms such as "correct," "beautiful," or "healthy." In other words, these adjectives establish a structural correlation between aesthetics (visual, vocal, taste, smell, and kinaesthetic) and morality. The combination between sensory metaphors linked to moral judgment, and sensory metaphors linked to enjoyment, leads to a correlation between aesthetics and morality. This correlation is demonstrated in the syntagmatic parallel between the words "beautiful" and "good," and the use of taste and smell images to describe people's character. Good tastes and smells are associated with positive behaviour. Negative tastes and smells are associated with negative behaviour.

To summarize, the following table displays terms derived from the sensory world, and which appear in the contextual pattern of moral judgment and subjective opinion, as well as moral characteristics. Lack of perception is lack of judgment, which is an immoral act by itself: "Ah,

261. Synnott, "A Sociology of Smell," 437, 444.
262. Ong, "Shifting Sensorium," 28. Contrary to Ong, we find that moral judgment is not modern, and is found in the Hebrew Bible, including in the examples above.

you who call evil good (לרע טוב) and good evil (לטוב רע), who put darkness for light (חשך לאור) and light for darkness (אור לחשך), who put bitter for sweet (מר למתוק) and sweet for bitter (מתוק למר)!" (Isa 5:20).

Table 7. *Sensory Phrases and Metaphors for Moral Judgment*

Sight	Hearing	Kinaesthesia	Speech	Taste	Smell	Tactile[263]
ראה	שמע	הלך בדרך	אמר	טעם	ריח?	
ראה כי	לב שמע	הלך בשרירות לב	דבר Piel	אכל	באש	
עין	משמע אזן	ישר לכת	שפה	טוב למאכל		
טוב/רע בעיני	שמע בקול		לשון	טעם		
מראה עין	Hiphil אזן נטה		פה	מתוק/מר		
יפה			אמת/שקר			

Life, Experience, Ability, Autonomy

This final section describing a contextual pattern in which sensory vocabulary appears in the Hebrew Bible will demonstrate the spectrum of contexts shared by the various senses, contexts which all hint at a perception of the senses as representing human sovereign action. By sovereign action, I refer to human ability to act autonomously, and to experience the world subjectively. All contextual patterns described thus far would appear to support this perception: the use of the senses to harm or to help is an indication of strength and ability, and is frequently associated with metaphors of control; thought and learning sensory idioms and metaphors relate to the way the human experiences and is aware of the world, and also serve as a metaphor for one's very way of life; sensory imagery serves to describe emotional experience, not just for intellectual or physical experience;[264] and, finally, the senses as an epistemic tool, also tools for moral judgment of reality, a subjective, aesthetically based perception. In the following pages I will present several frequently appearing idioms and metaphors linked to the different senses which extend our understanding of the senses as an indicator of human action.[265] The metaphors that will be presented include sensory

263. The absence of one sense from a specific contextual pattern is detailed in Table 10 and the subsequent discussion.

264. The distinction between emotional, cognitive, and physical experience is made for the convenience of the discussion, and is by no means meant to reflect biblical epistemology.

265. See also pp. 182–83, below.

actions that represent abilities, together with sensory organs that represent strength and power. I will also present passages where the sensory organs constitute a synecdoche for the person as an active agent, as well as idioms in which sensory organs and sensory experiences symbolize vitality and life.

Meanings of strength, vitality, ability, and sovereignty frequently overlap. As we saw earlier with control imagery (help or harm), the senses and sensory organs can express control over reality. The understanding that the senses provide control is linked to two notions: the senses are tools for learning and thought,[266] and the use of the senses indicates a person's strength and ability. In this last context, too, we find concrete descriptions of sensory experience side-by-side with derived imagery. Eating, and even just tasting, delivers strength, as we see in Saul's description during his visit to Endor: "Immediately Saul fell full length on the ground, filled with fear because of the words of Samuel; and there was no strength in him (גם־כח לא־היה בו), for he had eaten nothing (לא אכל לחם) all day and all night" (1 Sam 28:20).[267] The concrete description of the link between eating and strength is extended and derived into an image of sight as strength. Such meaning is expressed in the narrative of Jonathan in Michmash:

> But Jonathan had not heard his father charge the troops with the oath; so he extended the staff that was in his hand, and dipped the tip of it in the honeycomb, and put his hand to his mouth (וישב ידו אל־פיו); and his eyes brightened (ותארנה עיניו)... Then Jonathan said, "My father has troubled the land; see (ראו־נא) how my eyes have brightened (ארו עיני) because I tasted (טעמתי) a little of this honey." (1 Sam 14:27, 29)[268]

Elsewhere, the light of the eye serves as a metaphor for strength: "My heart throbs, my strength fails me (עזבני כחי); as for the light of my eyes (ואור עיני)—it also has gone from me" (Ps 38:11). As I will demonstrate below, the correlation between light and sight, as well as the correlation between eating honey and strength, are a concrete idiom that becomes a metaphor for life.

In addition, the hand (tactile organ) too can signify strength and ability: "See, the Lord's hand is not too short (לא־קצרה יד) to save, nor

---

266. For the associative link between learning and control in biblical epistemology, see *MKCS*.

267. As well as vv. 22, 23, 25; cf. 1 Kgs 19:5–8.

268. See Chapter 2 n. 137. Clearly Jonathan's eating is contrasted to Saul's fasting, which in both cases proves useful and symbolizes his inability; see M. Garsiel, *The First Book of Samuel: A Literary Study of Comparative Structures, Analogies and Parallels* (Ramat-Gan: Revivim, 1983 [Hebrew]), 90–93.

his ear too dull (לֹא־כָבְדָה אָזְנוֹ) to hear" (Isa 59:1). In many biblical passages, the hand signifies strength, power, or divine rule:

> Yours, O Lord, are the greatness, the power, the glory, the victory, and the majesty; for all that is in the heavens and on the earth is yours; yours is the kingdom, O Lord, and you are exalted as head above all. Riches and honour come from you (מִלְפָנֶיךָ), and you (אתה) rule over all. In your hand (בידך) are power and might; and it is in your hand (בידך) to make great and to give strength to all. (1 Chr 29:11–12)[269]

In contrast, weak hands signify lack of ability: "But you, take courage (חִזְקוּ)! Do not let your hands be weak (אַל־יִרְפּוּ יְדֵיכֶם), for your work shall be rewarded" (2 Chr 15:7).[270] Similarly, the foot represents power and control, as we saw above, and weakness is portrayed through failures associated with the foot: "Vengeance is mine, and recompense, for the time when their foot shall slip (תָּמוּט רַגְלָם); because the day of their calamity is at hand, their doom comes swiftly" (Deut 32:35). The image of the slipping foot is also used in symbolism of life and death: "Bless our God…who has kept us among the living (נַפְשֵׁנוּ בַחַיִּים), and has not let our feet slip" (לַמּוֹט רַגְלֵנוּ, Ps 66:9).[271] Speech is also regarded as ability and strength, and can appear both as ability in general, and as an image for life: "my vigor (כֹּחִי) is dried up like a shard; my tongue (לְשׁוֹנִי) cleaves to my palate; You commit me to the dust of death" (Ps 22:16, JPS).[272] Lastly, the nose (olfactory organ) as the locus of breath and life, is mentioned as strength and ability: "…for when angry (בְאַפָּם) they slay men, And when pleased (בִרְצֹנָם) they maim oxen" (Gen 49:6, JPS). The parallelism in this verse assumes a similarity between the words אַף ("nose, anger") and רצון ("self-will"). It seems to me that אַף here is not just a syntagmatic representation of חרון אף[273] but also an abstract reference to the nose as a source of power, and, by extension, will. The nose, as the seat of life and breath, is imagined as an organ with strength and power similar to that of the hand or the foot. When strength has a negative connotation, it means anger, when it is positive, it means mercy.

---

269.   And many more, see P. R. Ackroyd, "יָד *yād*; זְרוֹעַ *zeroa*; יָמִין *yāmîn*; כַּף *kap*; אֶצְבַּע *ʾṣbaʿ*," *TDOT* 5:393–426 (419–20).

270.   Cf. 2 Sam 4:1; Jer 6:24; 50:43; Ezek 7:17; Zeph 3:16. For this contrast, see also Ackroyd, *TDOT* 5:413; Malul, *Society, Law, and Custom*, 164–65.

271.   Cf. Pss 38:17; 94:18.

272.   Some suggest to replace the word "strength" (כֹּחִי) with the word "palate" (חכי) as a parallel to "tongue" (לְשׁוֹן), yet without textual evidence (NRSV, BHK; HALOT 1:333; H. Ringgren, "כֹּחַ *kōaḥ*," *TDOT* 7:122–28 (124).

273.   See pp. 105–6, 128, above

The sensory organs and experiences that indicate strength and ability also serve as a synecdoche for the person/human as an active agent in the world. The nose as the seat of life is an example of this synecdoche: "as long as my breath is in me (בִּי) and the spirit of God is in my nostrils" (בְּאַפִּי, Job 27:3). In this synonymous parallelism the physical and abstract are merged, and the nose parallels the person as a whole. Yitzhak Zedaka demonstrates that different bodily organs appear as initiators of action, and constitute a semantic alternative to the living man. Zedaka explains some of the metaphors associated with sight in this way: "Therefore I (אֲנִי) will act in wrath; my eye (עֵינִי) will not spare, nor will I (Ø) have pity…" (Ezek 8:18). In this example, the expression "the eye pities" (חוּס עַיִן) can be substituted with the verb "to take pity" alone, while retaining the meaning of the verse. In the following verse too, the sight phrase can be substituted by the first person verb: "…my eyes have seen (רָאוּ עֵינַי) the King, the Lord of hosts!" (Isa 6:5). Here, "my eyes have seen" could easily be replaced with "I have seen." Similarly, it is possible to explain the correlation between eye and jealousy, will, expectation and thought, with the eye representing thought, as in the expression "in the eyes of" (בְּעֵינֵי).[274] Finally, the eye appears in parallelism to humans in general: "People (אָדָם) are bowed down, everyone (אִישׁ) is brought low, and the eyes (עֵינֵי) of the haughty are humbled" (Isa 5:15).

The ear and the hand can also signify action of the whole person. The proverb "An intelligent mind (לֵב) acquires knowledge, and the ear (אֹזֶן) of the wise seeks knowledge" (Prov 18:15), really means that the wise men will seek knowledge, not their ears. When the elders proclaim "…Our hands (יָדֵינוּ) did not shed this blood, nor did our eyes (עֵינֵינוּ) see it done" (Deut 21:7, JPS), they actually mean that they did not shed the blood, nor witness it.[275] Similar to the last example, the phrases "in the hand" (בְּיַד), "from the hand" (מִיַּד), and "to the hand" (לְיַד) all mark the entire person referred to.[276] Similarly, the expressions "to the mouth" (לְפִי) and "at the mouth" (עַל פִּי), which originate in the context of speech, signify the entire action, whether human or divine:[277] "Is it by your wisdom (בִּינָתְךָ) that the hawk soars, and spreads its wings toward the south? Is it at your command (עַל־פִּיךָ) that the eagle mounts up and makes its nest on high?" (Job 39:26–27).[278] The parallel between speech

---

274. Zedaka, "And Noah Found Favor," 116–18; Stendebach, *TDOT* 11:36–40. As well as pp. 258–62, below.

275. Examples taken from Zedaka, "And Noah Found Favor," 116–17.

276. Ackroyd, *TDOT* 5:410–12.

277. Garcia-López, *TDOT* 11:495.

278. Cf. Gen 41:40; Num 27:21; Deut 21:5; 1 Chr 12:33.

and between the speech organ and the whole person is found also using the synecdoche of the tongue: "The spirit of the Lord speaks through me (בי), his word is upon my tongue (לשוני)" (2 Sam 23:2).

The foot also indicated man (or God) in a synecdoche that characterizes synaesthetic thought in the Hebrew Bible.[279] For example, take the words of Jacob to Laban: "For you had little before I came, and it has increased abundantly; and the Lord has blessed you wherever I turned (לרגלי). But now when shall I provide for my own household also?" (Gen 30:30; cf. Deut 11:6). Here, we could easily translate the word לרגלי as "on my behalf." A similar meaning is found in the expression "in the foot" (ברגל), which means "together with": "...Leave us, you and all the people who follow you (lit. 'at your feet,' לרגליך)..." (Exod 11:8).[280] This is clearly not a neutral expression of joining and accompanying, but is used to describe a particular status. In all the biblical passages where the phrases "in the feet of" (ברגל) and "to the feet of" (לרגל) appear, they are used to describe those who are hierarchically subordinate to the person whose feet are mentioned. This phrase echoes the concept of the foot as an indicator of power and control. The control metaphor itself is a synecdoche where the foot represents the action of the whole body, as we see in the following parallel: "He subdued peoples under us (תחתנו), and nations under our feet" (רגלינו, Ps 47:4).

The foot as a symbol of control and power, and as representing the whole person, can also be seen in descriptions of bowing down: "She fell at his feet (על־רגליו) and said, 'Upon me alone, my lord, be the guilt; please let your servant speak in your ears, and hear the words of your servant'" (1 Sam 25:24).[281] This concrete description is parallel to the image of bowing before a king's nose (אפים): "Then Ahimaaz called out to the king, 'All is well!' He bowed low before the king, at his face (lit. 'nostrils,' לאפיו), and said..." (2 Sam 18:28, my translation).[282] This phrase is clearly influenced associatively by the image of bowing down until the person's face touches the ground (אפים ארצה). In this verse, however, the "face" referred to is that of the king, as indicated by the preposition ל, and the phrase represents the king and his presence.

Thus far I have shown how the sensory organs represent the active agent in general and its operative strength in the world. This is also the

---

279. Stendebach, *TDOT* 13:317.
280. Cf. Judg 8:5; 1 Sam 25:27; 1 Kgs 20:10; 2 Kgs 3:9 as well as the infinitive of רגל Piel (1 Sam 25:42). For other idioms of authority through the foot, see Malul, *Mesopotamian Legal Symbolism*, 403ff.
281. Cf. 2 Kgs 4:37.
282. As well as 2 Sam 14:33; 24:20; 1 Sam 20:41; 25:23.

perception that underpins sensory imagery that describes a way of life or human behaviour. Walking a path, for example, is a metaphor for human behaviour, where the walking foot signifies the person and his/her behaviour.[283] Walking a path and hearing a voice are a common metaphor for describing human behaviour: "Today you have obtained the Lord's agreement: to be your God; and for you to walk in his ways (ללכת בדרכיו), to keep his statutes, his commandments, and his ordinances, and to obey him (לשמע בקלו)" (Deut 26:17, and many other verses). In fact, this imagery assumes that the action of the senses is not neutral, but carries a moral load. Similarly, walking a path is parallel to speaking the truth: "I resolved I would watch my step (דרכי) lest I offend by my speech (חטוא בלשוני); I would keep my mouth muzzled while the wicked man was in my presence" (Ps 39:2, JPS). Here too speech and walking are judged according to a moral/ethical scale: "True instruction was in his mouth (פיהו), and no wrong was found on his lips (שפתיו). He walked (הלך) with me in integrity and uprightness, and he turned many from iniquity" (Mal 2:6).[284]

Eating also serves as a metaphor for behaviour, as we see in the proverb "the parents have eaten sour grapes, and the children's teeth are set on edge" (Jer 31:28).[285] This image of eating as behaviour underpins the warning against inappropriate eating that we find in Proverbs (23:20–21; 28:7).[286] The experience of life itself is also described in imagery taken from the realm of taste: "Another dies in bitterness of soul (נפש מרה), never having tasted of good (אכל בטובה)" (Job 21:25). Appropriate living is described as a life of eating and drinking (Qoh 2:24; 3:13), particularly eating sweet food: "My child, eat honey, for it is good, and the drippings of the honeycomb are sweet to your taste" (Prov 24:13). Such imagery is associated with sensory action, but we also find imagery of human moral behaviour that originates in the substance of sensation, such as taste and smell. Taste and smell signify moral and personal qualities, as we see in several verses, including: "Moab has been at ease from his youth, settled like wine on its dregs; he has not been emptied from vessel to vessel, nor has he gone into exile; therefore his flavour (טעמו) has remained and his aroma (ריחו) is unspoiled" (Jer 48:11).[287] Taste as signifying the person can be seen in the use of taste as a

---

283.　Stendebach, *TDOT* 13:317–19.

284.　Cf. pp. 167–75, above.

285.　As well as Ezek 18:2; cf. Prov 1:31.

286.　Excessive eating is tied to immoral behaviour through the link hunger–lust, which is also found in the field of sight. In both cases we find an attempt at social control over sensory experience.

287.　Cf. 1 Sam 21:14; 25:33; as well as pp. 167–75, above.

synecdoche for the acting agent, similar to the examples we saw earlier, and in the polysemy taste/decree found in the word טעם (see Jonah 3:7 and elsewhere).

We therefore see that the senses, the sensory organs, and the way they are used, symbolize the active agent, his/her ability to function in the world, and his way/her of behaving. These three aspects of the use of the senses are associated with a perception of the senses as a symbol of life. We have already seen that the nose is the seat of the spirit of life (e.g. Gen 2:7). We have also seen how standing on one's feet signifies life: "I prophesied as he commanded me, and the breath (רוח) came into them, and they lived (ויחיו), and stood on their feet (ויעמדו על־רגליהם), a vast multitude" (Ezek 37:10).[288] In contrast, pulling the feet symbolizes death, as found in the description on Jacob on his deathbed: "When Jacob ended his charge to his sons, he drew up his feet (ויאסף רגליו) into the bed, breathed his last, and was gathered to his people" (Gen 49:33).[289] Similarly, sight, especially seeing the light, is compared to life: "Or why was I not buried like a stillborn child, like an infant that never sees the light (לא־ראו אור)?" (Job 3:16).[290] A long life and the quality of life are also compared to sight: "What man is he that desireth life, and loveth many days, that he may see good (לראות טוב)?" (Ps 34:13, KJV; cf. Ps 128:8). In other biblical passages, the phrase "to see life" (ראה חיים) simply means to live: "Enjoy (lit. 'see,' ראה) life with the wife whom you love, all the days of your vain life that are given you under the sun, because that is your portion in life and in your toil at which you toil under the sun" (Qoh 9:9).[291] The parallel between eye, foot, and life is also apparent in Ps 116:8: "For you have delivered my soul (נפשי) from death, my eyes (עיני) from tears, my feet (רגלי) from stumbling."

In addition to the mentioned idioms and metaphors, we find a prominent metaphor in the biblical text associated with the sensory world, even if somewhat indirectly; the metaphor is "eating is sovereignty and success." This image originates in concrete reality—eating gives strength, eating one's own crops means independence—and extends to a derived image.[292] From a concrete perspective, it is clear that the production and storing of food—as in the story of Joseph in Egypt, for example—indicates independence and sovereignty. In contrast, the purchase of food or water indicates dependence and lack of sovereignty, as we see in the

---

288. Cf. Ezek 2:12; 3:24; 2 Kgs 13:21; Zech 14:12.

289. See Stendebach, *TDOT* 13:314.

290. Cf. Qoh 7:11; 11:7.

291. There are other images linking sight to life and presence. See pp. 155–58.

292. This is a common image in the Hebrew Bible; as such, I shall not present or discuss all sources, but will discuss it further shortly.

story of the Israelites' crossing the Transjordan (Deut 2:6, 28). Similarly, we find that eating one's harvest is a blessing, while the enemy's eating of the harvest is a curse:

> Your threshing shall overtake the vintage, and the vintage shall overtake the sowing; you shall eat your bread to the full (אכלתם לחמכם לשבע), and live securely (וישבתם לבטח) in your land… I will bring terror on you; consumption and fever that waste the eyes and cause life to pine away. You shall sow your seed in vain, for your enemies shall eat it (ואכלהו איביכם). (Lev 26:5, 16).[293]

This idea leads to the more general notion of harming the enemy as eating, as we saw above (pp. 146–50). The concrete description becomes a more general statement in the words of the prophet Isaiah: "If you are willing and obedient (ושמעתם), you shall eat the good of the land (טוב הארץ תאכלו); but if you refuse and rebel, you shall be devoured (תאכלו) by the sword; for the mouth of the Lord has spoken" (Isa 1:19–20). The image of eating one's own harvest as an indication of sovereignty and independence is also associated with the image of food as earning a living, even outside of an agricultural context: "…O seer, go, flee away to the land of Judah, earn (lit. 'eat,' אכול) your bread there, and prophesy there" (Amos 7:12).[294] Another example where food serves as a metaphor for sovereignty, and where eating from someone else's table is a metaphor for dependence, is the phrase "the ones that eat at the table" (אכלי שלחן), referring to those accompanying the king. While eating at the king's table is receiving royal patronage, it also means giving up some independence, and being subordinated to a certain hierarchy and inspection.[295]

In this section I demonstrated how different expressions and phrases from the field of sensory organs, and sensory experiences indicate independent human action, ability, and strength. This very general contextual pattern is the basis for the other contexts mentioned earlier: help, harm, thought, emotional experience, and moral judgment. The centrality of this context is also clear from the inclusion of all the senses in this field. As we saw in the previous tables, some contexts included reference to only part of the senses. In the context of strength, ability, and sovereignty, in contrast, we find metaphors and phrases that represent the seven modalities mentioned in the previous chapter. To sum up, I offer the following table:

293.   Cf. Deut 8:10; 28:5; 1 Sam 14:30–34; Jer 29:28 and many more.
294.   Cf. 1 Kgs 17:15; Ps 128:2 and more.
295.   1 Sam 20:29; 2 Sam 9:13; 19:29; 1 Kgs 2:7; 5:7; 18:19. See also MacDonald, *Not Bread Alone*, 154–63.

Table 8. *Sensory Phrases and Metaphors for Life, Ability, and Autonomy*

Sight	Hearing	Kinaesthesia	Speech	Taste	Smell	Tactile
ראה	שמע	הלך	פה	אכל	אף	יד
אור עינים	אזן	עמד	לפי	פה	ריח	ביד
עין		רגל	על פי	טעם	רוח	מיד
בעיני		ברגל	לשון	מטעם		ליד
אור עינים		לרגל	שפתים			

Towards a Definition

The examples that have been used thus far represent the complexity of meanings embedded in sensory vocabulary, and the common contexts in which sensory vocabulary is used. Among the numerous examples, few verses represented an absence of sensory ability and/or organ, and hence lack of ability or strength. This is particularly evident in descriptions of the helplessness of idols that are portrayed as being unable to use their senses: "The makers of idols all work to no purpose; and the things they treasure can do no good (בל־יועילו), as they themselves can testify. They neither look (בל־יראו) nor think (בל־ידעו), and so they shall be shamed" (Isa 44:9, JPS). Further discussion of the meaning of non-functioning sensorium will be found in the next chapter, including disabled sensorium due to birth, symbolic punishment, or old age. We shall see that non-functioning sensorium can indicate lack of ability and lack of independence. In this paragraph, as in this chapter as a whole, I have attempted to demonstrate how sensory imagery which appears in contextual patterns helps us understand the sensory category. The main conclusion that emerges from these metaphors is that we must understand the senses as abilities. In this wider context, we find a group of meanings represented by the following contrasts:

Table 9. *Dichotomy in Sensory Imagery*

Sensory Abilities	Sensory Disabilities
Vigour	Weakness
Ability	Disability
Sovereignty, independence	Dependence
Life	Death

In order to attempt to define the sensory category—or the term "sense"—in the Hebrew Bible, had it existed in Biblical Hebrew, we must clarify that the modern definitions of the words "sense" and "sensation" are both based on a Western epistemology that defines the senses as a means of receiving information from the world. But as this chapter has shown, the Hebrew Bible sees the senses as something more complex, something that cannot be defined using such simplistic terms. This is in contrast to deuterocanonical sources, which present a reflective picture of the senses, and even give them names such as "action" (*energèma*, Sir 17:5);[296] "spirit" (*pneuma*, T. Reub. 2:2–9), or "senses" (*aistheseis*, T. Naph. 2:8).[297] Nevertheless, the existence of a septasensory category, which includes the modalities described in the previous chapter, is self-evident. The definition of this category may not be explicit, but it is incorporated within the contexts presented in the current chapter. One can state that the senses are a physical experience which mark human ability to act in a sovereign manner in the world.

The current study started with a question: What is included in the biblical sensory category? After examining the contextual patterns in which sensory vocabulary appears, it is possible to assert that the senses included in the category are those provided as an answer to the following questions: Through what means does man learn about the world? Through what means does man control the world? And, What characterises human autonomy? In addition to these categorical questions, it is also evident that various senses share characteristics, such as being open or closed, being turned toward or away and more. Nevertheless, when a particular human experience shares a contextual or associative pattern with another one, it is not clear-cut whether both belong to the same category or not. For example, is sexuality another sense, or is it merely described in terms of other sensory experiences, without sharing all of the categorical definition with them? Alternatively, are hot and cold sensations a measure of temperature in the Hebrew Bible? Do they belong to the tactile sense, or are they shared characteristics of all senses? Furthermore, is it a matter of quality vs. quantity? Must a certain sense be found in *all* contextual patterns to be included in the sensory category? A firm answer to these questions can only be found in a systematic philosophical system. But since the Hebrew Bible only presents us with a reflection of the experienced cultural reality, and not with an analysis of that reality, these questions will be answered as well as possible. Below, I present a summary table of the different contextual patterns presented in

296.   See Chapter 2, n. 158.

297.   One must note that these verses contain stoic influence, which has a different categorization of the senses to the platonic one. For example, the "spirit" (*pneuma*) had eight parts, which partially overlap the senses; see Hollander and de Jonge, *The Testament of the Twelve Patriarchs*, 93; Segal, *Ben-Sira*, 105.

this chapter. The table shows how the seven senses presented in Chapter 2 apply to each context. Naturally, in terms of associative contexts, these senses constitute a single category, as was demonstrated before.

Table 10. *The Contextual Patterns of Sensory Experience*

	Help	Harm	Learning, Understanding, and Knowledge	Emotional Experience	Moral Judgment	Life, Ability, and Autonomy
Sight	+	+	+	+	+	+
Hearing	+		+	+	+	+
Kinaesthesia	+	+	+	+	+	+
Speech	+	+	+	+	+	+
Taste		+	+	+	+	+
Smell	+	+	298	+	+	+
Tactile	+	+	+			+

This table demonstrates visually the contextual patterns examined, which are, in fact, the characteristics of the sensory category in the Hebrew Bible. The table demonstrates how the modern meaning of the word "sense" does not suffice when considering the biblical sensorial category. It seems that there are two axes around which we should understand the sensory category in the culture reflected in the Hebrew Bible. The first axis is ability, the second is experience. That is, the senses are abilities through which the world is experienced. Another way of putting this is that the senses are a physical way of functioning, and are closely correlated to various limbs and organs, and to humanity as a whole. These ways of functioning include thought and action, obedience and disobedience, enjoyment and suffering. Our understanding of the sensorium and its characteristics, as reflected in biblical literature and language, differs markedly from the epistemological definition of the senses as physical tools for understanding the world. In the biblical sense, it is pointless to make a clear distinction between the experience/ability to study, and other experiences or abilities.

At a first and even second glance, there is no explicit or linguistic representation of the word "sense" or the like in Biblical Hebrew. Yet after the survey of examples, associations, and contexts, I want to suggest that there are phrases that do refer to the sensory category and represent a

---

298. Using the olfactory sense for moral judgment testifies to its place in perception, and its relevance to the field of thought and study, even though this aspect was not stressed. See pp. 157–63, above.

sort of alternative to the word "senses." These phrases use "sight" and "hearing," or "the eye" and "the ear," side-by-side in different contexts, as all-purpose representations of the senses. As will be discussed below, the senses are created by God. This prevalent biblical view is demonstrated most concisely by two proverbs: "The hearing ear and the seeing eye—the Lord has made them both" (Prov 20:12); "He who planted the ear, does he not hear? He who formed the eye, does he not see?" (Ps 94:9). I maintain that the associative and contextual patterns presented in this book are enough to claim that Proverbs in fact refers to "God who created the senses," except that the word "senses" is represented verbally by the action of seeing and hearing. This phenomenon should come as no surprise. Biblical Hebrew often uses phrases rather than individual words to describe various phenomena. In fact, naming a category by using part of its members is a known semantic phenomenon.[299] One example is the use of merism—using two words to describe something in its whole or complete form.[300] There is no Biblical Hebrew equivalent to "universe" or "cosmos." But the expression "heaven and earth" expresses that meaning, and the concept of "universe" is clearly found in biblical thought. Similarly, despite the absence of a specific term to describe it, we must accept the existence of a sensory category.

Once we assume that sight and hearing can refer to the sensory category as a whole, we can further explain the frequent use of parallels and clusters of terms from the world of sight and hearing in various contexts. Examples include the context of understanding: "Look, my eye has seen all this, my ear has heard and understood it" (Job 13:1), which describes a complete understanding. Note also the context of help: "The eyes of the Lord are on the righteous, and his ears are open to their cry" (Ps 34:16)—which describes complete attentiveness. The use of sight and hearing verbs is especially prevalent when describing experience and understanding in general: "...Son of man, see with your own eyes, and with your own ears listen, and attend your heart to everything I tell you..." (Ezek 44:5, my translation). The frequent use of sight and hearing as representative of sensory experience is based on their centrality in biblical perception. This centrality is also expressed by the large number of words, phrases, metaphors, and even names that use sight and hearing vocabulary.[301]

---

299.   I wish to Eve Sweetser for discussing the matter with me.

300.   See A. M. Honeyman, "Merismus in Biblical Hebrew," *JBL* 7 (1952): 11–18 (16–17).

301.   See also pp. 69–75, above.

Experiences that can be interpreted as experiential synaesthesia are usually described in phrases of sight and hearing. The two verses that most probably attempt to document experiential synaesthesia refer to sight and hearing.[302] The first verse describes the revelation at Mt. Sinai: "When all the people witnessed (lit. 'saw,' ראים) the thunder and lightning, the sound of the trumpet, and the mountain smoking, they were afraid and trembled and stood at a distance" (Exod 20:18).[303] The second verse describes Eliphaz's dream: "It stood still, but I could not discern its appearance (מראהו) [although] a form was before my eyes (עיני); I heard (אשמע) silence (דממה) and voice (קול)" (Job 4:16).[304] The synaesthetic experience is described as a change in the normal way we recognize the world, as a change in sight and hearing. This also explains the alternation between sight and hearing in a prophetic context, which will not be discussed here.[305]

Although, as we have seen, sight and hearing, or the eye and the ear, symbolize the sensory category as a whole, there is not a total semantic synchronicity between sight and hearing. While sight appears in all the contextual patterns explored in this chapter, hearing is markedly absent from the context of harm and control. There are other differences between the two. The biblical perception seems to distinguish between understanding through sight and understanding through hearing. Sight is perceived as a direct experience, as first-hand knowledge. Hearing, on the other hand, could be an experience that is further from its origin: "As we have heard, so have we seen (כאשר שמענו כן ראינו) in the city of the Lord of hosts, in the city of our God, which God establishes forever. Selah" (Ps 48:9). This gap between hearing and sight is highlighted in the story

302. Most synaesthetic idioms are linguistic synaesthesia, as explained in Chapter 1.

303. The more common interpretation is that ראה in this verse expresses, generally, perception through the senses, and therefore, can include both sight and hearing; see Kedar-Kopfstein, "Synästhesien," 50; U. Cassuto, *A Commentary on the Book of Exodus* (trans. I. Abrahams; Jerusalem: Magnes, 1967), 252.

304. This verse too attracts attempts at non-synaesthetic explanation. See, for example, the voice is *like* silence, in comparison to the storm (Tur-Sinai, *The Book of Job*, 83); "I heard a murmur, a voice" (JPS). Moreover, Tur-Sinai claims that there is no visual revelation and that the first part of the verse should be amended: יעמוד ולא אכיר מראה וַתמונה לנגד עיני, meaning, "I have not seen a vision, nor an image" (cf. Exod 12:8).

305. The question of prophetic experience as sight, hearing, or synaesthesia is not dealt with in detail here. In the past there were attempts to find a development in prophecy reflected in differing sensory experiences, normally from sight to hearing (see n. Chapter 1, n. 64).

of the Queen of Sheba, who heard about King Solomon (1 Kgs 10:1) and came to Jerusalem (v. 2) in order to see for herself (v. 4). The Queen of Sheba summarizes her visit in the following words: "So she said to the king, 'The report was true that I heard (שמעתי) in my own land of your accomplishments and of your wisdom, but I did not believe the reports until I came (באתי) and my own eyes had seen it (ותראינה עיני). Not even half had been told me; your wisdom and prosperity far surpass the report (שמועה) that I had heard (שמעתי)'" (vv. 6–7). The use of sight and hearing as representing the sensory category, and of the eye and the ear as representing the senses, reveals both what is common to the two actions and what differentiates them. Some of the biblical passages that feature both the eye and the ear refer to all the sensory organs. Other passages that feature sight and hearing refer to the overall sensory experience. In other cases, sight and hearing can describe opposite experiences.

Chapter 4

THEOLOGY OF THE SENSES

In this chapter I will examine the common understanding of the senses as divinely created. This notion is quite essential in biblical literature and sheds much light on the biblical septasensory category. After reviewing the information found within the Hebrew Bible about the creation of the senses, I will discuss harming the senses, which bears symbolic load closely related to the divine origin of sensory experience. I will then discuss sensory disability and demonstrate how the definition of the senses as described in the previous chapter, together with the notion of divine creation of the senses and divine punishment of harming the senses, explain the cultural-social evaluation of those with sensory disability.

Who Created the Senses?

I opened my discussion of the sensorium in Chapter 2 by examining human actions that cannot be performed by idols.[1] The mentioned verses teach us two major traits of the senses. The first is that these experiences characterize vitality and autonomy. Inability to experience through the senses signifies inability to act. The second is that humans cannot create the senses, just as they cannot create life. Humans can only form raw materials to create idols, without the ability to give them any vitality. The helplessness of idols rests not only in the fact that they do not possess senses, or have no autonomy, or lack life, but in the fact that they are created by humans, not by God. In a kind of dark prophecy, Moses describes the actions of his people in a future exile: "There you will serve other gods made by human hands, objects of wood and stone that neither see, nor hear, nor eat, nor smell" (Deut 4:28). One must note that the main issue in this verse is not idolatry! Rather, it is the fact that the

---

1. Deut 4:28; Pss 115:4–5; 135:15–17; Dan 5:28.

Israelites will worship helpless gods and therefore will get into trouble. Moreover, the oxymoron "gods made by human hands" is a true mockery of the idols and those believing in them.[2] In the two other "sensory lists" which describe the inabilities of the idols, the stress on the link between the lack of sensory experience and human creation is further developed. Since Ps 135:15–17 is an echo of Ps 115:4–7, we will focus on the latter.[3] In Ps 115:2–8, the psalmist compares his omnipotent God to the helpless gods worshipped by the nations:

> Why should the nations say, "Where is their God?"
> Our God is in the heavens; he does whatever he pleases.
> Their idols are silver and gold, the work of human hands.
> They have mouths, but do not speak; eyes, but do not see.
> They have ears, but do not hear; noses, but do not smell.
> They have hands, but do not feel; feet, but do not walk; they make no sound in their throats.
> Those who make them are like them; so are all who trust in them.

In this passage, the inability of the idols is contrasted to the ability of God; the inability of the idols is detailed through their sensory inabilities; and lastly, the list of disabilities follows the expression "works of human hands"—the idols are the work of human hands and therefore they lack sensory experience. Furthermore, the psalmist is not content simply to highlight the lack of senses; rather, he demonstrates that the creation of sensory organs is no guarantee that they can be used. The human creators of the idols are highlighted again in v. 8, where they are named "their makers" (עשיהם). The term hints at the creative pretentiousness of idol makers, when naturally it is God who makes (עשה) the heaven and the earth (v. 15). The message is clear: creative abilities belong to God alone, God has created the senses and he is the source of ability.[4] In other verses that describe the helplessness of idols, we again find an emphasis on the material nature of the idols, even when their human-made characteristic is not specifically mentioned. For example, "Their idols are like scarecrows in a cucumber field, and they cannot speak (לא ידברו); they have to be carried, for they cannot walk (לא יצעדו). Do not be afraid of

---

2. Other verses that describe the idols as a human creation are Isa 41:6–7; 44:12–20; Jer 10:3–5; Ps 106:19–20. Similarly, we must understand the title given to the idols, "wood and stone" (עץ ואבן, Deut 28:3, 64), as denoting human formation. See Tigay, *Deuteronomy*, 53–54.

3. The similarity between Ps 115:4–7 and Ps 135:15–17, with the awkward position of the last within Ps 135, led to claims of the dependency of the latter on the former. See Briggs and Briggs, *The Book of Psalms*, 480.

4. Dahood, *Psalms III*, 141.

them, for they cannot do evil, nor is it in them to do good" (Jer 10:5).[5]
Here again, the idols' helplessness is indicated by the absence of senses.
They do not speak, they do not walk, and they have to be carried. This
inability to talk or walk indicates an overall inability to act, either in a
good or in a harmful way. Indeed, this verse strengthens the evidence for
the phenomena mentioned earlier—sensory experience signifies neutral
ability, an ability that can be used positively or negatively.

In another description of idols, Isaiah claims that they do not see and
do not understand: "The makers of idols all work to no purpose; and the
things they treasure can do no good (בל־יועילו), as they themselves can
testify. They neither look (בל־יראו) nor think (בל־ידעו), and so they shall
be shamed" (Isa 44:9, JPS). These passages teach us about the perception
of the divine, but also about the perception of the senses. Reflected in
these verses is an understanding that the senses represent the ability to
act autonomously, and that the origin of the senses lies in the act of
creation. In this respect, the senses resemble the spirit or the breath of
life, which is also presented in the Hebrew Bible as an ability that God
alone can create. In that matter, there is an essential difference between
Ps 115 and Ps 135. In the latter, the idols not only have no sensory
ability, they also have no breath in their mouths (v. 17), meaning they
have no life.[6] From the context, this statement would seem to be a kind of
summary of the previous claims regarding the inability to speak, see, or
listen. The phrase "they even have no breath in their mouth" (אַף אֵין־יֶשׁ
רוּחַ בְּפִיהֶם), which is used here for emphasis, neutralizes any counter-
argument regarding any ability of the idols.[7]

Thus far I have presented evidence for divine creation of the sensorium by examples of negation—the idols are human creations that lack
senses, implying that God is the only creator of sensory experience.
However, there are also verses that state this concept more explicitly. In
a somewhat tautological manner, the psalmist claims: "He who planted
the ear, does he not hear? He who formed the eye, does he not see?"
(Ps 94:9). God is the source of the senses, and at the same time God has

---

5. For similar verses, see n. 2; and cf. Isa 46:7: "They must carry it on their backs
and transport it; When they put it down, it stands, It does not budge (יָמִישׁ) from its
place. If they cry out to it, it does not answer (יַעֲנֶה); It cannot save them from their
distress" (JPS).

6. Briggs and Briggs, *The Book of Psalms*, 480.

7. For further and at times similar discussion of the matter, see S. M. Olyan,
"The Ascription of Physical Disability as a Stigmatizing Strategy in Biblical Iconic
Polemics," *JHS* 9, no. 14 (2009): Article 14:1–15. Online: www.arts.ualberta.ca/
JHS/Articles/article_116.pdf.

sensory abilities. On the other hand, humans have sensory abilities, but cannot create the senses. Lastly, idols have no senses, nor can they create them. As in previous verses, this verse too appears in a polemic context, within a psalm of polemic structure. The psalmist offers the argument of the wicked—"...The Lord does not see (יִרְאֶה); the God of Jacob does not perceive" (יָבִין, v. 7)—and responds by claiming that God indeed can see and hear (v. 9), and know (v. 10).[8] Verse 9 clearly refers to the creation of the senses as the verbs "to plant" (נטע) and "to form" (יצר) are used elsewhere to describe God's acts of creation. We find an example of the psalmist praising God the creator: "he who fashions (יֹצֵר) the hearts of them all, and observes (מֵבִין) all their deeds" (Ps 34:15).[9] Here too the significance of the verse for our purpose is twofold: the verse teaches us that God is the creator of mind, and the verse teaches us that God has the ability to observe or understand. The logical link between the two is implied.

In God's rebuke to Moses we also see the prominence of the creation of the senses: "...Who gives speech to mortals? Who makes them mute or deaf, seeing or blind? Is it not I, the Lord?" (Exod 4:11). Although the verse addresses Moses, it does not refer to him alone. The verse is a general statement that uses the term "mortal" (אדם), which is usually used to describe humankind in creation accounts. In fact, the verse describes the initial creation of sensory abilities, as well as the constant control (continuous creation) of God over sensory perception and its content.[10] While at the first part of the verse, it is possible to understand the statement as a motif of placing words in the mouth of the prophet,[11] it is clear from the second part that a more general statement is involved:

---

8. R. J. Clifford, *Psalms 73–150* (Abingdon Old Testament Commentaries; Nashville: Abingdon, 2003), 114; cf. Isa 29:16: "You turn things upside down! Shall the potter (יֹצֵר) be regarded as the clay? Shall the thing made say of its maker, 'He did not make me'; or the thing formed (יֵצֶר) say of the one who formed it (יֹצְרוֹ), 'He has no understanding'?"

9. Briggs and Briggs, *The Book of Psalms*, 289. For the root יצר in descriptions of creation, see Pss 74:17; 105:5. Cf. H.-J. Kraus, *Psalms 1–59: A Commentary* (trans. H. C. Oswald; Minneapolis: Fortress, 1988), 378, and S. Paas, *Creation and Judgment: Creation Texts in Some Eighth Century Prophets* (OTS 47; Leiden: Brill, 2003), 58–60.

10. C. Houtman, *Exodus* (HCOT; Kampen: Kok, 1993), 109–310. For the term "human being" (אדם) in the context of creation, see Gen 1:26–27; 5:1–2; Deut 4:32 and elsewhere.

11. E.g. M. Noth, *Exodus* (trans. J. S. Bowden; OTL; London: SCM, 1962), 62. Cf. Num 22:38; 23:16; Deut 18:18.

God controls the creation of humans in terms of their bodily organs, as well as their usage.[12]

The idea of God as the creator of the senses does not appear in the Genesis account of creation, where we read that "the Lord God formed man from the dust of the ground, and breathed into his nostrils the breath of life (וייפח באפיו נשמת חיים); and the man became a living being" (Gen 2:7). That is, man is a functioning, living being and the use of sensory perception involved is not detailed. Interestingly, in the Aramaic translations of *Onkelos* the expression "breath of life" (נשמת חיים) becomes within Adam an "uttering speech" (רוח ממללא). Such translation could be the result of later perceptions of speech being created for the purpose of prayer, a notion that was common during the Second Temple period and throughout early Christianity.[13] *Pseudo-Jonathan* goes further and translates this verse as follows: "And he breathes into his nostrils the breath of life, and the breath became in the body of Adam as spirit capable of speech (רוח ממללא), to give light to the eyes (אנהרות עיינין) and to give hearing to the ears (מצתות אודנין)."[14] Both translations echo the perception presented already in Exod 4:11, namely, that God created speech.

Further evidence for this tradition is found in a number of biblical verses that seem difficult to interpret. Amos 4:13, for example, reads: "Behold, the former of mountains, the creator of wind (רוח), the one who tells man his speech (שחו), who makes the morning darkness, and treads upon the heights of the earth—Yahweh, the God of hosts is his name" (my translation). Clearly, this verse refers to God as the creator and sovereign of the world, as the verbs "to form" (יצר) and "to create" (ברא)

---

12. For the terms, antonyms, and their various readings, see Houtman, *Exodus*, 410–12, as well as p. 90, above.

13. E.g. "you have created the breath of the tongue, and you have known its utterance" (1QHa 9 [1] 27–31, my translation); "And I lifted up my hands in righteousness and blessed the Great Holy One, and I spoke with the breath of my mouth and with a tongue of flesh, which God has made for the sons of the flesh of man, that they might speak with it {and he has given the, a breath and tongue and mouth that they might speak with it.}" (*1 En.* 84:1, translation from G. W. E. Nickelsburg and J. C. VanderKam, *1 Enoch: A New Translation Based on the Hermeneia Commentary* [Minneapolis: Fortress, 2004], 119). A detailed discussion of both is found in H. Arnon, "The Creation of Speech in the Qumran Sectarian Literature (1QHa 9 [1] 27–31)" (M.A. diss., The University of Haifa, 2006 [Hebrew]).

14. Translation from M. Maher, *Targum Pseudo-Jonathan: Genesis* (Aramaic Bible; Collegeville: Liturgical, 1992), 22.

highlight.[15] But the expressions "wind" (רוח) and "speech" (שֶׂח*) in this context are more controversial. The first term, רוח, could refer to the wind as a power of nature, in parallel to the mountains, as translated above. It could, however, indicate human spirit as well.[16] The term translated here as "his speech" (שחו) differs from the other phrases in this verse, which all refer to wondrous natural phenomena. This word can either refer to speech or thoughts, and the third person pronominal suffix could be attributed to God or to humans. Most translations, contra to my view, translate here "reveals his thoughts to mortals" and hence lose the possibility of reference to the creation of speech.[17] As we find elsewhere that the creation of earth and the creation of human spirit are the greatest wonders (Zech 12:1; cf. Isa 44:24), it seems that here too Amos describes the creation of the mountains, the spirit/breath of humans, as well as speech.[18] Such an idea is expressed also in the phrase "creating the fruit of the lips" (Isa 57:19 [18]),[19] as well as the notion of God's knowledge of the content of speech: "Even before a word is on my tongue, O Lord, you know it completely" (Ps 139:4).[20]

We find further evidence that God created the senses in the prophecies of Isaiah. In his description of the upturn of the natural order of creation, the mountain becomes a plain, the desert blossoms. The upturn is possible due to God's initial creation of the mountains and the desert. Similarly, the fate of sensory experience will be reversed: "Then the eyes

15. M. Weiss, *The Book of Amos* (Jerusalem: Magnes, 1992 [Hebrew]), 125–27. The root "to create" (ברא) is unique in describing divine action. The root "to form" (יצר) originated in pot-making. The image of creating humans by forming, similar to pot-making, is widespread in the prophecy; e.g. Isa 29:16; Jer 18:6. See Paas, *Creation and Judgment*, 73.

16. Weiss, *Amos*, 221 n. 64.

17. E.g. NRSV (given above), JPS, NIV, KJV and more.

18. Rözal views רוח as the human soul and the third person pronominal suffix in שחו refers to humans, not to God. However, like most translations he views the word as "thoughts," i.e. God knows the thoughts of humans as he created them; see H. N. Rözal, *Amos* (Haifa: Ah, 1990 [Hebrew]), 128–29. Normally, however, the lexeme שׂיח (of which שֶׂח is a by-form) represents speech, and the meaning "thought" is its derived meaning. See S. M. Paul, *Amos* (Mikra Le'Israel; Tel Aviv: Am Oved, 1994, [Hebrew]); Weiss, *Amos*, 223 n. 76.

19. For the interpretation of the verse as describing the creation of speech, see Oswalt, *Isaiah: Chapters 40–66*, 491.

20. Similarly God controls walking: "I know, O Lord, that the way of human beings is not in their control, that mortals as they walk cannot direct their steps" (Jer 10:23). The verse is a general claim about humanity in contrast to God; Jer 17:5–11 is similar. See R. P. Carroll, *The Book of Jeremiah* (OTL; London: SCM, 1986), 263.

of the blind shall be opened (תפקחנה), and the ears of the deaf unstopped (תפתחנה); then the lame shall leap (ידלג) like a deer, and the tongue of the speechless sing (תרן) for joy. For waters shall break forth in the wilderness, and streams in the desert" (Isa 35:5–6). This verse mentions four senses—sight, hearing, kinaesthesia, and speech—all of them controlled by the all-powerful God. Even though the verse does not explicitly state that God created the senses, he clearly controls them. It is God who decides on the existence of the senses, and he decides on their absence. A similar reference to sight and hearing appears in other passages in Isaiah: "On that day the deaf shall hear (ושמעו) the words of a scroll, and out of their gloom and darkness the eyes of the blind shall see (תראינה)" (Isa 29:18); "Listen (שמעו), you that are deaf; and you that are blind, look up and see (הביטו לראות)!" (42:18); "to open (לפקח) the eyes that are blind, to bring out the prisoners from the dungeon, from the prison those who sit in darkness" (Isa 42:7).[21] God's ability to change sensory disability is demonstrated elsewhere, and clearly related to his creative power. Psalm 146 describes God as the creator, "who made heaven and earth, the sea, and all that is in them" (v. 6). It goes on to describe God as the righteous judge and supporter of the downtrodden (v. 7).[22] Finally, God is able to change the existing order: "The Lord opens (פקח) the eyes of the blind. The Lord lifts up those who are bowed down..." (v. 8).

To sum up this section, it is enough to use a biblical proverb: "The hearing ear and the seeing eye—the Lord has made them both" (Prov 20:12). From this verse we can also understand that while all the senses were divinely created, prominence is given to the hearing, speech, and sight senses. The creation of the senses is alluded to at different levels of the text, explicitly and implicitly. The theological argument that God controls the senses teaches us that the functioning of the senses is an essential part of human vitality, similar to the "breath of life" mentioned in the creation narrative. The absence of the senses, on the other hand, and especially the absence of all the senses, is compared to the absence of any real existence or power.[23] This correlation between the creation of life and the creation of the senses appears frequently in metaphors that compare the use of the senses to life, and compare the lack of use of the senses to death.[24]

---

21. In these verses, physical and metaphorical blindness merge; see L. Wächter, W. Von Soden, and H.-J. Fabry, "עִוֵּר *'iwwēr*; עור *'wr* I; עִוֶּרֶת *'wweret*; עִוָּרֹון *'iwwārôn*; סַנְוֵרִים *sanwērîm*; שׁעע *š'ʿ*," *TDOT* 10:574–77.

22. Descriptions of God as supporter of the sensorily disabled, and its parallel to human support, will be mentioned below.

23. Houtman, *Exodus*, 412.

24. For more details, see pp. 255–58, below.

Harming the Senses

Different human abilities, what we call senses, appear in various biblical passages that relate to God's creation and control over the sensorium. The same notion is expressed when divine punishment is carried out through harming of the senses, and particularly the sense of sight. Within the long curse concluding Deuteronomy, a fine example is found: "The Lord will afflict you with madness (שגעון), blindness (עורון), and confusion of mind (תמהון לבב); you shall grope about at noon as blind people (עור) grope in darkness, but you shall be unable to find your way; and you shall be continually abused and robbed, without anyone to help" (Deut 28:28–29). Divine punishment includes various diseases (also v. 27), and the meaning of each individual disease is not always clear. Blindness, however, is described in detail, with a focus on the blind person's kinaesthetic problems and orientation challenges.[25] The biblical text could also be hinting at the blind person's socio-economic status. The blind are constantly being exploited and robbed, probably because of their physical disabilities.[26] We find a similar threat in the prophecy of Zechariah:[27] "On that day, says the Lord, I will strike every horse with panic (תמהון), and its rider with madness (שגעון). But on the house of Judah I will keep a watchful eye (אפקח את־עיני), when I strike every horse of the peoples with blindness (עורון)" (Zech 12:4). Blindness is portrayed as divine punishment which will be inflicted on Israel's enemies in battle and will render the enemy helpless. Later in Zechariah, we see another threat against the enemies that go to war with Judah: "This shall be the plague with which the Lord will strike all the peoples that wage war against Jerusalem: their flesh shall rot while they are still on their feet; their eyes shall rot in their sockets, and their tongues shall rot in their mouths" (Zech 14:12). Kinaesthetic, sight, and speech disabilities are mentioned together, and the severity of God's punishment is highlighted by the fact that the nations will be punished while they are still alive.[28] Moreover, the punishment is in fact that which happens to the dead, thus the symbolic load of sensory disability at death is evident.

25. As will be demonstrated, this image repeats in other biblical texts.

26. In this context, blindness is compared to a legal state of helplessness. See Malul, *Society, Law, and Custom*, 170. In the present study I do not discuss the definition of disability. For the possible terms and their implications, see the Introduction to Avalos, Melcher, and Schipper, eds., *This Abled Body*, written by the editors.

27. Clearly alluding to and using the vocabulary of Deuteronomy; see Wächter, Von Soden, and Fabry, *TDOT* 10:576.

28. Stendebach, *TDOT* 13:314.

Other biblical passages describe concrete and metaphorical blindness accompanied by kinaesthetic and even speech disabilities:

> Therefore justice is far from us, and righteousness does not reach us; we wait for light, and lo! There is darkness; and for brightness, but we walk in gloom. We grope like the blind along a wall, groping like those who have no eyes; we stumble at noon as in the twilight, among the vigorous as though we were dead. We all growl like bears; like doves we moan mournfully. We wait for justice, but there is none; for salvation, but it is far from us. (Isa 59:9–11)

In this prophecy, there is an immediate, direct correlation between crime and punishment, which implies a kind of divine punishment, even though this is not stated explicitly. The prophecy is a simile which compares the helplessness of Jacob (Israel) to blind people groping around and stumbling, and to animals that "speak," yet are not understood (= heard). Blindness here, therefore, marks both divine punishment and helplessness. Blinding as divine punishment repeats alongside kinaesthetic and orientation difficulties: "I will bring such distress upon people that they shall walk like the blind (והלכו כעורים); because they have sinned against the Lord, their blood shall be poured out like dust, and their flesh like dung" (Zeph 1:17); "Blindly they wandered (נעו עורים) through the streets, so defiled with blood that no one was able to touch their garments" (Lam 4:14). Indeed, even when the punishment is not blindness, the state of the punishment is compared to blindness. Temporary blindness, which is mentioned twice in the Hebrew Bible, is also described as divine punishment that leads to temporary loss of sight and loss of orientation. The men of Sodom were "struck with blindness...so that they were unable to find the door" (Gen 19:11), and the Aramean army that surrounded Samaria is struck with temporary blindness by God, which enabled Elisha to lead them into the city (2 Kgs 6:18–19). Only once inside did their temporary blindness disappear, and "the Lord opened their eyes, and they saw that they were inside Samaria" (v. 20).[29] Without a doubt, temporary, constant, or symbolic blindness are all a sign of divine punishment and human disability—blindness becomes a hallmark for divine punishment.

In addition to blindness, divine punishment can influence the mouth, thus disabling the possibility of harming: "O God, break the teeth in their mouths; tear out the fangs of the young lions, O Lord! Let them vanish like water that runs away; like grass let them be trodden down and

29. For סנוורים as loss of orientation, and not merely sight, see Wächter, Von Soden, and Fabry, *TDOT* 10:577.

wither" (Ps 58:7–8). Divine punishment can also harm the hand: "When the king heard what the man of God cried out against the altar at Bethel, Jeroboam stretched out his hand from the altar, saying, 'Seize him!' But the hand that he stretched out against him withered so that he could not draw it back to himself" (1 Kgs 13:4). In this verse too, harming the hand has a symbolic load, as it marks the lack of power and divine punishment of Jeroboam. In a furious prophecy to the leader, Zechariah too wishes harm on the hand and the eye: "Oh, my worthless shepherd, who deserts the flock! May the sword strike his arm and his right eye! Let his arm be completely withered, his right eye utterly blinded!" (Zech 11:17).[30] Note again that in addition to the physical harm, harming the eye and the hand marks the loss of authority. Lastly, harming the sense as a form of divine punishment appears as prevention of understanding: "…Go and say to this people: 'Keep listening, but do not comprehend; keep looking, but do not understand.' Make the mind of this people dull (הַשְׁמֵן), and stop their ears (הַכְבֵּד), and shut (הָשַׁע) their eyes, so that they may not look with their eyes, and listen with their ears, and comprehend with their minds, and turn and be healed" (Isa 6:10).[31] In this verse the control of God over the sensorium is so vast that it contrasts free will and understanding. From the above-cited verses there is no evidence of the perception that congenital sensory disability implies divine punishment.[32] The evidence lies in prophetic curses and rhetoric which portray damage to the senses as divine punishment. The punishment can be actual harm to the senses, or other harms which are compared to sensory disability. The main harmful acts associated with divine punishment are those harming sight, mobility, and speech, and are usually part of a broader description of extinction or failure.

30. Such descriptions (and Ps 137:5) are mostly explained as a stroke; see A. Ohry and E. Dolev, "Disabilities and Handicapped People in the Bible" (Hebrew), *Koroth* 8, no. 5–6 (1982): 57–67 (64).

31. Moreover, God's control over speech is demonstrated by causing muteness: "And I will make your tongue cling to the roof of your mouth, so that you shall be speechless (וְנֶאֱלַמְתָּ) and unable to reprove them; for they are a rebellious house" (Ezek 3:26). Similarly, some interpreters understand Exod 4:11 as a threat for Moses (see B. S. Childs, *Exodus: A Commentary* [OTL; London, SCM, 1974], 78–79), and Ezek 29:7 as harming movement and posture (see D. I. Block, *The Book of Ezekiel: Chapters 25–48* [NICOT; Grand Rapids: Eerdmans, 1998], 136).

32. Such a view is found in the New Testament as the common sense which Jesus negates: "As he walked along, he saw a man blind from birth. His disciples asked him, 'Rabbi, who sinned, this man or his parents, that he was born blind?' Jesus answered, 'Neither this man nor his parents sinned; he was born blind so that God's works might be revealed in him'" (John 9:1–3).

The evidence for harming the senses presented thus far is clearly linked to the perception of God as the creator of the senses, as presented earlier in this chapter. However, it is also possible that divine harm of the senses is an idiom based on punishment practices prevalent in the biblical era, and mentioned in the Hebrew Bible and in other texts from the ancient Near East.[33] Below, I will present examples of the harm to the senses that was implemented as an act of punishment and humiliation. Adoni-bezek, who receives a poetic punishment, is an example of harm to the ability to grasp and move: "Adoni-bezek fled; but they pursued him, and caught him, and cut off his thumbs and big toes (בהנות ידיו ורגליו). Adoni-bezek said, 'Seventy kings with their thumbs and big toes cut off (בהנות ידיהם ורגליהם מקצצים) used to pick up scraps under my table; as I have done, so God has paid me back.' They brought him to Jerusalem, and he died there" (Judg 1:6–7). The punishment mentioned twice in the narrative—as Adoni-bezek's own punishment, and as the punishment he used to mete out to his enemies—leads to a lack of equilibrium and a dramatic reduction in kinaesthetic ability. Clearly, a soldier who is punished by having his fingers and toes cut off, can no longer fight.[34] This is also a symbolic damage as the foot and stepping marks in the Hebrew Bible and the ancient Near Eastern independence and control.[35] The description of kings licking food scraps under the table hints at their dependence, and at the humiliation they were subjected to. Not only did they not dine with the king, they had to gather food scraps. We find a similar punishment in the story of Ish-Bosheth (Ishbaal), the supposed inheritor of the Saulide monarchy. Those who assassinated him were severely punished by David: "So David commanded the young men, and they killed them; they cut off their hands (ידיהם) and feet (רגליהם), and hung their bodies beside the pool at Hebron. But the head of Ishbaal they took and buried in the tomb of Abner at Hebron" (2 Sam 4:12). In this narrative, the limbs were cut off after the men were killed, a punishment with clear rhetorical character, mortification indeed.

Punishment, including restricting freedom of mobility in both a practical and a symbolic sense (denying autonomy), often appears in the Hebrew Bible as reversible and temporary. The poetic description of Joseph's imprisonment includes the shackling of his legs and neck: "His feet were hurt with fetters, his neck was put in a collar of iron; until what

33. Mainly in the apocalyptic parts of the book of Zechariah.
34. A. Katznelson and M. Katznelson, "Locomotor Disfunction in the Bible" (Hebrew), *Koroth* 8, no. 5–6 (1982): 57–62 (61–62); Huber-Bechtel, "The Biblical Experience of Shame/Shaming," 81–82.
35. Stendebach, *TDOT* 13:319.

he had said came to pass, the word of the Lord kept testing him. The king sent and released him; the ruler of the peoples set him free" (Ps 105:18–20). Note how the physical aspect is merged in this psalm with the abstract and theological aspect, and compare this with the description of Abner: "Your hands were not bound, your feet were not fettered; as one falls before the wicked you have fallen…" (2 Sam 3:34).[36] It seems that temporary harm to kinaesthetic ability is based on the same poetics as an irreversible one. Note as well that within the legal material we find only one example of the cutting off of a limb as punishment: "If men get into a fight with one another, and the wife of one intervenes to rescue her husband from the grip of his opponent by reaching out and seizing his genitals, you shall cut off her hand; show no pity" (Deut 25:11–12). This is also the only instance where cutting off a limb does not serve symbolic/rhetoric purposes. At the same time, it is impossible to assert whether such law was enforced, or was an idealized description by the biblical narrator.[37]

Cutting off the nose and ears is another harmful act described in the Hebrew Bible as part of the punishment and humiliation meted out in war: "I will direct my indignation against you, in order that they may deal with you in fury. They shall cut off your nose and your ears, and your survivors shall fall by the sword. They shall seize your sons and your daughters, and your survivors shall be devoured by fire" (Ezek 23:25).[38] Like other descriptions of war, the harm caused by the enemy is based on divine decision, and therefore it is, symbolically at least, divine harm as well.[39] Cutting off the ears and nose harms sensory abilities such as hearing, posture, smell, and breathing. Even when the purpose of the punishment is symbolic, its results have a real effect on the senses.

The human punishment described in greatest detail in the Hebrew Bible is gouging out the eyes, which appears in three different biblical stories. The first is the story of Samson, who is shackled and has his eyes gouged out: "So the Philistines seized him and gouged out his eyes. They brought him down to Gaza and bound him with bronze shackles; and he ground at the mill in the prison" (Judg 16:21). Samson is punished by

---

36. Cf. 2 Kgs 17:4; Jer 39:7; 40:1; 52:11; Ezek 3:25; Ps 149:8; 2 Chr 36:6.

37. Assuming that *lex talionis* laws (Exod 21:24; Deut 19:21) are moral and not practical. More generally, as the question of the applicability of biblical law is too broad to be dealt with in this context, we present evidence for harming of the senses which is mentioned innocently.

38. Cf. the Egyptian practice of nose-cutting for prisoners (Z. Rosen, "The Healthy and the Diseased Nose in the Bible" [Hebrew], *Koroth* 8, no. 5–6 [1982]: 79–85 [82]).

39. The nose and the ears were decorated with jewelry (Ezek 16:12).

temporary restraint of his movement, as well as complete blinding. The punishment is carried out by the Philistines, but marks God's rejection of Samson. Samson himself uses the routine description of blindness in order to get the young man to lead him to the pillars: "Samson said to the attendant who held him by the hand, 'Let me feel (הימשני) the pillars on which the house rests, so that I may lean against them'" (Judg 16:26). This verse highlights the practical need of the blind person for guidance, and the assumption that a blind person's ability to move is damaged.[40]

Someone else whose eyes are gouged out as part of his imprisonment is Zedekiah the king of Judah: "Then they captured the king and brought him up to the king of Babylon at Riblah, who passed sentence on him. They slaughtered the sons of Zedekiah before his eyes (לעיניו), then put out (עור) the eyes (עיני) of Zedekiah; they bound him in fetters and took him to Babylon" (2 Kgs 25:7).[41] Here too damage to the eyes is accompanied by harming or controlling movement, and it serves symbolic and practical elements. Zedekiah's blindness is his loss of authority, and loss of divine support.[42] The third narrative mentioning gouging the eyes is the narrative of Nahash the Ammonite and his threat over Jabesh: "But Nahash the Ammonite said to them, 'On this condition I will make a treaty with you, namely that I gouge out (נקור) everyone's right eye (עין ימין), and thus put disgrace (חרפה) upon all Israel'" (1 Sam 11:2).[43] This verse reveals the true symbolic nature of eye-gouging. It only talks of gouging out one eye, which leads to neither blindness nor immobility. The correlation to reproach in this verse makes it clear that even partial blindness is a symptom of disgrace and inferiority. These extended narratives give the impression that gauging the eyes was a most common practice, and that divine blinding is based on real practices, and not merely theological perceptions.

There are two more references to gouging of the eyes, and both are worth mentioning. During the challenge to Moses' leadership, Dathan and Abiram complain: "It is clear you have not brought us into a land flowing with milk and honey, or given us an inheritance of fields and vineyards. Would you put out the eyes of these men (העיני האנשים ההם תנקר)? We will not come!" (Num 16:14). Some commentators see this verse as an allusion to the custom of punishment by gouging out the eyes. It seems more probable, though, that Dathan and Abiram are

40. Note that the root מוש/משש appears only in the context of blindness (physiological or metaphorical), see pp. 106–9, above.

41. Cf. Jer 39:7; 52:11. This detail is lacking from 2 Chr 36:11–20.

42. See Jer 21; 24.

43. For the longer version in the LXX and 4QSam[a], see A. Rofé, "The Acts of Nahash According to 4QSam[a]," *IEJ* 32 (1982): 129–33.

simply saying that Moses cannot deny what everyone knows, he cannot prevent people from seeing and witnessing the exact state of affairs.[44] The other example of eye gouging refers to post-mortem punishment, where harming the body has only a symbolic purpose: "The eye that mocks a father and scorns to obey a mother will be pecked out by the ravens of the valley and eaten by the vultures" (Prov 30:17). The eye in this verse is synecdoche for the person, and the punishment is in proportion to the offence. This clearly refers to a contempt for the dead, who do not merit burial.[45]

To sum up the above references, inflicting damage on the senses was a recognized custom in biblical times, especially in times of war. The purpose was two-fold: to undermine the ability of the warriors to fight, and to create moral damage to the vanquished, with physical damage symbolizing the loser's surrender and inferiority.[46] In biblical theology, these two are accompanied by the idea that loss in war is divine rejection. Biblical passages focus mainly on damage to mobility, grasping, and sight abilities. However, other forms of physical damage may have existed that do not get a mention in the biblical text.

In contrast to the damage to the senses described above, the deterioration of sensory abilities in old age is described as a natural human process, rather than a response to any specific human action.[47] This damage to the senses is regarded as a natural phenomenon, and anyone of advanced age who does not suffer from sensory aging is considered particularly special. One case is Moses on his deathbed: "Moses was 120 years old when he died; his sight was unimpaired (עינו לא־כהתה) and his vigor had not abated" (Deut 34:7).[48] However, in another passage, Moses

---

44. See also p. 238, below.

45. This verse demonstrates the biblical link between hurting the parents' honour and a punishment including inappropriate death/burial. See S. M. Olyan, "Honor, Shame and Covenant Relations in Ancient Israel and Its Environment," *JBL* 115 (1996): 201–18.

46. The symbolic background for damaging of the senses as "lowering" will be discussed below, pp. 212–20.

47. A short description is found in I. G. Papayannopoulos, "Information Revealed from the Old Testament Concerning Diseases of Old Age" (Hebrew), *Koroth* 8, no. 5–6 (1982): 68–71.

48. Normally, the phrase לא נס לחה is translated "Moses' vigor did not fade," yet the exact meaning of the word לח is debatable. Scholars and dictionaries derive the noun from the root לחח ("to be moist, fresh"); see the full discussion in J. H. Tigay, "'לא נס לחה He Had Not Become Wrinkled' (Deuteronomy 34:7)," in Zevit, Gitin, and Sokoloff, eds., *Solving Riddles and Untying Knots*, 345–50. It seems to me that the noun should be derived from the Semitic root *l̥y*, known from Akkadian and Ugaritic/Canaanite. The root appears with a middle *ḥeth* in Old Babylonian (*CAD* 9,

says about himself: "...I am now 120 years old. I am no longer able to get about (לצאת ולבוא)..." (Deut 31:2). In other words, Moses has difficulty in walking, or his strength has given out on him, and he has difficulty ruling.[49] The two descriptions are, therefore, contradictory in a way. We hear of other leaders, whose kinaesthetic abilities are damaged in old age. King Asa, for example, "...in his old age he was diseased in his feet" (1 Kgs 15:23).[50] And the LXX translation of the book of Samuel has these words in Samuel's mouth: "And now, behold, the king *goes about* before you, and I am old, and I will *sit still*,[51] and behold, my sons are with you. And behold, *I have gone* about before you from my youth even until this day" (1 Sam 12:2, NETS).[52] In his words, Samuel describes ruling over the people as walking, in contrast to sitting still. His words could describe a physical state, but also have symbolic load.

Other senses that get damaged because of old age include hearing and taste, as Barzillai attests: "Today I am eighty years old; can I discern what is pleasant and what is not? Can your servant taste what he eats or what he drinks? Can I still listen to the voice of singing men and singing women?" (2 Sam 19:36). Barzillai's old age is highlighted in the opening verse of this incident: "Barzillai was a very aged man, eighty years old..." (19:33). His advanced years are a factor in his difficulties, which include an inability to use his senses for his pleasure, as well as implied cognitive difficulty.[53] These difficulties are part of the aging process that leads to death: "Please let your servant return, so that I may die in my own town, near the graves of my father and my mother..." (19:38).

Damage to sight is the most frequently mentioned damage that occurs in old age. At least four biblical characters are described as suffering from sight problems associated with old age. Unlike deliberate damage that leads to blindness, the blindness of old age is portrayed as gradual

---

152–53), and means "to be strong," "to be able." See a similar parallel between sight and strength (כֹּחַ): "My heart throbs, my strength (כֹּחִי) fails me; as for the light of my eyes—it also has gone from me" (Ps 38:11); cf. "Do not cast me off in the time of old age; do not forsake me when my strength (כֹּחִי) is spent" (Ps 71:9, NRSV). See also Chapter 3, n. 271 and Chapter 5, n. 99.

49. Papayannopoulos, "Diseases of Old Age," 68.

50. Cf. 2 Chr 16:12, where a theological explanation is given to the disease. Such interpretations of the verse prevailed since antiquity. For a summary, see J. Schipper, "Deuteronomy 24:5 and King Asa's Foot Disease in 1 Kings 15:23b," *JBL* 128 (2009): 643–48 (645–47).

51. The assumed Hebrew *Vorlage* of the LXX, "I will sit still" (יֹשַׁבְתִּי), is orthographically close to the Hebrew of the MT, "I am gray" (שַׂבְתִּי).

52. See also LXX for Ps 90:10 and Sir 25:20.

53. See also Sir 42:8 for the parallel old||fool||stupid.

damage. We see this in the use of verbs like כהה and כבד ("to become dim") which describe a gradual action, as in the description of Eli's blindness: "At that time Eli, whose eyesight had begun to grow dim (עיניו החלו כהות) so that he could not see (לראות), was lying down in his room" (1 Sam 3:2; cf. 4:15). Eli's old age is the cause for blindness, he lies down without movement, and he is losing his authority.[54] Isaac too lost sight in old age, and lacks the ability to see (understand) things properly: "When Isaac was old and his eyes were dim so that he could not see (ותכהין עיניו מראות)..." (Gen 27:1). Jacob too loses sight in old age: "Now the eyes (עיני) of Israel were dim (כבדו) with age, and he could not see well (לראות)..." (Gen 48:10). From the perspective of the narrative, these three men suffer from some form of mental blindness, not just visual blindness. Isaac fails to recognize his son; Jacob fails to recognize his grandsons, and Eli fails to control his sons. Only Ahijah of Shiloh, whose blindness is also due to old age, can still "see" clearly because of his prophetic powers—"Now Ahijah could not see, for his eyes were dim (קמו עיניו) because of his age" (1 Kgs 14:4)—and it seems that there is a reversal of the type scene in this case.[55]

There are examples throughout the Hebrew Bible of the disintegration of the abilities of mobility, hearing, taste, and sight in old age. Clearly, this gradual damage is irreversible: "Remember that my life is a breath; my eye will never again see good" (Job 7:7).[56] The correlation between old age and death requires no explanation. Sometimes, damage to sensory abilities parallels mental damage,[57] indicating the difficulty that the elderly have in retaining their social place, even if they continue to be honoured.[58] Similar descriptions of old age are found throughout the

---

54. See J. Sasson, "The Eyes of Eli: An Essay on Motif Accretion," in *Inspired Speech: Prophecy in the Ancient Near East. Essays in Honor of Herbert B. Huffmon* (ed. J. Kaltner and L. Stulman; JSOTSup 372; London: T&T Clark International, 2004), 171–90.

55. Some scholars point to Qoh 12:3 as a reference to loss of sight in old age. From ancient times, Qoh 12:2–7 has been interpreted as a description of old age. However, most terms in these verses are not clear enough, and besides the loss of sight, we cannot be sure that the rest of the paragraph describes problems of posture, hearing, sleep, etc. For detailed analysis, including allegoric and others, see C. L. Seow, *Ecclesiastes: A New Translation with Introduction and Commentary* (AB 18C; New York: Doubleday, 1997), 351–67.

56. See Kedar-Kopfstein, "Decoding of Polysemantic Lexemes," 22.

57. For initial discussion of mental illness and old age in the Hebrew Bible, see E. Perl and D. Irsai, "Aspects in the Biblical Approach to Mental Sanity in Old Age" (Hebrew), *Koroth* 8, no. 5–6 (1982): 72–78.

58. See pp. 212–20, below.

ancient Near East, including speech difficulties.[59] Here is an example from an Aramaic inscription discovered in Nerab, estimated to be from the seventh century B.C.E. (*KAI* 226:3–5): "Because of my righteousness before him, he gave me a good name and prolonged my days. On the day I died, my mouth was not closed to words, and with my eyes, what do I see? Children of the fourth generation…"[60] This inscription is dedicated to the priest Agbar, who is depicted as sitting in front of an altar. In this inscription, as with the description of Moses (Deut 34:7), we learn about the common sensory state of the elderly through description of the extraordinary. Such an extraordinary state, and specifically the ability to speak and see, receives special mention. Speech as an ability that one loses in old age does not appear in the Hebrew Bible, yet it is mentioned in other sources from the ancient Near East.[61]

We have looked at the disabilities caused by divine punishment, human punishment, or old age, and have seen that all are linked to some extent to divine rejection. In addition, we find in the Hebrew Bible congenital disabilities. Despite the fact that most passages that mention the lack of senses do not indicate the circumstances of the disability, we must assume that not all the disabilities were the result of punishment. Different adjectives are used to describe people with disabilities, all of them in the *kittel* paradigm:[62] the blind is עִוֵּר,[63] the deaf is חֵרֵשׁ,[64] the mute

59. Such as in Egyptian (Seow, *Ecclesiastes*, 373–75), Akkadian (*ANET*, 311), and Sumerian (Seow, *Ecclesiastes*, 374; H. Tawil, "Some Literary Elements in the Opening Sections of the Hadad, Zākir, and the Nērab II Inscriptions in the Light of East and West Semitic Royal Inscriptions," *Or* 43 [1974]: 60–63 [58]).

60. Translation by F. Rosenthal, *ANET* 504–5; see also G. A. Cooke, *A Text-Book of North Semitic Inscriptions, Moabite, Hebrew, Phoenician, Aramaic, Nabataean, Palmyrene, Jewish* (Oxford: Clarendon, 1903), 189–91. And original there: שמני שם טב והארך יומי ביום מתת פמי לאתאחז מן מלן ובעיני מחזה אנה בני רבע. Full discussion of this inscription is found in Tawil, "Some Literary Elements," 58–65. In the Hebrew Bible, see David's words in 1 Kgs 1:48, which stress his ability to see, despite his old age. See also pp. 155–58, above.

61. For details, see Tawil, "Some Literary Elements," 60–63.

62. D. T. Stewart, "Deaf and Blind in Leviticus 19:14 and the Emergence of Disability Law," unpublished paper delivered in the "Biblical Scholarship and Disabilities Consultation" section, SBL Annual Meeting, Philadelphia, Pa., November 19, 2005.

63. Exod 4:11; Lev 19:14; 21:18; Deut 15:21; 27:18; 28:29; 2 Sam 5:6, 8; Isa 29:18; 35:5; 42:7, 16, 18, 19; 43:8; 56:10; 59:10; Jer 31:8; Zeph 1:17; Mal 1:8; Ps 146:8; Job 29:15; Lam 4:14. Some of these verses describe symbolic blindness (= lack of knowledge) through images of real blindness. Note that people of old age and with visual impairment are never termed "blind" (עור).

64. Exod 4:11; Lev 19:14; Isa 29:18; 35:3; 42:18–19; 43:8; Pss 38:14; 58:5.

is אִלֵּם,[65] and the lame is פִּסֵּחַ,[66] or "of crippled feet" (נכה רגליים).[67] Other disabilities appear in a list of disabilities that preclude the priest from making a sacrifice (Lev 21:18–20; cf. 22:22–24; Deut 15:21). The list includes damage to various organs, but there is no indication that this included damage to the senses. Only damage to bodily perfection is called a deficiency (מום). That is why David Stuart claims that the biblical deficiency category only incorporates external damage that can be immediately discerned, even if the disabilities have no adverse effect on the senses or do not lead to actual lack of capacity.[68] We see that the names given to people with disabilities relate to four senses: sight, hearing, speech, and mobility. People whose sense of taste or sense of smell have been damaged, like people with damage to their upper limbs, do not receive a permanent descriptor.[69] In sum, references to sensory disability with no clear source are to be further explored in order to establish their place in the theology of the senses. The next section will discuss the status of the sensorily disabled, and the link of this status to the divine creation of the senses.

Sensory Disabilities

There are two types of information to be gathered about people with sensory disability in the Hebrew Bible. First, evidence of practical-concrete difficulties experienced by people who have one or more damaged senses, and who have been cast to the margins of society.

65. Exod 4:11; Isa 35:6; 56:10; Hab 2:18; Ps 38:14; Prov 31:8.

66. Lev 21:18; Deut 15:21; 2 Sam 5:6, 8; 9:13; 19:27; Isa 33:23; 35:6; Jer 31:8; Mal 1:8; Job 29:15; Prov 26:7.

67. 2 Sam 4:4; 9:3. Cf. the term "of broken (נכה) spirit" in Isa 66:2. Mephiboshet is the one called "of crippled (נכה) legs," or "lame" (פסח) in the Hebrew Bible. His description in 2 Sam 4:4 is the only description of a disability which results from an accident (rather than congenital, punishment, or old age). This verse also parallels the two terms used for describing Mephiboshet's disability: "Saul's son Jonathan had a son who was crippled in his feet (נכה רגלים). He was five years old when the news about Saul and Jonathan came from Jezreel. His nurse picked him up and fled; and, in her haste to flee, it happened that he fell and became lame (ויפסח). His name was Mephibosheth" (2 Sam 4:4, JPS).

68. E.g. deafness is not a deficiency (מום), and hence not mentioned in the list, see J. Milgrom, *Leviticus: A Book of Ritual and Ethics* (Continental Commentary; Minneapolis: Fortress, 2004), 266.

69. The exception is the adjective אטר, which describes a dysfunctional hand (Judg 3:15; 20:16). The meaning of the root is "to shut," "to close" (see Ps 69:16). The adjective belongs to the context of ability of the senses, imagined as open and closed organs (see pp. 127–29, above).

Practical-concrete difficulties mean physical difficulties that affect the ability to earn a living or to move,[70] or the legal status and societal restrictions placed on the sensorily disabled. Second, evidence of a prejudice against people whose senses have been damaged, as expressed through the negative contexts associated with disabilities and sensory damage. One example is the perception that sensory damage reflects divine punishment, a perception that creates negative attitudes towards such people, and highlights the fact that they were marginalized, quite apart from the practical-concrete problems.

These two insights complement each other. The concrete difficulties and restrictions add to the existing negative associative contexts of the sensorily disabled, while being based on the very same semantics. For example, the public approbation against harming the blind person, "Cursed be anyone who misleads a blind person on the road..." (Deut 27:18), describes both the physical-concrete problem that a blind person might encounter, and its context also indicates the negative semantic correlation of blindness as helplessness. The next verse demands a fair trial for the marginalized members of society: "Cursed be anyone who deprives the alien, the orphan, and the widow of justice..." (Deut 27:19). The proximity of the two verses indicates a contextual correlation between blindness and the alien, orphan, and widow. All are marginalized people who are dependent on society for their survival. Another example of a dialectic relationship between the two marginal aspects is the series of public approbations in the Holiness Code: "You shall not revile the deaf or put a stumbling block before the blind; you shall fear your God: I am the Lord" (Lev 19:14). The instruction not to harm the deaf and the blind highlights their physical disabilities. The juxtaposition of the blind and the deaf, coming between the instruction not to mistreat and not to withhold wages (v. 13), and the instructions relating to fair justice (v. 15), are an indication of their status in society. Once again, people with sensory disability appear in correlation with weak people who cannot protect their rights by themselves.[71] Below, I will discuss the associations and semantic load that affect the marginalization of people with sensory disabilities.

70. Cf. N. H. Walls, "The Origins of the Disabled Body," in Avalos, Melcher, and Schipper, eds., *This Abled Body*, 13–30 (15–16).

71. Later on in Lev 19, the elderly are described as those in need of legal protection, in proximity to the directive to protect the alien, and to keep a righteous judgment (vv. 33–37): "You shall rise before the aged and show deference to the old; you shall fear your God: I am the Lord" (Lev 19:32, JPS). As discussed above, this verse serves as another example of the liminal status of old people.

The two examples cited above (Deut 27:18 and Lev 19:14) focus on the difficulty of the blind and the deaf to receive fair justice. Elsewhere, the mute is in the same situation, and like other marginalized people they cannot protect themselves, and must therefore be protected by the fair judge. Take, for example, the following teaching: "Speak up for the dumb (אלם), for the rights of all the unfortunate. Speak up, judge righteously, champion the poor and the needy" (Prov 31:8–9, JPS). The mute here symbolizes those unable to protect themselves physically in a court of law, which is why the mute is mentioned parallel to the poor and needy. The problems of the mute in court can also be deduced from the metaphors of helplessness: "But I am like the deaf (חרש), I do not hear (אשמע); like the mute (אלם), who cannot speak (יפתח פיו). Truly, I am like one who does not hear (שמע), and in whose mouth (פיו) is no retort" (Ps 38:14–15). Lack of verbal ability, which poses physical difficulty, becomes an image of inability, and in turn, this image becomes associated with the mute in other contexts.

Job, who highlights his righteousness of his path as a judge, also mentions his support of people with sensory disabilities: "I put on righteousness, and it clothed me; my justice was like a robe and a turban. I was eyes to the blind (עינים...לעור), and feet to the lame (רגלים לפסח). I was a father to the needy, and I championed the cause of the stranger" (Job 29:14–16). Again, the blind and the lame are compared to marginal, helpless people. The concrete legal state becomes a metaphor for God's guidance, returning his people to Zion: "I will lead the blind (עורים) by a road they do not know, by paths they have not known I will guide them. I will turn the darkness before them into light, the rough places into level ground. These are the things I will do, and I will not forsake them (Isa 42:16). Note how in this prophecy, too, sight and kinaesthesia are closely linked. Moreover, God's fair judgment is described elsewhere as "opening the eyes of the blind" (Ps 146:8), alongside the protection of the alien, orphan, and widow (v. 9). These biblical passages reveal how difficult it was for people with sensory disabilities to receive fair justice in society and in the court, in addition to their daily struggle with regular functioning.

Further evidence of the marginalization of people with disabilities is the prohibition on priests with deficiencies to perform priestly acts:

> For no one who has a blemish shall draw near, one who is blind or lame,
> or one who has a mutilated face or a limb too long, or one who has a
> broken foot or a broken hand, or a hunchback, or a dwarf, or a man with a
> blemish in his eyes or an itching disease or scabs or crushed testicles. No

descendant of Aaron the priest who has a blemish shall come near to offer the Lord's offerings by fire; since he has a blemish, he shall not come near to offer the food of his God. (Lev 21:18–21)[72]

For the purpose of our discussion, I will examine the four terms appearing in v. 18, since they reflect a name for the person carrying the deficiency, rather than a description of it. The blind (עִוֵּר) and the lame (פִּסֵּחַ) as people with disabilities are mentioned several times in the Hebrew Bible and were mentioned above. The term חָרֻם, which appears only in this verse, is usually interpreted as someone with a damaged nose.[73] The term שָׂרוּעַ, which appears only in this verse and in a description of disabilities that exclude an animal for sacrifice (Lev 22:23), is usually interpreted as someone who has a limb that is stretched or is too long.[74] This prohibition is supported by the prohibition to sacrifice an animal which has "anything blind, or injured, or maimed, or having a discharge or an itch or scabs…a limb too long or too short…its testicles bruised or crushed or torn or cut…" (Lev 22:22–24). A similar prohibition appears in Deuteronomy, where it is forbidden to sacrifice an animal that "has any defect—any serious defect, such as lameness or blindness…" (Deut 15:21). The correlation between the two prohibitions lies in the fact that the priests, like the sacrifices, are sacred to God.[75] Humans and animals with deficiencies are both perceived as "incomplete." All the deficiencies mentioned are visible, and not all of them affect a particular sensory ability.[76] This contrast is highlighted by the juxtaposition of the words "flaw" (מוּם) and "flawless" (תָּמִים): "When anyone offers a sacrifice of well-being to the LORD, in fulfilment of a vow or as a freewill offering, from the herd or from the flock, to be acceptable it must be perfect (תָּמִים); there shall be no blemish (מוּם) in it" (Lev 22:21).[77] Indeed, the adjective תָּמִים recurs frequently as a criterion for choosing an animal for

72. Cf. Lev 22:22–24; Deut 15:21, where mutilated animals are forbidden from sacrifice.

73. So most interpreters (e.g. G. J. Wenham, *The Book of Leviticus* [NICOT; Grand Rapids: Eerdmans, 1979], 292). Hurting the nose could have caused anosmia.

74. This interpretation, similar to the interpretation of the word חָרוּם, is consistent from old translations through modern scholarship. It is based mainly on cognate Semitic roots.

75. For the comparison between deficiencies of the sacrificed animal and of the priests, see Milgrom, *Leviticus*, 266, and further his claim that the prohibition on priests with deficiencies (מוּם) from serving in the holy comes from the conceptual parallel between physical and moral deficiency (pp. 260–66).

76. Stewart, "Deaf and Blind in Leviticus."

77. Cf. "…to bring you a red cow without blemish (תְּמִימָה), in which there is no defect (מוּם)…" (Num 19:2, JPS).

various sacrificial purposes, even though the details of the disabilities appear only in the two verses cited.[78] As the blind and the lame are mentioned in these lists, one should assert that at least these two sensory disabilities receive further negative association of distance from God.

We can assume that even if these prohibitions did not normally affect people who are not priests, they further reinforced the marginalization of people with disabilities. Many commentators also point to the proverb prohibiting against affected members of the general public from entering the sanctuary: "The blind and the lame shall not come into the house" (2 Sam 5:8). The expression used is "blind and lame" (עור ופסח), standing for any defect from head to foot (cf. Deut 15:21).[79] Coming in the middle of a description of David's conquest of Jerusalem, this expression is an etiological juxtaposition designed to explain the removal of the blind and the lame during battle (2 Sam 5:6–8). The role of the blind and the lame in this battle is uncertain, and two explanations are offered to explain it. The first is that the Jebusites placed the lame and the blind on the walls of their city as part of psychological warfare. The message they wished to project was that even the weak can defend the city; the second is that placing the blind and the lame on the walls (or, according to some commentators, models of blind and lame people) is a kind of magical curse on the enemy's army.[80] The first explanation could indicate the weakness of people with disabilities, the second indicates that people with disabilities are regarded as cursed; both indicate a level of semantic marginality of the blind and the lame.

There is also a mention of the lame in Isaiah's description of the destruction of the Temple: "Your rigging hangs loose; it cannot hold the mast firm in its place, or keep the sail spread out. Then prey and spoil in abundance will be divided; even the lame (פסחים) will fall to plundering" (Isa 33:23). Here too the actions of the lame are not entirely clear. Will there be so much plunder that even non-combatants will get some? Or does the prophet mean that God will fight for Jerusalem, and that even if the fighters are lame, they will still win? Either way, the lame symbolize the disabled who under normal circumstances do not fight and do not

---

78.   Exod 12:5; 29:1; Lev 1:3, 10; 3:1, 6; 4:3, 23, 28, 32; 5:15, 18, 25; 9:2, 3; 14:10; 22:19, 22; 23:12, 18; Num 6:14; 19:2; 28:3, 9, 11, 19, 31; 29:2, 8, 13, 17, 20, 23, 26, 29, 32, 36; Ezek 43:22, 23, 25; 45:18, 23; 56:4, 6, 13.

79.   See Olyan, "Anyone Blind or Lame," 221–26. Others interpret the house (2 Sam 5:8) as the royal house; see Vargon, "The Blind and the Lame," 500; A. R. Ceresko, "The Identity of 'the Blind and the Lame' ('iwwēr ûpissēaḥ) in 2 Samuel 5:8b," *CBQ* 63 (2001): 23–30 (25).

80.   For both interpretations, see Vargon, "The Blind and the Lame," 513–14.

earn plunder. The last example, albeit a most prominent one, of the marginalization of the lame emerges from the description of the history of Mephibosheth who "was lame in both his feet" (2 Sam 9:13),[81] and was allowed to lean on the king's table, apparently as an act of pity.[82] Mephibosheth's lameness seems to have limited his ability to function, as we see in his words to David, after being accused of treachery:

> My lord, O king, my servant deceived me; for your servant said to him, "Saddle a donkey for me, so that I may ride on it and go with the king." For your servant is lame. He has slandered your servant to my lord the king. But my lord the king is like the angel of God; do therefore what seems good to you. (2 Sam 19:27–28)

Although his words are cut short, it is clear that Mephibosheth's physical disabilities limit his independence and make him dependent on his servants. In the story, this dependent relationship leads to an attempt to harm Mephibosheth, thus exposing his weakness as an invalid, and explaining his dependence on the righteousness of the king.

Thus far, I have presented sparse evidence of the physical and practical difficulties of people with damaged senses. This evidence covers two areas. One deals with the marginalization that results from the invalid's objective physical difficulties: the blind and the lame who cannot move independently and who lose their way, the mute who cannot defend himself in court, the deaf person who cannot protect himself against ridicule and contempt, and so on. These difficulties marginalize people with disabilities when they encounter the justice system. They appear alongside the poor and the foreigner as people who require fair justice and societal support. The second area deals with ritual restrictions placed on people with disabilities, pushing them even further to the margins of society.[83] Such restrictions are associated with perceptions of physical perfection and perceptions of disabilities as divine punishment.

81. As well as "crippled (נכה) legs" (2 Sam 9:3). For a full discussion of the semantics of disability in the story of Mephiboshet, see Schipper, *Figuring Mephibosheth*.

82. Vargon, "The Blind and the Lame," 504. Sitting at the king's table demonstrates proximity, but at the same time creates a clear hierarchy, and possibly indications of control (cf. MacDonald, *Not Bread Alone*, 154–63). In the case of Mephiboshet, the last Saulide to claim the throne, all three aspects seem to play a role.

83. Rabbinic literature does not forbid the sensorily impaired from entering the temple, yet does not require them to come either. Moreover, people with sensory disability are not allowed to testify, and are described as liminal figures. Generally, the perception that bodily impairment indicates cognitive and/or moral impairment is strengthened.

The difficulties posed for the sensorily disabled are exposed through laws designed to restrict and/or protect these people. In addition, it is exposed through semantic marginalization, which doubtlessly affected their status.

What I call semantic marginalization is the prejudice anchored in cultural perceptions about sensory experience. If the ancient Israelites assumed that sensory experience marks a basic physical and cognitive ability that positions man as a functioning, independent being, then the lack of one of the senses immediately affects that same person's functioning. If the ancient Israelites assumed that damage to the senses is the result of punishment and sin, then people with damaged senses are regarded as inferior or as sinners. The most obvious example that we find in the Hebrew Bible is blindness. Sight symbolizes knowledge and thought. Symbolically, someone who cannot see, cannot know. That is why society perceives the blind person as someone who cannot think or know. In addition, the custom of punishing by gouging out the eyes and the perception of blindness as divine punishment makes it seem that every blind person is punished. Below, I will examine how damage to any one of the senses created associative layers of semantic marginality on top of the concrete difficulties that contributed to their creation.

The derived meanings of sensory vocabulary (related to the contextual patterns examined in the previous chapter) are the main key to understanding the semantic marginality of the sensorily disabled. In the Hebrew Bible, sight symbolizes knowledge, and hearing indicates understanding;[84] logically, lack of hearing and a lack of sight symbolize a lack of knowledge and a lack of understanding. The rebukes uttered by the prophets make frequent use of these cultural assumptions. The prophet Isaiah complains that Israel are "...the people who are blind (עִוֵּר), yet have eyes, who are deaf (חֵרֵשׁ), yet have ears!" (Isa 43:8). He also complains that its leaders "...are blind (עִוְרִים), they are all without knowledge (לֹא יָדְעוּ); they are all silent (אִלְּמִים) dogs that cannot bark; dreaming, lying down, loving to slumber" (56:10).[85] The prophet Ezekiel expresses a similar attitude about his people, "...who have eyes to see but do not see, who have ears to hear but do not hear" (Ezek 12:2). Similarly, Jeremiah accuses the "foolish and senseless people, who have eyes, but do not see, who have ears, but do not hear" (Jer 5:21).[86] The

---

84. See pp. 159–60, above.

85. See also Isa 5:12; 6:10; 42:20; 44:18; 59:1; 74:3; 75:12 and more.

86. As well as Jer 6:10; 7:24, 26; 11:8; 17:23; 25:4; 34:14; 35:15; 44:5; cf. Deut 29:1–3.

prophet's rebuke provides us with several core concepts: (1) lack of sight and hearing is foolish; (2) lack of sight and hearing is a sin; (3) lack of sight and hearing are the attributes of the blind and the deaf. If we accept these three concepts, an associative pattern is created: foolishness–sin–deafness–blindness.

The correlation between disabilities and foolishness is further high-lighted in the wisdom tradition: "As legs hang limp on a cripple (פסח), so is a proverb in the mouth of a fool" (Prov 26:7, JPS). The parallel between the lame and the fool places the lame person on the wrong side of the wisdom continuum. Similar parallels are found between sight and foolishness: "Then I saw that wisdom excels folly as light excels dark-ness. The wise have eyes in their head, but fools walk in darkness..." (Qoh 2:13–14).[87] Blindness as interfering with thought and regular functioning is also used as a warning against bribery: "You must not distort justice; you must not show partiality; and you must not accept bribes, for a bribe blinds (יעור) the eyes of the wise and subverts the cause of those who are in the right" (Deut 16:19); "Do not take bribes, for bribes blind (יעור) the clear-sighted and upset the pleas of those who are in the right" (Exod 23:8, JPS). Here again we see the semantic contrast between sight and wisdom, and between blindness and foolish-ness, based on the assumption that blindness damages normal cognitive ability. These examples demonstrate how the cultural context of the perception of the senses (thought, wisdom, understanding) influences the marginalization of people whose sensory ability has been damaged. The correlation between lack of physical ability and lack of "mental" ability is also clear from the correlation between blindness and mental illnesses, as demonstrated in Deut 28:28–29 (cf. Zech 12:4) mentioned above. The paradigmatic comparisons between people with disabled feet and people with disabled spirit also demonstrate this similarity (Isa 66:2).[88]

As we saw in the previous chapter, the senses do not only appear in the context of knowledge and understanding. Sensory vocabulary is used to describe life and vitality.[89] Death, the end of life, is sometimes described as an end of sensory experience, and the deterioration process of the senses in old age leads to death (see Job 7:7). The metaphor "seeing the sun is life" demonstrates this correlation: the unborn infant

---

87. The image of light and darkness expands the contrast between sight and blindness.

88. The distinction between cognitive and mental abilities is modern. In the Hebrew Bible, mental disability is any interruption of normative perception. See Chapter 3, n. 251.

89. See pp. 175–83, above.

"has never seen (ראה) or experienced (ידע) the sun" (Qoh 6:5, JPS).[90] The psalmist wishes his enemies to be like a miscarriage, "that never sees (חזו) the sun" (Ps 58:9), namely non-existent. The correlation between death and darkness is also evident and linked to sight: "he has made me sit in darkness like the dead of long ago" (Lam 3:6).[91] But it is not just blindness and darkness that are likened to death—the inability to move or walk is also likened to death. Jacob's death is described thus: "…he drew up his feet into the bed, breathed his last, and was gathered to his people" (Gen 49:33). By contrast, people who are reborn will stand on their feet: "…and the breath came into them, and they lived, and stood on their feet, a vast multitude" (Ezek 37:10). Similarly, the dead man who came alive when he touched Elisha's bones: "As a man was being buried, a marauding band was seen and the man was thrown into the grave of Elisha; as soon as the man touched the bones of Elisha, he came to life and stood on his feet" (2 Kgs 13:21).[92]

Since life itself is likened to mobility, death comes when mobility stops. We see this in Hezekiah's thanksgiving after recovery from sickness: "I said in the cutting off (דמי) of my days, I shall go to the gates of the grave: I am deprived of the residue of my years. I said, I shall not see (אראה) the Lord, even the Lord, in the land of the living: I shall behold (אביט) man no more with the inhabitants of the world" (Isa 38:10–11). The first verse describes stopping and ending of days, which leads to death;[93] the second verse likens the cessation of sight to death. Losing the ability to walk or speak describes death, as we see in the following verses: "Assuredly, her young men shall lie fallen in her squares. And all her warriors shall be stilled (ידמו) in that day…" (Jer 49:26).[94] The basic meaning of the root דמה here could be interpreted as halting and stopping, but also silence; in this verse it parallels "falling,"

90. *HALOT* 2:710–11; cf. Job 3:16. For the associative link between "seeing light" and "life," see pp. 248–51, below. See also the words of Gilgamesh: "Let my eyes see the sun and be sated with light! The darkness is hidden, how much light is there left? When may the dead see the sun?" (IX '38–'39, based on the Old Babylonian version; A. George, *The Epic of Gilgamesh* [London: Penguin, 1999], 71).

91. Cf. Ps 143:3.

92. For this image, see Stendebach, *TDOT* 13:314, and a reference there to Ezek 2:1–2; 3:24. Similarly, Stendebach interprets the phrase "while standing on his feet" (Zech 14:12) as meaning "while he is still alive."

93. A. Baumann, "דָּמָה *dāmāh* II; דמם *dmm*; דום *dwm*; דָּמִי *domî*; דְּמָמָה *demāmāh*; דֻּמָּה *dummāh*; דּוּמָם *dûmām*; דּוּמִיָּה *dûmîyyāh*; דּוּמָה *dûmāh*; חָשָׁה *chāshāh*; חָרַשׁ *chārash* II; חֶרֶשׁ *chērēsh*; חֶרֶשׁ *cheresh*," *TDOT* 3:260–65 (263).

94. Cf. Jer 50:30; Hos 10:15. For more sources, see ibid., 263.

that is, dying.[95] The correlation between stopping sensory experience, and specifically the ability to see and move, creates a semantic correlation between people with damaged senses and death. Later on, the Talmud states this correlation explicitly: "Four kinds of people are regarded as dead, and they are: the poor man, the blind person, the leper, and the man who has no children" (*b. 'Abod. Zar.* 5:1).[96] This saying relates directly to the social standing of these four unfortunates, and reinforces the notion that people with disabilities are regarded by society as marginalized. This social marginalization is sometimes described in death metaphors, or by the use of the concept of death to describe social marginalization.[97] Yet in contrast to the dead man and the leper, it seems that people with sensory disabilities are not regarded as unclean.[98]

The only verse in the Hebrew Bible that can indirectly link blindness and leprosy recounts how Nahash the Ammonite's proposal to gouge out eyes, which is called "reproach" (חרפה, 1 Sam 11:2), is similar to the way leprosy is often described.

This indirect correlation leads us to a further associative space in which vocabulary of sensory disability is used—an associative space that links fear, pain, shame, and inferiority.[99] The use of such vocabulary in these contexts contributes to the semantic marginalization of the sensorily disabled. One of the characteristics of situations of fear and pain in the Hebrew Bible is a kind of paralysis (which also appears in images of death) and helplessness. Since the senses are abilities, they are damaged by situations of fear and pain.[100] When Elihu fumes to Job about his silent friends, he accuses them of cowardice: "They are dismayed (חתו), they answer no more (העתיקו מהם מילים); they have not a word to say. And am I to wait, because they do not speak (ידברו), because they stand there,

---

95. See Levine, "Silence, Sound," and for a similar image in Akkadian, M. Malul, "*Eṭūṭu* 'Darkness' and *ṭiṭṭu* 'Clay' (Gilg. XI 106, 118)—Poetic License or Corruption Due to Etymological Similarity? Another Interpretation," in *An Experienced Scribe who Neglects Nothing: Ancient Near Eastern Studies in Honor of Jacob Klein* (ed. Y. Sefati; Bethesda, Md.: CDL, 2005), 548–56.

96. Similarly in *Gen. Rab.* 71; *Exod. Rab.* 5; *Lam. Rab.* 3.

97. See, for example, "When Rachel saw that she had borne Jacob no children, she became envious of her sister; and Rachel said to Jacob, 'Give me children, or I shall die'" (Gen 30:1, JPS). See *MKCS*, 222, 359; and also my "Honour and Shame," 35–36.

98. Stewart, "Deaf and Blind in Leviticus."

99. These fields partially coincide through shared images. See my "Honour and Shame," 86–88.

100. For the senses as an idiom for ability, see pp. 175–83, above.

and answer (ענו) no more?" (Job 32:15–16).[101] Job is also silent when God reveals himself: "See, I am of small account (קלתי); what shall I answer you (אשיבך)? I lay my hand on my mouth" (Job 40:4). Job himself utters a similar response to that used by others to him, while he still had a high status: "When I went out to the gate of the city, when I took my seat in the square, the young men saw me and withdrew, and the aged rose up and stood; the nobles refrained from talking (עצרו במלים), and laid their hands on their mouths; the voices of princes were hushed (נחבאו), and their tongues stuck to the roof of their mouths" (Job 29:7–10). In all three examples, the confrontation of a stronger party is responded to by silence. Such a response is not always negative, and can express a respectful attitude in an asymmetric relationship, such as between Job and God. Job's comment, "I am of small account (קלתי)," explains his silence in terms of his relative status. The command "Hush!" (הס) that demands silence usually appears in the context of silence before God.[102] Similarly, the root "to be silent" (חשה) describes passivity more than it describes actual silence.[103] To sum up, silence marks passivity and inferiority, and very often a sense of fear. Such a response is evaluated as positive when directed at God, yet evaluated as weakness when directed at other people.

Negative evaluation of sensory disability in the context of helplessness is widespread. For example, it can describe oppression: "He was oppressed, and he was afflicted, yet he did not open his mouth (נעוה); like a lamb that is led to the slaughter, and like a sheep that before its shearers is silent (נאלמה), so he did not open his mouth" (Isa 53:7). While the previous idioms could be based on any human response to fear, this idiom specifically refers to the behaviour of the animal being slaughtered. Even the lamb is silent before it is slaughtered. In any case, silence indicates weakness and helplessness, a weakness that the prophet Micah wishes on the nations: "The nations shall see and be ashamed of all their might; they shall lay their hands on their mouths; their ears shall be deaf (תחרשנה)" (Mic 7:16, KJV). The weakness of the nations is accompanied by shame, stemming from God's revelation (v. 15) and parallel to their fear of him (v. 18). This introduces damage to another sense, the sense of hearing. The psalmist's appeal shows the correlation between silence and

---

101. The usage of "to stand" (עמד) to denote "to stop (talking)" is found in other synaesthetic phrases, such as "his eye stopped" (lit. "stood," קום, 1 Sam 4:15) and the parallel "to be silent" (דמם) and "to stand" (עמד, 1 Sam 14:9).

102. Amos 6:10; 8:3; Hab 2:20; Zeph 1:7; Zech 2:17.

103. Baumann, *TDOT* 3:262.

shame:[104] "Do not let me be put to shame, O Lord, for I call on you; let the wicked be put to shame; let them go dumbfounded (יִדְּמוּ) to Sheol. Let the lying lips be stilled (תֵּאָלַמְנָה) that speak insolently against the righteous with pride and contempt" (Ps 31:18–19). Inability to speak in this verse is a sign for downfall. In Hannah's prayer, we see her inability to speak as a result of her stormy emotions: "Hannah was praying silently; only her lips moved, but her voice was not heard…" Eli interprets Hannah's temporary muteness in a negative light—"therefore Eli thought she was drunk" (1 Sam 1:13)—and he even rebukes her for this: "How long will you make a drunken spectacle of yourself? Put away your wine" (v. 14).

Unlike descriptions of silence that are caused by fear, descriptions of weeping in the Hebrew Bible refer specifically to the eyes and sight, and are often accompanied by weeping and wailing, not by silence. For example: "My eyes are spent with weeping" (Lam 2:11); "Because of this our hearts are sick, because of these things our eyes have grown dim" (5:17).[105] Hunger is also described as a factor in weak sight: "The wild asses stand on the bare heights, they pant for air like jackals; their eyes fail because there is no herbage" (Jer 14:6).[106] And lastly, grief also damages sight: "My eye has grown dim from grief, and all my members are like a shadow" (Job 17:7). We find that emotions and situations of distress are described as silence and/or as blindness. What would one think of a person who spends their whole life in silence, or without sight?

Psalm 69, which is full of descriptions of suffering, has the psalmist wish complete failure and destruction on his/her enemies, including the following: "May their eyes grow dim (תֶּחְשַׁכְנָה) so that they cannot see; may their loins collapse (הַמְעַד) continually" (v. 24, JPS). It is unclear whether this is a reaction of fear and shame, or an actual wish for blindness. In addition, this verse presents us with a motif of trembling and shock, which is repeated in a description of fear, shame, and pain. Similar phrases appear to reflect Ezekiel's sorrow and the reactions of fear that he prophesies:

> And you, O mortal, sigh; with tottering (שִׁבָּרוֹן) limbs and bitter grief, sigh before their eyes. And when they ask you, "Why do you sigh?" answer, "Because of the tidings that have come." Every heart shall sink (נָמֵס) and

---

104. I use the English term "shame" to refer to a range of meanings sprouting from the Hebrew root בּוֹשׁ. In this verse and others, however, the meaning is closer to "disappointment" or "failure." See further my "בּוֹשׁ in the Psalms."

105. See Collins, "Physiology of Tears."

106. Cf. Lam 4:17; Pss 38:11; 119:81–82; Job 31:16. See ibid., 20–22.

all hands hang nerveless (רפו); every spirit shall grow faint (כההה) and all knees turn to water because of the tidings that have come… (Ezek 21:11–12, JPS)

Again, we find the emotional response of sadness or fear described as trembling of the body, feebleness, and lack of strength and ability.

The description of the greatness of God in the Song of the Sea in Exodus includes the response of the nations:

The peoples heard, they trembled (ירגזון); pangs (חיל) seized the inhabitants of Philistia. Then the chiefs of Edom were dismayed (נבהלו); trembling (רעד) seized the leaders of Moab; all the inhabitants of Canaan melted away (נמגו). Terror and dread (אימתה ופחד) fell upon them; by the might of your arm, they became still (ידמו) as a stone until your people, O Lord, passed by… (Exod 15:14–16)

These verses demonstrate how the fear of God is expressed in trembling of the body and silence (or paralysis) of the body. Similar descriptions are found elsewhere:[107] "Dread (פחד) came upon me, and trembling (רעדה), which made all my bones shake (הפחיד)" (Job 4:14); "The sinners in Zion are afraid (פחדו); trembling (רעדה) has seized the godless…" (Isa 33:14).[108] We see a similar fear-induced description of trembling of the body in images of fearful men being compared to women during labour: "trembling (רעדה) took hold of them there, pains as of a woman in labour" (Ps 48:7); "Damascus has become feeble (רפתה), she turned to flee, and panic (רטט) seized her; anguish (צרה) and sorrows (חבלים) have taken hold of her, as of a woman in labour" (Jer 49:24).[109] These descriptions clarify the biblical perception of the essence of the trembling that grips a body when fear strikes, a trembling that cannot be controlled. Humans lose control over their bodies, as we see in the verses cited—trembling grips, vibration holds. Elsewhere, damage to other senses is added to kinaesthetic damage: "Therefore my loins are seized with trembling (חלחלה); I am gripped by pangs like a woman in travail, too anguished to hear, too frightened to see" (Isa 21:3, JPS).[110]

---

107. Baumann, *TDOT* 3:263. Cf. Lev 10:3; Jer 47:5 (describing mourning, and hence the silence of Ashkelon does not result from fear). See Levine, "Silence, Sound," for the root דמם in the context of mourning, and the question of its meaning.

108. Cf. Ps 2:11.

109. Cf. Isa 13:8.

110. Philip claims that the verse describes damage to sight and hearing, basing her claim on ancient Near Eastern spells, which describe the difficulties of seeing, hearing, and speaking during labour; T. Philip, "Menstruation and Childbirth in the Bible" (Ph.D. diss., The Hebrew University of Jerusalem, 2003 [Hebrew]), 188. It seems to me, however, that in this verse the fear is a result of sight and hearing.

The use of childbirth metaphors to describe a man in distress and fear also explains the associative correlation that we find between childbirth, the blind, and the lame in the prophecy of Jeremiah: "See, I am going to bring them from the land of the north, and gather them from the farthest parts of the earth, among them the blind (עור) and the lame (פסח), those with child (הרה) and those in labour (ילדת), together; a great company, they shall return here" (Isa 31:8). At first sight, it seems inappropriate to compare the woman in labour or the pregnant woman, who symbolize reproduction and fertility, to people with disabilities. It seems therefore that we are to interpret the words of Jeremiah as a merism—God will bring back all the people, from the downtrodden and the cursed to the blessed. Looking at it again, however, the description of women in labour throughout the Hebrew Bible highlights their dangerous (and thus marginal) situation and helplessness during childbirth, despite the centrality of the principle of reproduction. The cluster of terms in this prophecy describes the weakest people, who lose autonomy over their own body. Taria Philip claims that this metaphor is based on the very limited knowledge of males of the childbirth process in the ancient Near East: the men saw the first contractions, heard the cries, and had first-hand knowledge of women who died during childbirth. It is not a great leap to turn childbirth into a metaphor for fear, pain, and death.[111]

I have presented here two main expressions of prejudice against people with sensory disabilities: first, use of vocabulary of malfunctioning sensorium to describe a lack of understanding, a lack of knowledge, and a lack of ability. This is partly based on realistic difficulties of people with sensory disabilities in biblical times, and partly on cultural assumptions that regarded use of the senses as a means of knowledge and involvement in society, and a symbol of human life. Thus people who lack knowledge, who are marginalized and near death, are compared with people whose senses have been damaged. Second, I have presented expressions of prejudice that do not relate directly to people who are missing some of their senses, but that locates them in a negative and marginalized associative context: fear–shame–inferiority–weeping–helplessness–birth. All the situations in this associative context feature damage to the senses, especially muteness, blindness, and trembling. Although this damage may be temporary, it symbolizes the marginalization and helplessness that the sensorily disabled carry permanently.

---

111. Ibid., 190.

Summary

This chapter looked at the marginal status of the sensorily disabled in ancient Israel. In total, the associations linked with the sensorily disabled contrast the positive associations with sensory experience (see also Table 9). Concepts such as wisdom, understanding, ability, independence, and life are reflected in the Hebrew Bible by sensory vocabulary. Similarly, concepts such as foolishness, lack of understanding, dependence, lack of ability, and death (as well as old age) are reflected in the Hebrew Bible by metaphors of temporary or permanent sensory disability. These metaphors create a negative image of disabled people, in addition to the actual prohibitions or restrictions placed upon them. This imagery places them in the margins of society together with the poor, the foreigner, and the widow. Punishment customs, including damage to the senses (particularly gouging out the eyes) as a way of harming a person's independence and ability to function, were also designed to humiliate and shame. The lack of sensory ability is thus portrayed as a disgrace, which is why the vocabulary used to describe situations of shame and fear includes elements from the field of lack of sensory ability: muteness, deafness, and lameness. Divine punishment too is described in terms of damage to the senses, a theology which further diminishes the sensorily disabled. Presumably, people with sensory disabilities were regarded as sinners, as those who God had rejected and punished. Such a perception was also prevalent in Qumran and in rabbinical literature, but is effectively refuted in the New Testament.[112]

The marginality of the sensorily disabled is not clear-cut from the above evidence. There is no proof that such people were actually forcibly excluded from society, as may have been the case with other marginalized people.[113] It is possible that we do not hear about the status of the sensorily disabled because it did not undergo change, unlike the status of people who were excluded and then included again in society (e.g. leprosy).[114] Damage to the senses is usually irreversible, so that the person with a defect remains marginalized all their life, requiring the protection of society. Their marginalization is caused by objective difficulties

---

112.   See n. 32, and below. For the history of the tie between blemished and sin, see R. Raphael, *Biblical Corpora: Representations of Disability in the Hebrew Biblical Literature* (LHBOTS 445; London: T&T Clark International, 2008), mainly Chapter 2. It seems that a conceptual shift is already found in Isa 42. Similar notions are present in J. Schipper, *Disability and Isaiah's Suffering Servant* (Oxford: Oxford University Press, 2011).

113.   See n. 97.

114.   For the legal meaning of the root אסף, see *MKCS*, 360.

that made it hard to work and earn a living. This is another reason why damage to sight and the ability to stand or move are so prevalent in the Hebrew Bible. In cases of oppression or exploitation, such a person— especially the mute—also experienced difficulty standing up to the justice system. People with sensory disabilities also suffered humiliation due to the associative contexts of their disabilities. The senses are presented in several passages as a yardstick for independence and ability, for wondrous characterization, like the creation of the mountains and the wind. A perception that regards the senses as part of a human's ontological essence could also lead to people without all their senses being regarded as essentially inferior, as almost "non-persons."[115] Like all marginalized people, they are betwixt and between, part person, part non-person, between life and death, between society and the outside.[116]

Theology and the Sensory Category

The matters discussed in this chapter lead to some refinement of the biblical sensory category. It is now possible to assert that according to biblical epistemology the senses were a *divinely created* physical experience, one which symbolized human ability to act in a sovereign manner in the world. The fact that the senses are a divine creation, like the breath of life, broadens our understanding of the contextual patterns described in the previous chapter. Sensory experience as control (harm or aid) is closely linked to the idea that God has given humans dominion over the world. Sensory experience as knowledge and understanding is linked to the idea that God is the source of wisdom. Sensory experience as vitality is linked to the idea the God is the giver of life. Most important from the theological perspective, however, is that once sensory experience is damaged, it implies lack of divine support.

The belief in divine creation of the senses, together with the emphasis on the embodied aspect of sensory experience, means that in ancient Israel carnal experience is a positive and important experience. Only when the senses are used excessively or inappropriately[117] are they condemned.

At the same time, the prohibitions against animals with mutilations being sacrificed, and against priests with mutilations from serving in the sanctuary, add to the semantic marginality of the sensorily disabled. At

---

115. Similarly, the linguistic-cultural feature of calling those fluent in the language "people," in contrast to those who do not (see *MKCS*, 146–49).

116. See V. Turner, *The Ritual Process: Structure and Anti-Structure* (London: Routledge & Kegan Paul, 1969), 95.

117. See pp. 180–81, above.

Qumran we find that disabled were excluded from ritual practice, and in rabbinical literature, not only were they exempt from ritual practice, but they could not give evidence. The animals to be sacrificed and the priest that serve God were both regarded as belonging to God, and must have perfect appearance. Such understanding raises the possibility that the Hebrew Bible reflects an ideal of physical perfection. Support for this is evident in the perception that having a limb removed (such as hands, feet, or eyes gouged out) after death, as well as being denied a proper burial, indicated a dishonouring of the dead. This dishonouring did not draw its significance from damage to the dead person's abilities, but from damage to the completeness of his body. We will not examine this principle of body perfection in detail. However, if we want to demonstrate the bodily perception reflected in the Hebrew Bible, we can consider the very different view presented in the New Testament. While, as was demonstrated above, in the Hebrew Bible sin leads to damage to the senses, the New Testament rejects this view: "As he [Jesus] walked along, he saw a man blind from birth. His disciples asked him, 'Rabbi, who sinned, this man or his parents, that he was born blind?' Jesus answered, 'Neither this man nor his parents sinned; he was born blind so that God's works might be revealed in him'" (John 9:1–3). This short narrative encapsulates the implicit understanding of blindness as punishment in the Hebrew Bible, and negates it. Moreover, while in the Hebrew Bible sin leads to harming the senses, in the New Testament the senses can lead to sin:

> If your hand or your foot causes you to stumble, cut it off and throw it away; it is better for you to enter life maimed or lame than to have two hands or two feet and to be thrown into the eternal fire. And if your eye causes you to stumble, tear it out and throw it away; it is better for you to enter life with one eye than to have two eyes and to be thrown into the hell of fire. (Matt 18:8–9)

The approach presented in the Gospel of Matthew is only possible once a distinction between the body and the soul is accepted, following Greek or other influence, and separating the senses from the mind. In the Hebrew Bible, such separation is not evident, and the completeness of the body, including the appropriate sensory experience, is part and parcel of the completeness of moral behaviour and the thinking mind.[118]

---

118. See also Van der Hoek, "Endowed with Reason." Although an echo of Prov 16:17–19 could be found in these verses, note that in the Hebrew Bible the wrongdoing of the senses does not lead to complete annulment of their value.

Chapter 5

THE CENTRALITY OF SIGHT IN
BIBLICAL EPISTEMOLOGY

In this chapter I will focus on one particular sense within the biblical sensory category: the sense of sight. While the previous chapters took a macro look at the sensorium, this chapter will examine the micro picture: understanding the associative patterns and semantic load associated with sight and its use in practice. At the same time, the biblical perception of sight will be explored in light of our understanding of the entire sensorium: how sight plays such a dominant role—conceptually, linguistically, and practically—in the Hebrew Bible.

The centrality of sight in the biblical perception will be demonstrated by using terms derived from the field of sight; the metaphors and images that emerge from the field of sight; and the evidence of the use of sight in practice in various social and cultural contexts. We will also examine the status of the sense of sight compared to the other senses within the biblical perception of the sensorium. In particular, we will address the research dispute regarding the superiority of sight. While the focus will be on the sense of sight, our conclusions will also affect our understanding of the entire sensorium.

Hierarchical Sensorium?

Having decided to explore a particular sense in detail, it has to be noted that the selection of sight for analysis is not accidental, but based on two factors. First, the sense of sight is linguistically prominent and highly elaborated in Biblical Hebrew, and thus must have been highly developed in biblical culture. The sense of sight stood out when I examined the characteristics of the whole sensorium, and therefore it deserves an in-depth treatment. Second, the sense of sight is associated with one of the most crucial questions raised by previous scholars: How important was the sense of sight compared with hearing or other senses in biblical perception? As presented in my Introduction (pp. 22–31), scholars are divided on the matter. Some claim that hearing is the central and most important sense in biblical perception. Others claim that sight is more central and more important. As a result, the expanded discussion on sight has significant implications for our understanding of the sensorium in biblical epistemology.

Previous research presents us with an unresolved dispute: Is hearing or sight the dominant sense in biblical epistemology? Those who champion the superiority of hearing point to the confrontation between biblical culture and Greek/modern culture. Biblical culture, they say, is just like any oral or performative culture that prioritizes the sense of hearing over the sense of sight. This view mirrors the age-old philosophical dispute between Judaism and Hellenism, which in Jewish sources is often presented as a dispute between hearing and seeing.[1] Those who champion the superiority of sight claim that this is a biological fact, which is only mirrored in the culture reflected in the biblical text. However, despite the opposing conclusions, most scholars debating the matter share some presuppositions in common. Both sides of the debate assume that there is a hierarchy of the senses, and that the scholar must reveal this hierarchy. Such an assumption is, naturally, based on the Western perception, originating with Plato, which determined a sensory hierarchy, with sight in top spot. In other words, even those scholars who claim that hearing is the superior and most important sense in biblical perception, base their argument on the existence of a sensory hierarchy that originates in another culture. Another similarity between the sides is that they are both based on theory rather than on detail. The perception that the sense of hearing is more central assumes that there are only two types of culture when it comes to sensory experience. The perception that the sense of sight is more central assumes that the use of the senses is merely physiological-universal.

In light of the associative patterns described in previous chapters, it seems to be necessary to re-examine this question. Despite careful study of all biblical verses mentioning the senses in the Hebrew Bible (and it has not been possible to cite every verse in the present book), I found no evidence of a structural hierarchy of the senses. What I did find is a prominence given to sight within the associative and contextual patterns, as well as elaborate use of sight vocabulary to express the derived meanings related to the sensory category. It seems that the large number of metaphors and contexts in which sight is mentioned hint at the centrality of sight in biblical culture—a centrality which is neither a superiority, as in the platonic perception, nor an exclusivity of sight, as we find in

1. See the discussion on pp. 14–27, above.

modern Western perception.[2] In this chapter, I will revisit some of the contexts mentioned in Chapters 3 and 4 which are crucial for the understanding of sight. The examination will suggest that in some cases sight is the root metaphor for a specific context, and that other sensory vocabulary draws on it. In addition, I will look into some legal idioms and aspects unique to sight and their theological implication; at the biblical scheme of knowledge; at the scarce evidence for the explicit preference of sight over hearing or other sensory experiences; and finally at the central role that sight vocabulary plays in biblical narrative. All these aspects will point out the improbability of the supremacy of hearing in ancient Israel, and demonstrate at least some level of preference being given to sight.

Sight and Evidence

Sight and Public Evidence

This section will examine the centrality of sight within the juridical system of the Hebrew Bible. It is customary to analyse the sensory hierarchy in terms of the evidence experienced by a particular sense, such as the preference of sight over other senses in legal literature.[3] However, because we do not have a sufficient grasp of the laws of evidence in the Israelite juridical system, this will not be the avenue of research taken below. Instead, I will focus on the centrality of sight in another core aspect of the juridical system, namely, the public aspect which validates it. Clearly, the communal and participatory nature of justice in a performance-based oral society such as biblical society is essentially multisensory. Touch, mobility, eating, speech, and hearing are integrally related to the legal act. However, the validity of the legal act is based on its being a public action,[4] and sight is the dominant metaphor used to describe the public's involvement in the process.[5] Even when the other senses are involved in the public's participation, such as hearing an announcement, or ritual eating,[6] it is the fact that the act was seen that

2. See pp. 17–20, above.

3. See Leventhal, "The Torah and the Senses (A)," 95–97. There are many sensory aspects to the juridical system (evidence, testimony, symbolic acts, etc.), see *MKCS* 2002, 197–216; Malul, "Ceremonial and Juridical Background," part b:1.

4. Malul, *Mesopotamian Legal Symbolism*, 27–28; Hibbits, "Coming to Our Senses," 946–47.

5. As will be demonstrated, this image sprouts from the concept of sight as personal learning and inquiry, and of sight as participation.

6. Dee M. Bareket, "Food and Eating in the Bible as a Means of Communication" (M.A. diss., The University of Haifa, 2004 [Hebrew]), 55–60.

expresses the participatory element. Below, I will show how sight represents this public aspect in the Hebrew Bible, and how sight is extended
metaphorically ("sight is evidence") to contexts that are not purely legal.
This includes sight as a symbol of the responsibility of the observer;
sight as proof of miracles having happened; and sight as first-hand
knowledge.

As this study is not focused of the juridical system per se, I will not
distinguish below between actual legal events and other public events
which are described using legal vocabulary. In fact, similar terms are
frequently used both within and without the pure juridical context as
portrayed in the Hebrew Bible: "It is probably inappropriate to say that
psalms and prophecy 'borrowed' legal phraseology, for there is ample
evidence that in ancient Israel the judicial realm had not yet become as
specialized as it has in the modern legal system."[7] It is safe to assume,
therefore, that movement of idioms and metaphors between different
realms, such as juridical, historical, prophetic, cultic, etc., indicates a
conceptual unity. It is difficult to prove a phenomenological gap between
the experience of participation in a legal event and that of participation in
other public events. A fine example of this is the conceptual proximity
between the juridical system and the religious system. The experience of
relating to God in a covenant relationship, where sanctions are applied if
this relationship is harmed, demonstrates the haziness of the boundaries
between the different realms—justice, religion, society.

Turning to the evidence, I will first explore how the public nature of
events in general is described using sight idioms. The twelve spies,
coming back to report from Canaan (Num 13–14), brought back with
them evidence of what they found—grapes, figs, and pomegranates—as
Moses had instructed them (13:20). Notably, the spies bring back more
than a mere verbal report:

> And they came to Moses and Aaron and to all the congregation of the
> Israelites in the wilderness of Paran, at Kadesh; they brought back word
> (וישיבו...דבר) to them and to all the congregation (כל־העדה), and showed
> them (ויראום) the fruit of the land. And they told him (ויספרו־לו ויאמרו),
> "We came to the land to which you sent us; it flows with milk and honey,
> and this is (זה) its fruit." (Num 13:26–27)

As these verses demonstrate, the spies accompany their report with
visual proof, proof that is brought before the whole community.[8] The

---

7. Buss, "The Idea of Sitz im Leben," 168.

8. The terms "all the congregation (עדה) of Israel" and "the whole congregation
(עדה)" appear in this story and highlight that it is a public event, with legal aspects.
For the term עדה as "legal community," see *HALOT* 2:289. According to the popular

fruit that they brought back to demonstrate the nature of the land is not consumed, nor valued through taste; rather, it is valued through sight and constitutes visual evidence in the report. In other words, the fruit serves as evidence for the truthfulness of their words, and the public viewing of the proof validates it. The practice of showing an artefact and talking about it also characterizes the actions of the prophets. In several biblical passages the prophets present a visual picture and then interpret it. Indeed, drawing public attention requires more than just linguistic rhetorical devices—it requires the use of visual rhetorical devices, such as an unusual act or phenomenon. The case of the spies is no different. Besides its legal function as evidence, the over-sized fruit (v. 23) serves both the rhetoric of the spies, claiming that the land and its people are too strong to fight, as well as the rhetoric of the author, claiming the fertility of the land.

The rhetoric and evidential aspect of visual presentation in prophetic context is evident in the dispute between Jeremiah and the prophet Hananiah (Jer 28:1–11), which takes place "in the presence (lit. 'eyes') of the priests and all the people" (vv. 1, 5, 11).[9] Moreover, during the dispute Jeremiah refers to the public (semi-legal) aspect of their debate when he claims that future events will prove who was a true and who was a false prophet (v. 9).[10] It is assumed that the public setting creates evidence in public memory, which serves as an archive. Against such a background, note that the whole congregation is summoned to view the unexpected acts of Jeremiah (ch. 27), and that Hananiah too is not content with words alone, but highlights his words with action:

---

dictionaries, the word "witness" (עֵד) is derived from the root עוד, meaning "repetition," "memorization," just like the words "decree" (עֵדוּת) and "testimony" (תְּעוּדָה); see BDB, 729; *HALOT* 2:795; and H. Simian-Yofre and H. Ringgren, "עוּד ʿwd; עֵד ʿēd; עֵדוּת ʿēdût; תְּעוּדָה teʿûdâ," *TDOT* 10:495–517 (195). The word "congregation" (עֵדה), however, is derived from the root יעד, meaning "to appoint," similar to the term "appointed time," "place of meeting"; see מוֹעֵד in BDB, 729; *HALOT* 2:795; and D. J. Levy, J. Milgrom, H. Ringgren, and H.-J. Fabry, "עֵדָה ʿēdâ," *TDOT* 10:468–81 (469). Despite these etymologies, there are semantic-associative links between the terms "congregation" (עֵדה) and "witness" (עֵד), mainly in cases where the congregation serves as an audience, which watches and approves the occurrences. Note that some scholars claim for etymological link as well; see Simian-Yofre and Ringgren, *TDOT* 10:496.

9. Cf. Jer 19:10; 43:9; Ezek 4:12; 12:3–7; 21:11.

10. The possible link to Deut 18:15–22 enhances the legal aspect of the event. See W. McKane, *A Critical and Exegetical Commentary on Jeremiah* (2 vols.; ICC; Edinburgh: T. & T. Clark, 1996), 2:711–14.

> Then the prophet Hananiah took the yoke from the neck of the prophet Jeremiah, and broke it. And Hananiah spoke in the presence of all the people (לעיני כל־העם), saying, "Thus says the Lord: This is how I will break the yoke of King Nebuchadnezzar of Babylon from the neck of all the nations within two years." At this, the prophet Jeremiah went his way. (Jer 28:10–11)

Both the vocal and the visual aspects of the prophetic symbolic act are validated by the sight of the people, not their hearing. Both the narrative of the spies and the dispute between Jeremiah and Hananiah describe public events that have no explicit legal aspect. Yet in both accounts it is assumed that public evidence provides proof for generations through sight.

The public nature of an event characterizes its legal status, a matter elaborated in the juridical system presented in the book of Deuteronomy. According to David Daube, the public nature of personal affairs gives legal validity to "the culture of the book of Deuteronomy." This public nature of the juridical process is not restricted solely to procedures associated with investigation, but also with legal processes associated with a change of status and possession. Punishment is also meted out publicly and viewed by the community. In fact, according to Daube, public punishment is the main sanction in Deuteronomy. The biggest implicit threat in the legal system presented in Deuteronomy is the threat of losing social status, or, in other words, shame.[11] To phrase it differently, the visual terms discussed in this section serve as the main metaphor, or perhaps synecdoche, for the public nature of the legal system. These terms highlight different aspects of the public action: creating evidence of the legal act, emphasizing legal responsibility, and creating a social deterrent factor.

An example is found it the law of levirate marriage (Deut 25:5–10), which describes the legal setting of "pulling of the sandal"—a legal symbolic act in which the descendant's brother withdraws from the duty of Levirate marriage. After the claims of the parties have been heard by the elders, the widow removes her brother-in-law's sandal, the widow spits in his face, and a statement of his refusal is read out. The symbolic legal act, as well as the solemn declaration, hint at the multi-sensory nature of this ceremony. But importantly, it is the public nature of this legal act that gives it its validity. This public nature is evident in the expression "in view of": "then his brother's wife shall go up to him in the presence (lit. 'eyes,' לעיני) of the elders, pull his sandal off his foot, spit in his face, and declare, 'This is what is done to the man who does

---

11. D. Daube, "The Culture of Deuteronomy," *Orita* 3 (1969): 27–52.

not build up his brother's house'" (Deut 25:9). In other words, for the acts to be valid, the elders must view them—the elders are the eyewitnesses to what is happening. The public nature of this act has a dual social function: denouncing (i.e. sanction against) the brother-in-law who refuses levirate marriage, and creating a kind of collective archive. Visual witnessing proves the actual occurrence, a crucial aspect of a legal system in oral society.[12]

The term "in the eyes of" (לעיני) is used to describe the legal aspect of a public event also in the narrative.[13] The description of the purchase of the Cave of Machpelah (Gen 23) reflects what was undoubtedly a widespread custom or legal procedure—the transmission of ownership. The purchase is preceded by negotiations between Ephron and Abraham. When Ephron offers to give Abraham the cave for nothing, Ephron insists: "No, my lord, hear me; I give you the field, and I give you the cave that is in it; in the presence of (לעיני) my people I give it to you; bury your dead" (Gen 23:11). Ephron's words highlight that there will be witnesses to the act, so no one will be able to make further demands at any later date. This is precisely the reason that Abraham insists on paying. He wants the plot of land to become an acquisition (מקנה), his own property "in the presence (לעיני) of the Hittites, of all who entered the gate of his town" (v. 18, JPS). In this verse too, the public aspect of the legal act is emphasized through the use of the term לעיני and the inclusion of the whole congregation. Such a stress is meant to create evidence of the purchase, or to reflect such evidence to the intended audience. In any case, it reflects the common law in biblical times, according to which the sale only becomes valid when the purchase was witnessed. Abraham probably had to stand on his plot as a sign of his ownership,[14] and the whole assembled crowd probably heard Ephron announce his renouncement of the field and the cave. However, the medium that transformed the selling act from a concrete act associated with a

---

12. The public aspect of the legal system is not unique to Deuteronomy. The phrase לעיני appears with a similar meaning in other law codes, for example, the punishment on incest in Lev 20:17 is carried out "in front of the eyes" of the people. Here, like in Deuteronomy, the public nature of punishment is a deterrent. See also B. Danet, "Speech, Writing and Performativity: An Evolutionary View of the History of Constitutive Ritual," in *The Construction of Professional Discourse* (ed. B.-L. Gunnarson, P. Linell, and B. Nordberg; Language in Social Life Series; New York: Longman, 1997), 13–41 (17).

13. For the fundamental discussion and definition of "law in the Narrative," see D. Daube, *Studies in Biblical Law* (Cambridge: Cambridge University Press, 1947), 1–73.

14. Cf. *MKCS*, 169–77.

particular time and place, into an act with a validity that transcends that time, was the public witness, described as seeing. This very same function is fulfilled by a written legal document in other cultures. Lastly, while other Hebrew terms could be used to express public witnessing, such as "in front of them," "in their face" (לפני), "in their ears" (לאזני), "in their midst" (בקרב), or any other expression derived from a bodily synecdoche, the Hebrew Bible consistently chooses the term "in their eyes" (לעיני), a choice which cannot be accidental, and must reflect a broader cultural perception.

Sight is used to create evidence of a legal act, a kind of "memorandum" of the event, also through the verb "to see" (ראה), used to open a declaration with the imperative. Such opening is meant to "call to witness," and appears frequently in a legal context. Most prominent is its appearance in public pronouncements: "See (ראה), I am setting before you today a blessing and a curse" (Deut 11:26); "See (ראה), I have set before you today life and prosperity, death and adversity" (30:15).[15] Such imperatives are meant to stress and create evidence for the given statement, and the legal responsibility sprouting from it. Despite the statements being read out aloud, it is to be seen (witnessed). An echo of legal appeal is found in literary passages. When Potiphar's wife, after being refused by Joseph, tells the servants, "...See (ראו), my husband has brought among us a Hebrew to insult us! He came in to me to lie with me, and I cried out with a loud voice" (Gen 39:14), she is clearly attempting to establish witnesses to support her accusation. Elijah says to the widow from Zarephath, "See (ראי), your son is alive" (1 Kgs 17:23). Here, Elijah draws her attention to his powers, and indeed she affirms: "Now I know that you are a man of God, and that the word of the Lord in your mouth is truth" (v. 24). When Jonathan is condemned for having eaten despite the oath, he is put on trial. Notably, he calls attention to the positive aspect of his act: "...see (ראו) how my eyes have brightened because I tasted a little of this honey" (1 Sam 14:29). When Ben Haddad asks Ahab for further payment, Ahab declares his innocence to the elders: "Look now! See (דעו־נא וראו) how this man is seeking trouble; for he sent to me for my wives, my children, my silver, and my gold; and I did not refuse him" (1 Kgs 20:7). Ahab's words "for the record" help him gain support from his people. Lastly, a similar announcement occurs several chapters later, when the king of Aram asks the king of Israel to help his general, Naaman, with his skin disease. The king of Israel interprets the request as an attack, and attests his servants: "...Am I God, to give death or life, that this man sends word to me to cure a man of his

---

15. As well as Deut 1:8, 21; 2:24, 31; 4:5; 11:26; 1 Sam 12:24; Jer 1:10.

leprosy? Just look and see (דְּעוּ־נָא וּרְאוּ) how he is trying to pick a quarrel with me" (2 Kgs 5:7).[16] In all these examples, the imperative "see" is used to create evidence and affirm the speaker's position.

Similar appeal to acknowledgment of evidence can be framed as a question rather than as an imperative:

> Now Elisha was sitting at home and the elders were sitting with him. The king had sent ahead one of his men; but before the messenger arrived, [Elisha] said to the elders, "Do you see (הַרְאִיתֶם)—that murderer has sent someone to cut off my head! Watch (רְאוּ) when the messenger comes, and shut the door and hold the door fast against him. No doubt the sound of his master's footsteps will follow. (2 Kgs 6:32, JPS)

The first occurrence of ראה in Elisha's words is meant to create evidence of his innocence, in a way similar to previous examples. The second is a call for action. Similar phraseology is used in the description of the public anointing of Saul: "Samuel said to all the people, 'Do you see (הַרְאִיתֶם) the one whom the Lord has chosen? There is no one like him among all the people.' And all the people shouted, 'Long live the king!'" (1 Sam 10:24). In his call, Samuel not only legally validates the choice of the new king,[17] but also gives some of the responsibility for the choice to the people, who have agreed with it.

The encounter between David and Saul in the cave further reinforces the usage of "to see" (ראה) in the creation of potential legal evidence:

> David said to Saul, "Why do you listen (תִשְׁמַע) to the words of those who say, 'David seeks to do you harm'? This very day your eyes have seen (רָאוּ עֵינֶיךָ) how the Lord gave you into my hand in the cave; and some urged me (וַאֹמֶר) to kill you, but I spared you. I said (וָאֹמַר), 'I will not raise my hand against my lord; for he is the Lord's anointed.' See (רְאֵה), my father, see (רְאֵה) the corner of your cloak in my hand; for by the fact that I cut off the corner of your cloak, and did not kill you, you may know for certain (דַע וּרְאֵה) that there is no wrong or treason in my hands. I have not sinned against you, though you are hunting me to take my life..." (1 Sam 24:10–12)

This passage, which is only part of David's speech, reflects several important notions. First, it aspires to create public knowledge of the fact that David is not pursuing Saul in order to harm him. Four times Saul is asked to see, and at the same time he is asked to abandon what he has heard. Furthermore, the term used, "your eyes have seen" (רָאוּ עֵינֶיךָ), highlights that Saul himself experienced the rescue first-hand, while his

---

16. See also Jer 2:19, 23.
17. For more on sight as evidence for leadership transfer, see p. 245, below.

previous knowledge was acquired second-hand (hearing). The repetition of the imperative "see" (ראה גם ראה) accompanies the display of the evidence—the edge of Saul's robe—proving that he was indeed rescued. Finally, the expression imperatives "know and see" (דע וראה) call on Saul to acknowledge David's innocence. At the very least, this entire story takes place in the presence of David's entourage, which is mentioned frequently in the exposition of this scene. In all probability, the events were also witnessed by Saul's own entourage. The correlation between the speech and legal procedure is explicit in the text, when David asks for fair judgment of Yahweh on the matter (v. 13).

To sum up, we saw that in the Hebrew Bible sight is presented as the primary medium for proving a legal event, and for creating a collective memory of events with legal and other ramifications. In other words, sight is the primary sense through which the public nature of the judicial system operates. This public aspect creates a kind of living documentation, as well as the foundation for social sanctions. Importantly, sight becomes a metaphor for public witnessing, even when other sensory experiences are involved.

Sight and Responsibility

In the preceding section I briefly mentioned that seeing (i.e. witnessing) not only created documentation of evidence and social sanction, but also responsibility of the observer. In fact, some examples of sight as public witnessing in legal contexts can only be explained thus. The deuteronomic legislator used the phrase "in your sight" (לעיניכם) while warning against excessive punishment. The person proved wrong in trial was to be punished with flogging. However, the lawmaker restricts the punishment: "Forty lashes may be given but not more; if more lashes than these are given, your neighbour will be degraded (נקלה) in your sight (לעיניך)" (Deut 25:3). Normally, the severity of the act is understood to be expressed in the words "be degraded in your sight." The term translated here as "degraded" is נקלה, and could be used to describe either social humiliation or serious physical harm, and in any event is associated with the semantic field of shame in the Hebrew Bible.[18] In other words, this law indicates that a punishment of social humiliation should not be added to the physical punishment, or that the physical punishment should be limited in order not to cause irreversible damage. According to this explanation, the use of the phrase "in your sight" (לעיניך) does more than indicate the public nature of punishment. Rather, it indicates the public responsibility of the observer. To phrase it differently, in previous

18. See my "Honour and Shame," 51–54.

examples, the public nature of punishment was meant to deter trans-
gressors, while in this verse, it is meant to provide balance and super-
vision of the legal system. The verse thus represents a perception that
anyone observing an unjust action bears some responsibility to act.

We find another example of this social/legal responsibility in the
grouping of laws of lost property: "You shall not watch (לא־תראה) your
neighbour's ox or sheep straying away and ignore (והתעלמת) them; you
shall take them back to their owner" (Deut 22:1).[19] In this directive seeing is contrasted to ignoring, expressed through the verb עלם (Hithpael).
The root עלם has the basic meaning "hidden,"[20] and often describes the
unknown[21]—whether something that cannot be seen, or something that is
not acknowledged. The Hithpael form found in this verse should indicate
the pretentiousness of action, and therefore we should translate: "You
shall not see (לא־תראה) your neighbour's ox or sheep straying away and
pretend not to have seen (והתעלמה) them" (Deut 22:1, my translation).[22]
The biblical text does not detail any punishment attached to a person
who ignores what he saw. It could therefore be claimed that, practically
speaking, there is no way of applying sanctions to someone who behaves
this way. Nevertheless, the text does express an expectation of behaviour, an expectation of social responsibility. Maybe the sanction applied
to acts that are performed in the private domain (and which, by definition, have no witnesses) is not a punishment determined by law, but is
based on the deterrent factor of a public curse:

> The same day Moses charged the people as follows: When you have
> crossed over the Jordan, these shall stand on Mount Gerizim for the bless-
> ing of the people: Simeon, Levi, Judah, Issachar, Joseph, and Benjamin.
> And these shall stand on Mount Ebal for the curse: Reuben, Gad, Asher,
> Zebulon, Dan, and Naphtali. Then the Levites shall declare in a loud voice
> to all the Israelites: "Cursed be anyone who makes an idol or casts an
> image, anything abhorrent to the Lord, the work of an artisan, and sets it
> up in secret." All the people shall respond, saying, "Amen!" "Cursed be
> anyone who dishonours father or mother." All the people shall say,
> "Amen!" "Cursed be anyone who moves a neighbour's boundary marker."

19. Cf. vv. 3, 4, as well as Lev 4:13; 5:3, 4; 20:4.

20. BDB, 761; C. Locher, "עָלַם ʿālam; תַּעֲלֻמָה taʿalumâ," *TDOT* 11:147–54
(mainly p. 150, and see p. 148 for the meaning "something dark"; yet see *HALOT*
2:834–35, which finds homonymic root with such meaning).

21. See *MKCS*, 259–61. The root עלם is found with the object "eye" (עין) six
times (Lev 20:4 [×2]; 2 Sam 12:3; Ezek 22:26; Job 42:3; Prov 28:27, and once with
the object "ear" (אזן, Lam 3:56).

22. For the meaning "pretending" embedded in the Hithpael (e.g. התחלה, התנדל,
התחכם), see Gesenius §54:3.

All the people shall say, "Amen!" "Cursed be anyone who misleads a blind person on the road." All the people shall say, "Amen!" "Cursed be anyone who deprives the alien, the orphan, and the widow of justice." All the people shall say, "Amen!" "Cursed be anyone who lies with his father's wife, because he has violated his father's rights." All the people shall say, "Amen!" "Cursed be anyone who lies with any animal." All the people shall say, "Amen!" "Cursed be anyone who lies with his sister, whether the daughter of his father or the daughter of his mother." All the people shall say, "Amen!" "Cursed be anyone who lies with his mother-in-law." All the people shall say, "Amen!" "Cursed be anyone who strikes down a neighbour in secret." All the people shall say, "Amen!" "Cursed be anyone who takes a bribe to shed innocent blood." All the people shall say, "Amen!" "Cursed be anyone who does not uphold the words of this law by observing them." All the people shall say, "Amen!" (Deut 27:11–26)[23]

This passage closes the deuteronomic law code with a public oath which differs from previous chapters in content and style. These verses do not mention any punishment, and seem to relate to unprovable transgressions. The entire description reflects the public nature of signing a covenant, and precedes the description of the blessing and the curse that closes the covenant. In fact, the curse that appears later in Deut 28:15–29:69 is the sanction (i.e. punishment) for those who commit these transgressions.[24] Another example of this perception is found in the Book of Covenant:

When someone delivers to another a donkey, ox, sheep, or any other animal for safekeeping, and it dies or is injured or is carried off, without anyone seeing it (אין ראה), an oath before the Lord shall decide between the two of them that the one has not laid hands on the property of the other; the owner shall accept the oath, and no restitution shall be made. (Exod 22:9–10)

This verse reflects both the importance of sight as evidence (as presented in the previous paragraph), and the use of an oath when visual evidence is absent.

The use of curse or oath sanctions makes it easier to understand the prohibition against ignoring an animal that has gone astray (above, Deut 22:1), or the prohibition against excessive punishment (above, Deut 25:3). The legal logic seems to be sight → knowledge → responsibility. The link between sight and responsibility is further clarified in the declaration to be made at the rite of the red heifer: "Our hands did not shed this blood, nor did our eyes see (עינינו לא ראו) it done" (Deut 21:7). This verse describes two ways of evading responsibility—responsibility for

---

23. The way in which the Masoretic division into *parshiyot* preserves the oral background of these verses is notable.

24. Daube, "The Culture of Deuteronomy," 39.

the deed, and responsibility for knowing about the deed. The first is described using a tactile metaphor (touching is doing), while the second uses a sight metaphor (seeing is knowledge); the verse clusters and puts side-by-side both types of responsibility. The idea that sight bears responsibility is found also in the Priestly code, within the instructions of guilt offering: "When any of you sin in that you have heard (תשמע) a public adjuration to testify and—though able to testify as one who has seen (ראה) or learned of the matter (ידע)—does not speak up (יגיד), you are subject to punishment" (Lev 5:1).[25] This verse describes an iniquitous deed in terms of hearing, while the verses that follow describe sins caused by touch (vv. 2–3) and speech (v. 4). If one does not respond when a sin is being committed, even though he sees it (i.e. witnesses), he must bring a guilt offering, just as if one ignores (עלם Niphal, vv. 2–4) other sins. Most importantly, the metaphor "sight is responsibility" occurs across the legal codes of the Pentateuch. Indeed, it appears in prophetic material which uses legal metaphors: "Is it not to share your bread with the hungry, and bring the homeless poor into your house; when you see (תראה) the naked, to cover them, and not to hide yourself (תתעלם)[26] from your own kin?" (Isa 58:7).[27] Isaiah reflects an expectation for action and social responsibility based on sight.

Earlier, I suggested that this social/legal responsibility is enforced through the sanction of curse or oath. I would like to propose that this social/legal responsibility is also based on the legal commitment of the dominant partner in the covenant to protect the weaker partner.[28] This legal commitment also uses sight as a metaphor for providence.[29] Moreover, God's authority over the committed person or group is expressed in idioms of sight. For example, Samuel is dedicated to God as a child, and thus says his mother: "As soon as the child is weaned, I will bring him, that he may appear (lit. 'be seen,' נראה) in the presence of the Lord, and remain there forever" (1 Sam 1:22). The verb "to be seen" (ראה Niphal) in this verse describes a continuous action, and indicates that Samuel belongs to God, as Hannah had promised earlier, "…I will dedicate him to the Lord for all the days of his life…" (1 Sam 1:11).[30] In other biblical

25. See also Num 35:23.

26. Literally, "act as if you do not see," see n. 26.

27. For the legal meaning of the phrases "to reach out (שלח) the finger," and "to talk (דבר) deceptively" found in v. 9, see Malul, "Ceremonial and Juridical Background," part a:1.

28. Mendenhall and Herion, "Covenant," 1180–81.

29. Cf. pp. 130–40, above.

30. Elat, *Samuel and the Foundation of Kingship*, 19–20. Elat notes that the term repeats in legal treaties, and is comparable to the Akkadian phrase *dagālu ana pān*.

passages, God is described as all-seeing (knowing).[31] God's authority over the individual or the collective in terms of the parties to the covenant is also described as sight, and therefore responsibility.[32] These common perceptions strengthen the idea that sight involves legal and social responsibility, especially when sight has hierarchical elements.

The social/legal responsibility that originates from sight, especially from the sight of the Lord in a covenant relationship, is also embedded in narratives regarding human relationships. A fine demonstration is found within the Joseph story. The famine in Egypt starts while Joseph holds a senior position in the kingdom (Gen 41:42–45; 47:13–26). At first, Joseph sells the stored grain for money; but once the money ran out, "all of Egypt" (כל־מצרים) comes to Joseph and asks for food, with a serious complaint: "Give us food! Why should we die before your eyes (lit. 'in front of you,' לנגדך)? For our money is gone" (Gen 47:15). Following this grave complaint, Joseph agrees to sell food in exchange for livestock. When these run out, the Egyptians return to Joseph and again complain: "Shall we die before your eyes (לעיניך), both we and our land? Buy us and our land in exchange for food. We with our land will become slaves to Pharaoh; just give us seed, so that we may live and not die, and that the land may not become desolate" (v. 19). Subsequently, each and every Egyptian, with the exception of the priests of Pharaoh, are enslaved. It seems that mentioning "all of Egypt" in this narrative expresses both the desperate condition of the Egyptians,[33] and Joseph's responsibility over them (cf. Gen 41:43). The rhetoric that the Egyptians use is that Joseph, who has a high standing in the kingdom, sees (= knows) their difficult situation, and therefore has the responsibility to act. The words "in your presence" (לנגדך) and "before your very eyes" (לעיניך) highlight the notion that seeing a situation leads to responsibility, and that ignoring the situation is not an option.

See also the command to "be seen (לראות) the face of Yahweh" (Exod 34:24; cf. 34:23; Deut 17:13; 31:11). These verses, like the description in the book of Samuel, stress the sight of God, yet in other verses, the human actor is the one who comes to see God. For example, see Isa 17:7–8, and the words of Jacob to Esau: "No, if I find favour in your eyes, you would accept this gift from my hand; for I see your face like seeing the face of God, and you have received me with favour" (Gen 33:10, my translation). Due to this dual description, it is assumed that the usage of Niphal ראה is *tiqqun soferim* for an assumed original Qal ראה (לְרְאוֹת), "to see the face of Yahweh."

31. Jer 23:24; Pss 33:13; 113:6; 138:6; Job 34:21.

32. See pp. 151–52, above.

33. The despair is expressed through the threat of death (cf. Gen 30:1), as well as through the loss of independence (see pp. 212–20, above).

Another example involving responsibility that comes from sight and knowledge is the fable of the watchman in Ezek 33:1–6.[34] In times of war, the watchman must issue a warning when he sees the enemy approaching. Failure to issue his warning, failure to report what he sees (= knows), makes him responsible for the death of the people. In this fable, and partially in the Joseph story, the issue is professional responsibility based specifically on the sense of sight. But even the professional responsibility presented in the watchman fable is based on the parallel between "doing" and "seeing" presented above (Deut 21:7). Just as the responsibility of someone who knows of a crime resembles the responsibility for the crime itself, so the responsibility of the person who knows is only discharged when the message is delivered—either by giving evidence in court, or by reporting as an observer. The moral of the watchman fable (Ezek 33:7–9) follows the same logic: the prophet is responsible for what he sees and knows. It should therefore come as no surprise that in other biblical passages, the prophet is called "the seer" (ראה, חזה).[35] Earlier, we identified different aspects of the notion that sight is the primary vehicle of knowledge. Now it is clear that knowledge acquired through sight (i.e. first-hand) places a degree of social/legal responsibility on the observer.

To sum up, sight is the main vehicle for evidence that proves that a legal event took place, by creating a memory of the event and "extending" it apart from the boundaries of the time it happened. Carasik reaches the conclusion that "for Deuteronomy, seeing was believing—perception with the eye represented direct, undeniable experience. This use of the eye as the characteristic organ by which one becomes aware of events is matched by a characteristic verb that describes the maintaining of that awareness."[36] In this section I have demonstrated that this notion is not restricted to the book of Deuteronomy. Moreover, the rhetoric of the relationship between Israel and God uses these metaphors as proof that miraculous historical events actually took place, as explored in the next

34. Compare with the other biblical texts which refer to the watcher and his duty: 2 Sam 18:24–27; Isa 26:6; Jer 48:19.

35. Clearly, the titles "seer" (ראה, חזה) demonstrate an understanding of prophecy as visual-cognitive experience of reality beyond the normal one. As elsewhere in the ancient Near East, the seer was expected to see things that others could not (e.g. Elisha, 2 Kgs 2:10; 6:17), and predicted the future via "visions" or through the examination of the vital organs of animals. In this parable, the responsibility of sight is stressed, despite the fact that sight as prophetic experience is not mentioned, and despite the fact that the titles "prophet" (נביא), "watcher," or "seer" are not used. For more on sight and prophecy, see pp. 266–69, below.

36. Carasik, "To See a Sound," 259.

section. In this mutual relationship, as in reality, sight leads to knowledge, and knowledge leads to responsibility. To finish with a last example, the direct correlation between sight and knowledge is demonstrated in the challenging words of Dathan and Abiram: "It is clear you [Moses] have not brought us into a land flowing with milk and honey, or given us an inheritance of fields and vineyards. Would you put out the eyes (עיני...תנקר) of these men? We will not come!" (Num 16:14). In other words, Dathan and Abiram claim that Moses cannot blind the whole community, as everyone sees (= knows) his failure. The direct correlation between sight and knowledge is what leads to the responsibility of the observer, and this is the basis of the legal prohibition against disregarding. The unseen and unknown, however, leads to no personal responsibility, and remains in the realm of the divine: "For God will bring every deed into judgment, including every hidden (נעלם) thing, whether it is good or evil" (Qoh 12:14, NIV).

Seeing is Believing

Sight as an indicator for public witnessing is, then, used frequently in legal metaphors, especially, but not solely, those used by the deuteronomist. The correlation between the rhetoric of the book of Deuteronomy and legal perceptions is well demonstrated in the notion of the covenant, which shapes significant parts of the book. As a legal code, Deuteronomy includes a historical introduction, the conditions of the loyal covenant, the clauses of the agreement, a call for witnesses, curses, and blessings.[37] And as Moshe Weinfeld points out, expressions from the field of sight recur:

> The deuteronomic orator often employs rhetorical phrase such as: "your eyes see" עיניכם הראות, "you have seen" אתם ראיתם (11:7; 29:1 et al.) to implant in his listeners the feeling that they themselves have experienced the awe-inspiring events of the Exodus; and he repeats these phrases again and again as if to hypnotize his audience. The device of the rhetorical question is also used significantly with purpose: "Did a people ever hear the voice of a god"…? (4:33).[38]

Weinfeld regards the mentioned phrases (אתם ראיתם עיניכם הראות) as characteristic of the deuteronomic phraseology. However, as will be demonstrated below, the description of the experience and perception of divine revelation are not confined to these visual phrases, nor to the book of Deuteronomy. Evidence of revelation and miracles is described in a range of idioms from the semantic field of sight, such as "to see" (ראה),

37. Weinfeld, *Deuteronomy and the Deuteronomic*, 61.
38. Ibid., 173.

"to show" (ראה Hiphil), "stand and see" (יצב Hithpael + ראה), "know and see" (ידע + ראה), "seeing eyes of" (ראה + עיני), "to the eyes" (לעיני), and "to observe" (בין Hithpael). In the following pages, I will examine these phrases and their use as proof of miracles. Clearly, such use is based on sight metaphors as personal experience and first-hand knowledge.[39]

The terms and phrases mentioned by Weinfeld, as well as other expressions from the field of sight, usually appear as part of the rhetoric of proving the events and miracles experienced by the people. In other words, the miracles happened publicly, with all the people watching. This created a collective memory that could not be denied—a kind of non-verbal recording of the events. The public nature of miracles resembles the public nature of the juridical system; the validity of the covenant is based on the fact that the entire congregation saw, witnessed the miraculous deeds of God.[40] God's wonders in Egypt, for example, are presented as an historical event that serves as background to the demand for obedience. The rhetoric that proves that these historical events took place is the rhetoric of sight: "Moses summoned all Israel and said to them: 'You have seen (אתם ראיתם) all that the Lord did before your eyes (לעיניכם) in the land of Egypt, to Pharaoh and to all his servants and to all his land, the great trials that your eyes saw (ראו עיניך), the signs, and those great wonders'" (Deut 29:1-2).[41] Sight is overly stressed in these verses, which describe participation and (possibly) multisensory experience. A more detailed list of events that the Israelites witnessed appears elsewhere in the book:

> Remember today that your children were not the ones who saw and experienced (ידעו...ראו) the discipline of the Lord your God: his majesty, his mighty hand, his outstretched arm; the signs he performed and the things he did in the heart of Egypt, both to Pharaoh king of Egypt and to his whole country; what he did to the Egyptian army, to its horses and chariots, how he overwhelmed them with the waters of the Red Sea as they were pursuing you, and how the Lord brought lasting ruin on them. It was not your children who saw what he did for you in the wilderness until you arrived at this place, and what he did to Dathan and Abiram, sons of Eliab the Reubenite, when the earth opened its mouth right in the middle of all Israel and swallowed them up with their households, their tents and every living thing that belonged to them. But it was your own eyes that saw (עיניכם הראות) all these great things the Lord has done. (Deut 11:2-7, NIV)

39. For more on the matter, see below, pp. 248-51.

40. For the historical introduction as part of the covenant (and specifically in the book of Deuteronomy), see Mendenhall and Herion, "Covenant," 1183-84.

41. Cf. Deut 1:30; 4:34; 6:22; 7:19; 10:21; 14:6; Josh 24:7, 17.

In this list, all wonders of the exodus and wilderness are listed, and all are claimed to have been personally watched by the Israelites. Such a claim validates the argument of divine providence by reference to the living archive, and precedes the demand for obedience (vv. 8–9). The book of Deuteronomy is not alone in claiming that the proof of a miracle lies in the fact that it was seen. The Exodus as described in Numbers mentions the Egyptians as the audience: "They set out from Rameses in the first month, on the fifteenth day of the first month; on the day after the Passover the Israelites went out boldly "in the sight of all the Egyptians" (לעיני כל־מצרים, Num 33:3). Stating that other nations viewed the exodus is an attempt to validate its historicity further, and is echoed elsewhere: "As in the days when you came out of the land of Egypt, show us (אראנו)[42] marvellous things. The nations shall see (יראו) and be ashamed of all their might; they shall lay their hands on their mouths; their ears shall be deaf" (Mic 7:15–16). Here too witnessing can be multi-sensory, yet it is described as sight. Moreover, it serves as the ultimate proof of divine action. I will mention a final example from the book of Judges, where a distinction is made between those who saw (= knew/experienced) the miracles and those who did not see (= know/experience) them:

> The people worshiped the Lord all the days of Joshua, and all the days of the elders who outlived Joshua, who had seen (ראו) all the great work that the Lord had done for Israel. Joshua son of Nun, the servant of the Lord, died at the age of one hundred and ten years… Moreover, that whole generation was gathered to their ancestors, and another generation grew up after them, who did not know (ידעו) the Lord or the work that he had done for Israel. (Judg 2:7–8, 10)[43]

Notable in these verses is that "to see" is structurally parallel to "to know," and that seeing the wonders implies a strong response on behalf of the viewer. Together with the previous example, these verses neatly express the miraculous nature of the events that took place in Egypt and the wilderness (the plagues of Egypt, the parting of the Red Sea, the journey through the wilderness, the opening up of the ground, and the exodus as a whole). The recurring statement that the Israelites saw the events with their own eyes is proof of the historic veracity of the events. In other words, this rhetoric acknowledges the difficulty that some people had in believing that these events in fact took place.

---

42. The NRSV changes the person in this translation, due to some difficulty in the verse (cf. *BHS*). Such difficulty, however, is not relevant to the understanding of the rhetoric of sight.

43. Cf. Josh 23:3–4.

Other events associated with the exodus from Egypt, and described in the Hebrew Bible, include the victory over the Amorite kings (Deut 3:21) and the Baal-peor incident: "You saw with your own eyes (עיניכם הראת) what the Lord did in the matter of Baal-peor, that the Lord your God wiped out from among you every person who followed Baal-peor" (Deut 4:3). An examination of the detailed description of the Baal-peor events as told in the book of Numbers demonstrates that the public nature of the event is evident outside Deuteronomy. The leaders of the rebellious people are to be hanged in broad daylight (נגד השמש, Num 25:4),[44] and as Moses speaks to the officials, "...one of the Israelites came and brought a Midianite woman into his family, in the sight (לעיני) of Moses and in the sight (לעיני) of the whole congregation (כל־עדת) of the Israelites, while they were weeping at the entrance of the tent of meeting." Clearly, the punishment too was viewed by the whole community, and the use of sight here is meant to deter, and not only prove a past event.

Similarly, the story of Dathan and Abiram/Korah, and especially their being swallowed up in the ground, is a public event, as is stressed both in Deuteronomy and in Numbers. In Deuteronomy, the miraculous swallowing up is described as taking place in front of the whole community (above, Deut 11:6–7) and their sight (עיניכם הראת).[45] In Numbers, the story also highlights the public nature of the miracle by describing the fact that it was widely observed: "Then Korah assembled the whole congregation (כל־העדה) against them at the entrance of the tent of meeting. And the glory of the Lord appeared to the whole congregation (כל־העדה)" (Num 16:19). The active involvement of the community is repeatedly highlighted (vv. 20, 21, 23, 25, 26).[46] While the Deuteronomy account has a polemic character that proves the occurrence of a miracle and divine intervention, the Numbers account has an etiological character that explains why the altar was covered.[47] The following chapter (Num 17:1–5) tells us that the staffs of the sons of Korah were used to prepare this cover. According to this version, the power of the memory acquired by public sight is not enough to endure down the generations. Thus, a physical object, a staff, had to be introduced into the story to bridge the

---

44. The link between "in front of the sun" (נגד השמש) and sight comes from the associative pattern sight–light. See also pp. 255–58, below.

45. For the relationship between the narrative in Numbers and in Deuteronomy, see von Rad, *Deuteronomy*, 84–85. The important matter here is the visual evidence.

46. See also n. 8, and T. R. Ashley, *The Book of Numbers* (NICOT; Grand Rapids: Eerdmans, 1992). The term "congregation" (עדה) has a legal meaning; see *HALOT* 2:789.

47. Cf. M. V. Fox, "The Sign of the Covenant," *RB* 81 (1974): 557–96.

time gap between those who witnessed the event and the following generations—"a reminder to the Israelites that no outsider, who is not of the descendants of Aaron, shall approach to offer incense before the Lord, so as not to become like Korah and his company—just as the Lord had said to him through Moses" (Num 16:40). This comparison of two versions of the same story demonstrates different subtleties in the use of sight to create documentation and memory.

Other miracles described in the Hebrew Bible are also experienced in a visual way for the sake of future generations. This is the essence of the miracle of the manna: "This is what the Lord has commanded: 'Let an omer of it be kept throughout your generations, in order that they may see (יראו) the food with which I fed you in the wilderness, when I brought you out of the land of Egypt'" (Exod 16:32). The tasteful experience (see Num 11:8) is transferred to a visual one for the sake of evidence. The need for a visual object to create a memory and proof of a historical event is found in the book of Joshua too, where the altar built by the Transjordanian tribes serves as a witness:

> Let us now build an altar, not for burnt offering, nor for sacrifice, but to be a witness between us and you, and between the generations after us, that we do perform the service of the Lord in his presence with our burnt offerings and sacrifices and offerings of well-being; so that your children may never say to our children in time to come, "You have no portion in the Lord." And we thought, If this should be said to us or to our descendants in time to come, we could say, "Look (ראו) at this copy of the altar of the Lord, which our ancestors made, not for burnt offerings, nor for sacrifice, but to be a witness (עד) between us and you." (Josh 22:26–28)

The argument in these verses is that the building of the altar, which would be visible for generations, is proof of the existence of the agreement between the tribes on both sides of the Jordan.[48] The altar in this story has a parallel function to a written legal document in other cultures, and it has precisely the ability to preserve visual evidence (rather than aural, taste, or odour) over time.[49]

---

48. For the link between sight and memory, which is shown in the examples, see also Carasik, *Theologies of the Mind*, 177–93. Another example of the same idea is found in Isa 66:23–24: "From new moon to new moon, and from sabbath to sabbath, all flesh shall come to worship before me, says the Lord. And they shall go out and look at the dead bodies of the people who have rebelled against me; for their worm shall not die, their fire shall not be quenched, and they shall be an abhorrence to all flesh."

49. Malul, *Society, Law, and Custom*, 159 n. 39.

We see that sight as proof of the truthfulness of a miraculous historical event is not limited to the rhetoric of the deuteronomist, which is nothing but a specific employment of imagery that suffuses the Hebrew Bible. Almost every miraculous description highlights the fact that there was an audience who viewed it. The very first time that Moses appears before the people as God's messenger, the public nature of the encounter is highlighted: "Aaron repeated all the words that the Lord had spoken to Moses, and he [Moses] performed the signs in the sight of the people (לעיני העם), and the people were convinced (ויאמן העם)" (Exod 4:30–31a, JPS). These verses demonstrate that seeing is believing, exactly because sight proves the authenticity of wonders. The plague of blood too it thus described, proving that it was a genuine miracle and not a natural phenomenon: Moses and Aaron did just as the Lord commanded. In the sight of Pharaoh (לעיני פרעה) and of his officials (לעיני עבדיו) he lifted up the staff and struck the water in the river, and all the water in the river was turned into blood (Exod 7:20). Noteworthy is the fact that the magicians of Egypt manage to do the same: "But the magicians of Egypt did the same by their secret arts (בלטיהם)" (v. 22), but in the sight of no one. Not only is an audience not mentioned, but also the word translated here as "secret art" (by-form of להטים) can easily be interpreted as a pun, meaning also "secretly" (לאט/לט), or "undercover."[50] In other words, the miracle performed by Moses is divine, and it is seen; the magic performed by the magicians is human, and indeed no one sees it and it cannot be approved.[51] The parting of the Sea of Reeds also took place in full view of the people, as Moses foretold: "...Do not be afraid (תיראו), stand and see (התיצבו וראו) the deliverance that Yahweh will work for you today; for what you have seen (ראיתם) in Egypt today you shall never see again (תוסיפו לראתם)" (Exod 14:13, my translation). Observing the parting of the Red Sea, like seeing the first signs (above, Exod 4:30), had the effect of reinforcing faith: "When Israel saw (וירא) the great power which Yahweh had exercised in Egyptians, the people feared (וייראו) Yahweh, and gained faith (ויאמינו) in Yahweh and in Moses, his servant" (Exod 14:31, my translation). Again, sight has rhetorical as well as historical purpose. Lastly, extracting the water from the rock also took place "in the sight (לעיני) of the elders of Israel" (Exod 17:6), or "before their eyes" (Num 20:8).[52]

50. For these forms and their etymology, see *HALOT*.
51. Cf. the plague of boils, which is performed "in the sight of Pharaoh" and further contrasts Moses and the magicians (Exod 9:8–11).
52. For the possibility that the verse involves speech as magic, see R. Kasher, "Theological Conception of the Miracle in the Bible" (Ph.D. diss., Bar-Ilan University, 1981 [Hebrew]), 204–6. Moses' sin (knocking the rock twice) was performed

We saw how the wonders of the exodus are viewed by a large audience in all pentatuechal traditions. In addition to these miracles, God's revelations are described as proven historical events, because they happened before the eyes of the entire community. This idea is highlighted in several biblical passages across the Pentateuch: "Moses and Aaron entered the tent of meeting, and then came out and blessed the people; and the glory of the Lord appeared (וירא) to all the people (כל־העם). Fire came out from the Lord and consumed the burnt offering and the fat on the altar; and when all the people (כל־העם) saw it (וירא), they shouted and fell on their faces" (Lev 9:23–24). Similarly, "the Lord will come down upon Mt. Sinai in the sight of all the people (לעיני כל־העם)" (Exod 19:11).[53] The completion of the building of Solomon's temple is also described as a public event that took place in the presence of the elders of Israel, all the heads of the tribes, all the men of Israel (1 Kgs 8:1–2), and generally the entire assembly (קהל ישראל, vv. 14 [×2], 22, 55). When the event is told in the book of Chronicles, it is stated explicitly: "When all the people of Israel saw (וכל בני ישראל ראים) the fire come down and the glory of the Lord on the temple, they bowed down on the pavement with their faces to the ground, and worshiped and gave thanks to the Lord, saying, 'For he is good, for his steadfast love endures forever'" (2 Chr 7:3). These descriptions are closely linked to the ones of the revelation in Sinai/Horeb. In fact, there is only one biblical passage that denies that the Israelites saw anything at Horeb:

> Then the Lord spoke to you out of the fire. You heard the sound (שמעים) of words but saw (ראים) no form; there was only a voice… Since you saw (ראיתם) no form when the Lord spoke to you at Horeb out of the fire, take care and watch yourselves closely, so that you do not act corruptly by making an idol for yourselves… (Deut 4:12, 15–16)

These words seem to contrast the prevailing perception that the Israelites saw the revelation in Horeb,[54] particularly because of possible cultic implications. The exception, in this case, emphasizes the rule.

"in front of the eyes" (לעיני) of Israel (Num 8:12; cf. 27:14, לעיניהם); the public nature of the sin is one of the reasons for the severe punishment.

53. Despite the tradition which claims danger in watching a revelation (Deut 18:16; Judg 6:22; 13:22; 1 Sam 6:19), seeing the revelation is essential for the rhetoric of the miracle. Note that in Exod 19, touching is dangerous, not sight. For ways of solving this contradiction, see the following note.

54. For the conceptual shift in these verses, see Carasik, "To See a Sound." Carasik also refers to Deut 5:4: "Face to face the Lord spoke to you on the mountain out of the fire." Note, however, that speaking "face to face" is common in the Hebrew Bible as a description of direct experience, and therefore we cannot find in this verse rejection of sight tradition.

Even when it is clear that Moses alone is privileged to speak to God face-to-face (Exod 33:11), this was seen by all the people (v. 10). This example demonstrates how the rhetoric of proving revelation is identical, that is, visual, whether the claim is that all the people were privileged to the revelation, or whether it is that all the people witnessed the choice of Moses by revelation. Notably, the transference of leadership to a new ruler is also described as a public act in other biblical passages, without miracles necessarily being part of the scene: "So the Lord said to Moses, 'Take Joshua son of Nun, a man in whom is the spirit, and lay your hand upon him; have him stand before Eleazar the priest and all the congregation (כל־העדה), and commission him in their sight (לעיניהם). You shall give him some of your authority,[55] so that all the congregation (כל־עדת) of the Israelites may obey (ישמעו)'" (Num 27:18–20).[56] The aim of the power transfer ceremony described is to establish the status of the new leader. As we see in these verses, the public act that Moses performs of transferring authority includes a symbolic act (lay your hand) and an announcement (commission), both of which are done in public.[57] This example demonstrates the link between the public nature of a legal act and the authentication of miracles. The two are blended in the transfer of authority from Elijah to Elisha, which is not accompanied by any cere-monial procedure, but happens miraculously, and is witnessed by the members of the prophetic guild. The fact that they saw Elisha's act per-suaded them that Elisha was Elijah's successor:

> He took the mantle of Elijah that had fallen from him, and struck the water, saying, "Where is the Lord, the God of Elijah?" When he had struck the water, the water was parted to the one side and to the other, and Elisha went over. When the company of prophets who were at Jericho saw him (ויראהו) at a distance, they declared, "The spirit of Elijah rests on Elisha." They came to meet him and bowed to the ground before him. (2 Kgs 2:14–15)

Also noteworthy are a few other public miracles that are mentioned outside the Pentateuch or the events of the exodus and the wilderness. For example, the miracle of the extended day during the war with the five kings is thus described:

> On the day when the Lord gave the Amorites over to the Israelites, Joshua spoke to the Lord; and he said in the sight (לעיני) of Israel, "Sun, stand still at Gibeon, and moon, in the valley of Aijalon." And the sun stood still,

---

55. Literally "splendor" (הוד), a term mostly referring to God.

56. Cf. Deut 31:7.

57. For the definition of symbolic legal gesture, see Malul, *Mesopotamian Legal Symbolism*, 20–22.

and the moon stopped, until the nation took vengeance on their enemies. Is this not written in the Book of Jashar? The sun stopped in mid-heaven, and did not hurry to set for about a whole day. (Josh 10:12–13)

Note how the first verse authenticates the miracle by the public *view* of the words, while the second one authenticates the miracle by textual reference. When Samuel finishes his criticism for Israelite kingship, he supports his view with a miracle: "Now therefore take your stand and see (התיצבו וראו) this great thing that the Lord will do before your eyes (לעיניכם). Is it not the wheat harvest today? I will call upon the Lord, that he may send thunder and rain…and all the people greatly feared the Lord and Samuel" (1 Sam 12:16–18).[58] Here too the emotional and evidential effects are intertwined. We saw earlier how the imperative "see" (ראה/ראו) denotes a call for attention and witnessing in a legal context. In the above example, this call is associated both with witnessing and with a call for personal impression.

Since the original context of the imperative "see" is the public domain, in which it is ascertained that everyone was aware of the rules ("see [ראו], I have commended you," Josh 8:8),[59] the command to witness a miracle is based on the legal meaning of sight as awareness and responsibility, as well as on the perception of sight as personal experience.[60] This complexity of notions is echoed in many biblical passages commencing with "see!" and which represent a call for awareness, witness, or knowledge. In other biblical passages, the command to see is accompanied by a command associated with physical mobility and posture. Examples of the former include phrases such as "Go and see" (לך וראה), "Come and see" (בוא וראה), "ascend and see" (עלה וראה), "move through and see" (עבר וראה),[61] all of which describe an intentional act of examination and

---

58. Cf. 2 Chr 20:17.

59. This image is used, even though in the case of oath-taking it would have been verbal (aural). There are common imperatives to hear or listen in the Hebrew Bible, ones which reflect the reality of public speech/reading. The opening serves to call the audience; see J. C. de Moor, "The Art of Versification in Ugarit and Israel," *UF* 12 [1980]: 311–15). Hence we find that the call to "see" is a call to witness a specific event.

60. See the similarity between "stand up (התיצבו) and see" (1 Sam 12:16), and "stand (עמד) in council" (Jer 23:18, 22). For more on the associative link between sight and movement, see pp. 77–80, above. For more on movement and sight as tools for acquiring knowledge, see *MKCS*, 140–54.

61. The references here are all imperatives: "see and go" (ראה + לך, Gen 37:14; Josh 2:1; 2 Kgs 6:13; 7:14; 10:16; Ps 66:5); "see and come" (ראה + בוא, Ezek 8:9); "see and ascend" (ראה + עלה, Num 27:12; Deut 3:27); "see and go up" (עלה + נבט, 1 Kgs 18:43); "see and cross over" (ראה + עבר, Amos 6:2).

clarification.[62] Examples of the latter include calls for seeing accompanied by standing, which usually describe an act of recognizing something. In many instances, this refers to the recognition of God's strength, as we saw in 1 Sam 12:16 and Exod 14:13 above.[63] Other passages also highlight sight as this kind of evidence—"Hear this, O Job; stop and consider (עמד והתבונן) the wondrous works of God" (Job 37:14).[64]

The command to witness an event is intended to create proof and memory, whether the event is legal or miraculous. The use of the rhetoric "you have seen with your own eyes" serves to create an unchallenged collective memory that proves that the miracles God performed took place. The events for which the biblical narrator uses the sight metaphor are often unnatural, miraculous events, such as the plagues in Egypt, the parting of the Red Sea, the opening of the ground, the revelation in Horeb, halting the plague, and extracting water from a rock. The miraculous deed is caused by speech, by touch, or by God's strength, but it is sight that proves that they actually happened.[65] This perception of proving miracles is based on using sight metaphors in a range of legal contexts.

All the descriptions of miracles and revelation that we have explored took place in the past. The emphasis on their being seen is proof that they took place. I will close this section by observing that this rhetoric is also used in prophecy, with the emphasis on future miracles and revelation. The proof of God's strength will be demonstrated in his future revelation, which will be seen by many witnesses. The following are some examples from the prophets, ranging through prophets of various times and schools: "As in the days when you came out of the land of Egypt, show us marvellous things. The nations shall see (יראו) and be ashamed of all their might…" (Mic 7:15–16); "I will display my glory among the nations; and all the nations shall see (וראו) my judgment that I have executed, and my hand that I have laid on them…when I have brought them back from the peoples and gathered them from their enemies' lands, and through them have displayed my holiness in the sight (לעיני) of many nations" (Ezek 39:21, 27);[66] "The Lord will bare his holy arm in

62. As well as "see and stand" (ראה + עמד, Jer 6:16); "watch and stand (עמד + צפה, Jer 48:19), which describe concrete examination.

63. Cf. 2 Chr 20:17.

64. For the root בין and sight, see Chapter 2, n. 23.

65. In the entire Hebrew Bible, there are only two cases of a miracle being performed without an audience: Elisha's miracle of oil (2 Kgs 4:4, 33), and the resuscitation of the child by Elijah (1 Kgs 17:19); see Kasher, "Theological Conception," 181–82.

66. Cf. Ezek 20:41; 28:25.

the sight (לעיני) of all the nations, and the very ends of earth shall see (וראו) the victory of our God" (Isa 52:10, JPS).[67] Notably, not only will the nations observe the revelation, but the forces of nature themselves will observe it, an idea which repeats also outside the prophetic corpus: "His lightnings light up the world; the earth sees (ראתה) and trembles. The mountains melt like wax before (מלפני) the Lord, before the Lord of all the earth. The heavens proclaim his righteousness; and all the peoples behold (וראו) his glory" (Ps 97:4–6). Ancient cultural knowledge regarding the centrality of sight in the juridical system, and the frequent use of sight vocabulary to indicate witness and the creation of collective memory, also form the background to these prophecies and psalms. These sight associations are intimately linked to the perception that sight means first-hand learning and knowledge, as will be expanded on below.

Sight and Sovereignty

Sight as First-Hand Knowledge

Through different levels of biblical perception, we have seen that the importance of seeing an event is an essential condition for proving that it took place. This is especially relevant in legal and historical contexts, as an expression of the public nature and involvement in the juridical process. This idea is linked to a perception that sight (as opposed to hearing) is a form of first-hand learning. That is, the perception of sight as a personal experience and involvement recurs as the basis for descriptions of justice and for descriptions of learning. In this section I will demonstrate how the use of sight metaphors to describe involvement in or being present at a non-legal event reinforces the semantic centrality of sight in biblical perception, to the extent that sight is used to describe life itself.

The correlation between sight and thought in biblical perception is so self-evident that we do not need to expand on it.[68] The correlation between the roots "to see" (ראה) and "to know" (ידע) that recurs in several contexts is especially prevalent. God's knowledge as well as his rule are described as sight: "God looked upon (וירא) the Israelites, and God took notice (וידע) of them" (Exod 2:25); "High though the Lord is, he sees (יראה) the lowly; lofty, he perceives (יידע) from afar" (Ps 138:6, JPS). Lack of understanding is also described as a problem of sight: "They do not know (ידעו), nor do they comprehend (יבינו); for their eyes

---

67. Cf. Isa 40:5; 62:2.

68. See also H.-F. Fuhs, "רָאָה *rā'âh*; רֹאֶה *rō'eh* I and II; רְאִי *re'î*; רְאוּת *reût*; מַרְאֶה *mareh*; מַרְאָה *mar'â*," *TDOT* 13:208–42 (213–16); *HALOT* 3:1157–58, and 2:3:3.

are shut, so that they cannot see (טחו מראות עיניהם), and their minds as well, so that they cannot understand" (Isa 44:18). This verse demonstrates how the associative pattern sight–knowledge is also absorbed in the eye–heart word pair.[69] This associative pattern is also reflected in the perception whereby what is unseen is also unknown: "Ha! You who hide a plan too deep for the Lord, whose deeds are in the dark, and who say, 'Who sees us (ראנו)? Who knows us (יודענו)?'" (Isa 29:15). The parallel between "to know" and "to see" is clearly not limited to information, but is also used to indicate comprehension, understanding, and learning. We also see these two roots used to describe legal affiliation: "...who said of his father and mother, 'I regard them not (לא ראיתיו)'; he ignored (לא הכיר) his kin, and did not acknowledge (לא ידע) his children..." (Deut 33:9).[70] In short, the association between sight and knowledge is more complex than the correlation between knowledge and other senses. Michael Carasik puts it thus: "We argued from the text of the Bible, too, that (with the extremely rare exception of taste) sight was the only sense used in biblical Hebrew as a metaphor for thinking."[71] Carasik distinguishes between learning/knowledge—actions that are also described using the other senses—and thought, which is described solely through the sense of sight.

This semantic correlation between sight and thought is based on a perception whereby sight is first-hand learning, and is based on personal experience. The following verse, which we cited earlier, is a good example: "Remember today that it was not your children (who have not known [ידעו] or seen [ראו] the discipline of the Lord your God)...for it is your own eyes that have seen [עיניכם הראות] every great deed that the Lord did" (Deut 11:2, 7). These verses (among others) distinguish between someone who has seen, and therefore knows; and someone who has not seen, and therefore does not know. In other passages in Deuteronomy, we see how future generations who did not witness the miracles themselves will learn about them through hearing:

> But take care and watch yourselves closely, so as neither to forget the things that your eyes have seen (ראו עיניך) nor to let them slip from your mind (לבבך) all the days of your life; make them known (והודעתם) to your children and your children's children—how you once stood before the Lord your God at Horeb, when the Lord said to me, "Assemble the

---

69. See also Watson, "Unnoticed Word Pair," as well as Chapter 3, n. 84.

70. For the legal background of the phrases, *MKCS*, 224. For similar legal meaning embedded in the terms "to acknowledge" (נכר Hiphil) and "good in the eyes of" (טוב בעיני); see Malul, "Law in the Narratives."

71. Carasik, *Theologies of the Mind*, 219.

people for me, and I will let them hear (ואשמעם) my words, so that they
may learn (ילמדון) to fear me as long as they live on the earth, and may
teach (ילמדון) their children so." (Deut 4:9–10)

In these verses the authenticity of the revelation in Horeb is affirmed,
and at the same the nature of information able to be transferred to the
following generations is specified: it is possible to transfer the things
heard, but transferring the personal experience is not required. The
learning schematic that emerges from these verses is as follows: sight →
persuasion → speech → hearing → learning. This process of creating
and passing on knowledge, in this case the knowledge of God, appears in
other biblical passages:

> For I know their works and their thoughts, and I am coming to gather all
> nations and tongues; and they shall come and shall see (ראו) my glory,
> and I will set a sign among them. From them I will send survivors to the
> nations, to Tarshish, Put, and Lud—which draw the bow—to Tubal and
> Javan, to the coastlands far away that have not heard of my fame
> (שמעו את־שמעי) or seen (ראו) my glory; and they shall declare (והגידו) my
> glory among the nations. (Isa 66:18–19)

Apart from the theological load inherent in these verses, there is also a
reflection of the perception of how knowledge is created: through
personal experience (= sight) being passed on (= speech). This explains
the widespread use of hearing metaphors to describe learning. The gap
between sight and hearing is further demonstrated in the book of
Proverbs. The call to listen to instruction is presented as a call to learn
the rules of wise behaviour: "Listen (שמעו), children, to a father's instruction, and be attentive (הקשיבו), that you may gain insight" (Prov 4:1).[72]
To see, on the other hand, is described as learning based on personal
experience: "I observed (אחזה) and took it to heart; I saw it (ראיתי) and
learned a lesson" (Prov 24:32).[73] So, if we accurately map the differences
between sight and hearing within the semantic field of knowledge, sight
means investigation and clarification, while hearing means learning.[74] As

---

72. Cf. Prov 19:26, 27 and many more.

73. Cf. Deut 11:2. For more on sight and hearing in the book of Proverbs, see
Carasik, *Theologies of the Mind*, 139–75.

74. The difference between Qohelet and Proverbs must be noted. Qohelet stressed
the personal process of learning and inquiry, mostly through the root "to see" (ראה).
In total, the root appears 51 times in the book, whereas it appears only ten times in
Proverbs. In the book of Proverbs, the process of transmission is the important one, a
process which is described through the root "to hear," "to obey" (שמע). This root
appears 34 times in Proverbs, and only eight in Qohelet. These statistics are just a
hint towards a possible inquiry of these books through the sensory prism.

I have already indicated, the perception of sight as first-hand learning is closely linked to the perception of sight as experience. When Qohelet opens his book, it is clear that he aims to share his own experience, rather than received tradition, with his audience: "I said to myself [...דברתי עם לבי], 'I [אני] have acquired great wisdom, surpassing all who were over Jerusalem before me; and my mind (לבי) has had great experience (lit. 'saw,' ראה) of wisdom and knowledge'" (Qoh 1:16).

Sight as Emotional Experience

There is widespread use of sight vocabulary as a metaphor for different shades of knowledge, as has been explored in previous studies. However, the metaphor of sight as experience, particularly emotional experience, is less discussed. As mentioned above, Menachem Kaddari demonstrates how the expression "to see at" (ראה ב) is used to describe an emotional experience caused by sight, indicating involvement in a particular event. For example, when Hagar despaired in the desert of Beer-Sheba, "she went and sat down opposite him a good way off, about the distance of a bowshot; for she said, 'Do not let me look on (אל־אראה ב) the death of the child.' And as she sat opposite him, she lifted up her voice and wept" (Gen 21:16). Hagar could not watch the event because of the suffering caused by witnessing it.[75] Similarly, God promises, through Hulda the prophet, that King Josiah will not have to experience the suffering of watching the disaster unfold: "Therefore, I will gather you to your ancestors, and you shall be gathered to your grave in peace; your eyes shall not see (ולא־תראינה עיניך ב) all the disaster that I will bring on this place..." (2 Kgs 22:20).[76] King Zedekiah, on the other hand, is punished by having to witness the disaster himself: "The king of Babylon killed the sons of Zedekiah before his eyes (לעיניו), and also killed all the officers of Judah at Riblah. He put out the eyes of Zedekiah (ואת־עיני צדקיהו עור), and bound him in fetters, and the king of Babylon took him to Babylon, and put him in prison until the day of his death" (Jer 52:10–11). Zedekiah in fact receives a triple punishment: he witnesses these difficult events, they are the last things he sees, and he is blinded.[77] Isaiah issues a similar dark threat, in his description of the catastrophe: "Their infants will be dashed to pieces before their eyes (לעיניהם); their houses will be plundered, and their wives ravished" (Isa 13:16). Here too we find a double threat: the events themselves, and having to watch them. One of the curses in

---

75. Kaddari, "What is the Difference?," 72. Cf. Gen 44:34; Num 11:15; Isa 33:15; Esth 8:6.

76. Cf. 2 Chr 34:28.

77. For blindness and gouging out of eyes as punishment, see pp. 196–98, above.

Deuteronomy demonstrates how difficult it is to experience terrible events by watching them: "Your sons and daughters shall be given to another people, while your eyes look on (ועיניך ראות), and strain (וכלות) for them all day but you will be helpless" (Deut 28:32, my translation). Witnessing children being taken captive is described as part of the punishment, and demonstrates how powerful this negative experience was.[78] The verb "to strain" (כלה) used as the second action of the noun "your eyes" (עיניך) usually describes eyes that are tired from weeping.[79] As clear from the examples above, the description of experience as sight is not limited to the phrase "to see at" (ראה ב). The power of personal experience is also described in other sight-related words, such as (ראה עין), "in front of the eyes" (לעיני), and "seeing eyes" (עינים ראות).[80]

The use of these sight expressions of punishment as an observed experience differ from descriptions of the public nature of the punishment, which also use sight metaphors. They imply emotional influence on top of the evidence caused by sight. Further examples will clarify: "Thus said the Lord: 'I will make a calamity rise against you from within your own house; I will take your wives and give them to another man before your very eyes (לעיניך) and he shall sleep with your wives under this very sun (לעיני השמש)'" (2 Sam 12:11, JPS); "...So they pitched a tent for Absalom upon the roof; and Absalom went in to his father's concubines in the sight of all Israel (לעיני כל-ישראל)" (16:22).[81] The description of Absalom's acts uses several sight nuances. The first, "before your eyes" (לעיניך), describes David's helplessness to act; "before the eyes of the sun" (לעיני השמש), means it will happen in broad daylight, that is, it will be open and known; "before the eyes of all Israel" (לעיני כל-ישראל) indicates the public nature of the deed. The public nature of the event holds two implications: the first, a legal implication—the whole of Israel knows that Absalom is the new king; the second, an experiential-emotional meaning—the public nature of the punishment makes the experience of the punishment even more extreme, and also magnifies the degree of shame that accompanies it.[82] That means that the

---

78. The contrast between sight and inability is further stressed here. The phrase אין לאל ידך in this verse represents lack of legal authority (Malul, *Society, Law, and Custom*, 170). It seems, therefore (and in light of pp. 232–38, above), that the principle of legal/social responsibility is reflected here again. Those who see the events are obliged to act in the legal sphere, but have no authority to do so.

79. See Lam 2:11: "my eyes waste away (כלו) with tears" (see Collins, "Physiology of Tears").

80. See also Jer 20:40 (ועיניך ראות); 29:21 (לעיניכם).

81. Cf. pp. 258–63, below.

82. For shame and publicity, see my "Honour and Shame."

legal and emotional connotations are not mutually exclusive, and both can be expressed using sight metaphors. Another example, from a quite different context, is the following description from the mouth of Moses: "So I took hold of the two tablets and flung them from my two hands, smashing them before your eyes (לעיניכם)" (Deut 9:17). The legal significance of smashing the tablets is that the covenant is cancelled, which is given further emphasis by the public nature of the deed. But it must also be recognized that witnessing this was an immediate experience. Smashing the tablets is therefore portrayed as a kind of punishment, which was experienced through sight.

Earlier we saw that personally experiencing a catastrophe (through sight) appears as a punishment or the threat of a punishment. A similar threat also drives the experience and involvement in positive events, and this drive is also described through sight metaphors. We see this in Jeremiah's threat to Shemaiah the Nehelamite: "…I am going to punish Shemaiah of Nehelam and his descendants; he shall not have anyone living among this people to see the good (ולא־יראה בטוב) that I am going to do to my people, says the Lord, for he has spoken rebellion against the Lord" (Jer 29:32). This verse shows us that not all sight leads to distress and pain. Sight is thus a neutral emotional tool, and it is the scene being witnessed that determines the response. Isaiah's prophecies also contain sight as a positive experience leading to joy: "Listen! Your watchmen lift up their voices; together they shout for joy. When the Lord returns to Zion, they will see it with their own eyes (עין בעין יראו)" (Isa 52:8).[83] In these passages, sight signifies experience and involvement, based on the perception that sight constitutes first-hand knowledge. Moreover, in the last cited verse, the intimacy of sight is highlighted in the expression עין בעין, which in other passages signifies an intimate encounter: "And you will not escape from his hand, indeed you will be captured and handed over to him; your eyes will see the eyes of the king of Babylon (עיניך את־עיני...תראינה) and his mouth will speak with your mouth; and you will go to Babylon" (Jer 34:3, my translation).[84] Speaking and seeing are a hallmark of personal and intimate encounter, and define the communication between Moses and God: "With him I speak mouth to mouth, plainly and not in riddles, and he beholds the likeness of the Lord (תמנת...יביט)…" (Num 12:8, JPS).

Another matter is involved in the complexity of derived meanings of sight vocabulary. Alongside personal experience, knowledge, empathy,

---

83. Kaddari, "What is the Difference?," 71, and further on sight as idiom for malicious joy.
84. Cf. Jer 32:4.

and involvement, descriptions of divine help frequently use the language of sight:[85] "Leah conceived and bore a son, and she named him Reuben (ראובן); for she said, 'Because the Lord has looked on (ראה ב) my affliction; surely now my husband will love me'" (Gen 29:32); "She [Hannah] made this vow: 'O Lord of hosts, if only you will look on (ראה תראה ב) the misery of your servant, and remember me, and not forget your servant, but will give to your servant a male child, then I will set him before you as a nazirite until the day of his death. He shall drink neither wine nor intoxicants, and no razor shall touch his head'" (1 Sam 1:11).[86] In both stories, God's sight refers not only to seeing or empathizing, but also to actual help. Importantly, divine help too, which is based on understanding and empathy, is not portrayed solely with the use of the phrase ראה ב. In other biblical passages, the same meaning is expressed using the phrase ראה את (e.g. "the Lord...saw [וירא את] our affliction," Deut 26:7)[87] or using the verb ראה ("to see").[88] The correlation between sight as empathy and sight as personal presence can be summarized through the words of the Ezekiel: "Mortal, have you seen (הראית) what the elders of the house of Israel are doing in the dark, each in his room of images? For they say, 'The Lord does not see (ראה) us, the Lord has forsaken the land'" (Ezek 8:12).[89] All in all, it seems that the strict distinction purposed by Kaddari, namely, that the phrase ראה ב means emotional experience or empathy, and that the phrase ראה את denotes cognitive experience or perception, cannot stand. Both meanings are found across phrases, and are based on the perception of sight as first-hand learning and as involvement. Both phrases are used to express an emotional experience, and perhaps the absence of distinction between cognitive and emotional experience in these phrases should teach us about lack of such distinction in biblical times.[90] As neither phrase is unique to any of these experiences,[91] this latter metaphor—sight is

85. Cf. pp. 130–40, above.

86. Kaddari, "What is the Difference?," 73. Cf. Exod 2:11; Ps 106:44.

87. Cf. Pss 9:14; 31:8; 119:153.

88. E.g. Isa 58:3; Dan 9:18.

89. The image for God, who refrains from sight, and therefore does not understand/help, repeats in a few places, including Ps 10:11; "They think in their heart, 'God has forgotten, he has hidden his face, he will never see it'" (NRSV); and Job 10:4: "Do you have eyes of flesh? Do you see as humans see?" (NRSV). The link between sight and life and blindness and death, which will be demonstrated below, might raise sombre theological questions; these, however, will not be dealt with in the present study.

90. This distinction is based on the mind vs. body supposition, see pp. 5–22, above.

91. Kaddari, "What is the Difference?," 68–70.

empathy—joins the spectrum of sight meanings identified earlier, such as first-hand learning, and sight as involvement and experience. This totality represents the background to the sight–light metaphor as a symbol of life that we will examine in the next section.

Sight as Life

Sight metaphors of experience and involvement are used in descriptions of seeing descendants as symbolizing long life and social involvement. Just as sight signifies curses or punishments in the examples above, sight signifies the blessing of long life and of having many descendants. See, for example, Joseph's old age: "Joseph saw (וירא) Ephraim's children of the third generation; the children of Machir son of Manasseh were also born on Joseph's knees" (Gen 50:23). This verse describes the length of Joseph's life, and his involvement in family life. This metaphor is so rooted in biblical language that even the blind Jacob uses it: "Now the eyes of Israel were dim (עיני...כבדו) with age, and he could not see (לראות). So Joseph brought them near him; and he kissed them and embraced them. Israel said to Joseph, 'I did not expect to see (ראה) your face; and here God has let me see (הראה) your children also'" (Gen 48:10–11). Even though Jacob cannot see his grandchildren, he uses this expression to highlight the fact that he was privileged to meet them, to know them, to be present in their company, and above all, to live a long life that enabled him to "see" his descendants. Job's long life is described in a similar manner: "After this Job lived one hundred and forty years, and saw (וירא) his children, and his children's children, four generations" (Job 42:16). The theme of seeing children also appears as a general blessing: "The Lord bless you from Zion. May you see (ראה) the prosperity of Jerusalem all the days of your life. May you see (וראה) your children's children. Peace be upon Israel!" (Ps 128:5–6).[92] The parallel between sight and life can also be used to achieve the opposite effect. In Numbers, we find Moses weighed down under the avalanche of the people's complaints: "If this is the way you are going to treat me, put me to death at once—if I have found favour in your sight—and do not let me see (אראה) my misery" (Num 11:15). Moses contrasts his suffering, which is portrayed in this passage as seeing trouble, to death.[93] Once again, sight is used as a metaphor for life, whether with a positive or a negative connotation.

---

92. Other blessings in the psalm talk about eating one's own produce, a typical blessing which points to the importance of the "sovereignty of action" (see pp. 181–82, above).

93. In other texts, death is a metaphor for liminality; see *MKCS*, 464.

Usually, expressing a wish that someone will see good things is parallel to a long life: "Whoever of you loves life and desires to see many good days (לראות טוב)" (Ps 3:13, NIV).[94] Job describes his suffering in a similar way: "Remember, O God, that my life is but a breath; my eyes will never see happiness again" (עיני לראות טוב) (Job 7:7, NIV). By complaining that his life is passing like a breath and that his sight is failing, Job makes the comparison between old age and death. This is supported by another passage from Job: "My days are swifter than a runner; they flee away, they see no good" (לא־ראו טובה) (Job 9:25).[95] Clearly, just as sight symbolizes life and long life, so blindness symbolizes old age and death.[96]

Two other biblical passages highlight the uniqueness of being able to see in old age, and the associated meanings of clear thought and independence: "Moses was one hundred and twenty years old when he died; his sight was unimpaired (לא־כהתה עינו) and his vigor had not abated" (Deut 34:7). This verse highlights Moses' uniqueness—even at such an old age, he was able to lead the people.[97] A similar almost cursory claim is made about David, in the context of Solomon's anointment. After hearing about the anointment, David proclaims: "Praised be the Lord, the God of Israel who has this day provided a successor to my throne, while my own eyes can see it (ועיני ראות)" (1 Kgs 1:48).[98] David is giving thanks for his fitness despite his age. He is giving thanks for being alive at the anointment of his son, and for the fact that his son's anointment is taking place with his knowledge and in his presence. There is a dual similarity between David's words and Jacob's words in Gen 48:10–11. Jacob is blind, and David is speaking from his bed (1 Kgs 1:47). The expression "and my eyes see" does not always signify an actual physical state, but is a metaphor for presence and clearness of mind.[99] The other

---

94. Cf. Qoh 3:13; 5:17.

95. For such interpretation, see Tur-Sinai, *The Book of Job*, 169, as well as his reference to Job 7:7 in p. 138. Tur-Sinai connects the expression לראות טוב to the Arabic root طيب (cognate of טוב), meaning "to live." Note, however, that in Arabic too this meaning derives from the general meaning "good," "proper," and therefore could have had a similar semantic shift.

96. Another link between blindness and old age, see pp. 203–5, above.

97. For the meaning of לא נס לחו, see Chapter 4, n. 48.

98. Note the translation to ועיני ראות, "while I am still alive to see it" (NEB).

99. Note the contrast between Moses having his strength and sight (Deut 34:7) and Moses no longer being able to get about (לצאת ולבוא, Deut 31:2). It seems that seeing offspring is a literary convention of describing the blessing of old age (cf. Ps 128:6; Job 42:16). For extra-biblical sources, see Tawil, "Some Literary Elements."

similarity is that both David and Jacob use the expression "and my eyes see" to provide a legal stamp for the blessing they are giving their descendants. That is, the situation could be interpreted as a deathbed statement. I suggest, therefore, that the phrase ועיני ראות can signify legal fitness, and not only experience or old age.

The frequent examples where blindness is correlated with old age, including the exceptional circumstances where people can see despite their old age, further demonstrate the centrality of sight in biblical perception. Although other senses can also become damaged in old age,[100] the main damage to one's abilities is loss of sight. Even when the loss of an ability is unconnected to old age, it is described as a loss of sight: "My heart throbs, my strength fails me; as for the light of my eyes (אור עיני)—it also has gone from me" (Ps 38:11). In this verse, sight is the light of the eyes, which is a fine example of the correlation between sight and light. This is particularly evident in verses that contrast sight with darkness, and blindness with light: "The wise have eyes in their head, but fools walk in darkness (בחשך)" (Qoh 2:14); "On that day the deaf shall hear the words of a scroll, and out of their gloom and darkness (מאפל ומחשך) the eyes of the blind shall see (עיני...תראינה)" (Isa 29:18).[101] The light of the eyes can also describe a positive experience in general: "The light of the eyes (מאור עינים) rejoices the heart, and good news refreshes the body" (Prov 15:30).[102]

Qohelet too uses adjectives like "good" (טוב) and "sweet" (מתוק) to describe enjoyment of the light/life: "Light is sweet (מתוק האור), and it is pleasant for the eyes (וטוב לעינים) to see (לראות) the sun" (Qoh 11:7). This verse also indicates the correlation between sight, light, and life, and like so many other verses in Qohelet, portrays life and death as a contrast between light and dark.[103] This contrast appears in the next verse: "Even those who live many years should rejoice in them all; yet let them remember that the days of darkness (ימי החשך) will be many. All that comes is vanity" (Qoh 1.8). Sight and light symbolize experiencing life to the full.[104] Seeing the light is also a metaphor for life as explicitly

100. Such as hearing, movement, and so on. See pp. 203–5, above.
101. Cf. Isa 42:7.
102. Cf. Ps 19:9; Ezra 9:8.
103. R. Gordis, *Koheleth: The Man and His World* (Texts and Studies of the Jewish Theological Seminary of America 19; New York: Jewish Theological Seminary of America, 1951), 324–25. Gordis refers to similar expressions in Greek literature (*Iphigeneia at Aulis* 1.1219, by Euripides; cf. C. Classen, D. Howes, and A. Synnott, eds., *Aroma: The Cultural History of Smell* [London: Routledge, 1994], 9), and in Mesopotamian literature (*Gilgamesh* 11.73).
104. Cf. the phrase "to see life" (Qoh 9:9).

expressed by the psalmist: "For with you is the fountain of life; in your light we see light (באורך נראה־אור)" (Ps 36:10).[105] The same sentiment of seeing the light can also be used in a negative connotation: "Or why was I not buried like a stillborn infant, like infants who have never seen the light (לא ראו אור)'" (Job 3:16). According to Job, the transition of the infant into the land of the living means seeing the light. In Isaiah, the transition of the dead into the land of the living is similarly described: "The people who walked in darkness (בחשך) have seen a great light (ראו אור); those who lived in a land of deep darkness (צלמות)—on them light (אור) has shined" (Isa 9:1). Light is thus associated not just with long life, or life as experiencing and involvement with the world, but it also describes life itself. Life begins with light and ends with darkness, sight is living, and the gradual loss of sight in old age is a sign of the approach of death.[106]

Sight as Subjective Opinion

We have seen several examples where sight expressions in the Hebrew Bible are associated with a perception of sight as experience and knowledge based on personal involvement. The term "in the eyes of" (בעיני) reflects—and even sharpens—this perception. All our examples to date have been of sight representing learning based on investigation and examination, as opposed to rote learning. The following examples show how sight can also symbolize personal or subjective opinion—that is, knowledge that is not shared by everyone. Scholars have offered different definitions for the phrase בעיני. Michael Carasik, who claims that sight is the only sense in the Hebrew Bible used as a metaphor for thought, interprets the expression as meaning "in so and so's opinion, as

---

105.   Cf. Ps 49:20. The image of God as the source of light appears in the legal context as well: "I must bear the anger of the Lord, since I have sinned against him, until he champions my cause and upholds my claim. He will let me out into the light (יוציאני לאור); I will enjoy (אראה) vindication by him" (Mic 7:9, JPS). The phrase "bring into light" (יצא לאור + Hiphil) in its legal contexts refers to: (1) releasing from prison (cf. "Opening eyes deprived of light, rescuing prisoners from confinement, from the dungeon those who sit in darkness," Isa 42:7, JPS); (2) to sentence the accused to life; or (3) to make judgment in daylight, during morning time (M. Malul, private communication). Cf. also Shamash as the symbol of judgment and justice in Mesopotamia.

106.   For more on sight and light, and a possible etymological link, see Palache, *Semantic Notes*, 68–69. Moreover, Palache finds the meaning of light in the root נבט (p. 45). See also the semantic field of blooming and prosperity, including the root ציץ, which is related to "being seen" (p. 62). See a full discussion of the matter in *MKCS*, 115–17.

far as so and so is concerned."[107] This is indirectly supported by Eliezer Rubinstein, who interprets the term "in front of" (לִפְנֵי), as indicating thought, mainly in evaluation contexts: "If it pleases the king, and if I have found favour from him (לְפָנָיו), and if I am pleasant in the king's sight (בְּעֵינָיו)..." (Esth 8:5, my translation).[108] In this verse, the term לִפְנֵי signifies "the king's discretion." Rubinstein cites other examples where the expression "in the eyes of" (בְּעֵינֵי) replaces לִפְנֵי and holds the very same meaning: "The Lord said to Joshua, 'This day I will begin to exalt you in the sight (בְּעֵינֵי) of all Israel...'" (Josh 3:7). Rubinstein interprets this verse as: "All of Israel will think that you are great."[109] The expression "in the eyes of" denotes not just thought but judgment. Based on this study, Yitzhak Zedaka analysed the expression "to find favour in the eyes of."[110] According to Meir Malul, the term "good in the eyes" (טוֹב בְּעֵינֵי) refers to agreement in a legal sense. The basic meaning of the expression is satisfaction and agreement.[111] Stendebach also examines various expressions that include the phrase "in the eyes of," and concludes that they indicate the personal aspect of sight.[112] All these studies support the notion that "in the eyes of" expresses opinion, including personal opinion. Below, I will demonstrate how the context in which the term appears often indicates the existence of an opinion that is personal, subjective, and unconventional. We have already discussed "found favour in the eyes of" or "good in the eyes of." The common expression "did evil in the eyes of God" requires more in-depth analysis, and will not feature in this discussion.

From the different uses of the term "in the eyes of" (בְּעֵינֵי) it is clear that in the Hebrew Bible too not everyone perceives factual, objective reality in the same way: "So Jacob served seven years for Rachel, and

---

107. Carasik, *Theologies of the Mind*, 219.

108. The marked part is given as an example in Rubinstein, "*lipneēy* + NP," 60–61, and is compared to Num 24:2; Deut 24:12; Neh 2:6, and others.

109. See Rubinstein, "*lipnēy* + NP," 62, and compare 1 Sam 21:14 and other verses.

110. Zedaka, "And Noah Found Favor." According to Zedaka, the term בְּעֵינֵי has no meaning of judgment in this case, but of action. The verse "And Noah found favor in the eyes of Yahweh" (Gen 6:8, my translation) is explained by Zedaka in the following way: "The phrase represents Yahweh himself... The meaning of the sentence is: Noah got grace and favor from Yahweh, and not—according to Yahweh's discretion" (113).

111. Malul, "Law in the Narratives," 30–32. According to Malul (see n. 43), only some of the occurrences of the phrase have legal meaning: Gen 34:18; Josh 22:30; 1 Sam 29:6–9; 2 Sam 3:36; 1 Kgs 21:2; Jer 40:4.

112. Stendebach, *TDOT* 11:37–38.

they seemed to him (בעיניו) but a few days because of the love he had for her" (Gen 29:20). In this verse, the phrase is used to demonstrate how different was Jacob's experience in comparison to reality. Objectively, he worked for seven years; subjectively, these seven years passed like just a few days. Similarly, the psalmist compares human time and the divine experience of time: "For a thousand years in your sight (בעיניך) are like yesterday when it is past, or like a watch in the night" (Ps 90:4). Here too, the phrase "in the eyes of" is used to describe personal experience of time. From Job, we also see how a personal opinion can sometimes contradict reality: the guests in my house have forgotten me; my serving girls count me as a stranger; I have become an alien in their eyes (בעיניהם)" (Job 19:15).[113] Job points to the absurdity of his situation, where members of his household (the objective reality) treat him (with their eyes) as a stranger (the subjective reality.) The term "in the eyes of" also highlights the relativity of how reality is perceived. Note the description of the twelve spies: "There we saw the Nephilim (the Anakites come from the Nephilim); and to ourselves (בעינינו) we seemed like grasshoppers, and so we seemed to them (בעיניהם)" (Num 13:33). The reports of the spies do not describe absolute facts. They describe facts that were experienced relatively. We see the same phenomenon in the words of Achish to David:

> Then Achish called David and said to him, "As the LORD lives, you have been honest, and to me it seems right (וטוב בעיני) that you should march out and in with me in the campaign; for I have found nothing wrong in you from the day of your coming to me until today. Nevertheless the lords do not approve of you (בעיני...לא טוב). So go back now; and go peaceably; do nothing to displease the lords of the Philistines." (1 Sam 29:6–7)

The term phrase "in the eyes of" can sometimes mean more than just a personal opinion. It can also signify a minority opinion, or even an opinion that is fundamentally mistaken. Job's companions do not agree with him, but they have given up trying to argue with him: "So these three men ceased to answer Job, because he was righteous in his own eyes (בעיניו)" (Job 32:1). The underlying assumption of this verse is that while Job may have been righteous in his own eyes, he was not righteous in the eyes of his companions. Job's companions are not convinced, and they have a different opinion. The use of the expression "in his eyes" to describe Job in this verse clearly indicates that his was just one opinion—the minority opinion. This is not the only biblical passage where "in the eyes of" is used to describe an opinion that the speaker regards as

---

113. Cf. Job 11:4; 18:3.

not matching the truth: "Ah, you who call evil good and good evil, who put darkness for light and light for darkness, who put bitter for sweet and sweet for bitter! Ah, you who are wise in your own eyes (עיניהם), and shrewd in your own sight (פניהם)!" (Isa 5:20–21). These verses make it clear that Isaiah believes that anyone who displays such faulty discernment and judgment is not wise at all. They are only wise in their own personal opinion. Proverbs provides us with a similar sentiment: "The way of a fool is right in his own eyes (בעיניו); but the wise man accepts advice" (Prov 12:15).[114]

The term "in the eyes of" recurs several times elsewhere to signify that the speaker perceives of the described opinion as mistaken: "the princes of the Ammonites said to their lord Hanun, 'Is David is honouring your father in your sight (בעיניך) just because he has sent messengers with condolences to you? Has not David sent his envoys to you to search the city, to spy it out, and to overthrow it?'" (2 Sam 10:3, my translation; cf. 1 Chr 19:3). The princes use the term "in your eyes" to indicate that Hanun has a different (and in their view mistaken) opinion. This term is used to describe the question posed previously,[115] presenting it as Hanun's personal opinion, which does not match the opinion of the ministers. Joab's rebuke to David uses the expression "in your eyes" in the same way, when reproaching David for the mourn of Absalom:

> Today you have covered with shame the faces of all your officers who have saved your life today, and the lives of your sons and your daughters, and the lives of your wives and your concubines, for love of those who hate you and for hatred of those who love you. You have made it clear today that commanders and officers are nothing to you; for I perceive that if Absalom were alive and all of us were dead today, then it would be right in your sight (ישר בעיניך). (2 Sam 19:7)[116]

The term "right in the eyes of" can be understood in a multitude of ways. The literal meaning is that if Absalom was alive and everyone else dead today, David would have been pleased or satisfied (so most translations). Compare this to what is written about Hiram: "But when Hiram came from Tyre to see the cities that Solomon had given him, they did not please him (לא ישרו בעיניו)" (1 Kgs 9:12).[117] But if we analyse the phrase

---

114. Cf. Prov 3:7; 16:2; 17:8; 21:2; 26:5, 12, 16; 28:11; 30:12.

115. Cf. ודאי, אולי. See Zedaka, "And Noah Found Favor," 123.

116. The final words of verse are my own translation.

117. The phrase "upright for the eyes" (ישר בעיני) parallels the phrase "good in the eyes" (טוב בעיני), and denotes contentment and agreement (Malul, "Law in the Narratives," 31; Y. Muffs, *Love and Joy: Law, Language and Religion in Ancient*

closely, Joab was in fact claiming that the hypothetical situation that he is describing is straight, correct, ethical—in David's opinion. At the start of his words, Joab already hints that David's judgment is suspect, and that his opinion is unreasonable. "Right in your eyes" could therefore mean "right in your eyes only." In this context, it is worth examining the term "each man doing what is right in his eyes," which explicitly expresses unseemly behaviour: "Ye shall not do after all the things that we do here this day, every man whatsoever is right in his own eyes (כל־הישר בעיניו)" (Deut 12:8, KJV).[118]

I have demonstrated how the phrase "in the eyes of" (בעיני) refers to a personal and subjective opinion. This can sometimes even mean an opinion that does not match the truth, or contravenes the rules. Although the phrase does not always denote a wrong opinion, it always describes a subjective perception of reality. The wide spectrum of meanings inherent in the phrase is reflected in this last example:

> He [Abraham] went in to Hagar, and she conceived; and when she saw that she had conceived, her mistress became as nothing in her sight (בעיניה). Then Sarai said to Abram, "May the wrong done to me be on you! I gave my maid into your bosom, and once she saw that she had conceived, I became as nothing in her sight (בעיניה). May Yahweh judge between me and you!" But Abram said to Sarai, "Lo, your maiden is in your hand; do to her what is right in your ryes (הטוב בעיניך)." Then Sarai treated her harshly and she ran away from her. (Gen 16:4–6, my translation)

Hagar's attitude, which is condemned by Sarai, breaks society's rules, and is based on Hagar's personal opinion. Abram permits Sarai to use her own personal opinion when deciding how to treat Hagar, that is, according to what "is good in her eyes."[119] The meaning of "in the eyes of" as a personal opinion is demonstrated in a context where this opinion is presented as subjective or mistaken. The common phrase "good in the eyes of" and "evil in the eyes of" are based on the very same metaphor of judgmental perception of reality, relative perception of reality, and subjective statement of reality.

Israel [New York: Jewish Theological Seminary of America, 1992], 178–79). For more on the parallel ישר‖טוב, see Josh 9:25: "And now we are in your hand: do as it seems good (טוב) and right (ישר) in your sight (בעיניך) to do to us."

118. Cf. Judg 17:6; 21:25.

119. Cf. Gen 19:8; Judg 19:24, where the phrase כטוב בעינכם is clearly marking non-normative behaviour.

Supreme Sight

Until now, I have looked at sight imagery which indicates the centrality of sight in descriptions of thought and emotional processes, and as a marker of the sovereign individual. In addition, there is incidental preference for sight over other senses, reflected in three horizons to be briefly presented below: the preference for sight-based evidence, the parallel between blindness and madness, and supernatural experience. As briefly discussed above, the precedence of sight in the epistemic process implies a preference for sight-based evidence: "Look (ראו) at the nations, and see (הביטו)! Be astonished! Be astounded! For a work is being done in your days that you would not believe if you were told" (Hab 1:5). This verse opens its description of the terrible deeds of the Chaldeans with the imperative "Look." As we saw earlier, this opening is not unique to Habakkuk, nor to prophecy in general, and serves as the basis for a call for attention and witnessing. What the verse from Habakkuk adds is the call to the community to see with their own eyes, to examine something that is under their very noses. The prophet also explains why they should examine it themselves (= sight): if they were to learn about it second-hand (= hearing), they would not believe what they were being told. This verse demonstrates an idea I discussed at length in the section "Seeing is Believing" (pp. 238–48), namely, that proof that wondrous events happened lies in their being seen. The implicit assumption found in Habakkuk is that sight is more convincing than hearing, because it is a way of firsthand knowledge and experience.

In the last section of Job we find a similar implicit notion. God's main claim in the first speech out of the whirlwind (28:1–29:30) is that Job does not know what God knows, a statement reinforced by the claim that Job was not present, did not walk, did not see, and did not know the process of creation.[120] Put simply, Job did not personally experience the creation. Following the second speech of God out of the whirlwind (40:6–41:26), Job give his final response (Job 42:1–6). In this response Job describes how he was convinced, and admits that he knows and understands nothing. He closes with the following words: "I had heard of you by the hearing of the ear (לשמע אזן שמעתיך), but now my eye sees

---

120.   In ch. 38 this idea is represented through the following verbs: *kinaesthesia/presence*—היה (v. 3), בוא (vv. 16, 22), הלך (v. 17); *sight*—ראה (vv. 17, 22), גלה (v. 17); *knowledge*—ידע (vv. 3, 4, 12, 18, 21, 33), בין (vv. 18, 20). Other verbs in the chapter describe God's acts of creation. Yet, the border between descriptions of knowledge and creation is blurred, and it seems that knowledge is creation; see the full discussion in Hartley, *The Book of Job*, 489–505.

you (עיני ראתך)" (v. 5). There is an underlying claim in this verse that Job only knew what he knew through hearing, hearsay, second-hand. Now that he has seen with his own eyes, he is able to conclude: "therefore I despise myself, and repent in dust and ashes" (v. 6). Although this verse is somewhat inscrutable, Job seems to be pointing to the difference between his acquaintance with God before the revelation, which was an acquaintance based on learning (= hearing); and his present acquaintance, which is based on personal experience (= sight). After Job sees God with his own eyes, he understands more than he understood through learning and hearing, which are considered so highly in the wisdom tradition.[121]

Another biblical passage that hints at this superiority is the story of Sodom: "Then the Lord said, 'How great is the outcry (זעקה) against Sodom and Gomorrah and how very grave their sin! I must go down and see (ארדה־נא ואראה) whether they have done altogether according to the outcry (הכצעקתה) that has come to me; and if not, I will know (אדעה)'" (Gen 18:20–21). In this verse God himself sets out (through motion and sight) personally to examine and investigate what he heard; indeed, these descriptions contrast other images of God as all-seeing, seated in heights,[122] yet matches the often anthropomorphic God of the book of Genesis. For the present discussion, the underlying assumption of these verses is that sight and personal presence are perceived as more convincing than hearing. The Queen of Sheba agrees with this notion: "…The report was true that I heard (שמעתי) in my own land of your accomplishments and of your wisdom, but I did not believe the reports until I came and my own eyes had seen it (באתי ותראינה עיני). Not even half had been told me; your wisdom and prosperity far surpass the report that I had heard" (השמועה אשר שמעתי)" (1 Kgs 10:7). Once again, we see how personal inspection through sight and presence is preferable to second-hand knowledge through hearing. In this verse this notion is verbally stressed by the repetition of the root שמע, in contrast to presence and sight. Isaiah hints at a similar conclusion: "so he shall startle many nations; kings shall shut their mouths because of him; for that which had not been told (לא־ספר) them they shall see (ראו), and that which they had not heard (לא־שמעו) they shall contemplate (התבוננו)" (Isa 52:15). This verse summarizes the reaction of fear at witnessing the servant of the

---

121. These words are Job's acceptance of the divine argumentation, yet they protest against the wisdom tradition, which is mostly represented in the book of Proverbs. This protest is added to the dispute with the wisdom tradition throughout the book.

122. See Jer 23:24; Pss 33:13; 113:6; 138:6; Job 34:21.

Lord.[123] This is a typical fear response—paralysis and muteness, which we discussed earlier. Importantly, this response is the result of seeing, which has a more powerful impact on the observer than hearing (cf. pp. 251–55).

As all these verses demonstrate, there is an underlying preference for sight-based experience or knowledge, which is justified because of the assumed stronger impression gained by sight. Hence, there is an essential and not only quantitative difference in the way that sight is used to express the various contexts discussed in Chapter 3. Before I conclude my discussion on the centrality of sight in biblical perception, I will briefly examine three additional cultural models. The first model deals with metaphors of madness as loss of sight, which hint at the notion that sight is the central ability in human functioning. This will only get a short treatment because of the paucity of material. The second model deals with the use of sight metaphors to describe an experience of something distinct from reality, including the prophetic experience. And the third model deals with the use of words from the linguistic field of sight at key moments in the biblical narrative. Our examination of these three models adds to our understanding of the centrality of sight in biblical perception

Sight and Sanity

One of the more interesting phenomena documented by anthropologists who examined the perception of the senses in different cultures is the description of madness as a disruption in the functioning of the senses. Different cultures highlight the disruption of different senses, according to a normative sensory preference: "Mental disorder is conceptualised in terms of perceptual disorder, and the modality affected is the most prominent modality in terms of the culture's sensory profile."[124] In the Hebrew Bible, we find madness expressed through the loss of the ability to think, which is symbolized by sight: "The Lord will afflict you with madness (שגעון), blindness (עורון), and confusion of mind (תמהון לבב)" (Deut 28:28). Even though this verse contains expressions that are unique and difficult to interpret, the commonly accepted translation is that its describes madness and loss of perception.[125] Blindness is clustered here with both. Notably, the root שגע describes behaviour that is not

---

123.   The meaning of the root יזז in this verse is "to scare," "to shock"; see Oswalt, *Isaiah: Chapters 40–66*, 374; BDB, 633.

124.   Howes, "Sensorial Anthropology," 190 n. 4.

125.   Translated as "madness," "blindness," "confusion of mind"; see von Rad, *Deuteronomy*.

normative,[126] while the term תמהון ascribed to the mind (heart) could either indicate confusion or disability to act. The parallel between this term and blindness appears in another (possibly linked) verse: "On that day, says the Lord, I will strike every horse with panic (תמהון), and its rider with madness (שגעון). But on the house of Judah I will keep a watchful eye (אפקח את־עיני), when I strike every horse of the peoples with blindness (עורון)" (Zech 12:4). These two verses use the same cluster, and indicate the use of sight as a main metaphor for thought, with the assumption that, without sight, the ability to think and judge is damaged. Sight is not the only sense that is used as a metaphor for madness in the Hebrew Bible. The phrase טעמו (Piel) שנה, literally "to change taste," means to have damaged perception, to be mad.[127] That is to say, in Biblical Hebrew I could not find a single sense that is consistently and widely used to express madness. Nevertheless, the very use of blindness alongside terms such as confusion and madness points to the centrality of sight as a perceptive sense in the biblical sensorium.

Sight and the Supernatural

There has long been a dispute about whether sight or hearing is the central sense that lies at the core of biblical descriptions of the prophetic experience.[128] The prophetic description makes alternate use of words for hearing and sight. The prophets hear voices and they see visions, and none of the prophets makes exclusive use of one sense to describe the experience of revelation. This is why any attempt to define a chronology or transition of prophecy from a hearing experience to a sight experience, or vice versa, is doomed to fail. In fact, prophecy is often described using both of these sensory components. See, for example, the description of Balaam: "the oracle of one who hears (שמע) the words of God, and knows (ידע) the knowledge of the Most High, who sees (יחזה) the vision of the Almighty, who falls down, but with his eyes uncovered (גלוי עינים)" (Num 24:16). This verse contains the same parallel between sight, hearing, and knowledge that we saw earlier.[129] The different Hebrew terms for "prophet" provide another hint in this direction. חוזה and רואה,

---

126.　1 Sam 21:16; 2 Kgs 9:20, and others. A distinction is drawn between the roots שנה and שגע, see *HALOT* 4:1415.

127.　See Chapter 3, nn. 250 and 251.

128.　Cf. Chapter 1, n. 64 and pp. 185–86, above.

129.　If my suggestion, namely, to see sight and hearing as the linguistic representation of the sensorium in the Hebrew Bible (pp. 185–86, above), is accepted, we can interpret the prophet who sees and hears as the prophet who knows "everything," or, alternatively, as the prophet who experiences through the whole sensorium.

both meaning "Seer," are derived from the field of sight, and show that the prophetic experience is similar to the visual experience. Furthermore, the root חזה, whose primary meaning is "to see," is nearly always used to describe prophecy.[130] The term "prophet" (נביא), on the other hand, indicates the action of the prophet, and not the prophetic experience. The original meaning of the word seems to be "to speak."[131] In total, the dispute over the essence of sensory prophetic experience relies on a vocabulary that describes the prophet's actions in the stories and in the prophecies themselves.

Given the focus of the present study, we will not become entangled in this spider's web. Instead, I will comment on this complex issue. Initially, any suggestion that prophetic experience shifts from sight (concrete) to hearing (abstract) as part of growing anthropomorphic sensitivity only further supports the assumption that sight is a more intimate and direct mode of perception.[132] Second, prophecy could be interpreted as an ability to absorb reality, which is beyond the sensory grasp of ordinary people. In terms of the sight–hearing dispute, how was this alternative reality absorbed—through sight or through hearing? Obviously, it is by no means certain that this reality was experienced by only one of the senses. Moreover, the vocabulary used in the prophetic books is not helpful in determining the answer. However, there is further evidence to be considered. Few narratives in the Hebrew Bible mention the experience of alternative reality. As I will demonstrate, the thread that links these different narratives is that a supernatural reality can be seen in them temporarily and exclusively.

I will present in detail three of these stories, all of which focus on a description of the prophet's ability to witness or experience the supernatural. The first story is the transfer of authority from Elijah to Elisha:

> When they had crossed, Elijah said to Elisha, "Tell me what I may do for you, before I am taken from you." Elisha said, "Please let me inherit a double share of your spirit." He responded, "You have asked a hard thing; yet, if you see (תראה) me as I am being taken from you, it will be granted you; if not, it will not." As they continued walking and talking, a chariot of fire and horses of fire separated the two of them, and Elijah ascended in a whirlwind into heaven. (2 Kgs 2:9–11)

---

130. As well as presence in non-prophetic revelation; see, e.g., Pss 17:15; 27:4; 46:9), cf. the nouns חזון and מחזה.

131. Only based on cognate Semitic roots, and hence debatable. See H.-P. Müller, "נָבִיא *nābî*; נבא *nbʾ* niphal and hitpael; נְבִיאָה *nebîʾâ*; נְבוּאָה *nebûʾâ*," *TDOT* 9:129–50 (130–36); *HALOT* 2:659.

132. I would like to thank Baruch Halpern for discussing the matter with me.

In these verses, Elisha begs to inherit Elijah's prophetic abilities, and wants to be blessed with the same ability to see. We learn that from the condition expressed by Elijah. Once Elisha will see the wondrous ascent of Elijah, he will know that he has gained the prophetic ability. Several chapters later, we find further proof for this prophetic ability. During the siege of Aram over Samaria, Elisha's attendant expresses his fear:

> When an attendant of the man of God rose early in the morning and went out, an army with horses and chariots was all around the city. His servant said, "Alas, master! What shall we do?" He replied, "Do not be afraid, for there are more with us than there are with them." Then Elisha prayed: "O LORD, please open his eyes that he may see (פקח־נא את־עיניו ויראה)." So the Lord opened the eyes of the servant, and he saw (ויפקח...את־עיני וירא); the mountain was full of horses and chariots of fire all around Elisha. (2 Kgs 6:14–17)

In this story, the existence of a reality that cannot normally be experienced by the senses is not questioned. Exceptional people (such as prophets), or ordinary people whose eyes have been temporarily opened, are able to witness this parallel reality and to experience it. Notably, the experience of this reality is the experience of sight.

A similar description occurs in the satiric part of the story of Balaam. I will cite Num 22:21–31 here in full:

> So Balaam got up in the morning, saddled his donkey, and went with the officials of Moab. God's anger was kindled because he was going, and the angel of the Lord took his stand in the road as his adversary. Now he was riding on the donkey, and his two servants were with him. The donkey saw (ותרא) the angel of the Lord standing in the road, with a drawn sword in his hand; so the donkey turned off the road, and went into the field; and Balaam struck the donkey, to turn it back onto the road. Then the angel of the Lord stood in a narrow path between the vineyards, with a wall on either side. When the donkey saw (ותרא) the angel of the Lord, it scraped against the wall, and scraped Balaam's foot against the wall; so he struck it again. Then the angel of the Lord went ahead, and stood in a narrow place, where there was no way to turn either to the right or to the left. When the donkey saw (ותרא) the angel of the Lord, it lay down under Balaam; and Balaam's anger was kindled, and he struck the donkey with his staff. Then the Lord opened the mouth of the donkey, and it said to Balaam, "What have I done to you, that you have struck me these three times?" Balaam said to the donkey, "Because you have made a fool of me! I wish I had a sword in my hand! I would kill you right now!" But the donkey said to Balaam, "Am I not your donkey, which you have ridden all your life to this day? Have I been in the habit of treating you this way?" And he said, "No." Then the Lord opened the eyes of Balaam, and he saw (ויגל...את־עיני...וירא) the angel of the Lord standing in the road, with his drawn sword in his hand; and he bowed down, falling on his face.

Apart from the mockery in this description of the donkey seeing something that her master, the prophet, cannot see,[133] this passage reflects the perception that unusual reality is perceived through sight. The angel of God cannot be seen by every man, only by someone whose eyes have been opened.[134] In this story, Balaam's eyes are opened temporarily, just like the eyes of the attendant in the Elisha story. The Hagar story is to be understood in the same way: "Then God opened her eyes and she saw (ויפקח...את־עיניה ותרא) a well of water. She went, and filled the skin with water, and gave the boy a drink" (Gen 21:19). Once Hagar has been privileged to receive prophecy from the angel (vv. 17–18), she is able to see something that she did not see earlier. In the framework of our discussion, the well was revealed to Hagar through a miracle, and not because her emotions had calmed down.[135]

These stories reveal the way in which experiencing supernatural reality was perceived in the Hebrew Bible—through sight. While exceptional people in exceptional circumstances can see things, others are only dimly aware of them: "I, Daniel, alone saw the vision (וראיתי...את־המראה); the people who were with me did not see the vision (לא ראו את־המראה), though a great trembling fell upon them, and they fled and hid themselves. So I was left alone to see this great vision (ואראה את־המראה). My strength left me, and my complexion grew deathly pale, and I retained no strength" (Dan 10:7–8). If the definition of a prophet is someone who has access to experiences that cannot be accessed by ordinary people, then these stories demonstrate that the prophet's ability to see is the one making him exceptional.

Sight and Literature

Despite its complexity and contradictory nature, when we examine biblical literature we can discern a few common themes. One such theme is the covenant, a characteristic thread that winds its way throughout the

---

133.   In contrast to other descriptions of Balaam as "seer," and see A. Rofé, *"The Book of Balaam" (Numbers 22:2–24:25): A Study in Methods of Criticism and the History of Biblical Literature and Religion* (Jerusalem: Simor, 1979 [Hebrew]).

134.   Compare the seeing of the messenger by Gideon (Judg 7:12, 22), as well as the seeing of the mother of Samson and Manoah (Judg 13:3–19). During the plague following the recording of the people by David, some people see the "angel" (2 Sam 24:17, and even more so 1 Chr 15–16), yet in this narrative there is no exclusivity of sight.

135.   See also the parallel to the binding, where Isaac's life is saved by sudden sight; see V. P. Hamilton, *The Book of Genesis: Chapters 18–50* (NICOT; Grand Rapids: Eerdmans, 1995), 85.

books of the Hebrew Bible across different genres and sources, different periods, and different schools. Describing such a theme is relatively easy when we are examining an identifiable term such as the covenant, with its concrete background in social-cultural reality and terminology. It is more difficult to identify and describe figurative themes that are very prominent in the text. I suggest here preliminarily that sight—as part of a semantic composite dichotomy (See Table 11, below)—is one such theme. An abstract notion of this kind can reflect cultural preferences and perceptions. It can also influence the language and the structure of individual stories and whole books. Clearly my claim deserves a monograph-length study of its own, and I will only present two already discussed examples hinting in such a direction. One fine example of such a study is the doctoral dissertation of Talia Sotskover (2006), who studied the semantic field of sight and the appearance of words from this semantic field throughout the book of Genesis. According to Sotskover, these words appear consistently at central turning points in the various stories. In other words, sight is a central theme throughout all the Genesis stories, a theme that runs like a characteristic connecting thread from the creation of the world up to the death of Joseph. Moreover, Sotskover uses this phenomenon not only to understand better the narrative, but also in order to prove the unity of the book.

It seems that a very closely related phenomenon is found in other biblical books, and that sensitivity to sight vocabulary can reveal much about plot direction and character design in the Hebrew Bible. The centrality of sight is thus not a characteristic that is unique to Genesis, but is a literary motif that runs through the entire Hebrew Bible. This is particularly well demonstrated in 1 Samuel, as has been shown (though not always fully) by previous scholars,[136] but apparent elsewhere in the narration of the fate of the Davidic line.

As the book of Samuel is constructed through contrasting and competing pairs of potential leaders,[137] it is interesting to find that these pairs are normally negated through sight imagery; that is, while one character sees, the other does not. The first example is found in the first chapters of the book. While Samuel comes from Zophim (lit. "watchers," 1 Sam

---

136.   My own work on sight in 1 Samuel is ongoing. My initial thoughts were presented in "To See or Not to Be: Did Saul Ever Have a Chance?" (unpublished paper presented at a conference titled "The Ancient Near East in the 12th–10th Centuries B.C.E.," Haifa, May 2010).

137.   See J. Rosenberg, "1 and 2 Samuel," in *The Literary Guide to the Bible* (ed. R. Alter and F. Kermode; Cambridge: Belknap Press of Harvard University Press, 1987), 122–43; Garsiel, *The First Book of Samuel*.

1:1),[138] dedicated to be seen in the presence of God (v. 22),[139] and receives a revelatory vision (3:1, 15, 21),[140] Eli's "eyesight had begun to grow dim so that he could not see, [and he] was lying down in his room" (v. 2; cf. 4:15). As Jack Sasson has demonstrated at length, this contrasting motif is accreted throughout ch. 3 and predicts the fall of Eli and the divine choice of Samuel.[141] Notably, Samuel is the ultimate "seer" (רואה),[142] and his loss of authority is marked by his loss of sight. While we do not hear of Samuel's physical blindness, he clearly uses his ability to see in ch. 16, when he is sent to anoint David. As Robert Alter has shown,[143] the chapter's leading words are used to demonstrate that Samuel is not the one who sees; rather it is God. When Samuel arrived at the house of Jesse, to anoint the one whom God had chosen (lit. "saw," ראיתי, 16:1),

> he saw (וירא) Eliab, he thought: "Surely the LORD's anointed stands before him." But the Lord said to Samuel, "Pay no attention to his appearance (מראהו) or his stature, for I have rejected him. For not as man sees (יראה) [does the LORD see]; man sees (יראה) only what is visible (לעינים), but the Lord sees (יראה) into the heart." (1 Sam 16:6–7)

After this episode, Samuel disappears from the scene and only regains his sight as a contrast to Saul at the end of the book (see below).

The character of Saul, too, can be evaluated through sight vocabulary. In fact, in all episodes that contrast Saul with another character (Samuel, Jonathan, and David), Saul does not see, while the other person does. Saul's first appearance in the book (ch. 9) is marked by his contrast to the seer. When his son Jonathan disobeys him and puts the dynasty in danger, Saul is the one presented as wrong, that is, as blind:

> But Jonathan had not heard his father charge the troops with the oath; so he extended the staff that was in his hand, and dipped the tip of it in the honeycomb, and put his hand to his mouth; and his eyes brightened

---

138. The debate over the exact name and meaning is not central for the image created by the existing MT.

139. See n. 30, above.

140. For Samuel as medium, see M. Malul, "'Out of the Mouth of Babes and Sucklings You Have Founded Strength…' (Ps 8:3): Did Children Serve as Prophetic Mediums in Biblical Times?," *JNSL* 33, no. 2 (2007): 1–32 (4–5).

141. Sasson, "The Eyes of Eli."

142. A term unique to Samuel in the books of the Former Prophets. Elsewhere it appears in Isa 30:10 as a general term, and in Chronicles it refers to Samuel in synoptic and non-synoptic passages (1 Chr 9:22; 26:28; 29:29), as well as to Hanani (2 Chr 16:7, 10). Note that in the MT the term appears only in ch. 9, while in the LXX it appears again in ch. 16, thereby weakening the literary motif presented above.

143. R. Alter, *The Art of Biblical Narrative* (New York: Basic, 1981), 157–58.

(הַאֲרֹנָה עֵינָיו)... Then Jonathan said, "My father has troubled the land; see (רְאוּ) how my eyes have brightened (אֹרוּ עֵינַי) because I tasted a little of this honey." (1 Sam 14:27, 29)

The contrast between Saul and Jonathan is emphasized by the fact that Jonathan's eyes are lightened. Clearly, Saul's eyes are not, as Jonathan makes all the people see (witness) his superiority.

In an article dealing with the role of word pairs in consecutive narratives, A. Frisch has demonstrated how narratives dealing with Saul tend to use the verb "to hear" (שמע) as a *leitwort*, while juxtaposed narratives dealing with David tend to use "to see" (ראה). Furthermore, he claims that this literary choice generated the preference for David over Saul.[144] Here I want to refer to the climax of enmity between David and Saul, to two incidents in which David could have harmed Saul but refrained from doing so. The first encounter happens in a cave. Saul does not see or notice David and his men. Only when Saul leaves the cave does David reveal himself to him, and calls him not to base his impression on hearing, but on his own sight: "This very day your eyes have seen (רָאוּ עֵינֶיךָ) how the Lord gave you into my hand in the cave... See, my father, see (רְאֵה גַם רְאֵה) the corner of your cloak in my hand...you may know for certain (דַּע וּרְאֵה) that there is no wrong or treason in my hands..." (1 Sam 24:11–12 [10–11]).[145] David's repeated call for Saul's sight demonstrates Saul's "blindness." And, indeed, Saul is not seeing David, as is clear from his question: "Is this your voice, my son David?" (v. 17 [16]). The allusion to blind Isaac is inevitable (Gen 27:21–22). The second encounter follows a similar pattern. David reaches Saul at night, and "No one saw (ראה) it, or knew it (ידע), nor did anyone awake; for they were all asleep..." (1 Sam 26:12). In this case too David expressed his innocence, and here too Saul cannot see him, even when awake: "Saul recognized David's voice, and said, 'Is this your voice, my son David?'" (v. 17). Indeed, Saul's explicit acknowledgment of David's superiority in both cases is accompanied by implicit, literary acknowledgment. Understanding the cultural poetics of sight and blindness presented in this chapter helps to unfold such acknowledgment. In other words, Saul's replacement by David is highlighted by the contrast between seeing and not-seeing, even when real blindness is not involved. Readers with eyes in their head can know in advance who the chosen leader is.[146]

---

144. Frisch, "*rʾh* and *šmʿ*," 93.

145. See pp. 230–32, above.

146. For "cultural poetics" and its link to biblical studies, see Seeman, "Where Is Sarah Your Wife?," 105.

Finally, the encounter between Saul and Samuel's spirit (ch. 28), which marks the final end to his reign, is also infused with words from the field of sight. Saul is in disguise, and he reaches the woman of Endor under cover of darkness. The conversation between Saul and the witch highlights Saul's "blindness":

> The king said to her, "Have no fear (תיראי); what do you see (ראית)?" The woman said to Saul, "I see (ראיתי) a divine being coming up out of the ground." He said to her, "What is his appearance (תארו)?" She said, "An old man is coming up; he is wrapped in a robe." So Saul knew that it was Samuel, and he bowed with his face to the ground, and did obeisance. (1 Sam 28:13–14)

The alliteration of "to see" (ראה) and "to fear" (ירא) is not unique to this verse, and is meant to attract the audience's attention.[147] The word "appearance" (תאר) refers to Samuel's looks, and is correlated associatively as well as through alliteration to "appearance" (מראה), and "to see" (ראה).[148] Here too, despite the richness of sight and sight-related vocabulary, Saul does not see, and that is enough to be suggestive of the unhappy end.

As this brief example from 1 Samuel shows, words from the field of sight, and the motif of sight vis-à-vis blindness (real or metaphoric), guide the biblical narrative in 1 Samuel, and mark the turning points throughout the book. As the story of the royal houses continues in 2 Samuel and in Kings, we see the same phenomenon. In this context, note that the central turning point in 2 Samuel—the encounter between David and Bathsheba—starts off with David's sight (2 Sam 11:2).[149] More importantly, the very end of the Davidic dynasty is marked by the recurring motif for generational and leadership change—blindness. Zedekiah's blindness symbolizes the end of the kingdom of Judah and the start of a new era.[150] This centrality of key words and motifs reinforces

147. Cf. Gen 42:35; Exod 14:13; Deut 28:10; 1 Sam 3:15; 1 Kgs 3:28; Isa 8:12; Ps 52:8; Dan 1:10. See also Childs, *Exodus*, 344.

148. The word "form" (תואר) parallels "appearance" (מראה, Gen 29:17; 39:6; Isa 52:14; 53:2; Esth 2:7), and is used as subject of "to see" (ראה, Gen 41:19; Deut 21:11; 1 Sam 16:18). Note that the word is derived from the root ראה.

149. For this chapter as a turning point in the book of Samuel, see Rosenberg, "1 and 2 Samuel" 132–33. David's encounter with Michal, which marks the end of the relationship between the two dynasties, is also rich with sight symbolism; see Seeman, "The Watcher at the Window."

150. See also Ceresko, "The Blind and the Lame," 27–29, which finds the reference to the blind and the lame in 2 Sam 5:8 to be a hint to the end of both dynasties: Saul's dynasty ends with the lame Mephiboshet, while the Davidic dynasty ends with the blind Zedekiah.

our statement that the sense of sight is a central sense in biblical perception, based on the reflection of the figurative idea (sight–good–life) in the biblical narrative.

Conclusion

Throughout this book I have repeatedly claimed that there is no structural or conscious hierarchy of the senses in biblical perception. Nevertheless, if forced to choose a side in the age-old dispute of the supremacy of sight vs. hearing in biblical epistemology, one must choose sight. Indeed, there is no explicit hierarchy of the sensorium, so how is such a decision to be made? Is it based on statistics, that is, the more words from a specific semantic field are found in Biblical Hebrew, the more important is that modality? In a way it is and in a way it is not. The frequency of the root "to see" (ראה) and the word "eye" (עין) is not enough to prove any particular cultural perception. However, the metaphorical and contextual richness of the use of terms from the field of sight indicates that this sense was very highly developed, linguistically as well as performatively.[151] The world of images and metaphors associated with sight words is extremely broad. It includes imagery that is shared with other senses (see Chapter 2), as well as imagery that is unique to sight. After discussing the centrality of sight to the legal system, to theology, and to perception of perception, it is easy to reject the following view:

> Visualism grows to its present strength under the aegis of modern science... It has, of course, earlier roots too, which can be discerned in ancient Greece but grew much sturdier in the European Middle Ages... Modern theological and biblical studies have made it a commonplace that the ancient Hebrew concept of knowing expressed by *yadha* takes knowing as something like hearing—personal and communal—whereas the ancient Greek concept expressed in *gignosko* takes knowing as something like seeing—impersonal, fractioning, and analytic.[152]

Ong bases his conclusions on Thorlief Boman's *Hebrew Thought Compared with Greek*, which has been widely criticized in the general literature and in the Introduction to this book.[153] The main problem with Ong's view is his underlying assumption about the character of each sense. There are no grounds for assuming the existence of an inner-essential characteristic of the sense of sight that determines the semantic

151.   See Chapter 1, n. 194.
152.   Ong, "World as View," 636.
153.   See pp. 23–25, above.

load of the field of terms associated with it, or its actual use. As Ullendorff emphasized: "They do not see what we see, and what they do see they receive and digest in a manner fundamentally different from our own."[154] In my own words: similarity in action is not evidence of similarity in meaning, and the difference in meaning must also lead to a difference in action. Like Boman and Ong, I found that knowledge was perceived in the Hebrew Bible as something communal/public on the one hand, and as something acquired through personal experience on the other. But contra these scholars, the biblical evidence expresses this perception through sight vocabulary at least to the same—if not a greater—extent as by the hearing vocabulary. Sight is a medium, a central tool for acquiring knowledge and passing it on (memory). As the school of thought so eloquently represented by Ong likes to say, "the medium is the message." As demonstrated in this chapter, the Hebrew Bible reflects an implicit schematic of knowledge that originates in sight, and which is later passed on through speech-hearing. It is the very background of sight as a direct experience (interpreted as involvement and witnessing) that leads to the centrality of sight in various spheres of life, such as religious practice and the juridical system.

In his *Anthropology of the Old Testament*, Hans Wolff posed the following question: Which ability is the pre-condition for defining humans?[155] In my Introduction, I showed how different cultures give different answers to this question. Wolff's answer is that the sense of hearing and speech is the most central, and provides the essential condition of humanity in the Hebrew Bible.[156] There are two fundamental problems with Wolff's definition, however. The first one is his reliance on a universal definition of humanity; in other words, Wolff is still concerned with "how they thought" rather than "what they thought."[157] Second, Wolff devotes nearly no discussion to sight—an essential ingredient is missing:

> It seems odd that Wolff discusses the eye only cursorily in his *Anthropology of the OT*. It is impossible to support his statement that the priority of the ear and speech for truly human understanding is clear. The eye and the ear stand rather in a relationship of equivalence. Kraus describes the situation more accurately: No organ of the human body reflects the totality of life more impressively than does the eye... All the motions and emotions of the inner life are manifested in the eye.[158]

154. Ullendorff, "Thought Categories," 275.
155. Wolff, *Anthropology of the Old Testament*, 74.
156. Ibid., 78.
157. See p. 26, above.
158. Stendebach, *TDOT* 11:38.

Johnson is therefore correct in saying that the eye is associated with a wide range of "physical" activities, so that at times the use of ʿayin is almost synonymous with *nepesh* and *panim* (cf. Job 24:15).[159]

To Standebach's critique I would add that even if we do as Wolff suggests, and take account of the evidence regarding the sense of sight, then we have an equally good candidate for providing the essential condition for understanding humanity. As I have shown in this chapter, sight symbolizes thought and investigation, experience and life, and subjective opinion. Furthermore, the use of blindness imagery parallel to madness also demonstrates how sight is the central perceptive medium in biblical perception. Finally, sight is also the sense used to perceive supernatural events, as found in prophetic narratives.

When examining the various concrete, derived, and metaphoric meanings of sight vocabulary, it was also evident that sight is placed within a larger group of contrasting concepts, as summarized in the table below:

Table 11. *Dichotomy Between Sight and Blindness*

Sight	Blindness
Life	Death/old age
Light	Darkness
Wisdom	Foolishness
Choice	Rejection
Good	Evil

These contrasts emerge from the different metaphors associated with sight, and create a broader semantic whole that also supports the centrality of sight in biblical perception. This centrality is demonstrated in two ways. First, the very widespread use of these images and metaphors indicates their centrality in the worldview reflected in the Hebrew Bible. Second, these contrasts appear at key plot crossroads in the biblical narrative through the use of sight (and sightless) words. In fact, it is often the sight words that generate the associations of these contrasts, further clarifying the logic of the narrative. In sum, even if the supremacy of sight cannot be proved, it is nonetheless impossible to claim the inferiority of sight in biblical epistemology.

159.   Ibid., 11:36. Cf. Johnson, *The Vitality of the Individual*, 47–48; Kraus, "Hören und Sehen," 84.

CONCLUSION:
THE SENSES OF SCRIPTURE

The Concordia Sensoria Research Team provides us with four basic principles for cultural study of the senses (see p. 15). First and foremost, the categorization and hierarchy of the senses depends on the cultural tradition, which varies from culture to culture. As this book has hopefully demonstrated, the culture reflected in the Hebrew Bible had its own sensory category, implicitly embedded in language, proverbs, and narratives. The reflection of sensory perception in language is the second principle. Thirdly, the senses encode ethical values that are learned as part of the socialization process, in practice during childhood. Although childhood and education practices of ancient Israel are not clear to us, we did find that sensory vocabulary is used to describe moral behaviour. Furthermore, the wisdom tradition reveals at times sensory instructions and preferences, either for hearing or sight, and restricts the excessive use of taste and touch. Clearly, the sensory category is experienced as natural, and forms the basis for physical experience, which is also why it goes unexplained. The last principle of CONSERT is harder to examine, and deals with various sensory models within different parts of the same culture, based on religious, political, or gender factors. Further study must be done to reach a conclusion on the matter. As I mentioned briefly, there seems to be a basic dispute over sensory precedence between the wisdom classics of the Hebrew Bible—while Proverbs prefers hearing, Qohelet prefers sight.

Furthermore, any study of sensory perception making use of texts from the ancient Near East will enrich the conclusions of this book, and further explain the cultural similarities and differences between the respective cultures. It seems to me that great surprises await the scholar choosing this path. In at least two sensorily related idioms Akkadian and Hebrew differ greatly—namely, those related to hearing and smell. The wisest of the Akkadian gods, Ea, had big ears, an image very far from the wisest seeing God presented in the Hebrew Bible; the anger of Gods in Akkadian is seated in the heart (*libbu*), while in the Hebrew Bible it is seated in the nose (אף). Such a difference implies a completely different evaluation of the sacrificial system, a matter I hope to explore elsewhere.

To conclude the book, I will summarize the main conclusions. It seems that in the culture reflected in the Hebrew Bible there was a septasensory model which included the senses of sight, hearing, kinaesthesia, speech, touch, taste, and smell. Within this model, sight, hearing, kinaesthesia, and speech were considered closer or more similar to each other. Each of these senses was closely linked to a particular organ and perceived to have functioned through it. When the sensory organ was open, the sense functioned. When it was closed, it was disabled. Moreover, sensory perception was perceived to include various types of experience, including cognitive, emotional, and social experiences. Using the senses was a symbol for autonomy, subjectivity, and sovereignty. This symbol was based on the derived experienced attributed to the senses as well as to the perception that God had created the senses. As a result, people with sensory disabilities suffered not only from physical difficulties, but also from semantic liminality.

Although there is no way to prove that the above conclusions were reflected upon by the ancient Israelite, the vast evidence for the use of sight vocabulary and metaphors in various rhetorical contexts implies some kind of awareness of them—a common sense awareness, in which things are as they are. What is clear, however, is that presumptions about biblical thought, and specifically contrasting biblical thought to Greek, modern, or Western thought, prevent us from exploring the philosophical richness embedded in biblical language and narrative.

In this context, I would like to suggest that the commonplace dichotomy between biblical thought and Greek/Western/modern thought in fact misses a crucial point, and I will restrict my claims to the biblical sensory category as described in this book, and to the platonic sensory model. While these two models differ in many aspects—the number of senses, their strict hierarchy, their evaluation as tools for gaining accurate knowledge about the worlds, and more—both models give primacy to sight. I want to suggest that, while most summaries of Western epistemology ascribe the primacy of sight to Plato alone (see Chapter 1), this primacy in fact owed much to the centrality of unconscious biblical thought in the West. While Plato and successive philosophers talk about the senses, and greatly value sight, the imagery of sight embedded in the Hebrew Bible was widely experienced and embodied. Notions such as light and darkness, or sight and blindness, bear associative load in our own culture, including good and bad, wise and foolish, life and death. They do so because the biblical language is loaded with the same associative patterns. And thus, the pentasensory hierarchy, which places sight at the top of the pyramid, together with particular technological developments starting in the eighteenth century, managed to create the exclusivity of sight in Western contemporary culture precisely because of, and not despite of, its biblical heritage.

BIBLIOGRAPHY

Abrahami, P. "Masculine and Feminine Personal Determinatives before Women's Names at Nuzi: A Gender Indicator of Social or Economic Independence?" *CDLB* 1 (2011). No pages. Online: http://cdli.ucla.edu/pubs/cdlb/2011/cdlb2011_001.html.

Abu Lughod, L., and C. A. Lutz. "Introduction: Emotion, Discourse and the Politics of everyday Life." Pages 1–23 in *Languages and the Politics of Emotion*. Edited by C. A. Lutz and L. Abu-Lughad. Cambridge: Cambridge University Press, 1990.

Ackerman, D. *A Natural History of the Senses*. New York: Random House, 1990.

Ackroyd, P. R. "A Note on the Hebrew Roots באש and בוש," *JTS* 43 (1942): 160–61.

Aitken, J. K. *The Semantics of Blessing and Cursing in Ancient Hebrew*. ANESSup 23. Leuven: Peeters, 2007.

Alter, R. *The Art of Biblical Narrative*. New York: Basic, 1981.

Anderson, G. A. *A Time to Mourn, a Time to Dance: The Expression of Grief and Joy in Israelite Religion*. University Park: Pennsylvania State University Press, 1991.

Arnon, H. "The Creation of Speech in the Qumran Sectarian Literature (1QHa 9 [1] 27–31)." M.A. diss., The University of Haifa, 2006 (Hebrew).

Asad, T. *Genealogies of Religion: Discipline and Reasons of power in Christianity and Islam*. Baltimore: The Johns Hopkins University Press, 1993.

Ashbrook Harvey, S. *Scenting Salvation: Ancient Christianity and the Olfactory Imagination*. Berkeley: University of California Press, 2006.

Ashley, T. R. *The Book of Numbers*. NICOT. Grand Rapids: Eerdmans, 1992.

Atzmon, T. "How Many Senses Do We Really Have?" No pages. Online: http://www.ynet.co.il/articles/0,7340,L-2975031,00.html.

Augustin, M., and K.-D. Schunck, eds. *"Dort Ziehen Schiffe dahin…": Collected Communications to the XIVth Congress of the International Organization for the Study of the Old Testament*. Frankfurt am Main: Lang, 1996.

Avalos, H. "Introducing Sensory Criticism in Biblical Studies: Audiocentricity and Visiocentricity." Pages 47–60 in Avalos, Melcher, and Schipper, eds., *This Abled Body*.

Avalos, H., S. Melcher, and J. Schipper, eds. *This Abled Body: Rethinking Disabilities in Biblical Studies*. Semeia Studies 55. Atlanta: Society of Biblical Literature, 2007.

Avrahami, Y. "בוש in the Psalms—Shame or Disappointment?" *JSOT* 34 (2010): 294–313.

———. "Honour and Shame in the Hebrew Bible." M.A. diss., The Hebrew University of Jerusalem, 2002 (Hebrew).

———. "The Sensorium and Its Operation in Biblical Epistemology with Particular Attention to the Senses of Sight and Smell." Ph.D. diss., The University of Haifa, 2008 (Hebrew).

Bachar, S. "Perfume in the Song of Songs: An Erotic Motif and Sign of Social Class." *Shnaton* 15 (2005): 39–51.

Bakan, D. "Infanticide and Sacrifice in the Biblical Mind." *Midway* 8 (1967): 37–47.

Balentine, S. E. *The Hidden God: The Hiding of the Face of God in the Old Testament.* Oxford: Oxford University Press, 1983.

Bar-Am, A. "The Story of the Five Senses" (Hebrew). *De'ot* 5(1999): 76–87.

Bareket, M. "Food and Eating in the Bible as a Means of Communication" M.A. diss., The University of Haifa, 2004 (Hebrew).

Bark, F. "Listen Your Way In with Your Mouth: A Reading of Leviticus." *Judaism* 48, no. 2 (1999): 198–209.

Barr, J. *The Semantics of Biblical Language.* London: Oxford University Press, 1961.

Barthes, R. *Mythologies.* Translated by A. Lavers. London: Cape, 1972.

Bechtel, M. L. "Shame as Sanction of Social Control in Biblical Israel: Judicial, Political and Social Shaming." *JSOT* 49 (1991): 47–76.

Beck, B. E. F. "The Metaphor as Mediator Between Semantic and Analogic Modes of Thought." *Current Anthropology* 19, no. 1 (1978): 83–97.

Benedict, R. *Patterns of Culture.* Introduction by F. Boaz. Preface by M. Mead. New York: New American Library, 1960.

Ben-Yehuda, E. *The Dictionary of Hebrew Language, Old and New.* Jerusalem: Ben-Yehuda, 1948–1959.

Berger, P. L. *The Sacred Canopy: Elements of a Sociological Theory of Religion.* New York: Anchor, 1990.

Berlin, A. "Parallel Word Pairs: A Linguistic Explanation." *UF* 15 (1983): 7–16. Repr. pages 64–72 in *The Dynamics of Biblical Parallelism.* Bloomington: Indiana University Press, 1985.

Blackham, H. J. "An Introduction to Existentialist Thinking." Pages 1–15 in *Reality, Man and Existence: Essential Works of Existentialism: Essential Works of Existentialism Reality, Man and Existence.* Edited by H. J. Blackham. New York: Bantam, 1965.

Block, D. I. *The Book of Ezekiel: Chapters 25–48.* NICOT. Grand Rapids: Eerdmans, 1998.

Boer, P. A. H. de. "An Aspect of Sacrifice: II. God's Fragrance." Pages 27–47 in *Studies in the Religion of Ancient Israel.* VTSup 23. Leiden: Brill, 1972.

———. "Job 39:25—מלחמה יריח ומרחוק." Pages 29–38 in *Words and Meanings.* Festschrift David Winton Thomas. Edited by P. R. Ackroyd and B. Lindars. Cambridge: Cambridge University Press, 1968.

Boman, T. *Hebrew Thought Compared with Greek.* Translated by J. L. Moreau. New York: Norton, 1970.

Brenner, A. "Aromatics and Perfumes in the Song of Songs." *JSOT* 25 (1983): 75–81.

Brichto, C. H. *The Problem of "Curse" in the Hebrew Bible.* JBL Monograph Series 13. Philadelphia: Society of Biblical Literature and Exegesis, 1963.

Briggs, C. A., and E. G. Briggs. *Critical and Exegetical Commentary on the Book of Psalms.* ICC 16. Edinburgh: T. & T. Clark, 1969.

Brockington, L. H. "Audition in the Old Testament." *JTS* 49 (1948): 1–8.

Buber, M. *The Dialogue on Man and Being.* Chapters 1–3 translated by T. Wislovsky. Philosophical Writings 1. Jerusalem: Bialik Institute, 1959 (Hebrew).

Buss, M. J. "The Idea of Sitz im Leben—History and Critique." *ZAW* 90 (1978): 157–70.

Carasik, M. *Theologies of the Mind in Biblical Israel.* New York: Lang, 2006.

———. "To See a Sound: A Deuteronomic Rereading of Exodus 20:15." *Prooftexts* 19, no. 2 (1999): 257–65.

Carroll, R. P. *The Book of Jeremiah.* OTL. London: SCM, 1986.

Cassuto, U. *A Commentary on the Book of Exodus*. Translated by I. Abrahams. Jerusalem: Magnes, 1967.

Ceresko, A. R. "The Identity of 'the Blind and the Lame' (ʿiwwēr ûpissēaḥ) in 2 Samuel 5:8b." *CBQ* 63 (2001): 23–30.

Chance, J. K. "The Anthropology of Honor and Shame: Culture, Values and Practice." *Semeia* 68 (1994): 139–51.

Chandler, D. "Biases of the Ear and Eye: 'Great Divide' Theories, Phonocentrism, Graphocentrism and Logocentrism." No pages. Cited 7 October 2000. Online: http://www.aber.ac. uk/media/Documents/litoral/litoral.html.

Childs, B. S. *Exodus: A Commentary*. OTL. London, SCM, 1974.

Chomsky, N. *Language and Problems of Knowledge*: The Mangua Lectures. Current Studies in Linguistics 16. Cambridge: MIT, 1988.

Classen, C. "Foundations for the Anthropology of the Senses." *ISSJ* 153 (1997): 401–12.

———. "The Sensory Orders of 'Wild Children.'" Pages 47–60 in Howes, ed., *The Varieties of Sensory Experience*.

Classen, C., D. Howes, and A. Synnott, eds. *Aroma: The Cultural History of Smell*. London: Routledge, 1994.

Clifford, R. J. *Psalms 73–150*. Abingdon Old Testament Commentaries. Nashville: Abingdon, 2003.

Cohen, C. "The 'Held Method' for Comparative Semitic Philology." *JANES* 19 (1998): 9–23.

Cohen, H. R. *Biblical Hapax Legomena in the Light of Akkadian and Ugaritic*. SBL Dissertation Series. Atlanta: Scholars Press, 1978.

Collins, J. J. *Daniel: A Commentary on the Book of Daniel*. Hermeneia. Minneapolis: Fortress, 1993.

Collins, T. "The Physiology of Tears in the Old Testament." *CBQ* 33 (1971): 19–38, 185–97.

Cooke, G. A. *A Text-Book of North Semitic Inscriptions, Moabite, Hebrew, Phoenician, Aramaic, Nabataean, Palmyrene, Jewish*. Oxford: Clarendon, 1903.

Cranefield, P. F. "On the Origin of the Phrase NIHIL EST IN INTELLECTU QUOD NON PRIUS FUERIT IN SENSU." *Journal of the History of Medicine* (1970): 77–80.

Csordas, T. J. "Somatic Modes of Attention." *Cultural Anthropology* 8, no. 2 (1993): 135–56.

Dahood, M. *Psalms III*. AB 17a. Garden City: Doubleday, 1970.

Danet, B. "Speech, Writing and Performativity: An Evolutionary View of the History of Constitutive Ritual." Pages 13–41 in *The Construction of Professional Discourse*. Edited by B.-L. Gunnarson, P. Linell, and B. Nordberg. Language in Social Life Series. New York: Longman, 1997.

Daube, D. "The Culture of Deuteronomy." *Orita* 3 (1969): 27–52.

———. *Studies in Biblical Law*. Cambridge: Cambridge University Press, 1947.

Davidson Kalmar I., and D. Penslar. "Orientalism and the Jews: An Introduction." Pages xiii–xl in *Orientalism and the Jews*. Edited by I. Davidson Kalmar and D. Penslar. Waltham: Brandeis University Press, 2005.

De Saussure, F. *Course in General Linguistics*. Translated by R. Harris. London: Duckworth, 1982.

Desjarlais, R. *Sensory Biographies: Lives and Deaths Among Nepal's Yolmo Buddhists*. Berkeley: University of California Press, 2003.

Devereux, G. "Ethnopsychological Aspects of the terms 'Deaf' and 'Dumb.'" Pages 43–46 in Howes, ed., *The Varieties of Sensory Experience.*

Dhorme, P. *L'emploi métaphorique des noms de parties du corps en hébreu et en akkadien.* Paris: Gabalda, 1923.

Dorman, J. H. W. "The Blemished Body: Deformity and Disability in the Qumran Scrolls." Ph.D. diss., Rijksuniversiteit Groningen, 2007.

Dundes, A. "Seeing is Believing." Pages 86–92 in *Interpreting Folklore.* Bloomington: Indiana University Press, 1990.

Durham, J. I. "The Senses Touch, Taste, and Smell in Old Testament Religion." Ph.D. diss., University of Oxford, 1963.

Durkheim, E. *The Elementary Forms of Religious Life.* Translated by C. Cosman. Abridged with an Introduction and notes by M. S. Cladis. Oxford: Oxford University Press, 2001.

Eilberg-Schwarz, H. "The Problem of the Body for the People of the Book." Pages 53–73 in *Women in the Hebrew Bible.* Edited by A. Bach. New York: Routledge, 1999.

———. *The Savage in Judaism.* Bloomington: Indiana University Press, 1990.

Eisenstadt, S. N., ed. *Origins and Diversity of Axial Age Civilizations.* SUNY Series in Near Eastern Studies. New York: State University of New York Press, 1986.

Eisenstein, J. D. *Ozar Midrashim.* 2 vols. New York: Eisenstein, 1915 (Hebrew).

Elat, M. *Samuel and the Foundation of Kingship in Ancient Israel.* Jerusalem: Magnes, 1998 (Hebrew).

Elliott, J. H. "The Evil Eye in the First Testament: The Ecology and Culture of Pervasive Belief." Pages 147–59 in *The Bible and the Politics of Exegesis.* Festschrift Norman K. Gottwald. Edited by D. Jobling, P. L. Day, and G. T. Sheppard. Cleveland: Pilgrim, 1991.

Feld, S. "Sound as a Symbolic System: The Kaluli Drum." Pages 79–99 in Howes, ed., *The Varieties of Sensory Experience.*

Feldman, L. H. "Hebraism and Hellenism Reconsidered." *Judaism* 43, no. 2 (1994): 115–26.

Ford, J. N. "'Ninety-Nine by the Evil Eye and One from Natural Causes': *KTU*² 1.96 in Its Near Eastern Context." *UF* 30 (1998): 201–78.

Foucault, M. *The Birth of the Clinic: An Archaeology of Medical Perception.* Translated by A. M. Sheridan Smith. New York: Tavistock, 1973.

Fox, M. V. "The Sign of the Covenant." *RB* 81 (1974): 557–96.

Frisch, A. "*rʾh* and *šmʿ* as a Pair of Leading Words" (Hebrew). *WCJS 12* (1997): 89–98.

Fritsch, C. T. "A Study of the Greek Translation of the Hebrew Verbs 'to See' with Deity as Subject or Object." *Eretz Israel* 16 (1982): 51ʾ–56ʾ.

Garsiel, M. *The First Book of Samuel: A Literary Study of Comparative Structures, Analogies and Parallels.* Ramat-Gan: Revivim, 1983 (Hebrew).

Geertz, C. "From the Native's Point of View." Pages 225–42 in Rabinow and Sullivan, eds., *Interpretive Social Science.*

———. *The Interpretation of Cultures: Selected Essays.* New York: Basic, 1973.

Geller, S. A. "Fiery Wisdom: Logos and Lexis in Deuteronomy 4." *Prooftexts* 14, no. 2 (1994): 103–39.

———. "Textual Juxtaposition and Comparative Study." Pages 72–79 in *Approaches to Teaching the Hebrew Bible as Literature in Translation.* Edited by B. N. Olsen and Y. S. Feldman. New York: Modern Language Association of America, 1989.

George, A. *The Epic of Gilgamesh.* London: Penguin, 1999.

Gibson, A. *Biblical Semantic Logic: A Preliminary Analysis*. New York: St. Martin's Press, 1981.

Ginat, J. *Blood Disputes Among Bedouin and Rural Arabs in Israel: Revenge, Mediation, Outcast and Family Honor*. Pittsburgh: University of Pittsburgh Press in cooperation with Jerusalem Institute for Israel Studies, 1987.

Goering, G. S. "Sapiential Synesthesia: The Conceptual Blending of Light and Word in Ben Sira's Wisdom Instruction." Unpublished.

Goldberg, H. E. *Jewish Passages: Cycles of Jewish Life*. Berkeley: University of California Press, 2003.

Goldberg, H., O. Ziv, and E. Basker. *Anthropology: Man, Society, Culture*. Tel Aviv: Cherikover, 1978 (Hebrew).

Good, B. "The Heart of What's the Matter: The Semantics of Illness in Iran." *Culture, Medicine and Psychiatry* 1 (1977): 25–58.

Gordis, R. *Koheleth: The Man and His World*. Texts and Studies of the Jewish Theological Seminary of America 19. New York: Jewish Theological Seminary of America, 1951.

Green, D. A. *The Aroma of Righteousness: Scent and Seduction in Rabbinic Life and Literature*. University Park: Penn State University Press, 2011.

———. "Soothing Odors: The Transformation of Scents in Ancient Israelite and Ancient Jewish Literature." Ph.D. diss., University of Chicago, 2003.

Greenstein, E. L. "Some Developments in the Study of Language and Some Implications for Interpreting Ancient Texts and Cultures." Pages 441–79 in *Semitic Linguistics: The State of the Art at the Turn of the Twenty-First Century*. Edited by S. Izre'el. Israel Oriental Studies 20. Winona Lake: Eisenbrauns, 2002.

Gruber, M. I. *Aspects of Non-Verbal Communication in the Ancient Near East*. Studia Pohl. Dissertationes scientificae de rebus Orientis antiqui 12/1–2. Rome: Biblical Institute, 1980.

———. "Was Cain Angry or Depressed? Background of a Biblical Murder." *BAR* 6, no. 6 (1980): 35–36.

Guerts, K. L. *Culture and the Senses: Bodily Ways of Knowing in an African Community*, Berkeley: University of California Press, 2002.

Gumperz, J. J. "Sociolinguistics and Communication in Small Groups." Pages 203–24 in *Sociolinguistics: Selected Readings*. Edited by J. B. Pride and J. Holmes. Harmondsworth: Penguin, 1972.

Gunkel, H. *The Legends of Genesis : the Biblical Saga and History*. Translated by W. H. Carruth. Introduction by W. F. Albright. New York: Schocken, 1964.

Habel, N. C. *The Book of Job*. OTL. London: SCM, 1985.

Hagedorn, A. C. *Between Moses and Plato: Individual and Society in Deuteronomy and Ancient Greek Law*. FRLANT 204. Göttingen: Vandenhoeck & Ruprecht, 2004.

Hallpike, C. R. *The Foundations of Primitive Thought*. Oxford: Clarendon, 1979.

Hamilton, V. P. *The Book of Genesis: Chapters 18–50*. NICOT. Grand Rapids: Eerdmans, 1995.

Hartley, J. E. *The Book of Job*. NICOT. Grand Rapids: Eerdmans, 1988.

Hartom, E. S. *Ben-Sira: Partially Translated and Interpreted*. Tel Aviv: Yavneh, 1963 (Hebrew).

Herzfeld, M. "Anthropology: A Practice of Theory." *International Social Science Journal* 153 (1997): 301–18.

Hibbits, B. J. "'Coming to Our Senses': Communication and Legal Expression in Performance Cultures." *Emory Law Journal* 41 (1992): 874–960.

Hollander, H. W., and M. de Jonge. *The Testament of the Twelve Patriarchs: A Commentary.* SVTP 8. Leiden: Brill, 1985.

Honeyman, A. M. "Merismus in Biblical Hebrew." *JBL* 7 (1952): 11–18.

Houtman, C. *Exodus.* HCOT. Kampen: Kok, 1993.

Howes, D. "Sensorial Anthropology." Pages 167–92 in Howes, ed., *The Varieties of Sensory Experience.*

———. *Sensual Relations: Engaging the Senses in Culture and Social Theory.* Ann Arbor: University of Michigan Press, 2004.

———. "To Summon all the Senses." Pages 3–21 in Howes, ed., *The Varieties of Sensory Experience.*

———., ed. *The Varieties of Sensory Experience: A Sourcebook in the Anthropology of the Senses.* Toronto: University of Toronto Press, 1991.

Huber-Bechtel, L. "The Biblical Experience of Shame/Shaming: The Social Experience of Shame/Shaming in Biblical Israel in Relation to Its Use as Religious Metaphor." Ph.D. diss., Drew University, 1983.

Hunt, P. N. "Sensory Images in Song of Songs 1:12–2:16." Pages 69–78 in Augustin and Schunck, eds., *Dort Ziehen Schiffe dahin....*

Hurvitz, A. *A Linguistic Study of the Relationship Between the Priestly Source and the Book of Ezekiel: A New Approach to an Old Problem.* CahRB 20. Paris: Gabalda, 1982.

Jackson, M. "Phenomenology, Radical Empiricism, and Anthropological Critique." Pages 1–45 in *Things as They Are: New Directions in Phenomenological Anthropology.* Edited by M. Jackson. Bloomington: Indiana University Press, 1996.

Jaynes, J. *The Origin of Consciousness in the Breakdown of the Bicameral Mind.* Boston: Houghton Mifflin, 1976.

Johnson, A. R. *The Vitality of the Individual in the Thought of Ancient Israel.* 2d ed. Cardiff: University of Wales Press, 1964.

Kaddari, M. Z. "Ma raʾita ki... (Gen 20, 10)." Pages 79–84 in Augustin and Schunck, eds., *Dort Ziehen Schiffe dahin....*

———. "What is the Difference between 'raʾah b-' and 'raʾah et' in Biblical Hebrew?" (Hebrew). *Mehkarim be-Lashon* 5–6 (1982): 67–78.

Kaminsky, J. S. *Corporate Responsibility in the Hebrew Bible.* JSOTSup 196. Sheffield: Sheffield Academic, 1995.

Kasher, R. "Theological Conception of the Miracle in the Bible" Ph.D. diss., Bar-Ilan University, 1981 (Hebrew).

Katznelson, A., and M. Katznelson. "Locomotor Disfunction in the Bible" (Hebrew). *Koroth* 8, no. 5–6 (1982): 57–62.

Kedar-Kopfstein, B. "On the Decoding of Polysemantic Lexemes in Biblical Hebrew." *ZAW* 7 (1994): 17–25.

———. "Synästhesien im biblischen Althebräisch in Übersetzung und Auslegung." *ZAH* 1, no. 1 (1988): 47–60; 1, no. 2 (1988): 147–58.

Kessler, R. "Der antwortende Gott." *Wort und Dienst* 21 (1991): 43–57.

Khalil, Gibran. "The Eye." Page 33 in *The Madman* (repr.; Whitefish: Kessinger Publishing, 2004.

Knight, D. A. "The Understanding of 'Sitz im Leben' in Form Criticism." *SBLSP* 1 (1974): 105–25.

Köhler, L. *Old Testament Theology*. Translated by A. S. Todd. Philadelphia: Westminster, 1957.

Kotzé, Z. "A Cognitive Linguistic Methodology for the Study of Metaphor in the Hebrew Bible." *JNSL* 31, no. 1 (2005): 107–17.

Kraus, H.-J. "Hören und Sehen in der althebräischen Tradition." Pages 84–101 in *Biblische-theologische Aufsätze*. Neukirchen–Vluyn: Butzon & Bercker 1972. Reprint from *Studium Generale* 19 (1966): 115–23.

———. *Psalms 1–59: A Commentary*. Translated by H. C. Oswald. Minneapolis: Fortress, 1988.

Kruger, T. *Qohelet: A Commentary*. Hermeneia. Philadelphia: Fortress, 2004.

Kurek-Chomycz, D. "Making Scents of Revelation: The Significance of Cultic Scents in Ancient Judaism as the Backdrop of Saint Paul's Olfactory Metaphor in 2 Cor 2:14–17." Ph.D. diss., Katholieke Universiteit Leuven, 2008.

Lacocque, A. *The Book of Daniel*. Translated by D. Pellauer. Atlanta: John Knox, 1979.

Lakoff, George, and Mark Johnson. *Metaphors We Live By*. Chicago: University of Chicago Press, 1980.

Leach, E. R. "The Comparative Method in Anthropology." *IESS* I (1968): 339–45.

Leventhal, M. D. M. "The Torah and the Senses (A)" (Hebrew). *Zohar* 6 (2001): 87–102.

———. "The Torah and the Senses (B)" (Hebrew). *Zohar* 7 (2001): 83–100.

Levin, S. "The More Savory Offering: A Key to the Problem of Gen. 4:3–5." *JBL* 98 (1979): 85.

Levine, B. A. "Silence, Sound, and the Phenomenology of Mourning in Biblical Israel." *JANES* 22 (1993): 89–106.

Levine, E. "Biblical Women's Marital Rights." *PAAJR* 63 (1997): 87–135.

Levinson, B. M. *Legal Revision and Religious Renewal in Ancient Israel*. New York: Cambridge University Press, 2008.

Lévi-Strauss, C. *The Savage Mind*. Translated by D. Weightman. Chicago: University of Chicago Press, 1966.

———. *Structural Anthropology*. Translated by C. Jacobson and B. Grundfest Schöpf. New York: Basic, 1963.

Livnat, Z. "*Beᶜeiney* + Noun Phrase in Biblical Hebrew: Semantic–Syntactic Investigation." *WCJS 11* 4, no. 1 (1994): 9–14. Repr. in *Beit Mikra* 164 (2000) (Hebrew).

MacDonald, N. *Not Bread Alone: The Uses of Food in the Old Testament*. Oxford: Oxford University Press, 2008.

Machinist, P. "Fate, *miqreh*, and Reason: Some Reflections on Qohelet and Biblical Thought." Pages 159–75 in Zevit, Gitin, and Sokoloff, eds., *Solving Riddles and Untying Knots*.

Maher, M. *Targum Pseudo-Jonathan: Genesis*. Aramaic Bible. Collegeville: Liturgical, 1992.

Malul, M. "The Ceremonial and Juridical Background of Some Expressions in Biblical Hebrew." Pages 299–327 in *Studies in Bible and Exegesis*. Festschrift M. Garsiel. Edited by S. Vargon, Y. Kaduri, R. Kasher, and A. Frisch. Ramat Gan: Bar-Ilan University Press, 2009 (Hebrew).

———. "*Eṭūṭu* 'Darkness' and *ṭiṭṭu* 'Clay' (Gilg. XI 106, 118)—Poetic License or Corruption Due to Etymological Similarity? Another Interpretation." Pages 548–56 in *An Experienced Scribe who Neglects Nothing: Ancient Near Eastern Studies in Honor of Jacob Klein*. Edited by Y. Sefati. Bethesda, Md.: CDL, 2005.

———. "Fabrication of Evidence in the Bible: Jacob's Imposture and Joseph's Blood-Stained Coat" (Hebrew). *Diné Israel* 22 (2003): 203–20.

———. "A Holistic-Integrative Investigation of Biblical Culture: A Case Study: The Motif of Spying and Conquering a Territory in the Bible" (Hebrew). *Shnaton* 14 (2004): 141–57.

———. *Knowledge, Control and Sex: Studies in Biblical Thought, Culture and World-view.* Tel Aviv-Jaffa: Archaeological Center, 2002.

———. "Law in the Narratives: A Study of the Expressions הִכִּירוֹ and וַיִּיטַב בְּעֵינֵיהֶם in 2 Sam 3:36." *JNSL* 17 (1991): 23–36.

———. "'Out of the Mouth of Babes and Sucklings You Have Founded Strength…' (Ps. 8:3): Did Children Serve as Prophetic Mediums in Biblical Times?" *JNSL* 33, no. 2 (2007): 1–32.

———. *Society, Law, and Custom in the Land of Israel in Biblical Times and in the Ancient Near Eastern Cultures.* Ramat-Gan: Bar-Ilan University Press, 2006 (Hebrew).

———. "Some Idioms and Expressions in Biblical Hebrew Originating in Symbolic Acts in the Realm of Treaty-Making" (Hebrew). *Halvrit WeAhyoteha* 4–5 (2004–2005): 189–208.

———. *Studies in Mesopotamian Legal Symbolism.* AOAT 221. Kevelaer: Butzon & Bercker, 1988.

———. "What is the Relationship Between Piercing a Slave's Ear (Ex. 21:6) and Circumcising Him within the Passover Sacrifice (Ex. 12:43–53)?" *ZAR* 13 (2007): 135–58.

Marks, L. E. *The Unity of the Senses: Interrelations among the Modalities.* New York: Academic, 1978.

McKane, W. *A Critical and Exegetical Commentary on Jeremiah.* 2 vols. ICC. Edinburgh: T. & T. Clark, 1996.

Mead, M. "The Study of Culture at a Distance." Pages 3–53 in *The Study of Culture at a Distance.* Edited by M. Mead and R. Métraux. Chicago: University of Chicago Press, 1953.

Mendenhall, G. E., and G. A. Herion. "Covenant." *ABD* 1:1179–202.

Merleau-Ponty, M. *Phenomenology of Perception.* Translated by C. Smith. Repr. 1958. London: Routledge, 2004.

———. *Signs.* Translated by R. C. McCleary. Northwestern University Studies in Phenomenology and Existential Philosophy. Chicago: Northwestern University Press, 1964.

Meshorer Y. "Two Extraordinary 'YHD' Coins." *Eretz Israel* 25 (1996): 434–37.

Milgrom, J. *Leviticus: A Book of Ritual and Ethics.* Continental Commentary. Minneapolis: Fortress, 2004.

Moor, J. C. de. "The Art of Versification in Ugarit and Israel." *UF* 12 (1980): 311–15.

Muffs Y. *Love and Joy: Law, Language and Religion in Ancient Israel,* New York: Jewish Theological Seminary of America, 1992.

Nickelsburg G. W. E., and J. C. VanderKam. *1 Enoch: A New Translation Based on the Hermeneia Commentary.* Minneapolis: Fortress, 2004.

Noth, M. *Exodus.* Translated by J. S. Bowden. OTL. London: SCM, 1962.

O'Connor, M. *Hebrew Verse Structure.* Winona Lake: Eisenbrauns, 1980.

Ohry, A., and E. Dolev. "Disabilities and Handicapped People in the Bible" (Hebrew). *Koroth* 8, no. 5–6 (1982): 57–67.

Olyan, S. M. "'Anyone Blind or Lame Shall not Enter the House': On the Interpretation of Second Samuel 5:8b." *CBQ* 60 (1998): 218–27.

———. "The Ascription of Physical Disability as a Stigmatizing Strategy in Biblical Iconic Polemics Strategy in Biblical Iconic Polemics," *JHS* 9, no. 14 (2009): Article 14:1–15. Online: http://www.arts.ualberta.ca/JHS/Articles/article_116.pdf.

———. "Honor, Shame and Covenant Relations in Ancient Israel and Its Environment." *JBL* 115 (1996): 201–18.

Ong, W. J. "The Shifting Sensorium." Pages 25–30 in Howes, ed., *The Varieties of Sensory Experience*.

———. "World as View and World as Event." *American Anthropologist* 71 (1969): 634–47.

Ortner, S. B. "Theory in Anthropology Since the Sixties." *Comparative Studies in Society and History* 26, no. 1 (1984): 126–66.

Oswalt, J. N. *The Book of Isaiah: Chapters 1–39*. NICOT. Grand Rapids: Eerdmans, 1986.

———. *The Book of Isaiah: Chapters 40–66*. NICOT. Grand Rapids: Eerdmans, 1997.

Paas, S. *Creation and Judgment: Creation Texts in Some Eighth Century Prophets*. OTS 47. Leiden: Brill, 2003.

Palache, J. L. *Semantic Notes on the Hebrew Lexicon*. Translated by N. J. Z. Werblowsky. Leiden: Brill, 1959.

Palmer, G. B. *Toward a Theory of Cultural Linguistics*. Austin: University of Texas Press, 1996.

Papayannopoulos, I. G. "Information Revealed from the Old Testament Concerning Diseases of Old Age" (Hebrew). *Koroth* 8, no. 5–6 (1982): 68–71.

Parpola, S., and R. M. Whiting, eds. *Sex and Gender in the Ancient Near East*. CRRAI 47/2. Helsinki: Neo-Assyrian Text Corpus Project, 2002.

Paul, S. M. *Amos*. Mikra Le'Israel. Tel Aviv: Am Oved, 1994 (Hebrew).

———. "Euphemism and Dysphemism." *EncJud* 6:959–61.

———. "Euphemistically 'Speaking' and a Covetous Eye." *HAR* 14 (1994): 193–204.

———. "The Shared Legacy of Sexual Metaphors and Euphemisms in Mesopotamian and Biblical Literature." Pages 489–98 in Parpola and Whiting, eds., *Sex and Gender in the Ancient Near East*.

Pedersen, J. *Israel: Its Life and Culture*. 2 vols. London: Cumberlege, 1954.

Perl, E., and D. Irsai. "Aspects in the Biblical Approach to Mental Sanity in Old Age" (Hebrew). *Koroth* 8, no. 5–6 (1982): 72–78.

Philip, T. "Descriptions of the Birthing Women in the Bible and in the Ancient Near East: The Birthing Women and the Prophet Who Do Not See and Hear" (Hebrew). Pages 415–26 in *Shai le-Sara Japhet: Studies in the Bible, Its Exegesis and Its Language*. Festschrift S. Japhet. Edited by M. Bar-Asher, D. Rom-Shiloni, E. Tov, and N. Wazana. Jerusalem: Bialik Institute, 2007.

———. "Menstruation and Childbirth in the Bible." Ph.D. diss., The Hebrew University of Jerusalem, 2003 (Hebrew).

———. "Woman in Travail as a Simile to Men in Distress in the Hebrew Bible." Pages 499–505 in Parpola and Whiting, eds., *Sex and Gender in the Ancient Near East*.

Polak, F. H. "Linguistic and Stylistic Aspects of Epic Formulae in Ancient Semitic Poetry and Biblical Narrative." Pages 285–304 in *Biblical Hebrew in Its Northwest Semitic Setting*. Edited by S. E. Fassberg and A. Hurvitz. Winona Lake: Eisenbrauns, 2006.

Rabinow P., and M. W. Sullivan. eds. *Interpretive Social Science*. Berkeley: University of California Press, 1979.

———. "The Interpretive Turn: Emergence of an Approach." Pages 1–24 in Rabinow and Sullivan, eds., *Interpretive Social Science*.

Rad, G. von. *Deuteronomy: A Commentary*. Translated by D. Barton. OTL. London: SCM, 1966.

Raphael, R. *Biblical Corpora: Representations of Disability in the Hebrew Biblical Literature*. LHBOTS 445. London: T&T Clark International, 2008.

Ritchie, I. D. "Fusion of the Faculties: A Study of the Language of the Senses in Hausaland." Pages 192–202 in Howes, ed., *The Varieties of Sensory Experience*.

———. "The Nose Knows: Bodily Knowing in Isaiah 11.3." *JSOT* 87 (2000): 59–73.

Rofé, A. "The Acts of Nahash According to 4QSamᵃ." *IEJ* 32 (1982): 129–33.

———. *"The Book of Balaam" (Numbers 22:2–24:25): A Study in Methods of Criticism and the History of Biblical Literature and Religion*. Jerusalem: Simor, 1979 (Hebrew).

Rogerson, W. J. "The Hebrew Conception of Corporate Personality: A Re-examination." *JTS* 21 (1970): 1–16.

Rosaldo, M. Z. "The Use and Abuse of Anthropology: Reflection on Feminism and Cross-Cultural Understanding." *Signs* 5, no. 3 (1980): 389–417.

Rosen, Z. "The Healthy and the Diseased Nose in the Bible." *Koroth* 8, no. 5–6 (1982): 79–85.

Rosenberg, J. "1 and 2 Samuel." Pages 122–43 in *The Literary Guide to the Bible*. Edited by R. Alter and F. Kermode. Cambridge: Belknap Press of Harvard University Press, 1987.

Rözal, H. N. *Amos*. Haifa: Ah, 1990 (Hebrew).

Rubinstein, E. "*lipnēy* + NP: From Place Indication to Indication of the 'Thinker' and the 'Cause': A study into Biblical Hebrew." *Leshonenu* 40 (1986): 57–66 (Hebrew).

Said, E. W. *Orientalism*. Translated by A. Zilber. Tel-Aviv: Am-Oved, 2000 (Hebrew).

Sandmel, S. "The Ancient Mind and Ours." Pages 29–44 in *Understanding the Sacred Text: Essays in Honor of Morton S. Enslin on the Hebrew Bible and Christian Beginnings*. Festschrift M. S. Enslin. Edited by J. Reumann. Valley Forge: Judson, 1972.

Sasson, J. "The Eyes of Eli: An Essay on Motif Accretion." Pages 171–90 in *Inspired Speech: Prophecy in the Ancient Near East*. Festschrift H. B. Huffmon. Edited by J. Kaltner and L. Stulman. JSOTSup 372. London: T&T Clark International, 2004.

Sawyer, J. F. A. *Semantics in Biblical Research: New Methods of Defining Hebrew Words for Salvation*. London: SCM, 1972.

Scheper-Hughes, N. *Death Without Weeping: The Violence of Everyday Life in Brazil*. Berkeley: University of California Press, 1992.

Schipper, J. "Deuteronomy 24:5 and King Asa's Foot Disease in 1 Kings 15.23b." *JBL* 128 (2009): 643–48.

———. *Disability and Isaiah's Suffering Servant*. Oxford: Oxford University Press, 2011.

———. *Disability Studies and the Hebrew Bible: Figuring Mephibosheth in the David Story*. LHBOTS 441. New York: T&T Clark International, 2006.

Schökel, L. A. "Contemplar y Gustar." *Estudios Bíblicos* 57 (1999): 11–21.

Schutz, A. "Phenomenology and the Social Sciences." Pages 119–42 in *Phenomenology and Sociology*. Edited by T. Luckmann. Harmondsworth: Penguin, 1978.

Seeman, D. "The Watcher at the Window: Cultural Poetics of a Biblical Motif." *Prooftexts* 24, no. 1 (2004): 1–50.

———. "'Where Is Sarah Your Wife?' Cultural Poetics of Gender and Nationhood in the Hebrew Bible." *HTR* 91, no. 2 (1998): 103–25.

Segal, M. Z. *The Complete Ben-Sira*. Jerusalem: Bialik Institute, 1953 (Hebrew).

Seow, C. L. *Ecclesiastes: A New Translation with Introduction and Commentary*. AB 18C. New York: Doubleday, 1997.

Shapira, A "On 'Dignity' in the Bible" (Hebrew). *Beth Mikra* 44, no. 2 (1999): 128–45.

Shupak, N. "Learning Methods in Ancient Israel." *VT* 53 (2003): 416–26.

———. *Where Can Wisdom Be Found? The Sage's Language in the Bible and in Ancient Egyptian Literature*. OBO 130. Fribourg: University Press Freiburg, 1993.

Silbermann, L. H. "Listening to the Text." *JBL* 102 (1983): 3–26.

Smith, J. Z. *Imagining Religion: From Babylon to Jonestown*. Chicago Studies in History of Judaism. Chicago: University of Chicago Press, 1988.

Soll, W. J. "Babylonian and Biblical Acrostics." *Biblica* 69 (1988): 305–23.

Steiner Y., C. Ormian, and Y. Leibovitch. "Senses" (Hebrew). *EH* 17 (1983): 213–23.

Stewart, D. T. "Deaf and Blind in Leviticus 19:14 and the Emergence of Disability Law." Biblical Scholarship and Disabilities Consultation. Society of Biblical Literature Annual Meeting, Philadelphia, Pa., November 19, 2005.

Stoller, P. *Sensuous Scholarship*. Philadelphia: University of Pennsylvania Press, 1997.

———. *The Taste of Ethnographic Things*. Philadelphia: University of Pennsylvania Press, 1989.

Sovran, T. *Semantic Fields: A Linguistic-Philosophical Study of Meaning Relations*. Jerusalem: Magnes, 2000.

Sutskover, T. "The Semantic Field of 'Seeing' in the Book of Genesis and the Coherence of the Text." Ph.D. diss., Tel-Aviv University, 2006 (Hebrew).

Synnott, A. "Foundations for the Anthropology of the Senses." *International Social Science Journal* 153 (1997): 401–12.

———. "Puzzling Over the Senses: From Plato to Marx." Pages 61–76 in Howes, ed., *The Varieties of Sensory Experience*.

———. "A Sociology of Smell." *Canadian Review of Sociology and Anthropology* 28, no. 4 (1991): 437–59.

Talmon, S. "The 'Comparative Method' in Biblical Interpretation: Principles and Problems." Pages 320–56 in *Congress Volume: Göttingen 1977*. Edited by J. A. Emerton. VTSup 29. Leiden: Brill, 1978.

Tawil, H. "Some Literary Elements in the Opening Sections of the Hadad, Zākir, and the Nērab II Inscriptions in the Light of East and West Semitic Royal Inscriptions." *Or* 43 (1974): 60–63.

Thomsen, M. L. "The Evil Eye in Mesopotamia." *JNES* 51 (1992): 19–32.

Tigay, J. H. "'לא נס לחה He Had Not Become Wrinkled' (Deuteronomy 34:7)." Pages 345–50 in Zevit, Gitin, and Sokoloff, eds., *Solving Riddles and Untying Knots*, 345–50.

———. *Deuteronomy: The Traditional Hebrew Text with the New JPS Translation*. JPS Torah Commentary. Philadelphia: Jewish Publication Society, 1996.

———. "'Heavy of Mouth' and 'Heavy of Tongue' on Moses' Speech Difficulty." *BASOR* 231 (1978): 56–67.

———. *You Shall Have No Other Gods: Israelite Religion in the Light of Hebrew Inscriptions*. Atlanta: Scholars Press, 1986.

Tsevat, M. "An Aspect of Biblical Thought: Deductive Explanation" (Hebrew). *Shnaton* 3 (1978): 53–58.

Tsur, R. "Literary Synaesthesia: A Cognitive Approach." *Hebrew Linguistics* 29–30 (1990): 75–86.

Turner, V. "Muchona the Hornet, Interpreter of Religion." Pages 333–56 in *In the Company of Man*. Edited by J. Casagrande. New York: Harper Bros, 1959. Repr. as Chapter 4 in *The Forest of Symbols: Aspects of Ndembu Ritual*. Ithaca: Cornell University Press, 1967.

———. *The Ritual Process: Structure and Anti Structure*. London: Routledge & Kegan Paul, 1969.

Tur-Sinai, N. H. *The Book of Job: A New Commentary*. Jerusalem: Kiryat Sefer, 1957.

Tylor, A. "The Wisdom of the Many and the Wit of One." Pages 3–9 in *The Wisdom of Many: Essays on the Proverb*. Edited by W. Mieder and A. Dundes. New York: Garland, 1981.

Tylor, E. B. *Primitive Culture: Researches into the Development of Mythology, Philosophy, Religion, Language, Art, and Custom*. 2 vols. London: John Murray, 1920 (1871).

Ullendorff, E. "Thought Categories in the Hebrew Bible." Pages 273–88 in *Studies in Rationalism, Judaism and Universalism*. Festschrift L. Roth. Edited by R. Lowe. London: Routledge & Kegan Paul, 1966.

Unterman, J. "The (Non)Sense of Smell in Isaiah 11:3." *Hebrew Studies* 33 (1992): 17–23.

Van der Hoek, A. "Endowed with Reason or Glued to the Senses: Philo's Thoughts on Adam and Eve." Pages 63–75 in *The Creation of Man and Woman: Interpretations of the Biblical Narratives in Jewish and Christian Traditions*. Edited by G. P. Luttikhuizen. Leiden: Brill, 2000.

Vargon, S. "The Blind and the Lame." *VT* 66 (1996): 498–514.

Walls, N. H. "The Origins of the Disabled Body." Pages 13–30 in Avalos, Melcher, and Schipper, eds., *This Abled Body*.

Wasserman, N. "'Sweeter than Honey and Wine…' Semantic Domains and Old Babylonian Imagery." Pages 191–96 in *Landscapes: Territories, Frontiers and Horizons in the Ancient Near East*. Edited by L. Milano, S. De Martino, F. M. Fales, and G. B. Lanfranchi. CRRAI 44/3. Padova: Sargon, 2000.

Watson, W. G. E. *Classical Hebrew Poetry: A Guide to Its Techniques*. JSOTSup 26. Sheffield: Sheffield Academic, 1984. Repr., New York: T&T Clark International, 2008.

———. "The Unnoticed Word Pair 'eye(s)' // 'heart'." *ZAW* 101 (1989): 398–408.

Weinfeld, M. *Deuteronomy and the Deuteronomic School*. Oxford: Oxford University Press, 1972.

Weisman, Z. "Patterns and Structures in the Visions of Amos" (Hebrew). *Beit Mikra* 14, no. 4 (1970): 40–57.

Weiss, A. L. *Figurative Language in Biblical Prose Narrative: Metaphor in the Book of Samuel*. VTSup 107. Leiden: Brill, 2006.

Weiss, M. *The Book of Amos*. Jerusalem: Magnes, 1992 (Hebrew).

Wenham, G. J. *The Book of Leviticus*. NICOT. Grand Rapids: Eerdmans, 1979.

Whitehead, A. N. *Process and Reality*. New York: Macmillan, 1929.

Wikan, U. *Managing Turbulent Hearts: A Balinese Formula for Living*. Chicago: University of Chicago Press, 1990.

Wilcke, C. "A Riding Tooth: Metaphor, Metonymy and Synechdoche, Quick and Frozen in Everyday Language." Pages 77–102 in *Figurative Language in the Ancient Near East*. Edited by M. Mindlin, M. J. Geller, and J. E. Wansbrough. London: School of Oriental and African Studies, 1987.

Williams, B. *Shame and Necessity*. Berkeley: University California Press, 1993.

Wober, M. "Sensotypes." *Journal of Social Psychology* 70 (1966): 181–89.

Wolff, H. W. *Anthropology of the Old Testament*. Translated by M. Kohl. London: SCM, 1974.

————. *Hosea: A Commentary on the Book of the Prophet Hosea*. Translated by G. Stansell. Hermeneia. Philadelphia: Fortress, 1974.

Yanai, T. *Following the Thoughts: On the Universe, Nature, and Man*. Ramat-Gan: Poetica, 1994 (Hebrew).

Zakovitch, Y. *The Song of Songs: Introduction and Commentary*. Mikra Le'Israel. Tel Aviv: Am Oved, 1992 (Hebrew).

Zedaka, Y. "'And Noah Found Favor in the Eyes of the Lord' (Semantic and Syntactic Analysis)" (Hebrew). *Bikoret u Parshanut* 24 (1988): 133–40.

Zeligman, Y. A. "The Problem of Prophecy in Israel, Its Origin and Its Character" (Hebrew). *Eretz Israel* 3 (1954): 123–32.

Zevit, Z., S. Gitin, and M. Sokoloff, eds. *Solving Riddles and Untying Knots: Biblical, Epigraphic, and Semitic Studies*. Festschrift J. C. Greenfield. Winona Lake: Eisenbrauns, 1995.

INDEXES

INDEX OF REFERENCES

INDEX OF AUTHORS

CPSIA information can be obtained at www.ICGtesting.com
Printed in the USA
LVOW10s1717050614

388782LV00005B/207/P